STORM WARNINGS!

STEVE HALE

RIVERSTONE GROUP PUBLISHING

ISBN: 978-0-9763092-7-7

Design and Production

Riverstone Group, LLC, Jasper, Georgia

Printed in ______

WHAT LEADERS ARE SAYING.....

"Steve Hale writes like he preaches—combining urgent biblical truth with the breaking news of the moment! As a revivalist/evangelist, Steve never loses sight of God's mercy and love for broken people, but *Storm Warnings!* is just that—a warning. It's an appropriate time for a book like this. Every believer with a sense of what the Lord is saying to the churches is on spiritual high alert today because judgment cannot be delayed indefinitely. Steve reminds us of the serious days just ahead, and the amazing grace available if we pay attention to the Storm Warnings!"

—Dr. J. Kie Bowman, Senior Pastor
Hyde Park Baptist Church
Austin, Texas

"God has given Steve Hale an incredible mind, heart, and passion for telling the truth as you will see in his newest book, *Storm Warnings!* I encourage everyone to read it, be blessed, and pass it on. In light of the Judgment Seat of Christ for believers, the Great White Throne Judgment for unbelievers, and the events taking place in our nation and around the world, we all must heed the warnings of the impending storm that Steve presents in this volume."

—Dr. Johnny Hunt, Senior Pastor
First Baptist Church
Woodstock, Georgia

"If you have read Evangelist Steve Hale's *Truth Decay*, you will be excited to read *Storm Warnings!* Steve always brings God's Word with power to current trends and current events. As you read Storm Warnings! I pray you will be blessed."

—Dr. Jerry Vines, Pastor Emeritus
First Baptist Church
Jacksonville, Florida
2-time President, Southern Baptist Convention

"In a time when America is living at a critical crossroads in its history, Dr. Steve Hale has penned a prophetic word. Thoroughly researched and fair in his assessments, Dr. Hale has given us a book that accurately diagnoses our nation's foundational problem and the necessity of God's intervention. *Storm Warnings!* is a must-read book for our time.!

—-Dr. Dwayne Mercer, Senior Pastor
CrossLife Church
Oviedo, Florida

"Dr. Steve Hale has added a prophetic voice to the needs of our day with his newest book, *Storm Warnings!* Steve has long held my admiration for his insight and character. He has preached for me and I've watched God use him in great ways. He understands our country, our needs, and more importantly, our hope found only in the Lord Jesus Christ. I urge you to read this book and ask God to send a great wave of repentance and revival to our Land!"

—-Dr. Doug Munton, Senior Pastor
First Baptist Church
O'Fallon, Illinois

"*Storm Warnings* gives us a picture of the world we are living in and the major storm that is brewing. Under God's leadership, Steve Hale has given us a clarion call for the Christian and the Church to wake up and wise up to the storm that is upon us. This book provides the directions we need for the approaching storm."

—Dr. David Gallamore, Senior Pastor
Rock Springs Baptist Church
Easley, South Carolina

"Sometimes warnings garnered about the state of affairs are completely overdone. But evangelist Steve Hale has carefully documented his warnings based on what God's Word says. *Storm Warnings! America's Race to a Day of Reckoning* points to exactly what the Bible says will happen unless America alters its course. It is not only true for America, but is true for any nation anywhere. Read this book and find out what God says about our nation."

—Dr. Paige Patterson, President
Southwestern Baptist Theological Seminary
Ft. Worth, Texas

CONTENTS

Acknowledgements

Every project of this magnitude is a collaborative effort involving multiple people. For *Storm Warnings!* there are two in particular whose tireless expertise made this volume a reality. While all of the writing and research was done by Yours Truly, it was my ministry assistant, Shelby Johnston, who re-typed my manuscripts and patiently displayed the fruit of God's Spirit in the midst of my many revisions and additions to the work she had already done. "Shelby, you were awesome throughout this project. Surely, there is a special reward awaiting you at the Judgment Seat of Christ!"

Secondly, you would not be holding this volume in your hand without our talented graphic designer and publisher, Ernest Pullen. Ernest has been responsible for all of our publications, but this 600-plus page work was a Mt. Everest in comparison to the others. His knowledge, insights, and counsel have been invaluable through the years. "Ernest, the creative juices that God has given you along with your godly perspective and the years of experience you bring to any project are truly a gift, one that I have never taken for granted. Thank you for helping bring dreams and visions into reality."

Finally, and most importantly, this assignment which I believe was birthed from the heart of God, would never have come to fruition without the constant encouragement from His indwelling Spirit. My golf game has suffered from declining the opportunities to "tee it up" in lieu of sitting at the computer doing research and writing instead. Every author understands there is a price to be paid, and often along the way those in his/her inner circle make sacrifices as well. Some have compared the completion of a project of this magnitude with giving birth to a child. I doubt that mothers would appreciate such an analogy because late night hours, self-imposed deadlines, and writer's block most likely do not compare with labor pains. Nevertheless, "Thank you, Lord, for Your sustaining grace, wisdom, and the constant motivation to complete what You placed upon my heart. I only pray that You are pleased and that Your intended purpose will be realized. I love you, Lord."

Introduction

The year, 1991. The day, October 28. Halloween was approaching, but most of the nation was unaware that something much more harrowing than goblins and ghosts was in the making. The Ocean Prediction Center warned that a "dangerous storm" of an unusual nature was forming in the next 36 hours. The National Weather Service issued similar warnings, but the public remained skeptical, and understandably so. After all, the skies were blue, the sun was shining, and children were playing. All seemed well with the world, but that was about to change on this fateful day. A strange convergence of weather patterns, in fact, a set of meteorological circumstances that occur only once every 50 to 100 years, was forming what would come to be known as *The Perfect Storm.*

This monster of a storm was popularized when author Sebastian Junger profiled the true story of a swordfishing boat, *the Andrea Gail*, was sunk by the towering waves of the Atlantic as described in his novel *The Perfect Storm.* The movie by the same name and starring George Clooney only served to extend the storm's fame.

From Massachusetts to Maine, thousands were evacuated, $200 million of damage incurred, and 38,000 homes without power. [1] Waves from the storm reached a height of 100.7 feet on October 30, the highest ever recorded in the offshore waters of Nova Scotia. [2] In laymen's terms, the storm was created from a collision between a high pressure system, a low pressure system and the remnants of a dying hurricane—all of which sent winds crashing into the East Coast. Today we are better equipped to predict storms of this variety, but in 1991 it was a challenge to forecasters.

Another Storm is Brewing

What meteorologists found challenging in 1991, and even hard to believe, political analysts and social engineers are struggling to grasp the magnitude of another storm that is approaching the horizon of the United States of America. Warnings have been, and are being, issued but often get muffled by a more dominant media. The messengers sounding the alarm are often discredited as rightwing extremists, Bible-thumping alarmists, or simply an uninformed populace that is over-reacting to a mere bump in our road to recovery. However, with increasing frequency prominent voices are echoing the same concerns and the alarms are beginning to sound off simultaneously through the radio, television, social media, print media, neighborhood gatherings, and yes, a few pulpits throughout the nation. Wall Street and the White House seem to be in a perpetual state of damage control by putting a positive spin on America's terminal illness lest the stock market plummets beyond a point of no return.

As you will see, *Storm Warnings* unfolds a convergence of social, moral, economic, political, military, and spiritual conditions that have all come together simultaneously to form the perfect storm for sinking the greatest nation in history. This is not hyperbole or speculation. You will see that no nation has ever survived the onslaught of such challenges apart from Divine intervention. And that, my friend, is the missing component in this catastrophic equation that must be heard.

Are We the Titanic?

In a previous book, *Truth Decay*, I compared America's path of destruction to that of the "unsinkable" Titanic. If you have read the book, I apologize for the redundancy. The analogy, however, is too poignant and the imagery is too vivid not to repeat.

On April 14, 1912, the waters out in the ocean were icy and the midnight air was frigid, but inside a luxurious ocean liner 2,000 people were comfortably sound asleep and totally oblivious to any impending danger. Little did they know that their ship had charted a course that would lead to a watery grave. The ship's captain was asleep, but the man who stood at the helm could see in the distance a huge iceberg blocking their path. In fact, they had been repeatedly warned that there was ice ahead and they should turn around. Yet, those warnings were ignored. After all, this was a state-of-the-art ship and supposedly unsinkable. It was a masterpiece of technology, weighing 46,328 tons, stretching over 882 feet long, and standing 11 stories tall.

When it became apparent that a collision was inevitable, the captain sounded the alarm and began yelling at the top of his lungs that danger lay ahead. The ship, which was thought to be unsinkable and took years to build, required only two hours and forty minutes to sink. With a glancing blow, the Titanic hit the ice, causing a 300-foot gash in the ship.

But here is what is interesting. Even after being awakened from their sleep, most of the people refused to believe that this great ship was actually sinking. In fact, many would not even get in the lifeboats. Instead, they laughed and joked as the band continued to play. They simply could not, or would not, believe that the great Titanic was about to sink. It wasn't long before the laughter and jokes turned into screams and prayers for those who were perishing. The band stopped playing ragtime music and began playing a hymn. Suddenly, the music stopped, and within seconds the Titanic disappeared 13,000 feet below the ocean's surface.

There came a point when it was too late to stop, too late to turn back, too late to sound the alarm, and too late to choose another direction. The only thing left to do was to gather the passengers on the deck for a final eulogy of one last prayer and one last hymn.

What happened to the Titanic is now happening to America. Understandably, most people do not want to believe it. We do not want to hear it, much less think about it. So, we continue to play on the deck. [3]

Our nation is hemorrhaging in the brain and we are on life support. Well-informed news junkies understand that such language is not an overreach, but to the casual reader this sounds a little "off the wall." Let's at least agree on this much: The good ship USS America is taking on water and while those on deck are frantically trying to plug the holes the water continues to rise. It's time for the band to stop playing, the passengers to stop laughing, and those at the helm to stop pretending. It is time for spiritual leaders throughout the nation to interrupt their regularly scheduled programming and call the churches of our Land to repentance and prayer. An uninformed people will never feel the desperate need for such. *Storm Warnings* is one more voice issuing a wake-up call. Indeed, we all have "skin in the game" because we are all passengers with water to the neck and rising. Our national destiny and life as we've known it, hang in the balance. For some, *Storm Warning*s will confirm what you already suspected. For others, it will be eye-opening. My prayer for all is that the cumulative impact of this information will compel us to stand for truth, fight for the founding principles that made us the greatest nation in history, be proactive in making a difference, bombard Heaven's Throne with effectual, fervent prayer, and seek personal as well as corporate revival in our local churches.

George Washington's Prayer for the United States of America

"Almighty God; We make our earnest prayer that Thou wilt keep the United States in Thy Holy protection; and Thou wilt incline the hearts of the Citizens to cultivate a spirit of subordination and obedience to Government; and entertain a brotherly affection and love for one another and for their fellow Citizens of the United States at large, and particularly for their brethren who have served in the Field.

And finally that Thou wilt most graciously be pleased to dispose us all to do justice, to love mercy, and to demean ourselves with that Charity, humility, and pacific temper of mind which were the Characteristics of the Divine Author of our blessed Religion, and without a humble imitation of whose example in these things we can never hope to be a happy nation. Grant our supplication, we beseech Thee, through Jesus Christ our Lord. Amen." [1]

An Excerpt from a Letter Written by President George Washington

"Much to be regretted indeed would it be, were we to neglect the means and depart from the road which Providence has pointed us to, so plainly; I cannot believe it will ever come to pass. The Great Governor of the Universe has led us too long and too far…to forsake us in the midst of it…We may, now and then, get bewildered; but I hope and trust that there is good sense and virtue enough left to recover the right path."[2]

— George Washington (1732-1799)
the first President of the United States and Commander-in-Chief of the Continental Army during the Revolutionary War

CHAPTER 1

A Nation In Crisis

Things have changed in America and everyone knows it. Corruption is rampant. Moral standards are in the gutter. Most Americans believe the government (i.e. Congress) is corrupt and inept. The nation is bankrupt. Political scandals seem to be an every month occurrence. Hostility toward Christian values is prevalent. But, "as long as the stock market continues to rise and social security checks keep arriving in the mailbox, all of this talk about an economic collapse is just empty rhetoric." So goes the thinking. What if the truth is being covered up? What if this is the calm before the storm? What if we're in the midst of a massive fraud?

By handing out billions of dollars in checks, thanks to the Federal Reserve printing trillions in fake dollars, big-government spending has managed to mask the true picture of our economy. In four short years $6 trillion was added to the debt and many in Washington want to legalize another 12 million illegal aliens, giving them access to $9 trillion in entitlements. [3] Record numbers of Americans now receive food stamps (50 million), disability income, welfare checks, and unemployment benefits while another 40 million are receiving free healthcare.

Most Americans fail to realize that our nation is living off the kindness of strangers. We are recklessly borrowing money to fund our entitlement system. As crazy as it sounds, we borrow from China to pay entitlement checks to Americans and to hand out billions of dollars in foreign aid to countries that hate us and support terrorism. You can't make this stuff up. It's insanity on steroids. The government borrows 46 cents of every dollar it spends. [4] Another study, as recent as 2012, claims that foreign nations own 33 percent of our national debt which means that one out of every three dollars that we have borrowed is owed to foreign creditors![5]

Free breakfasts and lunches at school make it seem like our children aren't going hungry. General Motors is propped up by a 79 percent increase in government purchases. Strip away the spending and printing of money, strip away the entitlements, including income tax credits to illegal aliens (who pay no taxes in the first place), and it would be 1929 all over again with bread lines stretching for miles. Distribution of food stamps is the only thing preventing such bread lines today. Of course, to avoid the panic and downplay this crisis, the government's printing presses are running day and night to fund its weapon of mass distraction. Yes, we are facing an economic Armageddon and teetering on the brink of disaster. As of this writing, 90 million able-bodied, working age Americans are unemployed. Here is a "comical" profile in the life of an unemployed American.

A Day in The Life of Unemployed John Smith

- John Smith started the day early having set his alarm clock (MADE IN JAPAN) for 6 am....
- While his coffee pot (MADE IN CHINA) was perking,
- He shaved with his electric razor (MADE IN HONG KONG).
- He put on a dress shirt (MADE IN SRI LANKA),
- Designer jeans (MADE IN SINGAPORE)
- And tennis shoes (MADE IN KOREA)
- After cooking his breakfast in his new electric skillet (MADE IN INDIA),
- He sat down with his calculator (MADE IN MEXICO) to see how much he could spend today.

- After setting his watch (MADE IN TAIWAN)
- To the radio (MADE IN INDIA),
- He got in his car (MADE IN GERMANY)
- filled it with gas (FROM SAUDI ARABIA)
- And continued his search for a good paying AMERICAN JOB.
- At the end of yet another discouraging day, checking his computer (MADE IN MALAYSIA),
- John decided to relax for a while.
- He put on his sandals (MADE IN BRAZIL),
- poured himself a glass of wine (MADE IN FRANCE),
- And turned on his TV (MADE IN INDONESIA),
- And then wondered why he can't find a good paying job in AMERICA. [6]

When the writing of this book began, our nation was in the process of electing a president to succeed Barack Obama. From the outset Donald Trump was the GOP frontrunner. Surprisingly, his profane language, derogatory remarks toward women, biblical illiteracy, and narcissistic personality did not prevent evangelicals from rallying to his campaign.

Given the desperate hour in which we live, it would have been refreshing to hear candidates allude to the nation's need for God and calling upon His assistance in solving the problems facing the nation. However, one can only imagine the firestorm that would have resulted from the politically-correct crowd and such emphasis would have undoubtedly distracted attention from the central message of the candidate. As we will see in subsequent chapters, the Election of 2016 was historic on several fronts and President Trump hit the ground sprinting like a stallion out of the gates, perhaps setting a record in the productivity category for a first-month presidency. Trump's selection of Mike Pence as his vice-presidential running mate was a stroke of genius and the deciding factor in swaying millions of evangelicals into his camp. However, in the early weeks of his presidency there was already a strong resistance from liberals, the continued biased reporting of the mainstream media, and intelligence leaks resulting in the early resignation of General Michael Flynn. As Trump drains the swamp, there are moles from the previous administration working as operatives to undermine everything that Trump is striving to accomplish.

Despite the headwinds of resistance, Trump is proving himself fully capable by exceeding all expectations, just as he did in the election. As we will see in the following pages, his plate is full, the challenges are daunting, and the hour has never been more consequential. He and his outstanding cabinet need our prayers. It is one thing for millions of Christians to vote, but quite another for those same believers to daily lift our leaders before the throne of grace in prayer. Yet, this is the admonishment of Scripture and to do otherwise is a failure to obey First Timothy 2:1-3. For we know that the average age for great civilizations is approximately two hundred years. Do the math. We also know that great civilizations pass through a series of stages from their birth to their decline to their death. Check out the following:

Stages in the Death of a Nation

1) From bondage to spiritual faith.
2) From spiritual faith to great courage.
3) From great courage to liberty.
4) From liberty to abundance.
5) From abundance to selfishness.
6) From selfishness to complacency.

7) From complacency to apathy.

8) From apathy to moral decay.

9) From moral decay to dependence.

10) From dependence to bondage. [7]

Our moral decay will be discussed in a subsequent chapter, but any objective person must agree that we are in category number 10. The majority of Americans are dependent on the government for support, food stamps, healthcare, hand-outs, and sustenance. We find this same degenerative decline in the book of Judges. Apart from God's intervention, nations decline and gradually fade from the scene. Nations die just as do individuals. The above progression was true of Israel, it was true of Greece, Persia, Babylon, Rome, and it will be true of America unless we are shaken to the very core of our beings and voices of righteousness rise above the hollow rhetoric of our politicians and talking pundits of the media. Of all the stages listed above, historians point to the spiritual decline as the hinge that accelerates the nation's demise. With Israel, it began by turning from God to idolatry. Today, such idolatry takes the form of worshipping money and self. It would be nice to see someone in the Oval Office with the moral backbone who is the antithesis of such a false value system, someone whose very countenance, demeanor, and disciplines reflect a deep love for Jesus Christ. The power of such an example has yet to be seen, at least in our lifetime.

Signs of America's Economic Decline

- America's child poverty levels are worse than in any developed country including the nations of Poland, Lithuania, and Estonia.
- Median adult wealth in the U.S. ($39,000) is 27th globally, putting it behind Cyprus, Taiwan, and Ireland.

Median wealth per adult ranks 27th out of 27 high-income countries. We may feel like global leaders, but per capita median income ($18,700) is low and unchanged since 2000.

- The U.S. ranked 36th out of 162 countries in people living below poverty. Officially, 45.3 million people are impoverished.
- The U.S. is 34th out of 35 nations surveyed when it comes to children living in poverty. Only Romania was lower. Children in all of Europe, Canada, Australia, and Japan fare better.
- Utilizing 52 economic indicators, the U.S. ranked 16th out of 133 countries for social progress. [8]
- Since 2001, an unbelievable 42,400 American factories have closed their doors.[9]

In addition to the above, the U.S. ranked 16th out of 23 countries educationally and at the bottom in a skills survey and 21st out of 23 in adult literacy. We scored below wealthier countries when it came to our citizens' health. Likewise, America has more prison incarcerations than anywhere in the world! [10] This is not a picture of the America we once knew.

Riding on a Runaway Train

In 2008, foreclosures skyrocketed by 81 percent, a single-year record. [11] Then, in 2009 an additional 918,000 lost their homes, over 50,000 more than the previous record. [12] This runaway economic train accelerated at a breakneck speed when 1.05 million American families lost their home to foreclosure in 2010, shattering all previous records. [13] In 2011, almost two million Americans received notices from their banks that they were in danger of foreclosure. [14] An estimated 7 to 8 million homes in the U.S. have now been vacated. [15] Where do these people go? What do they do? How do they feel? Their world has been turned upside down. Men tend to find their identity in what they do for a living. Millions feel emasculated. Tension in marriages escalates under such financial strain. Divorces increase. Children are depressed and embarrassed. The domino effect has impacted tens of millions as the financial tentacles of this crisis weave their way through the very soul and fiber of our nation. Undoubtedly, homeless shelters are over-populated, church benevolence funds are depleted, apartment rentals are at all-time highs, but so are anxiety levels as millions of Americans are prescribed medication for a host of emotional disorders. This can be partially attributed to the fact that in five short years (2006-2011) 7 million Americans filed for personal bankruptcy. [16]

For the Christian, we have a plethora of promises from God's Word to stand upon. These are not pious platitudes or wishful daydreaming nor the product of positive thinking. God's Word is time-tested, but so few take God at His Word. Of all people, we have hope and our joy does not fluctuate with the stock market. It rains on both the just and the unjust, so even the godliest among us will confront adversity and financial challenges, but we do so in the power of our risen Christ. Looking through the lens of the Bible, discerning Christians understand the signs of the times. Yet, like ostriches with their heads in the sand, many either fail to see or refuse to acknowledge the danger that looms on the horizon.

The tendency might be to discard this book or disregard the information out of frustration or feelings of futility, but until we understand the depth of our issues and the severity of our crises, we will not be informed nor will we be compelled to be difference-makers in pursuing solutions. That being said, it is difficult to overstate the trouble our economy is in. For this reason alone, two chapters are devoted to our financial peril. Every election cycle we hear politicians ranting about the need to balance the budget, but nothing gets done. Voters are irate! Their anger was never more clearly seen than in the election of 2016 when establishment politicians were rejected and a real estate billionaire (Donald Trump) and a brain surgeon (Ben Carson) surged onto the political stage with much fanfare. The two could not have been polar opposites in their personalities with Carson being soft-spoken and humble, and Trump being boisterous, unscripted, and arrogant. Yet, one by one, the more experienced politicians dropped out of the race as the political novices continued to rise and voters rushed to the ballot boxes expressing their disapproval for "do-nothing" career politicians. An exception was Ted Cruz, a first-term senator from Texas, who gained favor with voters by referring to the establishment as the "Washington Cartel," and pointing to his voting record that repeatedly opposed the Republican Establishment.

The point is this. While politicians from both sides of the aisle talk the talk, most have failed to walk the walk. Nevertheless, their hypocrisy does not discredit the validity of their talk. That is, reducing government spending, balancing the federal budget, and enacting reforms in Social Security, Medicare, and Medicaid are absolutely essential. The clock is ticking and we are approaching the point of no return. In other words, we are facing an economic implosion.

What the Experts Are Saying

- *"These deficits are like a cancer and they will truly destroy this country from within if we don't take care of them."* —Erskine Bowles, the Democrat co-chair of President Obama's National Commission on Fiscal Responsibility and Reform in 2010. [17]
- *"We are accumulating debt burdens that will rival a third-world nation within ten years. Once you end up losing the confidence of the markets, things happen very suddenly and very dramatically. We've seen that in Greece, we've seen it in Ireland, and we must not see it happen in the United States."*—David Walker, appointed by President Bill Clinton as the comptroller general of the United States—essentially the nation's chief financial auditor. [18]

- *"We are steadily becoming more vulnerable to economic disaster on an epic scale."*—Simon Johnson, a highly respected economist at Massachusetts Institute of Technology's Sloan School of Management and an advisor to the Congressional Budget Office in testimony before the Senate Budget Committee in 2010. [19]

- *America is on an unsustainable fiscal course and heading toward a fiscal train wreck. The risk is that something on the fiscal side will snap."*—Nouriel Roubini, professor of economics and international business at New York University's Stern School of Business who accurately predicted the collapse of the housing markets in 2008. [20]

- *"The United States cannot go on borrowing at projected rates. Without major policy changes, we risk a debt crisis that could severely damage our economy and weaken our influence in the world... We face the prospect of debt crisis and economic disaster if we do not act."*—Alice Rivlin, a Democrat on the president's Debt Commission and the founding director of the Congressional Budget Office, in testimony before the Senate Budget Committee in 2011. [21]

- *"It is only a matter of time until our financial house collapses. We are living on borrowed time and risk an economic catastrophe unless somebody in government exercises real leadership to reduce spending and borrowing."*—Stuart Butler of the Heritage Foundation. [22]

- *"We know we're going to have an economic collapse if we stay on the path we are on. And so to me it's unconscionable as an elected representative of people to know that that's coming and not try to do something to prevent it from happening."*—Republican congressman Paul Ryan, chairman of the House Budget Committee (and now Speaker of the House). [23]

- *"This debt is a mortal threat to our country. It is immoral to rob our children's future and make them beholden to China. No society is worthy that treats its children so shabbily."*—Republican congressman John Boehner (and house speaker at the time) [24]

These quotes are objective. They are sobering. They are a wake-up call. Knowing that Wall Street is listening, politicians do not typically use such extreme language for fear of plunging the Stock Market or risking damage to their own political image with their constituents.

How Much Is a Trillion?

In three years the nation's debt exploded from $5.8 trillion (2008) to $15.11 trillion (2011).[25] As of this writing, it is approaching $20 trillion. In 2011, our debt-to-GDP ratio was a staggering 100 percent—that is, the United States owed as much money as our entire national economic output was in 2010. [26] The national debt grew by a rate of $3 million a minute in 2011. [27]

Is it just me or does it seem that millions, billions, and trillions roll off our tongues like melted ice cream? It's one thing to wrap our tongues around these two syllable words, but the figures they represent are beyond human comprehension. A trillion is a million million or a thousand billion. It's a one followed by twelve zeroes. There, does that help? I didn't think so. Let's try again.

- If we were to pay one dollar every second of every hour of every day of every month to pay down our national debt, it would take us almost 32,000 years just to pay off $1 trillion; to pay off $14 trillion would take more than 443,000 years. [28]
- If we were to spend $10 million a day to pay down our national debt, it would take us about 273 years to get to $1 trillion—so it would take us about 3,822 years to pay off $14 trillion. [29]
- One trillion is more than the number of stars in the Milky Way Galaxy. [30]

- It would take more than ten thousand 18-wheelers to transport one trillion $1 bills. Our national debt today would fill up 30 of the largest container ships ever constructed, each holding more than 4,100 containers full of cash. [31]
- Fifteen trillion $1 bills laid end to end and side to side, would pave every interstate, highway, and country road in America—twice—with a good amount left over. [32]
- Going back in time 1 million seconds would take you back 12 days. One billion seconds would take you back 30 years and one trillion seconds would take you back 32,000 years. [33]
- The Federal Reserve issues new one-hundred dollar bills to your bank in banded packages of one hundred bills each. Each package equals $10,000. One hundred such stacks equal one million dollars. One billion dollars fills ten pallets of hundred-dollar bills. A Trillion dollars would fill ten thousand pallets of hundred-dollar bills—enough to fill the floor of a fair-size warehouse. [34]
- Let's try this one. If 16 trillion U.S. dollar bills were stacked on top of each other, they would create a pile that would reach 3.5 times the distance to the moon from the earth! If 16 trillion U.S. dollar bills were stretched out end to end, they would stretch from the sun to the orbit of Saturn! [35]
- If 18 trillion U.S. dollar bills were stretched out end to end, they would stretch from the sun to Pluto. [36]

How Does the Debt Affect You?

Let's think of the debt in per capita terms, which means dividing the entire national debt by the number of people who live in the country. After all, ultimately we are the ones responsible for paying off the debt. For comparison sake, in 1920 the per capita debt was only $137 and by 1940 it had risen to $281 per person. In 1967 it had risen to $1,700 per person and by 1980 it had more than doubled to $3,992 per person. In just a decade, the debt explosion tripled to $29,000 per person in 1990. In 2007, the numbers grew to $38,000. Keep in mind these figures are per person which exceeds $150,000 for a family of four. By 2020 it is estimated that our per capita debt will reach $59,000 which is a staggering $236,000 for a family of four. [37] We've not factored inflation into any of these figures, but when you shop for groceries, do you ever find yourself thinking, "How could I have spent $200 on those few items? It just seems that my money does not buy as much as it used to." And you're right. The purchasing power of $20 in 1970 now requires $116 in hard-earned cash. If we're to go back to 1913, $20 then would require $457 today. [38]

So, what is the plan to pay off such debt? You and I will be six feet under the ground, but liberals would propose raising taxes as an unavoidable option. We've been told that only two things in life are certain: death and taxes. Taxes have become such a way of life that we seldom stop to consider the extent to which we are taxed. "How may I tax you," says the government. "Let me count the ways." So, here is a short list:

1) Income Tax
2) Business Tax
3) Payroll Tax
4) Capital Gains Tax
5) Inheritance Tax
6) Sales Tax
7) Property Tax
8) Excise Tax
9) Gift Tax

10) Building Permit Tax
11) Corporate Income Tax
12) Fuel Permit Tax
13) Gasoline Tax
14) Local Income Tax
15) Marriage License Tax
16) Medicare Tax
17) Social Security Tax
18) School Tax
19) State Income Tax
20) Telephone Federal Excise Tax
21) Telephone Federal universal Service Fee Tax
22) Telephone Federal, State, and Local Surcharge Tax
23) Telephone Minimum Usage Surcharge Tax
24) Telephone State and Local Tax
25) Telephone Usage Charge Tax
26) Utility Tax
27) Vehicle Sales Tax
28) Workers Compensation Tax
29) Vehicle License Registration Tax
30) Workers Compensation Tax

I'll stop with these thirty, though we could have added another thirty. You get the picture. We are being taxed out the wazoo. As the axiom says, "We are born free and taxed to death." But now, due to irresponsible handling of our taxes, some in the Beltway are proposing additional revenue by hiking the tax rate. Washington's dysfunction is off the charts.

PAY YOUR FAIR SHARE

"It is time for folks like me who make more than $250,000 to pay our fair share." [39] Those words came from Barack Obama during his 2008 campaign and the underlying assumption was that "rich" people are greedy and not paying their fair share. "After all, they can afford it. They'll feel no pain." I cringed at such a statement, not because I make that kind of money, because I don't, but showing such partiality runs contrary to biblical thinking. Yes, the bible warns against treating the poor unjustly (Exod. 23:6) but it also condemns having a bias against the rich (Exod. 23:3). Taking money from the rich simply because they can afford it, is the same as stealing. While it is not right to steal from the poor, neither is it right to steal from the rich (Exod. 20:15).

This redistribution of wealth is socialism. First of all, who defines what is "fair?" How can the government force people to have equal amounts of possessions? Taking from those who have been most productive and frugal, and giving to those who have been least productive is to reward bad habits and penalize good habits. Can you imagine how demoralizing this would be for the wealthy, knowing they cannot enjoy the fruit of their labor? Biblically, the role of government is not to equalize the possessions of its citizenry. Rather, successful people employ many people who are provided for economically and thus, become contributing citizens to our society. God put Adam in the Garden of Eden "to work it and keep it" (Gen. 2:15). In 1 Thessalonians 4:11-12 Paul commanded those within the Church at Thessalonica to "work with your hands, as we instructed you, so that you may live properly before outsiders and be dependent on no one." He also said, "If anyone is not willing to work, let him not eat" (2 Thess. 3:10). Therefore, the primary goal of the government should be not more handouts, but providing incentives and the proper environment for job creation and the right conditions for small businesses to prosper and thus provide jobs. In so doing, poverty is stymied, self-respect is reinstated, and human dignity is increased. Clearly, this is not the case as of this writing.

SO, WHAT'S THE ANSWER?

There are four basic ways to solve our economic problems:

(1) Increase income by raising taxes on the citizens.

(2) Cut government spending by reducing public benefits.

(3) Borrow money through the issuance of government bonds.

(4) Print more money.

Given the lengthy, yet abbreviated, list of taxes you've just read, it might be reasonable to assume that to even suggest an increase in taxes would be political suicide....if it were not for one thing. And that is, 47% of the adult citizens pay no federal income taxes at all—71 million people. [40] Given the fact that nearly half of the voters in the United States pay no income tax whatsoever, this means they could care less if the government doubles or triples the tax because it does not affect them whatsoever. Wayne Grudem, in his outstanding book Politics According to the Bible, observes that "When a politician such as President Obama promises trillions of dollars in new government spending, half of the population doesn't think it matters at all, because they don't think it will cost them a dime. In this way the government is cut loose from accountability to the voters, and it can decide to tax and spend the nation into oblivion, with little fear that the majority of the population will care at all—until it is too late."[41]

The top 50% of wage earners pay 97% of all taxes and the bottom half of those who earned income paid less than 3%. The top 1% of wage earners paid 40% of the income taxes in 2006.[42] Here is the kicker. People who pay no taxes have become a majority of the voters in the United States which means that future election cycles favoring Republicans will be less and less likely only to accelerate our demise over the fiscal cliff. Republicans who advocate smaller government will have an uphill climb in convincing voters because to do so is to threaten the "freebies" and handouts that Big Government is offering. This is what made Trump's election all the more remarkable.

The government's preferred method of dealing with our economic challenges has been to print more money which leads to higher prices within the economy. Raising taxes and reducing spending is political suicide, at least, that's what is assumed among our politicians. Borrowing money is a convenient option, but we've borrowed until we're losing the confidence of our creditors. Printing money seems painless enough until inflation goes through the roof and the house of cards come tumbling down.

Economist Jerry Robinson says, "Search the pages of economic history and you will be hard-pressed to find another government that has relied so heavily upon deficit spending than the United States of America. Our nation has been allowed to delay the inevitable day of reckoning, but America's day of financial reckoning, which has been decades in the making, is nearer than ever before." [43] If we can determine the reasons for the dramatic rise in the national debt, then we should be able to arrive at some sensible remedies. Yes, there was the explosive government-subsidized healthcare bill. Yes, there has been excessive military spending on global wars. These two realities have been huge and not to be discounted. However, these pale in comparison when considering the nation's philosophy of excessive government and over regulation. For example, in 2012, the U.S. Census bureau reported that the federal government had just over 3 million employees on its payrolls. [44] In addition, there were another 19.6 million Americans who were employed by various state and local governments for a combined 22.6 million Americans employed by federal, state, and local governments! [45]

Having approximately 312 million American citizens, that's 1 out of every 14 Americans who are employed by the government. Much of the nation has grown weary of supporting a bloated bureaucracy that grows larger and larger while becoming less and less efficient.

Furthermore, in 2010, the U.S. Senate conducted an investigation into government waste and discovered that 250,000 deceased Americans had been receiving government checks. How embarrassing! Think about it. Benefit checks for over a decade, amounting to more than two million people, were being sent to dead Americans for prescription drugs, wheelchairs, electricity bills, and more. Comedians could have a field day with this, but it once again demonstrates the ineptness of the federal government.[46] Thus, downsizing the federal government and eliminating excessive waste, including things like the IRS and Department of Education, would be a good start. You think?

As of this writing, America owes more than $20 trillion to creditors, qualifying us from once being the world's biggest creditor nation to now being the world's biggest debtor nation. Undeniably, we are on the path to ruin....apart from Divine Intervention. In Deuteronomy 28, the Lord delineates blessings and curses that come upon a nation for either obeying or disobeying His commandments. One of those blessings is found in verse 12: *You will lend to other nations, but you will not need to borrow from them. The Lord will make you like the head and not like the tail; you will be on top and not on bottom."* The corresponding curse is found in verse 43: *"The foreigners who live among you will get stronger and stronger, and you will get weaker and weaker. Foreigners will lend money to you, but you will not be able to lend to them. They will be like the head, and you will be like the tail."* These two verses alone make it abundantly clear that America has fallen from the graces of God's blessing and is now under the curse of His judgment. The question that resides deep in the souls of many is, "Will the Lord, in His mercy, give America time to repent and implement the necessary changes or will He, in His justice, allow us to financially implode and thus, destroy ourselves?"

From the Diary of John Adams

"Suppose a nation in some distant region should take the bible for their only law book, and every member should regulate his conduct by the precepts there exhibited! What a Eutopia, what a Paradise would this region be." [1]

John Adams stated in his Address to the Military

"We have no government armed with power capable of contending with human passions unbridled by morality and religion. Our Constitution was made only for a moral and religious people. It is wholly inadequate to the government of any other." [2]

— John Adams (1735-1826), *was the 2nd President of the United States of America and the first to live in the White House. He served as the Vice-President for eight years under President George Washington.*
A graduate of Harvard University, he was a signer of the Declaration of Independence and is credited with urging Thomas Jefferson to write the Declaration.

CHAPTER 2

America's Economic Crisis (Part 2) Tornado Warning

Tornado warnings are common and I suspect they are ignored by much of the population….until one is actually sighted or until hearing the weather siren alerting everyone to take cover. Then, we run to the nearest basement, closet or bathtub. With tornadoes, there is typically a calm before the storm. Also, a cloud can spawn multiple twisters and obliterate entire communities.

I use this analogy when describing America's entitlement debt. Many are unaware of what it means. Others are ignoring the warnings. Much of the problem, however, is that the siren is seemingly silent. No one is running for shelter because our politicians are putting on their best game face and masking the catastrophe awaiting us. Make no mistake. We are in the calm before the storm. An F-5 tornado is fast approaching and we are directly in its path. Let me explain.

When President Barack Obama took office in 2009 the national debt was at a whopping $10.6 trillion. By the end of his first term, Obama and an irresponsible Congress ballooned the debt to $15.4 trillion, an increase of 44.5 percent. By April, 2015, it increased to over $18 trillion, a 71 percent rise in less than six years. If you were to put real numbers to how much each citizen owes in order to pay off this astronomical figure, it would be $56,900 per person.[3] However, the elephant in the room that few are talking about is not these figures. Oh, these are the ones we hear about on the nightly news, and rightly so. After all, the growth in debt for the past four years ($6 trillion) equals all the debt accumulated from the creation of the United States in 1776 to 2000! [4] So, this is a big deal. No, it's a HUGE deal. But there is something many times greater that is the primary contributor to the growth of our national debt. And that is, the nation's entitlement programs. The Big Three: Social Security, Medicare, and Medicaid. You may not be a "numbers" person and I completely "get" that. This stuff can make your head spin, even to the extent that you want to close the book and hope for the best. For others, that's being too kind. You would rather throw the book against the wall. Such anger, which I choose to call righteous indignation, is totally understandable. What our politicians have done is immoral and irresponsible. However, there is no way to discuss this Economic Armageddon without factoring in the numbers. So bear with me. I'll try to keep it simple....for both of us.

SOCIAL INSECURITY

I am part of the 76 million baby boomers who is cautiously optimistic (with the emphasis on "cautiously"), that one day I will join the other half of American households who open their mailboxes each month and pull out a check from my supposedly rich uncle—Uncle Sam. Frankly, I'm not holding my breath but when the average monthly payment is only $1,300, that's hardly enough to pay for our groceries and my wife's hair stylist. [5] What's scary is that for 55 percent of near-retirees this will be their only source of income. [6] No wonder this is the top worry for most Americans, especially when considering that the median retirement account balance among all households ages 55-64 is only $14,500. [7] You read that correctly. I can only imagine that these dear folks find themselves praying, "Even so, come Lord Jesus!" Add to this the fact that another one-third of Americans have NO money put away in any type of retirement account. [8]

Social Security is the largest federal government program and accounted for a fourth of all federal spending in 2015. [9] Newborn babies are sweet, innocent, and totally dependent on caring adults to help them mature, but these crying newborns need to be shedding tears over the fact that he/she has just inherited a share of the national debt at the tune of $58,000 as well as $155,000 in unfunded entitlement obligations. [10] Welcome to your new world, kid!

Richard Lamm, former governor of Colorado, summed it up like this: "Christmas is a time when kids tell Santa what they want and adults pay for it. Deficits are when adults tell the government what they want and their kids pay for it. [11] Indeed, the next generation is paying for this generation's Social Security.

Social Security is Bankrupt!

That's right. The rich uncle, ole Sam lost it all. Since 2010, Social Security has taken in less money from payroll tax revenues than it pays out in benefits. So, we have a cash flow deficit of about $69 billion, but over the next 10 years that figure will amount to $1.1 trillion. [12] The truth is, Social Security has promised $13.5 trillion more in benefits than it will receive in taxes over the next 75 years. [13] Our leaders in Washington knew this day was coming. I mean, they knew that 80 million Boomers would be retiring and so for years the government has been collecting more than it needed with the anticipation of paying Boomer's their benefits. But something happened along the way. Rather than putting those surpluses in an interest-bearing account, Washington has spent all of the money and replaced it with a big IOU. Who knew? But now time has run out. Washington has put the nation in such a deep fiscal hole that spending on entitlement programs and interest on our debt will consume all revenues in less than one generation. This hole is so dark and deep that by 2033 there will be nothing, no funds whatsoever, left to pay for other government spending, including our military. [14] So, when you hear politicians say that we are on an unsustainable path; this is what they're referring to. Is there a silver lining to this nightmare? To put it bluntly, no. And here's why.

Demographics are simply not in our favor either. Even the Social Security Administration acknowledges that "After 2014, cash deficits are expected to grow rapidly as the number of beneficiaries continues to grow at a substantially faster rate than the number of covered workers." For example, in 1950, there were 35 million workers paying Social Security taxes and 222,000 retirees collecting it. That's a 159 to 1 ratio. In 1975 there were 3.2 workers to every retiree. Now, with Baby Boomers retiring and job growth near zero, that ratio has begun plummeting. In 2010, the number of beneficiaries grew by 1.5 million, while the number of workers grew by 700,000. From 2000 to 2010, the number of recipients grew by 18.2 percent, while the number of payers grew by less than one percent. By 2031, the Social Security Administration forecasts there will be one retiree for every 2.1 workers. This is unsustainable. [15]

What's especially troubling is that in 2011 the Social Security Board of Trustees reported to Congress that incoming tax revenues will fall below program costs in 2023. The report stated that in 2036 the Social Security Trust Fund will be completely exhausted, with only enough tax revenue coming in to pay about 77 percent of benefits. [16] But then, in the same year the Medicare Board of Trustees reported to Congress that it will become insolvent in 2024. [17] Now, given these realities, you would think that somebody in the federal government would be sounding the alarm and running throughout the Beltway in a Paul Revere re-enactment warning our leaders to try and salvage the system we've created. But no, it has been seven years since that report and our policymakers have yet to come up with a viable plan to prevent our entitlement programs from being a weight around our necks and drowning the nation to a point of no return. To avoid this financial calamity, former U.S. Comptroller, David M. Walker, says, "The U.S. economy would need to grow by double digits every year for the next 75 years."[18] That's a polite way of saying, "We're sunk," because since 1970 the U.S. GDP growth has averaged around 3 percent per year.

Perhaps you are thinking, "If this is true, then how will Social Security survive long enough for me to benefit from it?" Fair question. After all, you've paid into it for years and now millions of Americans like yourself feel ripped off. The Heritage Foundation, one of the leading public-policy think tanks in Washington (at least somebody in Washington is thinking), published a study in 2010. Here was their chilling conclusion: To pay for all of Social Security and Medicare's unfunded liabilities alone (not to mention covering the cost of Medicaid, national defense, and the rest of the government), the federal corporate tax rate needs to be raised from 35 percent today to 88 percent. Considering that many American businesses are already gasping for oxygen, such a massive tax increase would amount to financial suicide. Top marginal federal tax rates on the wealthiest Americans would also need to be raised from 35 percent to 88 percent. Middle-income Americans would not escape a massive tax increase either. Rather they would see their federal tax rates skyrocket from 25 percent to 63 percent. [18]

The Heritage Foundation study also found that by 2037 Social Security benefits would need to be cut by 22 percent just to cover its costs. [19] So, those are two obvious options, (raising taxes or cutting benefits) neither of which is going to win any politician votes with their constituency. Ah, but what's behind door number three? The Fed could print more money, something it knows much about. While attractive on the surface, such a move would devalue the dollar, produce inflation, suffocate the economy and further harm American families. At what point do other nations look at our irresponsible approach to budget our money, our inability to pay back debt, and finally conclude that America is no longer a good credit risk? If this occurred, like the World Trade Center on 9/11, we would implode and our financial house would collapse.

Boston University professor of economics, R. Laurence J. Kotlikoff testified before the Senate Budget Committee, looked them in the eyes, and verbally took them to the proverbial "woodshed." He firmly stated, "Our country is broke. It's not broke in 75 years or 50 years or 25 years or 10 years. It's broke today. Indeed, it may well be in worse fiscal shape than any developed country, including Greece." [20] Are you sitting down? Take a deep breath. Here is why entitlement debt is the monster that the federal government refuses to talk about. Our real debt picture is in a financial stratosphere that none of us can wrap our brains around. When factoring in entitlement debt, our nation's debt picture now stands at $210 trillion. That's 16 times larger than our official U.S. debt. [21] Ok, now you can exhale. Can you imagine having this information in hand and being one of the 40 million Americans who carry an average student loan debt of $29,000? [22]

$210 TRILLION OF TOTAL DEBT!

Yes, that's the figure given to the Senate Budget Committee in 2015, something we cannot wrap our brains around. Several examples were given in the previous chapter on "How Much Is a Trillion?" We throw around words like a "trillion" and a "billion" with little thought as to the difference between the two, so you may find the following to be helpful in making the distinction:

- A billion seconds ago it was 1959.
- A billion minutes ago Jesus was alive.

- A billion hours ago our ancestors were living in the Stone Age.
- A billion dollars ago was only 8 hours and 20 minutes, at the rate Washington spends it.
- One million seconds is roughly equivalent to 12 days. That makes 118 million seconds equal to 1,416 days. Compare that with 118 billion seconds, which is equal to 3,740 years! 118 trillion seconds is almost 3.8 million years!
- The U.S. government spends $630 million every 13 hours just in interest payments on our debt.
- Suppose Congress set aside $1.00 per second to pay off $118 trillion in unfunded liabilities (although the earlier testimony to the Senate Budget Committee was $210 trillion). So, how long would it take our government to pay off $118 trillion dollars at $1.00 per second? It would be the year A.D. 3,778,012! Do you now see what a mess we're in! [23] Our children and grandchildren will not be able to retire. In a nutshell, we are in the eye of a massive financial hurricane created by inadequate planning, poor leadership, skyrocketing medical costs, military overextension, unrealistic political promises (in other words, lies), and moral rebellion against godly principles with the love of money at its root.

You want to hear something crazy? While 148 million Americans receive a government entitlement check, two-thirds of them say, "No, I have not used a government social program." [24] This must be who my parents were talking about when telling me that some people think money grows on trees.

From 1960 until as recently as 1985 workers at every income level could retire and expect to get more in benefits than they paid in Social Security taxes. Not anymore. In 2011, the Urban Institute found that a married couple who earned average lifetime salaries retiring that year had about $598,000 in Social Security taxes during their working years. However, they can only expect to receive about $556,000 in lifetime retirement benefits, assuming the husband lives to eighty-two and the wife lives to eighty-five. [25] Of course, given the financial landscape, this decrease in benefits will only get worse. Social Security is hemorrhaging money. There are simply not enough working people to subsidize beneficiaries. For this reason, commentator Mark Levin says, "the federal government's biggest program will stop with a crash, taking down the older recipients and the younger payers alike." [26] And who's to argue with him since, according to the Department of Treasury, 50 percent of our nation's public debt is owned by foreign governments. Russia is the eighth largest foreign holder, and guess who is first? You're right, China. [27] With these two nations being the worst enemies of freedom, we are held hostage due to our own greed. Knowing that these two nations, along with other foreign enemies, own 50 percent of our debt is not something you want to ponder just before going to sleep at night. Let's just say it. Apart from some unforeseen dramatic reversal, America is headed toward a financial meltdown. In 2009, interest on the national debt accrued at the rate of $41 million an hour. That's $690,000 a minute and $11,500 per second! [28] Remember, this is only interest. These payments do not touch the principal.

While we're on the subject, many Social Security recipients are depending upon this broken program as their primary means for financial sustenance in the sunset years. However, in looking at these numbers the golden years are quickly tarnishing and becoming rust. As a whole, Americans are $6.6 trillion short of the amount of money needed to retire. [29] A full 46 percent of all American workers have less than $10,000 saved for retirement, and 29 percent of all American workers have less than $1,000 saved for retirement. [30] Given this gloom and doom reality, 40 percent plan to work throughout the "retirement" years. [31]

GDP OR GPS

Ok, let's take a time-out and define GDP before taking too much for granted. Most everyone knows what GPS is, but economists throw around the term GDP as though it's common knowledge. Well, perhaps in their world, but not ours. Actually we need a little GPS (direction) on our GDP. The total value of all goods and all services produced by all individuals and all businesses in the entire United States in a single year is called the GDP (Gross Domestic Product). Experts have created what they call a debt ratio, which compares the national debt to the annual GDP. Using this ratio, each percentage point indicates that one year is necessary for the normal economic effect of the total output of individuals and business productivity to pay off the national debt. Did you follow that? Keep tracking with me. In 1980 the debt ratio was 32 percent of the GDP, meaning that it would take 32 years to pay off the debt as it existed at that point. Since 1980 the debt ratio has catapulted to 103 percent of the GDP, meaning that it will now take 103 years for national productivity to pay off the debt. [32] History and research confirm that this is a death sentence for any industrialized nation.

WELFARE

Those on welfare are faring well.In more than a dozen states a family of three receiving welfare support can live on a middle-class salary—all the while not holding a job! In eleven states welfare recipients make more than the starting salary for a schoolteacher, and in thirty-nine states they make more than the starting salary for a secretary. [33] We are told that 45 million people are deemed "poor" by the Census Bureau, but you may have a different opinion after reading the following:

- Eighty percent of poor households have air conditioning.

- Three-quarters have a car or truck; 31 percent have two or more vehicles.
- Nearly two-thirds have cable or satellite television.
- Half have a personal computer; one in seven has two or more computers.
- More than half of poor families with children have a video game system.
- Forty-three percent have Internet access.
- Forty percent have a wide-screen plasma or LCD TV.
- A quarter has a digital video recorder system such as a TIVO.
- Ninety-two percent of poor households have a microwave.[34]

Just a few decades ago these items would be considered luxuries. Furthermore, a USDA survey in 2009 revealed that 96 percent of poor parents stated that their children were never hungry at any time and 82 percent of poor adults reported that they were never hungry at any time. In fact, the average consumption of protein, vitamins and minerals is virtually the same for poor and middle-class children. Additionally, according to this study, poor children grow up to be (on average) one inch taller and 10 pounds heavier than the soldiers who stormed the beaches of Normandy in World War II.[35]

Now don't misunderstand, I'm not being uncompassionate toward the poor among us. Indeed, there are legitimate needs all around us and the Bible has much to say about helping the poor. However, the same Bible says that if a person refuses to work then he is not to eat. When the biggest health problem for the poor is obesity, then we've got a problem.

HEALTHCARE AND OBAMACARE

Healthcare comprises a large chunk of the national economy, one-fifth to be exact. Of course, Obamacare was a game-changer as this mandated socialized medicine policy increased premiums for young adults by as much as 44 percent and pre-retirement adults by 7 percent.[36] Republican House Speaker Paul Ryan summarized the Medicare crisis by saying, "Medicare faces the daunting demographic challenge of supporting the baby boomers as they retire. But it's much larger problem is that of medical costs, which are rising at roughly double the rate of growth in the economy. Today Medicare has an unfunded liability of $38 trillion over the next seventy-five years. This means that the federal government would have to set aside $38 trillion today to cover future benefits for the three generations of Americans: retirees, workers, and children. This translates to a burden of about $335,350 per U.S. household. Moreover, the problem worsens rapidly…By 2014, Medicare's unfunded liability is projected to grow to $52 trillion—or about $458,900 per household."[37]

Here's what I fail to understand. If the government hasn't proved the ability to make health care cheaper or better, then why is it even involved? The consequences of Obamacare have been disastrous. We're forced to pay for things we don't want. For example, if a family has six kids, they have no need for IVF, but they're still paying for insurance to cover it. Most likely, you're also paying for birth control coverage. This whole individual mandate to carry insurance is an unprecedented government overreach that exceeds the constitutional powers of Congress. Here's the thing. If Congress can force us to buy health insurance, it can force us to buy anything. And if it can force us to buy anything, it can prohibit us from buying anything. In my opinion, Obamacare was an intentional sabotage of the health-care system by those who have an agenda of transforming this nation from a democratic republic to one of socialism. This was Obama's intent from the beginning of his presidential campaign, to fundamentally change America into a socialized model like Europe and Canada. It has only added to the financial burden that we're already bearing and I know of not one physician who says anything positive about Obamacare. Quite the contrary. In a June 2012 survey of 36,000 doctors in active clinical practice, 90 percent of them believe the medical system is on the wrong track and 83 percent of them are thinking about quitting. Of this number, 65 percent blame the government for the current problems. In addition, 2 out of 3 physicians surveyed stated they were "just squeaking by or in the red financially." [38]

In a separate survey of 2,218 physicians, 34 percent plan to leave the field in the next decade. Of those physicians who plan to retire or leave medicine this year, 56 percent cited health reform as among the major factors and 55 percent were under age 55. [39]

Prior to the passing of Obamacare, a larger survey found that 45 percent said they would consider leaving their practice if the legislation was approved. That's 360,000 physicians! [40] For the first time, the number of U.S. physicians in their mid-50's (or older) has outpaced the number of physicians between the ages of 35 and 54.[41] A little known fact is that part of healthcare reform mandated that all physicians implement electronic health records which have further lit the emotional fuse of our physicians. One doctor said, "The introduction of electronic medical records in our office has created so much more need for documentation that I can only see about three-quarters of the patients I could before, and has prompted me to seriously consider leaving for the first time." [42] Remember Obama's promise: "If you like your doctor, you can keep your doctor. It will save your family thousands. It will save $77 billion a year, and thousands of jobs, and save lives as well." Famous last words, none of which were true.

One study in the American Journal of Emergency Medicine found that emergency-room doctors spend 43 percent of their time entering electronic records information and only 28 percent with patients. [43] You only have to reflect on your own doctor's visits. How much less listening, less examining, less eye contact goes on.

You're fortunate if you have eight minutes with him/her. My wife and I use a good, experienced chiropractor who serves our medical needs as much as a conventional physician. Suffice it to say, there is much anger seething under the surface of both physicians and patients due to this bad joke of legislation imposed on the backs of the American people.

IT'S NOT THE ECONOMY, STUPID!

When running for president in 1992, Bill Clinton adopted the slogan, "It's the economy, stupid!" Millions would still agree. And on the surface, it makes sense. After all, in 2009, 64.3 million Americans depended on the government for their daily housing, food, and health care. [44] That is about half of all American households. Federal welfare programs subsidize unwed births, single parenthood, and thus perpetuate a lifetime of government dependency. Government policies actually encourage women to stay single by giving them more money for doing so. Programs that may have had good intentions of helping the poor have instead actually institutionalized poverty by encouraging a life of single-parenthood—which only results in more poverty. Yes, Big Brother has stepped in and allowed welfare to serve as a substitute for a husband in the home. The welfare system penalizes low-income couples who do marry by eliminating or reducing benefits. So, as husbands left the home, the need for more welfare to support single mothers increased. Welfare has become a self-destructive cycle. Welfare promotes the decline of marriage which, in turn, generates the need for more welfare.

Seventy-one percent of poor families with children are headed by single parents. By contrast, 74 percent of all families with children above the poverty level are headed by married couples. [45] A USA Today editorial in 2011 reported that 41 percent of children born in the United States were born to unmarried mothers. This includes 73 percent of black children, 53 percent of Hispanic children, and 29 percent of white children. [46] If poor women who give birth outside of marriage were married to the fathers of their children, two-thirds would be lifted out of poverty. [47] The welfare state provides economic rewards to able-bodied adults who do not work. Even in good economic times, the median poor family with children has only 1000 hours of parental work per year. This is the equivalent of one adult working 20 hours per week. [48]

I'll not overload you with statistics, but most of the nation's ills, from crime to drugs to dropouts to mental disorders, and on it goes, can be traced back to fatherless homes. Here's the point. With nearly half of Americans dependent on the government for their income, housing, food, or healthcare and with half of Americans paying no income tax, do you think a majority of our citizens will vote for Republicans who support less spending and less government? I think not.

Return to God or Else...

The writing is on the wall: Our nation will either return to God and allow Him to heal our land, or we remain on this present budgetary path to destruction. Twenty-one of the last great empires all reflected the same common signs of decline. How many more warning signs do we need? The siren is blasting in our ears, but those within the beltway are deaf. More importantly, though, is the fact that God's Word is thundering on the deaf ears of Christians while His Church slumbers in a spiritual coma characterized by lethargy. Economists are saying that America's economy is in worse shape than most European nations. We are living on borrowed time. How long will it be before foreign lenders lose confidence or what happens if a national crisis strikes that only worsens our economic woes?

David Stockman is the former Reagan administration budget director. He is level-headed and cerebral in his approach with economic matters. He says, "The American Empire is done. We have reached a point of no return. The size of the government, the massive deficits, the precedents that have been established for bailouts and intervention in every sector of the economy....I'm not sure how they are going to be reversed or eliminated. This may be a permanent way of life." [49] Suffice it to say, we are fighting for the very soul of our country and at the heart of it all is the moral decline which is being clouded by economic concerns. They are woven together, interconnected, but focusing exclusively on the economy to the neglect of the moral is a strategic oversight. Granted, there is only so much the government can do when it comes to our morality, but we have judicial activists and congressional legislation that have accelerated our moral decay and only invoked the judgment of God rather than His blessing.

For example, since 1973 America has killed 58 million innocent, defenseless babies through abortion, the equivalent of our 72 largest cities. Aside from the horrific murder of a developing baby that is clearly seen on a sonogram, we also eliminated 58 million tax-paying citizens who would have aided the economy in ways beyond description. The wickedness from this one piece of legislation has invoked the anger of a holy God against our Land. I will show in a later chapter how, I believe, His judgment is finding expression throughout our Land. The American Holocaust of exterminating millions of innocent, unborn, defenseless babies has tightened the noose around the nation's economic neck and has validated the biblical principle called the Law of the Harvest which contains three tenets; We are reaping what we sowed, more than we sowed, and later than we sowed.

For now, there is another reaper marching throughout our nation wreaking havoc and leaving behind broken lives, fragmented homes, damaged emotions, and heartbreak beyond description, the Grim Reaper. The death and darkness imposed upon America can only be defeated by the penetrating Light and transforming power of the Gospel of Jesus Christ. The challenge is for the born-again community to embrace its responsibility, the mandate of Jesus, and the spirit of those First Century believers who said, "Whether it is right in the sight of God to listen to you more than to God, you judge. For we cannot but speak the things which we have seen and heard." (Acts 4:19-20)

From America's Founding Fathers...

"He therefore is the truest friend to the liberty of his country who tries most to promote its virtue, and who, so far as his power and influence extend, will not suffer a man to be chosen into any office of power and trust who is not a wise and virtuous man. The sum of all is, if we would most truly enjoy this gift of Heaven, let us become a Virtuous people."

— Samuel Adams (1722-1803)
known as the "Father of the American Revolution," signed the Declaration of Independence and called for the first Continental Congress. He later became Governor of Massachusetts.

CHAPTER 3

America's Military Crisis Rumbles of Thunder

Whether standing to sing the National Anthem at ballgames or when singing the theme songs of each military branch at church on Independence Day Sunday, I still get goosebumps. Patriotism flows through my veins. Riding up the tall escalator at Hartsfield International Airport in Atlanta upon returning home from a ministry engagement, there are veterans and other civilians with signs welcoming our men and women in uniform. Often, there is applause for these heroes. Indeed, America has been the proud beneficiary of a global military that is second to none, recognized throughout the planet as the most powerful military force in history. Our combined U.S. military budget of $700 billion exceeds the defense spending of the next ten nations combined. [1] Any nation that tries to take on the U.S. military in a direct confrontation does not have a chance, and they know it. Therefore, our military is being attacked on another front, the weakening of the U.S. economy. In the previous two chapters we saw the analogy of us on a sinking Titanic and headed toward an Economic Armageddon. The ramifications for our military are catastrophic and will impede the country's ability to defend itself.

The U.S. military maintains 716 bases and installations in approximately 150 nations and we are the only nation that can mobilize and deploy its armed forces through the air, on the ocean, in the ocean, and on land. [2] History has never seen such military might capable of projecting massive power at a few hours' notice anywhere in the globe. Our technology remains unequalled, almost something fictionalized in a *Star Wars* film. For example, on November 17, 2011 we successfully tested a hypersonic bomb that could be launched from any military base in the continental United States. Traveling more than five times the speed of sound (3,805 mph at sea level), this weapon can hit a designated military target thousands of miles away. The warhead can strike anywhere on the planet within one hour. Furthermore, it has the potential to fly at a flat trajectory within the atmosphere, rather than soaring upward and leaving the atmosphere as a ballistic missile would do. [3]

Despite the aforementioned positives, with each passing year our military is shrinking, even to the point that we are more vulnerable than ever. Here's why.

The Air Force

The United States Air Force is operating a geriatric fleet of planes, many of which are on life support. Our current fleet of planes is more than 26 years old, the oldest in USAF history. Some are more than 40 years old. The F-15, America's workhorse warplane since the Vietnam War, was designed to have a service life of 5,000 flight hours, but now has 18,000 hours and counting. [4] The Air Force's tactical aircraft squadrons number 26, down from 133 in the 1990's. [5] Airforce Chief of Staff, General Mark Welsh, says, "Airplanes are falling apart…There are just too many things happening because our fleets are too old. They're just too flat old." [6] "How old?" you ask. Well, the B-52 bomber is still the most common heavy bomber in the Air Force's active fleet, even though 90% of the 744 built have been retired. This plane took its first flight in 1951. Yet, can you believe that it is still the backbone of the nation's manned nuclear deterrent as well as a key player in most conventional bombing campaigns. But what is even more concerning are the plans to keep operating B-52s until at least 2040. "You can't be serious!" Fraid so. Most Americans are unaware that the nation's entire bomber fleet consists of only 170 planes, a third of which are not even available on any given day. The newest bomber in the fleet is 20 years old.[7] There are 400 tankers in the Air Force, most of which are over 50 years of age.[8]

Fox News ran an exclusive report on May 14, 2016 which exposed the severity of the problem. The U.S. Air Force is short 4,000 airmen to maintain its fleet, short 700 pilots to fly them and short vital spare parts necessary to keep their aircraft in the air. The shortage is so dire that some have been forced to scrounge for parts in a remote desert scrapheap known as "The Boneyard."[9] Only about half of the fleet of bombers at South Dakota's Ellsworth Air Force Base can fly. It was reported that since the end of the Gulf War, the U.S. Air Force has 30 percent fewer airmen, 40 percent fewer aircraft, and 60 percent fewer fighter squadrons. In 1991, the force had 134 fighter squadrons, today, only 55. The average U.S. Air Force plane is 27 years old.[10]

Staff Sgt. Tyler Miller, with the 28th Aircraft Maintenance Squadron based in Ellsworth, said, "When I first came in seven years ago, we had six people per aircraft and the lowest man had six or seven years of experience. Today, you have three-man teams with each averaging only three years of experience."[11] Embarrassing as it may be, they even search cannibalized museum aircraft to find the parts they need to get planes back into combat. One aircraft returned from deployment and was found to have 41 parts missing. To get the parts, they had to go to three separate aircraft! You're probably wondering, "Would America be ready for a conventional war with another major world power?" Colonel Stephen F. Jost even expressed the same concern and said, "If one broke out soon, the U.S. would take losses." Another officer echoed similar concerns by admitting, "It worries us all."[12] The same Fox News Report highlighted the fact that the decline of the U.S. military is occurring while Russia and China are building up their armaments.

The U.S. Army

The army is the smallest it has been since before World War II. The benchmark of readiness has been the ability to fight two major wars at once. (Think about the Cold War, when we were able to fight in Korea, Vietnam, and Desert Storm—while also maintaining forces in Europe and Asia capable of deterring the Soviet Union and China.) Those days are over. History has repeatedly shown the need to have 50 brigade combat teams. Today, we are at 32. [13] A more recent report puts the number at twelve. [14]

With the global threat of terrorism, the proliferation of nuclear weapons from rogue nations, and the aggressive military buildup from China along with the advancement of Russia's military invasions, the need for U.S. military presence has never been greater. Yet, we have never been weaker and we are about to lose 40,000 troops and 17,000 civilian employees by 2017 due to cuts in the budget. [15]

In 2010, Secretary of Defense Robert Gates announced that the United States would no longer be prepared to fight two wars simultaneously. [16] Once we lose the desire to maintain credible military primacy over all others, this can only deflate the morale of our soldiers.

Obama's Foreign Policy

Frankly, it's confusing. I am just a civilian watching the news, reading the papers, and subscribing to conservative journals, but then I hear this man speak and observe what appears to be an irrational, naïve view of the enemy. I'm left scratching my head and feeling less safe than before. According to top military brass, the U.S. can no longer handle multiple global threats. After Obama dismissed ISIS as a JV team, apparently the enemy did not get the memo. Just ask citizens in Istanbul, Paris, Brussels, Orlando,

Dallas, or San Bernardino or wherever the next ISIS attack occurs. Oh, we've made a half-hearted effort to scatter a few bombs in the Middle East, but our military strategists are telling us that President Obama's policy prevents them from aggressively pursuing the enemy. He has forcibly retired career generals and forced out hundreds of career majors and colonels. These men would have been promoted to General status in the future, but their absence leaves a huge void of experienced officers.

Furthermore, we know that jihadists are killing thousands of Christians, Jews, and others in the Middle East. So, what did the Obama Administration propose? Unbelievably, it recommended that a jobs program be created for the militants in the Middle East because military force alone would not achieve victory. What alternative universe are these people living in? Do they also believe in unicorns and the tooth fairy? And then, if you remember, Obama announced the date that we would be pulling out all our troops from Afghanistan. Former Secretary of Defense, Donald Rumsfeld, verbally chastised the president by saying, "He never should have said we'll be leaving on a certain date because it tells the Taliban, 'wait a while and then you can come in and take over.'" [17] As elementary as that announcement seemed to be, his administration trumped it by sending Secretary John Kerry to go on record in saying that "climate change is the greatest threat facing the United States and the world." What? He can't be serious. Are we supposed to be fighting melting icebergs or developing a strategy for potential threats from China, Russia, and radical Islamic terrorism? And then, we dare not forget the insane negotiation with our greatest enemy by signing a deal in which we gave Iran $150 billion in exchange for them curbing their nuclear programs and us lifting the imposed economic sanctions. President-elect Donald Trump says that we gave Iran $150 billion and we got nothing in return. From these brief examples alone, one can readily understand why our allies are feeling less secure than ever.

Former Vice President Dick Cheney echoed what many have been thinking: "If you had chosen somebody as President who wanted to take America down, who wanted to fundamentally weaken our position in the world and reduce our capacity to influence events, turn our back on allies, and encourage our adversaries, it would look exactly like what Barack Obama's doing." [18]

The Navy

Like our other branches of service, the United States Navy's fleet has only 274 warships, the smallest since World War I. [19] The Navy today is less than half the size it was during the Reagan administration. [20] We can no longer protect the seas nor our interests overseas. As the Navy gets smaller, the world's oceans are becoming more dangerous. Case in point is that we found it hard to fight Somali pirates, police the Persian Gulf, and deter Chinese expansion in the Western Pacific. Projections are that the Navy will shrink to around 240-250 ships and we will lose our naval supremacy. We are told that the Navy can only keep about a third of its ships at sea; ships must be maintained, and crews must train and rest.

A little known fact is that America has few shipyards even capable of building major warships. Add to this the fact that the vendor base for ship components has only one or two suppliers, which are small and cannot readily scale up to provide shipyards with more than the currently planned number of components, one can see that adding more ships is easier said than done. Yet, a failure to do so only makes the stakes higher. Free trade, commerce, navigation, and the very security of our nation hang in the balance.

The same scenario can be presented for the other branches of our armed forces as well. Most of us could find solace if we knew that the nation was moving forward in preparing for future conflicts by adding to our armaments. After all, the world has never been more unstable or dangerous. Yet, the United States is the only nuclear power without a modernization program. So, while the Russians and Chinese take modernization seriously, the Obama Administration focused on reduction. In fact, Russia possesses the largest nuclear weapons arsenal among the nuclear powers and has demonstrated a willingness to harm U.S. allies in recent years. [21]

No wonder that a Pew Poll found that only 15% of 18-29 year-olds believe that America is the greatest country in the world. [22]

Sequestration

Almost sounds like a surgical procedure, doesn't it? In some ways it is because by definition it is the imposing of automatic government spending reductions by withholding appropriations with a fixed percentage that applies uniformly to all government programs except those exempted. So, the Budget Control Act mandated that the government surgically extracts $1.2 trillion in funding for all federal agencies. It is most interesting to note that this was a ploy by Congress intended to motivate all congressional leaders to agree on a deficit reduction plan that was to replace the proposed federal spending cuts. In other words, sequestration was designed to be so unpalatable to both parties that surely they would be forced to compromise and join hands across the aisle in addressing the deficit, which now stands at $20 trillion. Please understand the rationale here. This proposed reduction was purposely designed to be so ridiculously outlandish that no one thought it would pass. However, to the disbelief of many, the strategy backfired and the sequester went into effect March 1, 2013. This amounted to a 15 percent reduction in defense spending or $500 billion. Just two years earlier Former Secretary of Defense Robert Gates had said, "If you took a 10 percent cut in defense, it would be catastrophic in terms of capabilities." [23] Congress is now looking ahead at its 2018 budget and on March 17, 2016 Defense Secretary Ash Carter said, "Russia, China, North Korea, Iran, and ISIS all pose threats, but the biggest strategic danger to U.S. national security would be a return to the sequester process. It would affect in future years our ability to recover full-spectrum readiness." [24] That is a huge admission and sober warning of just how vulnerable our national security is.

We are told in Proverbs, the Book of Wisdom, that there is safety in the multitude of counselors. Washington needs to listen to these counselors who issue warnings and advice from their years of experience.

Words of Warning and Wisdom

Former Secretary of Defense, Robert Gates

"The lessons of history tell us we must not diminish our ability or our determination to deal with the threats and challenges on the horizon, because ultimately they will need to be confronted.... We should learn from our National experience since World War I that drastic reductions in the size and strength of the U.S. military make armed conflict all the more likely with an unacceptably high cost in American blood and treasure. My greatest fear is that in economic tough times that people will see the defense budget as the place to solve the nation's deficit problem. As I look around and see a more unstable world, more failed and failing states, countries that are investing heavily in their militaries...I think that would be disastrous." [25]

Former Secretary of Defense William Cohen

"Cutting missile-defense funding at this critical juncture sends the wrong signal to both our adversaries and our allies. It would embolden North Korea, Iran, and other rogue states to pursue missiles of increasing range. It would also confuse our allies and undermine their trust in America's security guarantees." [26]

Senator Mark Begich (D-AK)

"I can't imagine a worse time to talk about cutting the missile defense program with North Korea playing games with international peace and security. Cutting the missile defense program is absolutely the wrong choice."[27]

(Senator Daniel Inouye ((D-HI)

"We can only substantially cut these programs at our Nation's peril." [28]

Senator Joe Lieberman (I-CT)

"We will not close the deficit by gutting the defense budget. Our real fiscal challenge and foremost responsibility lies in tackling the runaway cost of our entitlement programs." [29]

Senator John McCain (R-AZ)

"Defense spending is not what is sinking this country into fiscal crisis. And if the Congress and the President act on that flawed assumption, they will create a situation that is truly unaffordable—the decline of U.S. military power." [30]

Senator Jim Webb (D-VA)

"The size of the Navy's fleet has fallen to a 90-year low with less than 290 ships—an insufficient number to meet our national security requirements." [31]

Representative Doug Lamborn (R-CO)

"Threats do not always announce themselves in advance. In order to prepare for unpredictable threats, we must modernize our defense systems. We certainly cannot let them age and deteriorate." [32]

Representative Buck McKeon (R-CA)
Chairman, House Armed Services Committee

"It's my sense that White House defense decisions are putting this great Republic on the fast track for decline. The logic has been simply baffling to me: expand our military commitments while cutting the funding for our armed forces. Cutting defense will undermine our ability to project power, will strengthen our adversaries and weaken our alliances."[33]

House Speaker, Paul Ryan (R-WI)

"Our fiscal crisis is above all a spending crisis that is being driven by the growth of our major entitlement programs: Social Security, Medicare, and Medicaid. In 1970, these programs consumed about 20 percent of the budget. Today that number has grown to over 40 percent. Over the same period, defense spending has shrunk as a share of the federal budget from about 39 percent to just under 16 percent—even as we conduct an ambitious global war on terrorism. The fact is defense consumes a smaller share of the national economy today than it did throughout the Cold War. If we continue on our current path, the rapid rise of health care costs will crowd out all areas of the budget, including defense. Responsible budgeting must never lose sight of the fact that the first responsibility of the federal government is to provide for the common defense."[34]

Max Boot, Council on Foreign Relations

"The U.S. military is already operating at full capacity. It is already too small for all the missions thrown its way. It is already overstressed and over-deployed....There is an urgent need to recapitalize the force—and to expand the number of soldiers and marines, rather than to downsize the force, as currently planned."[35]

Frederick Kagan, American Enterprise Institute, and Kimberly Kagan, Institute for the Study of War

"Cutting U.S. defense spending would put the nation and the current global order at grave risk. International stability and American security are threatened by dangerous contingencies that are becoming increasingly likely."[36]

Gary Schmitt, American Enterprise Institute, and William Kristol, Foreign Policy Initiative

"It's far from clear that the U.S. military can withstand another eight years of flat or declining budgets and remain the preeminent global force it is today, continuing to spare us the costs that come with a world in which there is increasing anarchy and less order as American military power recedes."[37]

William Perry and Steven Hadley,
Quadrennial Defense Review Panel

The aging of inventories and equipment used by the services, the decline of the size of the Navy, escalating personnel entitlements, increased overhead and procurement costs, and the growing stress on the force means a train wreck is coming in the areas of personnel, acquisition, and force structure."[38]

Former Senator Malcolm Wallop, founder, Frontiers of Freedom

"The Obama administration's proposed defense budget cuts—particularly the deep cuts to our homeland missile defense system—are signaling to North Korea and Iran that we do not have the will to counter their aggressive actions."[39]

Despite the above warnings, all of which were in 2011, they were ignored and the cuts came and continue to come, which means we are living on borrowed time.

The Ultimate Warning

While the unified voice of these dignitaries is strong and should not have gone unheeded, the ultimate voice the nation must heed is God's. God is not a passive grandfatherly figure sitting in a celestial rocking chair turning a blind eye to our nation's plight. Instead, for decades God has been actively getting our attention by sending warning signals to America but no one seemingly is listening. Or, if they are, they have turned a deaf ear to His voice. The Bible is replete with insightful lessons on how He dealt with Israel in similar circumstances. One of His chosen means, though often a last resort, was to raise up foreign powers and allow Israel's enemies to become instruments in God's hand as a way of rebuking and chastising the nation for its departure from His principles.

One such example is found in Habakkuk 1:5-12: *"I will do something in your lifetime that you won't believe even when you are told about it. I will use the Babylonians, those cruel and wild people who march across the earth and take lands that don't belong to them. They scare and frighten people. They do what they want to do and are good only to themselves. Their horses are faster than leopards and quicker than wolves at sunset. Their horse soldier attack quickly; they come from places far away. They attack quickly, like an eagle swooping down for food. They all come to fight. Nothing can stop them. Their prisoners are as many as the grains of sand. They laugh at kings and make fun of rulers. They laugh at all the strong, walled cities and build dirt piles to the top of the walls to capture them. Then they leave like the wind and move on. They are guilty of worshiping their own strength....Lord, you have chosen the Babylonians to punish people; our Rock, you picked them to punish."*

Verse 7 says, "They scare and frighten people." These were the terrorists of Israel's day. Yet, God used them as His instruments to punish the nation for defying His laws and commandments. Wicked as they were, and holy as He is, it is no wonder that God said, "I will do something in your lifetime that you won't believe even when you are told about it." Yes, it is hard to believe that such a thing would happen to God's chosen people, but it did....and it will happen to America apart from massive spiritual awakening. In Amos 6:8 we find another example when God says, "I will let the enemy take the city and everything in it."

A popular verse that is often quoted is Romans 8:31, "If God is for us, who then shall be against us?" The converse is also true. If God be against us, it matters not who is for us. To think that ISIS, North Korea, Russia, or China could be allowed by God to prosper, rise to power, and overwhelm the United States of America is not far-fetched, given the fact that such occurred on numerous occasions to the nation of Israel. In His patience and mercy, God has spared our utter destruction in lieu of decades of repeated warnings (which I will mention in subsequent chapters) but God's Spirit will not strive forever. May Ezra 9:8 be our experience: "And now for a little while grace has been shown from the Lord our God….that our God may enlighten our eyes and give us a measure of revival in our bondage."

From America's Founding Fathers...

"Knowing that intercessory prayer is our mightiest weapon and the supreme call for all Christians, I pleadingly urge our people everywhere to pray. Believing that prayer is the greatest contribution that our people can make in this critical hour, I humbly urge that we take time to pray—to really pray.

Let there be prayer at sunup, at noonday, at sundown, at midnight—all through the day. Let us pray for our children, our youth, our aged, our pastors, our homes. Let us pray for our churches.

Let us pray for ourselves, that we may not lose the word "concern" out of our Christian vocabulary. Let us pray for our nation. Let us pray for those who have never known Jesus Christ and redeeming love, for moral forces everywhere, for our national leaders. Let prayer be our passion. Let prayer be our practice."

— Robert E. Lee
was the General of the Confederate Army and the son-in-law of George Washington's adopted grandson. He excelled at West Point.

CHAPTER 4

America's Immigration Crisis – Hail Stones

America no longer resembles the nation we once knew. Our language, culture, way of life, and moral decency have shifted dramatically in the last three decades. A partial explanation is the vast influx of illegal immigrants who are crossing our borders from 75 countries. [1] This chapter is not an attempt to denigrate our immigrant friends, belittle them, or prejudicially profile them by stereotypically blaming them for the nation's ills. We live beside them, worship with them, shop with them, and transact business with them. For more than two centuries, the United States has attracted immigrants in search of a better life and we have welcomed them with open arms. They are to be greatly admired for their courage, initiative, and work ethic.

Observing the numbers below, you can easily see a steady and controlled flow into our nation…until this century.

1901-1910 . . . . 8.8 million

1911-1920 . . . . 5.7 million

1921-1930 . . . . 4 million

1931-1940 500,000

1941-1950 . . . . 1 million

1951-1960 . . . . 2.5 million

1961-1970 . . . . 3.3 million

2000-2014 . . . . 14 million [2]

THE HISPANIC EXPLOSION IN AMERICA

Estimates are that 700,000 illegals enter America each year, [3] but of those who actually stay by avoiding deportation, the U.S. Border Patrol puts the number between 5,000 and 10,000 daily. [4] Unbelievably, America has already taken in more than one-quarter of Mexico's entire population, according to the Pew Research Center's analysis of census data. [5] The United States has more Hispanics than any other country besides Mexico. [6] The Hispanic population makes up 47 percent of New Mexico, 39 percent of California, 38 percent of Texas, 30 percent of Arizona, and 27 percent of Nevada. [7] California is an example of how rapidly this influx has occurred. In 1980, the state was home to 4.5 million Hispanics. Today, there are officially 14 million. [8] There are more Hispanics in California than there are people in 46 other states. [9] Los Angeles alone spends more than $1.6 billion a year on illegal aliens—$600 million for welfare, $550 million for public safety, and $500 million for their healthcare. [10] In 1970, there were fewer than a million Mexican immigrants here. Today there are 25 to 50 million Mexican immigrants, depending on whose estimate of the illegal population you accept. Keep in mind that these figures do not account for the children born to illegals who become automatic citizens of our country. So, how many illegals do we have residing in the United States? One Border Patrol Agent puts the number at 38 million which he claims to be a conservative estimate. Here's why. For each apprehension of an illegal, there are seven more that slip through the border. However, for the sake of this equation, let's assume that number is reduced to three instead of seven. The Department of Homeland Security claims there are 1.2 million apprehensions per year and multiplying it by 3 comes to 3.6 million illegal entries per year; then multiplying that number by 10 (for a decade), we arrive at 36 million illegal entries into the United States. When you add 2 million visa overstays, the total is now at 38 million illegal aliens. [11] Since this estimate only accounts for a decade, it is understandable why The Center for Immigration Studies claims the number to be more than 50 million with an additional 30 million who will arrive in the next 20 years. [12] Under Obama's watch, 2.5 million illegals have crossed the border. [13] On April 22, 2015, the Congressional Research Service reported to the Senate Judiciary Committee that "Between 1970 and 2013, the estimated foreign-born population in the United States increased from 9,740,000 to 41,348,066, an increase of 31,608,066 persons. This represents a 324 percent increase over this 43 year period. [14]

So, what is the significance of these numbers? Do they REALLY matter? Yes and here's why. Immigrants from Third World countries are pouring into our nation in unprecedented numbers and what's going under-reported is the fact that illegal aliens murder more people inside the USA every year than were killed in the attack on Pearl Harbor. [15] Illegal aliens murder more people inside the USA every year than were killed in the terrorist attack on 9/11 and they murder 25 times more people inside the USA every year than were killed in the Oklahoma City bombing. [16] Illegal aliens have murdered more people in the USA than were killed on 9/11, and in the wars in Afghanistan and Iraq *combined.* [17] In the first 3½ months of 2016, illegal aliens murdered more than 36,360 people inside the USA. [18] In a 79-page National Gang Report published in 2013 by the FBI, it was shown that 80 percent of the gangs in the Southwest were comprised of illegal aliens. [19] The crimes committed by these illegals include, weapons trafficking, alien smuggling, human trafficking, prostitution, extortion, robbery, auto theft, homicide, racketeering, money laundering, and drug-related crimes. The FBI estimates there to be 33,000 gangs operating in all 50 states totaling 1.4 million roaming our streets and neighborhoods. [20] In my own state of Georgia, between 2000-2007 we had a 152 percent increase of illegal immigrant population, the fastest rate of growth in the nation. [21]

Obviously, this is not suggesting that all illegal immigrants are murderers. I'm a news junkie by most definitions and I seldom, if ever, hear these facts reported. No doubt, the under-reporting is due to political correctness, wanting to show tolerance and diversity, and embracing a multi-culturally pluralistic society. It may sound harsh, and I may be perceived as racially prejudice, but such is not at all the case. I wholeheartedly support immigration as long as it's done legally. I simply fail to understand why we have yet to close our borders, especially given the crime statistics of illegals. Then, when you throw in the threat of terrorists invading our country, it's unconscionable and practically an act of treason that our borders remain so porous. Back in 2006, the DHS stated that 605,000 foreign-born criminals would be arrested by state and local law enforcement in 2007 alone. If their estimate is correct, then nearly a third of the 2 million prisoners in state and local facilities "that year" were foreign born. [22] We've not begun to scratch the surface in discussing rape, drugs, and other criminal activity. The stats are off the charts. Here are two that are especially interesting. In the United States, Hispanics are seven times more likely to give birth between the ages of ten and fourteen. [23] Welfare once again comes to the rescue thanks to the American taxpayer. Furthermore, Special Agent Laura Mark says that "Ninety to 95 percent of the marijuana in California is grown by Mexican nationals who work for the drug cartels." [24]

But despite the astronomical correlation between crime and illegal immigration, the Obama administration advocates Amnesty, a term the media and politicians falsely assume that the population understands. By definition, amnesty is a pardon for political offenses against a government, often granted without a trial or conviction. In other words, we simply overlook any past offenses, such as crossing our borders illegally. It seems impractical to deport millions back to Mexico, especially since their children are now U.S. citizens, so the simpler approach is to declare them to be citizens. That's a popular line of thinking.

The Political Impact

The political ramifications surrounding immigration policy is huge for both sides of the aisle. It is common knowledge that immigrants overwhelmingly vote democrat. Just a year before the 1996 presidential election, the Clinton White House naturalized 1 million immigrants just in time for his re-election. Criminal background checks were expedited for 200,000 applicants so that citizenship was granted to at least 70,000 people with FBI criminal records and 10,000 with felony records.[25] The Pew Hispanic Center reports that Hispanics will account for 40 percent of the growth in the electorate over the next two decades. By 2030, 40 million Hispanics will be eligible voters, up from 23.7 million today.[26] The Latino vote was certainly a key component in Obama's 2012 re-election bid over Mitt Romney. Making up 16 percent of the nation's population, Hispanics voted for Obama over Romney 71 percent to 27 percent.[27] Not surprisingly, illegal immigrants favor Democrats 54 percent to 19 percent.[28] No wonder that 53 percent of Democrats think tax-paying *illegal* immigrants should have the right to vote.[29] It is shocking to me that the percentage was not higher, but equally as surprising was the fact that 21 percent of Republicans agreed.[30]

Further proof that Democrats view immigrants as a huge voting block for their cause, on May 11, 2016, liberal groups launched a drive to register 1 million immigrants in key battleground states to try to stop Donald Trump's presidential bid. Headed by the National Partnership for New Americans, 500,000 people had already been contacted six months prior to the election in an aggressive effort to swing the vote to the Democrats.[31]

You might wonder why these millions of immigrants overwhelmingly align themselves with Democrats. For one thing, many immigrants come to America from other countries that are socialistic in government structure. Their home countries offered government-run healthcare, pension systems, and a host of other benefits. Thus, immigrants coming from these countries are predisposed to think of government in socialistic ways. From their perspective, a natural function of government is to redistribute economic resources. They expect government to act as a caregiver. While many of us adamantly disagree with this mindset, it makes perfect sense to the immigrant mind. Democrats believe in big government and whichever party offers the most "freebies" then that's the party immigrants (and a large percentage of Americans) will vote for. Case in point is Bernie Sanders, a self-proclaimed Democratic-Socialist who ran against Hillary Clinton for the Democratic nomination in the 2016 primary. Students were a primary demographic support for him because he campaigned for free college tuition. From the outset of the race, all the analysts and commentators were declaring an easy win for Clinton. It was supposed to be a simple walk in the park to victory. Much to everyone's surprise, Sanders' appeal for revolution and his "feel the bern" slogan caught on and he was consistently raising more money, out-numbering Hillary in rallies, and this 74-year old socialist was clearly generating more enthusiasm than Clinton.

The point is, there is a fundamental, deep-rooted assumption about government which the Republican Party must overcome if it is to reach the immigrant mind. The challenge for conservatives is how to explain to immigrants that the free enterprise system gives them more economic opportunity than a big government mentality that provides cradle-to-grave services. For one thing, immigrants need to learn about our American Heritage. Unfortunately, we have historians who are revisionists and often re-write history to fit their liberal worldview. By eliminating any reference to God or the Judeo-Christian heritage of our nation or the strong biblical stance of our Founding Fathers, then a chunk of American history has been omitted and is treason to what it means to be an American. Such is a betrayal, of our American heritage as Americans, but also of the journalistic code of ethics and objectivity as a historian. Nevertheless, compare any American history textbook with one used in a homeschool curriculum and you're in for a big surprise. The perspectives of history are astonishingly different.

Incidentally, in 2016 the governors of Maryland, Kentucky, and Virginia (maybe more, but at least these three) exercised executive order in restoring voting rights to people with felony convictions. For Virginia, the number was 200,000; for Maryland, it was 40,000. For Kentucky, it's approximately 100,000. The timing of this was not coincidental, just months prior to the 2016 presidential election. All three governors were Democrats. It's just one more "under the table" move to try and steal an election. Such action does not reflect the heart of the citizens, but it was this very kind of thing that created a desire to see someone run for President who did not have a political pedigree. Enter Donald Trump. Enter Ben Carson. Enter Carly Fiorina. No doubt, more will surface in future elections.

The Economic Impact

The most eminent economists in the nation concur that America's economy is teetering on total collapse and we are living on borrowed time. So, the last thing we need to do is enact an immigration policy that would perpetuate our economic peril. Sadly, political correctness is driving America over the fiscal cliff. Estimates indicate that 4 percent of the school-age population is comprised of children who are illegal immigrants. [32] Many require remedial assistance in language skills which only impedes other students and increases the cost of education. In fact, more than a third of all immigrants don't even have a high school diploma. [33] A decade ago, Standard & Poor estimated that our local school districts were educating 1.8 million illegal children at an average annual cost of $7,500 per student. Thus, the cost of providing education to these children is about $11.2 billion.[34] What's more perplexing is that illegal immigrants who have attended school in California for three years are eligible for reduced in-state tuition at public colleges.[35]

Illegal immigrants can also get emergency care through Medicaid. In 2010, the average immigrant household received around $24,721 in government benefits and services while paying $10,334 in taxes. The annual fiscal deficit of $14,387 per household is placed on the backs of U.S. taxpayers which, all total, amount to $54.5 billion annually.[36] Again, this was in 2010, so the cost is much more today. The cost to California in 2010 was $21.8 billion and for New York it is $9.5 billion annually.[37] Welfare consumption in Minnesota has more than doubled due to immigrants—only half of whom have jobs.[38] Corporate businesses are reaping the benefits of cheap labor while taxpayers pay the infrastructure cost. Over $60 billion are earned by illegal aliens in the U.S. each year with much of that money being sent home to Mexico, thus amounting to one of Mexico's largest revenue streams and a massive transfer of wealth from America. The total K-12 school expenditure for illegal immigrants costs the states $7.4 billion annually.[39] Here's the real kicker. According to the World Bank and the International Monetary Fund, Mexican immigrants send at least $20 billion out of America back to their relatives in Mexico each year.[40] Let that sink in. Those who are reliant on welfare are sending much of it back to their native country. This is money unavailable for investment in American companies or the purchase of American products. So, not only do taxpayers support Americans who have lost their jobs to low-wage immigrant laborers, but we support 75 percent of the immigrant families from Mexico who are on government assistance.[41] Seventy-three percent of legal Mexican immigrants send money back to their native land and 83 percent of illegal immigrants do.[42]

In all fairness, there are others who argue that undocumented immigrants have had a positive impact on the economy. I'm just not one of them, especially given the government expenditures for education, criminal justice, and emergency care services all of which are being borne by you and me, the U.S. taxpayer. We erase our borders, give them driver's licenses, let them continue to speak another language (which I detest when trying to call customer service), give them free education, free healthcare, social security benefits, and then allow them to threaten our way of life through documented murders of tens of thousands of American citizens who have paid hard-earned tax dollars for them to enjoy these freebies. Perhaps this is an unfair caricature. But, I agree with Ann Coulter's assessment: Third World immigration + massive welfare state + political correctness = *The End of America.* [43]

It seems that we are giving away our country without a shot being fired. The endless flow of immigrants is draining our economy and soaking up every last dollar of government aid. Enough already! Please do not misunderstand. This is nothing personal against these hard-working undocumented immigrants who desire to live a quiet, peaceful life and assimilate into our communities and truly love America. I harbor no anger toward these dear folks who walk through our porous borders and exploit our welfare system in order to make a better life for themselves and provide for their families. My beef is with our irresponsible, lax immigration policies and unwillingness to close the borders. My goodness, for the past 40 years, in each election cycle candidates rant and rave about this issue, but then do nothing about it once they're elected to office. We have now kicked the proverbial economic can down the road for so long that the can is now flat and can no longer be kicked. Furthermore, we've kicked the can so far that the road has now dead-ended. Now, we've grown a monster that is out of control and no politician, despite his negotiation skills, is going to come away unscathed from the tough choices facing him.

Joe Legal and Jose Illegal

From a sheer economic impact, consider the "real-life" scenarios of Joe Legal and Jose Illegal. Both men have two families, two parents, and two children. Joe Legal works in construction, has a Social Security Number and makes $25 per hour with payroll taxes deducted. Jose Illegal also works in construction, has NO Social Security Number, and gets paid $15 cash per hour "under the table."

Joe Legal's wages at $25 per hour, 40 hours per week, amounts to $1,000 per week or $52,000 per year. Now, after deducting 30% for state and federal tax, Joe's take-home pay is $31,231. Jose Illegal's wages at $15 per hour, 40 hours per week, amounts to $600 per week or $31,200 per year. Jose pays no taxes so he stays at $31,200.

Joe Legal pays Medical and Dental Insurance with limited coverage at a rate of $1,000 per month or $12,000 per year. Joe Legal now has $19,231. Jose Illegal, on the other hand, has full Medical and Dental coverage through the state and local clinics at a cost of $0.00 per year. Jose still has $31,200.

Joe Legal makes too much money to be eligible for Food Stamps or Welfare, so he pays $1,000 per month for food or $12,000 per year. Joe Legal now has $7,231. Jose Illegal has no documented income, so he is eligible for Food Stamps and Welfare. Jose still has $31,200.

Joe Legal pays rent at $1,000 per month, $12,000 per year. Whoa, now Joe is in the hole at minus $4,769. Jose Illegal receives a $500 per month Federal rent subsidy. Jose, therefore, pays rent at $500 per month (section 8 housing). This amounts to $6,000 per year. Jose Illegal still has $25,200.

Joe Legal now must work overtime on Saturdays or get a part time job to make up for slack. Of course, his wife could also work, but with two children, she prefers to be a stay-at-home Mom and invest her time into the kids. Jose has nights and weekends off with his family.

Joe Legal's and Jose Illegal's children both attend the same school. Joe Legal pays for his children's lunches. Jose Illegal's children get a government sponsored breakfast and lunch and they also qualify to be bused to school at taxpayer expense.

Jose Illegal's children have an after school ESL program. Joe Legal's children would have to find a way to get to school and go home after school as "latch-key kids" were it not for their Mom who has chosen to stay at home.

Joe Legal and Jose Illegal both enjoy the same police and fire services, but Joe paid for them and Jose did not. Jose Illegal sends money back home to Mexico to build a new home and retirement. He has money to buy a new truck. Joe Legal is still in the hole. [44]

You easily understand why, according to the monthly Bureau of Labor Statistics, "foreign-born" jobs numbers increased by 14,000 while those for "native-born" Americans fell off a cliff by 262,000. Over the past three months, the job numbers for native-born Americans dropped by nearly 1 million while jobs for immigrants grew by 218,000. [45]

When expressed in practical terms like this, we can easily see why illegal immigration is a lightning rod issue for much of the nation. We're simply tired of our elected officials putting political correctness over correct policy. And furthermore, we're tired of seeing immigrants who have no desire to assimilate themselves into the culture by learning to speak English, respect our flag, and respecting our rule of law, the Constitution. And don't ask me to set aside my American heritage and Christian traditions in order to accommodate political correctness that has run amuck. While Trump was not my first choice for the Republican nominee in the primaries, it was his courage in bringing this divisive issue to the forefront of the political narrative and his frank, straightforward language in addressing this problem that gained him favor in the minds of millions. Quite simply, he hit a nerve that resonated with a large percentage of the population.

It also needs to be said that 3.3 million Muslims live in the United States. Knowing that the terrorists associated with ISIS and other militant groups from the Middle East are primarily radical Islamists one cannot help but wonder how many of these Muslims within our borders have been radicalized. Conscientious objectors may say "only one percent," but that's still more than 33,000 jihadists, more than half of whom entered the country through immigration.[46]

Indeed, the face of America has changed. Hispanics comprise 15 percent of the population and by 2050; their numbers will have risen from 47 million to 133 million.[47] On average, it takes a minimum of 2.1 births per family to maintain a culture from generation to generation. America's average birth is now below the 2.1 required minimum, and has been for some time. On the other hand, third world immigrants are encouraged to have large families. After all, by law, any child born in the U.S. has automatic citizenship. The average Muslim family has eight children and over 25 percent of Hispanic women have three or more children.[48]

IS ILLEGAL IMMIGRATION PART OF A LARGER PLAN TO DESTROY AMERICA?

Some say that it is. For one thing, there are those who declare that President Obama has chosen for eight years to leave the borders wide open with the intent of bolstering the Democratic voter numbers five to ten years down the road. It is their contention that Obama does not believe in American exceptionalism and he purposely attempted to destroy the nation by his stance, or lack thereof, on immigration. The argument is five-fold: (1) Obama's lenient immigration policy and turning a blind eye to the porous nature of our borders in a time of heightened security due to terrorist threats has caused many to question his judgment on border security and love for America. (2) Adding thousands of illegals to our welfare system that is already hemorrhaging seems sorely irresponsible. (3)

Diseases such as Typhoid, measles, small pox, malaria and a host of other contagious diseases are being carried back into America through a flood of unchecked illegals. Thousands, if not millions, have not been immunized and can easily lead to an epidemic. (4) Increased crime in the nation is often traceable to illegal immigrants at a time when our police forces are already stressed to their limit. (5) Historically, immigrants have been vetted and assimilated into American culture, but today's illegal immigrants have no education of American culture, history, or values. They are simply moving their own culture, language, and values into our borders and it is accelerating our decline. We are a multi-racial, multi-lingual, multi-cultural society living in a nation where we no longer speak the same language, worship the same God, honor the same heroes or share the same holidays. So, given these five glaring realities surrounding immigration, the question of why any American President would refuse to close the borders, is a legitimate one. Either he is unbelievably naïve, grossly misinformed, asleep at the wheel, simply doesn't care, or misguided in his core principles as a politician. The other option is that he is fully cognizant, well-informed, eyes wide open, and does care, but not in a way that strengthens the nation. Rather, his covert agenda is to increase Democratic voters, eliminate the Republican Party and transform America into a Third World Socialist nation. You decide.

An Unprecedented Opportunity for Sharing the Gospel

The silver lining in this equation is the unprecedented opportunity to evangelize those around us. The world has come to us. Yes, go on mission trips to foreign countries, but you can also walk across the street and into a neighbor's home from a foreign country. Immigrants who have never heard the Good News of Jesus Christ are all around us. They do not know that the true and living God of history, the Maker and Creator of this universe, came to earth and revealed Himself in the person of Jesus Christ. Most have never understood that God loves them and demonstrated His love by shedding His own sinless blood on the Cross in order that we might be forgiven. When much of the nation celebrates Easter in honor of the resurrection of Jesus, most immigrants are oblivious to the fact that Jesus Christ conquered the grave and is alive today. Many of them are teachable and approachable. Never in the history of America have we seen a greater opportunity for spreading the Gospel within the borders of our own nation. The immigrants who give their lives to Christ will, in turn, share the same life-changing Gospel with their relatives back home in their native countries.

IS AMERICA BECOMING A THIRD WORLD COUNTRY?

Given what we've read, we cannot discount the possibility. Indeed, if we continue on our present path then we most certainly will be considered a third world nation. It sounds extreme. It sounds unpatriotic. It sounds anti-American. It sounds so pessimistic. So, before taking this proposition too lightly let's first understand what it means to be considered a third world country. Characteristics of Third World Countries include the following: (1) slow pace of industrialization (2) low levels of per capita income that is insufficient to generate savings for economic growth (3) low literacy levels but high population growth (4) poor health facilities and transport infrastructure (5) dependence on commodity exports as main foreign exchange earners.

America lags behind the rest of the developed world in education, health care, violence, and much more. With the above Third World profile in mind, consider where America stands in comparison.

(1) We have destroyed manufacturing. Not so long ago the United States was the world's largest exporter of manufactured goods. In the 1960's, one-in-three Americans worked in manufacturing. Today, only one-in-ten Americans work in manufacturing. Over the last decade, 50,000 manufacturing plants have closed down and millions of manufacturing jobs have been lost. [49] Not so long ago, the United States was the world's largest importer of raw goods and exporter of manufactured goods as well as the world's largest creditor. But today, we're the world's largest exporter of raw materials and importer of manufactured goods. We're also the world largest debtor.

(2) America's new economy can no longer support a middle class. At one time the middle class built TVs, or computers, or furniture on assembly lines. Today, they flip burgers at fast food chains and turn down the sheets in motels. Thus, local economies are collapsing, states are going bankrupt, and 50 million Americans are living in poverty and depend on food stamps for survival. In 2014, 38 percent of all American workers made less than $20,000; 51 percent made less than $30,000; 63 percent made less than $44,000; and 72 percent made less than $50,000. [50]

(3) Since the United States has transitioned from being the world's largest exporter of manufactured goods to the world's largest importer of manufactured goods, $588 billion U.S. dollars is being pocketed every year by developing nations that are now manufacturing the goods that once were made here in the United States. It comes as no surprise that foreign investors are now buying up American industries. Every single second, more than $4,000 of American industry is being sold off to foreign investors. [51] Think about it. In the past our wealth was recycled into the local community. For example, revenue earned by the local grocery store was invested in the local bank which then handed out loans to local businesses to hire local workers who collected paychecks to shop at the local grocery store. But today, with foreign investors,

larger chunks of wealth are not re-invested in the local economy but instead invested overseas in the developing world. When is the last time you saw a "Made in the USA" label?

(4) Our criminal justice system is flawed. We all know that. But most are unaware of how bad it is when compared to the rest of the world. The International Center for Prison Studies estimates that America imprisons 716 people per 100,000 citizens. Russia is second with 484, Iran with 284, and China with 121. In fact, the only country that incarcerates a higher percentage of its population than we do is North Korea. [52]

(5) The U.S. leads the developed world in firearm-related murders. According to the United Nations data, the U.S. has 20 times more murders than the developed world average. More than half of the most deadly mass shootings documented in the past 50 years around the world occurred in the United States. [53]

(6) When it comes to education, America has one of the highest achievement gaps between high income and low income students in the world. We'll address education in the next chapter, but suffice it to say that we are near the bottom of the industrialized world when it comes to education.

(7) America's infrastructure is slowly crumbling and in desperate need of repair. One study estimates that our infrastructure system needs a $3.6 trillion investment over the next six years. [54]

(8) The United Nations released a study stating that the biggest problem facing humanity today is overpopulation in third world countries. And then they provided a list of those third world countries: India, Nigeria, Pakistan, the Democratic Republic of the Congo, Ethiopia, the United Republic of Tanzania, the United States of America (USA), Indonesia, and Uganda. [55] Does it alarm you that our beloved nation finds itself categorized as a third world country by the United Nations? As we've sadly seen, the United

States is becoming more like the countries on this list. Other examples could be cited, but let's just say that the United States is declining at a rate never before witnessed in the history of the world. To say that we are being transformed into a Third World country is not a stretch.

THE BIBLE & IMMIGRATION

The Hebrew word translated "stranger," "alien," or "sojourner" derives from the verb ger, which occurs eighty-one times in the Old Testament. It means "to sojourn" or "to dwell as a stranger, become a refugee." [56] As a noun, ger is found eighty-two times in Hebrew. More than 160 occurrences of these words reveal just how common aliens were in ancient Israel's experience. But for our purposes it is important to note that the alien was a permanent resident and the foreigner was not. Foreigners were those who were passing through the land with no intention of taking residence. Perhaps they would be seasonally employed. So, in the Bible the foreigner and the alien were not the same and should not be confused. [57] In the Hebrew bible the alien (ger) was a person who entered Israel and followed legal procedures to obtain recognized standing as a resident alien. So, aliens were legal immigrants. And clearly Scripture makes a distinction between the alien and the foreigner. The word for alien occurs more than sixty times in the legal section of the Torah.

That being said, here is a small sampling of how Scripture says the alien should be treated:

Do not mistreat an alien or oppress him, for you were aliens in Egypt. (Exod. 22:21)

Do not oppress an alien; you yourselves know how it feels to be aliens, because you were aliens in Egypt. (Exod. 23:9)

And you are to love those who are aliens, for you yourselves were aliens in Egypt. (Deut. 10:19)

When an alien lives with you in your land, do not mistreat him. The alien living with you must be treated as one of your native-born. Love him as yourself, for you were aliens in Egypt. I am the Lord your God. (Lev. 19:33-34)

The community is to have the same rules for you and for the alien living among you; this is a lasting ordinance for the generations to come. You and the alien shall be the same before the Lord... (Num. 15:15-16)

The same law applies to the native-born and to the alien living among you. (Exod. 12:49)

But you must keep my decrees and my laws. The native-born and the aliens living among you must not do any of these detestable things. (Lev. 18:26)

You are to have the same law for the alien and the native-born. I am the Lord your God. (Lev. 24:22)

From these few passages alone, God made it abundantly clear to Israel that the alien was not to be oppressed and was to receive the same social benefits that were offered to others in Israel. As applied to our government, legal aliens should be treated the same as the rest of its citizenry. That is, Social Security, medical aid, tuition breaks, and so forth. Furthermore, God was adamant about integrating the aliens into the faith of Israel. For example, Deuteronomy 31:12-13 admonished, "*Assemble* the people—men, women, and children, and the aliens living in your towns—so they can listen and learn to fear the Lord your God and follow carefully all the words of this law. Their children, who do not know this law, must hear it and learn to fear the Lord your God as long as you live in the land you are crossing the Jordan to possess."

Once again, emphasizing the need for showing compassion to the alien and refusing to oppress him, the Lord speaks directly to Israel by declaring the following:

"Do what is just and right. Rescue from the hand of his oppressor the one who has been robbed. Do no wrong or violence to the alien, the fatherless or the widow, and do not shed innocent blood in this place." (Jer. 22:1-5)

"Do not mistreat an alien or oppress him, for you were aliens in Egypt." (Exod. 22:21)

"Do not oppress an alien; you yourselves know how it feels to be aliens, because you were aliens in Egypt." (Exod. 23:9)

"He defends the cause of the fatherless and the widow, and loves the alien, giving him food and clothing." (Deut. 10:17-18)

"When you are harvesting in your field and you overlook a sheaf, do not go back to get it. Leave it for the alien, the fatherless and the widow, so that the lord your God may bless you in all the work of your hands. When you bear the olives from your trees, do not go over the branches a second time. Leave what remains for the alien, the fatherless and the widow. When you harvest the grapes in your vineyard, do not go over the vines again. Leave what remains for the alien, the fatherless, and the widow. Remember that you were slaves in Egypt. That is why I command you to do this." (Deut. 24:19-22)

"In you they have treated father and mother with contempt; in you they have oppressed the alien and mistreated the fatherless and the widow." (Ezek. 22:7)

"The people of the land practice extortion and commit robbery; they oppress the poor and needy and mistreat the alien, denying them justice." (Ezek. 22:29)

"I will be swift to bear witness against the sorcerers, against the adulterers, against those who swear falsely, against those who oppress the hired workers in their wages, the widow, and the orphan, against those who thrust aside the alien, and do not fear me, says the Lord of hosts." (Mal. 3:5)

Suffice it to say that the Bible clearly takes seriously the offense of depriving or defrauding aliens of their pay.

God says in Isaiah 5:5, **"I will remove the hedge."** He refers to the hedge in a vineyard, but in verse 7 the vineyard is identified as **"the nation of Israel."** One way that God chooses to judge a nation is by removing His hedge of protection. More will be said on this in a later chapter, but I cannot read this without applying our open borders to this principle.

What was said of Israel in **Deuteronomy 4:6-8** could have once been said of America: **"Obey these laws carefully, in order to show the other nations that you have wisdom and understanding. When they hear about these laws, they will say, 'This great nation of Israel is wise and understand.' No other nation is as great as we are. Their gods do not come near them, but the Lord our God comes near when we pray to him. And no other nation has such good teachings and commands as those I am giving to you today."** This was the very thing observed by the French philosopher Alexis de Toqueville when he came to America for the purpose of determining the key to America's greatness. After looking at every other metric for greatness, not until he stepped inside our churches and found the pulpits aflame with righteousness, did he conclude this to be the reason America is the envy of the world.

Once again, to ensure that Israel's godly heritage was preserved, Deuteronomy 17:15 says, **"Be sure to appoint over you the king the Lord your God chooses. He must be one of your own people. Do not appoint as your king a foreigner who is not a fellow Israelite."** As you may remember, Barak Hussein Obama's ancestry roots were highly scrutinized prior to him taking office. His birth certificate became a thing of heated controversy. His upbringing in Muslim schools was also a point of contention. Historically and constitutionally, whoever leads the nation should embrace America's heritage and traditions, something many conservatives questioned when Obama took office. Now, eight years later, having observed his presidency and his liberal, radical policies, those suspicions have only been reinforced in the minds of millions.

SO, WHERE DO WE GO FROM HERE?

Should we adopt a policy of amnesty to undocumented immigrants? To do so would be in violation of our laws. Should we enforce harsh, massive deportation? Neither does this reflect the spirit of our nation nor the dignity of these hard-working, family-oriented people who desire to contribute to our society. This is a highly volatile, sticky issue, which is the very reason our politicians have continued to avoid it. There are no simple solutions, but I like the eight suggestions offered by Richard Land and Barrett Duke: [58]

(1) *Secure Borders.* A failure to do so, only invites infinite repetition of our dilemma.

(2) *Paths to Legal Status.* The United States should provide multiple paths to legal status, including paths that lead to citizenship, paths that allow a person to stay for a while and then return to their country, and paths that allow them to work here indefinitely, but retain citizenship in their home countries. Immigrants here illegally need not be deported but should have to "go to the back of the line" behind those who are already in line legally.

(3) *Appropriate and Adequate Penalties and Requirements.* Those who have come to our country illegally should not simply be granted amnesty. While we sympathize with their plight, they broke laws in order to immigrate and should be held accountable—but in an appropriate manner. Penalties might include a criminal background check or the requirement to pay back taxes for previously undocumented income.

(4) *Cut-off Date for Application for legal Status.* If there is no required cut-off date, many undocumented immigrants might not come forward in a timely manner.

(5) *Limits on Chain Migration.* We need to find a way to limit the influx of extended family members.

(6) *Incentive for Highly Skilled Immigrants.* We should provide incentives that draw highly skilled immigrants to our nation so we can bolster our long-term economic competitiveness.

(7) *Adequate Penalties for Hiring Undocumented Immigrants.* We should penalize businesses—again, appropriately and not cripplingly—for ignoring the legal status of their employees.

(8) *A Dependable Worker Verification System.* We need a responsive and up-to-date system that enables an employer to verify quickly an employee's status.

Russell Moore, president of the Ethics and Religious Liberty Commission (ERLC), along with Ralph Reed, coauthored an article in the *Wall Street Journal* advocating for a combination of justice and compassion. "People who entered the country illegally should admit their wrongdoing, pay fines and back taxes, submit to background checks, learn English, and demonstrate their ability to support themselves."[59] Moore also proposes the need of prioritizing certain immigrants—those with job skills or spouses and children of legal immigrants. Knowing that strong marriages and families produce better citizens, Moore does not think that law-abiding immigrants should be forced to wait years for their spouses and children to join them here.[60]

CONCLUSION

Finding the balance between compassion and justice on this issue is not easy. The two greatest commands are to love the Lord our God with all our heart, mind, and soul, and to love our neighbor as ourselves. It is not our right to ever be rude or unkind. Until we walk in someone else's shoes, we will never be able to fully embrace their perspective. Like so many of today's pressing issues that threaten the health and future of America, this is no time for a PC mentality. It is our love for America that we demonstrate concern for the reckless immigration policies that have been counterproductive to the health of our nation. So, while we welcome with open arms those who enter our borders legally through the right channels and desire to assimilate themselves into the American way of life by embracing the rich heritage that made us the greatest nation in world history, we also call upon our elected officials to lay aside their political agendas for the good of the nation and the preservation of our society by aggressively closing our borders to illegals....before it's too late.

Fisher Ames' Belief about Education

"Should not the Bible regain the place it once held as a schoolbook? Its morals are pure, its examples are captivating and noble...The reverence for the sacred book that is thus early impressed lasts long; and, probably, if not impressed in infancy, never takes firm hold of the mind....In no Book is there so good English, so pure and so elegant, and by teaching all the same they will speak alike, and the Bible will justly remain the standard of language as well as of faith. We have a dangerous trend beginning to take place in our education. We're starting to put more and more textbooks into our schools...We've become accustomed of late of putting little books into the hands of children containing fables and moral lessons...We are spending less time in the classroom on the Bible, which should be the principal text in our schools.... The Bible states these great moral lessons better than any other manmade book." [1]

— Fisher Ames (1758-1808)
was the one who suggested the wording of the First Amendment: "Congress shall make no law establishing religion, or to prevent the free exercise thereof, or to infringe the rights of conscience."

Harvard University's List of Foundational *Rules and Precepts*

"Number two in the list of eight reads as follows: "Let every student be plainly instructed, and earnestly pressed to consider well, the main end of his life and studies is, to know God and Jesus Christ which is eternal life, John 17:3 and therefore to lay Christ in the bottom, as the only foundation of all sound knowledge and Learning." [2]

CHAPTER 5

America's Education Crisis Dense Fog Alert

Spending $12,000 per year per student, one might assume that such an exorbitant investment would produce the best and brightest graduates who lead the industrialized world in academic achievement. After all, spending a cumulative $140,000 per student from grade one to grade twelve, why should anyone conclude otherwise? [3] Indeed, such was the case at one time in our nation's history. Unfortunately, those days are now a distant memory. For the past several years America's graduates consistently finish in the bottom quartile among leading industrialized nations of the world. Consider the following:

- In international math testing among fifteen-year-olds, by 2000 America had already fallen to nineteenth in the world and by 2012 we slipped to thirty-third, being surpassed by nations such as Vietnam, Singapore, Liechtenstein, Estonia, Iceland, and Portugal. [3]
- In international science testing among fifteen-year-olds, by 2000 America had dropped to fourteenth in the world and by 2012 had declined to twenty-fifth. Countries such as Poland, Germany, Ireland, Slovenia, and Latvia placed ahead of the United States. [4]
- In international reading testing among fifteen-year-olds, back in 2000 America had fallen to thirteenth in the world and by 2012 we dropped to twenty-second. Again, nations such

> as Korea, Estonia, Australia, the Netherlands, and Belgium scored ahead of America.

An astounding 19 percent of high school graduates are illiterate—that is, after twelve years of school and an average of $140,000 per student, one out of five graduates cannot read! [5] Yes, in the 1960's America led the world in literacy, but by 1991 we had fallen to sixty-fifth. [6] This equates to 32 million American adults who cannot read and 21 percent who cannot read above a fifth-grade level. [7] An unbelievable 63 percent of prison inmates are illiterate. [8] Any thinking person cannot read these stats without wondering, "What has gone wrong?" And then the follow-up question is, "What needs to be done to correct this alarming trend?" Some would actually lobby for more money. Clearly, a lack of money is not the problem and more money is certainly not the solution.

Incidentally, the above statistics are only a small sampling. For example, another recent study found that only 7 percent of America's fifteen-year-olds scored in the top levels of science proficiency—lower than 167 education systems and higher than only 27. [9] In 2013, 1.66 million students took the standardized Scholastic Aptitude Test (SAT) and only 43 percent of them scored high enough to be classified as "college ready." That was the fifth year in a row that fewer than half of our young people could not score above the 1550 threshold for demonstrating the capability to maintain a grade point average (GPA) of B-minus in a four-year degree college or university. [10] The 2013 National Assessment of Educational Progress (NAEP) reports that only 26 percent of the nation's twelfth graders are proficient in math and only 38 percent are proficient in reading. [11] Even more disturbing is the fact that 66 percent of all applicants for Special Forces in our military fail to meet the minimum educational standards on the tests. Eighty-six percent of African-American applicants and seventy-nine percent of Hispanic applicants fail. [12]

SO, WHERE DO PUBLIC SCHOOL TEACHERS SEND THEIR CHILDREN?

Nothing speaks more loudly or clearly about the condition of our public schools than the fact that urban public school teachers are twice as likely as non-teachers to send their own children to private schools. [13] In Philadelphia a staggering 44 percent of public school teachers send their own kids to private schools. In Cincinnati and Chicago, it's 41 and 39 percent respectively. In Rochester, New York, it's 38 percent. In Baltimore, it's 35 percent, San Francisco, 34 percent, and on it goes. You get the point. [14] Furthermore, a 2007 Heritage Foundation study found that 37 percent of representatives and 45 percent of senators sent their own children to private schools. [15] Nationwide, 28 percent of public school teachers have tried educational alternatives such as home schools, private schools, and charter schools. It is worth noting that this is 5 points higher than the general public. [16] In fact, the general public gives 1 of every 5 teachers a "D" or "F" grade. [17] Another article concluded, "School teachers are much more likely to use a private school than are other parents. As insiders, teachers presumably know the truth about the level of education that is being provided." [18] Indeed, no one knows the condition and quality of public schools better than the teachers who work in them every day. From personal experience, they have a first-hand understanding of the reasons their colleagues send their kids to private schools. Of course, much of the problem lies with what is not only being taught, but the environment in which it is being taught. Many of our best teachers are drained by the end of the school day from just trying to maintain control of their classroom. Much of their time is spent in classroom management because of "out of control" students who are distractive to other students.

Listen to a parent who spent 40 years as a public school teacher, but chose to send his own kids to private school. You see, he knew all too well that he would be compromising the quality of his children's academic pursuits. He sat in the classroom of a fellow colleague who taught at his own school and here is what he observed: "....a pencil being sharpened, a paper bag being crumpled and tossed, a few irrelevant jokes that ignited several side conversations, a tardy student sauntering in with a smirk, a student feeding yogurt to a friend, and a random class clown outside the window. The teacher is probably distracted by a disconcerting suspicion that he's talking primarily to himself." Then, this veteran teacher concluded, "I know most of the kids in this public school. They're not hurtful or malicious. They're just "cool" by default. No matter how diligently he teaches them about the appropriate time to sharpen a pencil, there will still be a culture of coolness, the norm of disengagement." [19]

IS THE COLLEGE LOAN DEBT WORTH IT?

It should be noted that the nation's two largest teachers' unions, the National Education Association (NEA) and the American Federation of Teachers (AFT) align themselves almost exclusively with the Democratic Party and have become two of the most liberal and influential lobbyist groups in Washington. One of many examples is when the teachers' union in California donated more than $1 million in an attempt to defeat a proposition to ban gay marriage. [20] Also, in 2011, over 62 percent of faculty members who teach full-time at undergraduate colleges and universities in America identified themselves as either "liberal" (50.3 percent) or "far left" (12.4 percent) on the political spectrum. [21] It should also be noted that college tuition debt is the fastest-growing type of indebtedness in the nation. In 1963-64, the average tuition, including room and board, (public and private) was $1,248. In 2013, the figure was $20,234. [22] It's understandable why 71 percent who graduated in the last few years owe an average of $29,400 in outstanding student loans. [23] Student debt now weighs on the backs of 41.4 percent of those under 35. [24] For those parents and students who already fall into the liberal camp, such an education only reinforces their ideology so it's not a big deal. But, for the millions of parents and students who are conservative politically, religiously, or both, they should not be surprised if that child emerges from the higher institution of learning wounded, bruised, and bleeding. Oh, he or she will walk across the stage with cap and gown and a big smile on the face as the president hands out the diploma. While those in the audience cheer with approval, often that student will be assimilated into society never again to return to his or her conservative roots. Academia says the student has been enlightened, while others would call it brainwashing. For those beginning careers, thousands of dollars in debt can take years for net worth to climb into the positive side of the ledger. Okay, you get the picture. It's ugly…..and it is not worth it.

IS IT REALLY EDUCATION OR INDOCRINIATION?

At the College of William and Mary, along with other universities, the following excerpt is found in a popular sociology textbook: *"You should be skeptical of any family arrangement that is deemed more functional than another, and you should hold the traditional family at a critical distance….clear rules no longer exist in our complex, diversified, and sometimes messy post- industrial society. Families today take on many shapes and sizes that best fit their members' needs and they are defined not by blood ties but by the quality of relationships. Let us count the ways."*[25] Without question, our public state universities have become bastions of liberalism indoctrinating the tens of thousands who graduate each year. The paradigm shift of our nation is largely attributed to liberal, tenured professors who have no fear of the system, no fear of censorship, and who see their role as social engineers to perpetuate a belief system that undermines the very foundation upon which America's educational system was built. Without core principles rooted in a strong and secure biblical worldview, today's students are vulnerable to such false doctrines and held captive by articulate professors who demand that they parrot such classroom lectures on their tests. If not, the student's grades will suffer dramatically. Too often the university classroom becomes an atmosphere of discomfort and intimidation where the primary purpose is a political indoctrination that contradicts our American heritage. To express opposite views or opinions is to run the risk of being humiliated, derided, and labeled a religious zealot or fanatic who is deserving of whatever persecution follows. Ironically, it is this very group of liberals who advocate tolerance and freedom of expression. Yet, our college campuses are often the least tolerant.

As further proof of this liberal bias, in 2015, liberal speakers outnumbered conservatives by at least 6 to 1 at the nation's top 100 schools as ranked by *U.S. News & World Report.* Among the top 10 of the list, none hosted conservative speakers. [26] Commentator Mark Levin boldly states, "Students are not lab rats to be subjected to endless educational experiments; they are not Pavlov's dog to be conditioned as societal malcontents; and they and their families (and the taxpayers) are not cash cows for reckless spending and debt assumption. The failure of American education is an unforgivable dereliction of one generation to the next." [27]

SEPARATION OF CHURCH AND STATE

As you may know, the phrase "separation of church and state" appears nowhere in our Constitution, the Declaration of Independence, or any of America's founding documents. The idea actually evolved from the First Amendment that was intended to prevent the federal government from establishing a national church or denomination. But it was in 1802 that Thomas Jefferson wrote a letter to the Danbury Baptist Association and created the phrase, "a wall of separation between Church and State." The Supreme Court used his phraseology as justification to purge God from local schools and most public forums. No one at the time of this ruling could have imagined the long-range consequences, but this was the tipping point, the game-changer, the pivotal decision that put into motion a series of catastrophic rulings that forever changed the face of America. It was in the 1962 *Engel v. Vitale* case that the Supreme Court ruled against a New York school board requiring every class to start each day with the following statement: *"Almighty God, we acknowledge our dependency upon Thee, and we beg Thy blessing upon us, our parents, our teachers, and our Country."*[28] This was a defining moment in our history when the Supreme Court banned the teaching of respect for God and thus, replaced the traditionalist worldview with a secular-socialist worldview, erroneously citing Jefferson's "wall of separation." Incidentally, America is rapidly becoming a socialist state as seen in the popularity of recent presidential candidate Bernie Sanders who garnered millions of votes in the Democratic Primary.

Socialism requires an all-powerful central government, so religion is a threat to socialists because it creates a cultural authority that supersedes government authority. It's no surprise that government and activist judges strive to silence evangelicals, censor sermons, and remove God from the public square and from classrooms. This is the cultural war we've been engaged in for decades. Prior to 1962, the First Amendment served its purpose for 150 years. Let there be no doubt, there are communists and enemies of our nation's heritage who want nothing more than to transform this nation into something that is hardly recognizable from yesteryear.

The tentacles of our over-bloated federal government reach into every facet of our daily lives. The air we breathe, the water we drink, the food we eat, the clothes we wear, the homes we live in, the fertilizer we put on our lawns, the phones we talk on, our jobs and businesses, our schools and colleges, the cars we drive, the roads we drive on, the gas we put in our cars, the electricity for our homes, our health care, our investments and retirement plans, how we raise our children, the words we speak. There is nothing that is not part of "the state." Sadly, "separation of church and state" now means "separation of God from government."

HOW COULD THIS HAVE HAPPENED?

The socialist activists found the key to promote their agenda, a cooperative unelected judicial branch that began to overrule existing laws and policy decisions made by the Congress and state legislatures. Keep in mind that most of these black-robed justices were educated, or indoctrinated, in our Ivy League bastions of liberalism. The federal courts began re-defining the Constitution as a "living" document that should be interpreted in light of the changing needs of society. That's why we've witnessed law suits against the Boy Scouts, the Pledge of Allegiance, and many other traditions and organizations that have had a long-standing acceptance in American culture. Through their distorted view of the First Amendment, our freedoms have been diminished because freedom is dependent on a decentralized form of government that trickles down to states, local governments, and institutions such as families, independent schools, churches, community organizations and businesses. The threat of expensive law suits is how the ACLU and other liberal groups replace traditional values with secularism. No school wants to be enthralled in such cases for two reasons: They don't have the money and they don't want the negative publicity. A high school principal in South Carolina was forced to resign because he refused to sponsor a gay club. This is the type of persecution is occurring throughout the nation for those who refuse to compromise biblical standards. Prior to the 1960's we had the freedom to incorporate faith and religious values without fear of interference from the federal government. No longer is that the case.

HOW RADICAL CAN IT GET?

We now have the legalization of same-sex marriage and states ruling in favor of transgender bathrooms. Wow, I didn't see one that coming! Bet you didn't either. It's only a matter of time before women will be sexually violated by perverts using their restroom. Some Ivy League scholar lawyer will probably come to the perpetrator's defense using the ever-evolving world of political correctness and find a loophole in the law that normalizes his sexual aggression in a transgendered society of diversity and the right of self-fulfillment and sexual expression.

But what about the most innocent and vulnerable among us....our children? In 2005 kindergartners and first graders in Massachusetts were being taught about the benefits of the gay lifestyle. Parents were irate. They, in turn, were "educated" by elitists who said, "It's the law in Massachusetts, and we're going to teach it." [29]

Sadly, students today do not learn that so many of our great explorers, artists, musicians, and scientists were motivated by their religious convictions. They do not learn of the improbability of evolution or the credible scientific evidence of a Creator God. You see, public schools do not typically advocate against religion, they just leave it out. It is a subtle, clever approach. Every subject is taught as though there is no God. There is no "right" or "wrong." This subtle omission of God and religion is basically an atheistic curriculum that blatantly denies His existence and His involvement in the formation of our nation. Nothing could be further from the truth.

PUBLIC SCHOOLS: SPIRITUAL WARZONES, ENTER AT YOUR OWN RISK

Before commenting on this aspect of our government-run education system, more commonly known as public schools, a disclaimer should be offered. There are untold thousands of God-fearing, church-going, Spirit-filled public school teachers who find themselves equally as frustrated by an education establishment that vigorously opposes any value or belief that can be remotely traced to the Bible, and yet, it endorses other values that Christians find repulsive. So, my opinions and assertions in this section are not intended as an indictment upon our men and women who work within the system. They are light in darkness, modern day standard-bearers who deserve our prayers and affirmation as they attempt to be missionaries and difference-makers for the glory of God. That being said, when every vestige of Christianity is removed from public schools, a void is created which must be filled. The following citations are just a fraction of examples, but hopefully enough to give you a glimpse of just how rotten the system has become. "Rotten" is probably not the best word. Let's try "militant".

It was in May of 1995 that Samuel B. Kent, a U.S. District judge for the Southern District of Texas decreed that any student uttering the word "Jesus" would be arrested and incarcerated for six months. Verbatim, here is a partial excerpt from his ruling:

And make no mistake; the court is going to have a United States marshal in attendance at the graduation. If any student offends this court, that student will be summarily arrested and will face up to six months incarceration in the Galveston County Jail for contempt of court. Anyone who thinks I'm kidding about this order better think again....Anyone who violates these orders, no kidding, is going to wish that he or she had died as a child when this court gets through with it.[30]

Seriously? Seriously. Most likely, Judge Kent was reacting to the hundreds of high school commencement services where Valedictorians, who love Jesus and pledge their allegiance more to Scripture than to a textbook, have stood and honored their Savior by giving Him credit for their academic accomplishments. One such example was Brittany McComb, the 2006 valedictorian of Foothill High School in Nevada. With a 4.7 GPA, Brittany had the highest grade point average in her graduating class. She wanted to thank God for her success. She made two references to the Lord, nine mentions of God, and one mention of Christ. Prior to delivering her speech, school officials censored her manuscript, deleting the reference to Christ and several other references to God and two Bible references. But when Brittany stood up to give her address, she also stood up for her right to freedom of speech. This was her speech, earned as a result of her academic record, and she believed she had the right to use her own words. Not surprisingly, school officials were monitoring her speech and cut off her microphone before she could mention the word "Christ." [31]

What further proof do we need that the America many of us grew up in no longer exists? This type of censorship and bullying is something we would expect in communist Russia or North Korea, but simply sheds further light on our path of socialism and also helps explain the transformation we've witnessed in American culture. The axiom that says, "Control the children, and you control the future" is true. The children of the 60's and 70's are now our presidents, congressmen, and leaders. They are a product of the social engineering under the guidance of our liberal education system.

A Vermont kindergartner was forbidden to tell his classmates that God is not dead because such talk "was not allowed at school." [32] This was a kindergartner for Heaven's sake! School administration officials at a Kentucky public school told a student he was not permitted to pray or even mention God at school. [33] A teacher in an elementary school in Florida overheard two of her students talking about their faith in Jesus and rebuked them, not for talking in class, but for talking about Christ in class. She ordered them not to discuss Jesus at school.[34] A school in Edison, New Jersey, reportedly rebuked a substitute teacher for leaving religious literature in the faculty lounge because of its potentially offensive content. Yet the school had allowed other teachers to leave literature trashing the "religious right."[35] Another teacher was singled out in a Denver elementary school where the principal "made" him remove his Bible from the library and also "made" him remove his personal Bible from his desk where he kept it to read during silent time. School officials didn't even want the Bible to be in the student's sight and made this teacher hide it during the day, even though he never read from it to his students.[36]

The 1985 case *Wallace v. Jaffree* held that public schools may NOT set aside a period of silence at the commencement of the school day if there is the mere suggestion that students might use the time for prayer.[37] What? Now the Court is monitoring the minds of our kids, forbidding them to have silent prayer. This is political correctness run amuck. Raymond Raines, a fourth grader at Waring Elementary School in St. Louis, Missouri, knows this all too well. He was sitting in his school cafeteria bowing his head and thanking God for providing his food. When a teacher recognized what he was doing, she immediately ushered him to the principal's office where he was ordered never to do it again. Oh, but he did, and he received a weeklong detention.[38]

And then there was the 1997 prayer case in DeKalb County, Alabama where a court injunction was issued stating that "any prayers spoken aloud in the classroom over the public address system, or as part of the program at school-related assemblies and sporting events, or at a graduation ceremony" were prohibited. Ok, no surprise there. But then the judge actually appointed an attorney to serve as a prayer monitor to oversee the school, making sure the order was complied with. [39] Over the next eight months the court-appointed prayer policeman cost the school $62,000. [40]

Let's call timeout for a moment. Take a deep breath. Step back and absorb what you've just read. Is this still the Land of the Free? Do we still have freedom of religion or freedom of speech? Where's the tolerance that we hear the left screaming for? Please be mindful that these incidents are not isolated. This type of thing is rampant. It has Christian principals and school administrators paranoid about having any association with Christianity. I'm a prime example. For almost four decades I have spoken in public school assemblies to hundreds of thousands of students. My *Be a Winner* presentation has received rave reviews from both students and teachers. It is a positive, high-energy, rapid-fire motivational approach to addressing drugs, alcohol, attitude, suicide, peer pressure, and the importance of staying in school. God, Jesus, Church, or the Bible are not mentioned in the presentation. Nevertheless, I am often forbidden to conduct such assemblies, even though there is no cost to the school. Hiding behind smoke screens, I hear various excuses given, but I know deep within that the principal fears an atheistic student or parent may get upset that a "preacher" spoke to the students. Again, I try to preclude any objection by submitting the manuscript, a DVD of the presentation, and a cover letter assuring the school that church/state guidelines will be followed. I dare say if a gay rights activist, a Moslem, or someone from another orientation wanted to conduct a program, then many of them would be welcomed under the banner of diversity and tolerance. Not anything Christian, though. This is discrimination on steroids.

In defense of our school administrators, I fully understand the political tightrope they're walking. Their job is on the line. When inviting me to their school, they are attaching their name to everything I say. They've never met me. Often, they are investing confidence in the local pastor that I will deliver the goods as advertised. So, while I do sympathize with these men and women, at some point we need to put on our "big-boy" pants, have a little backbone, and do what is in the best interest of our students by exposing them to a spiritually generic message of hope that will impact their lives for years to come.

In West Virginia, a federal district judge not only outlawed a student-led graduation prayer at St. Albans High School in Kanawha County; he ordered the offending school system to pay $23,000 in legal fees to the eighteen year-old atheist who filed the suit. [41]

To commemorate the first anniversary of the September 11 massacre, the Central Baptist Church in Sanford, Florida, organized a memorial service honoring the victims of the attacks. The church invited the local school board members, other community leaders, and the general public. The church asked the Seminole High School Gospel Choir to perform at the ceremony which was to be held at the church. The gospel choir had eighty-five members, every one of whom participated on a purely voluntary basis. Upon hearing of the invitation, school officials barred the choir from participating. School officials also said that the voluntary participation by individual choir members was forbidden and considered as "subversive of school policy." But that's not all. The school even prohibited choir members from praying among themselves prior to their practice sessions. When students respectively asked if they could share a moment of silence, the answer was no. [42] Actions by schools such as this are in blatant violation of our Constitutional right of religious freedom and free speech. The prevailing assumption in these schools seems to be that Christianity is offensive to all but Christians.

THERE'S SOMETHING ABOUT THAT NAME

In Frederick County, Maryland, a school employee was barred from distributing Christmas cards with a Christian message. A fourth grader in Ephrata, Pennsylvania was forbidden from handing out religious Christmas cards to his classmates. [43] A school district in California has forbidden teachers to utter the word "Christmas" in class and instructed them not to wear Christmas jewelry. [44] Throughout the country, school districts have discontinued references to "Christmas break" in favor of the politically correct "winter break" or "holiday break." In a Tupelo, Mississippi, elementary school, children had to sit through an assembly where Kwanzaa was celebrated, Chanukah was taught, and students were led to chant "Celebrate Kwanzaa." In contrast, in the Christmas hymns but not before officials removed any references to Jesus Christ or specifically Christian content. They even renamed the Christmas tree a "giving tree." [45] Pattison Elementary School in Katy, Texas banned the singing of Christmas songs, but threatened grade reductions for students who refused to participate in singing songs of other faiths. [46]

Obviously, the common denominator in each of these reprimands or prohibitions is the name of Jesus or Christ. The only reason that "Christmas" is offensive to these officials is because it contains the name of Christ. I could fill this book with example after example of our schools targeting Christian students, muzzling their witness and intimidating their faith. I find it interesting that many of the school systems throughout the nation have anti-bullying policies, but they themselves are perceived as bullying students who embrace high moral standards, but who simply want the right to exercise their constitutional freedoms of speech and religion. There is no reason that Christians should be seen as "the enemy." But Big Government wants to eliminate any resemblance of Christian values because to permit otherwise is a threat to their control upon our lives.

A STEP BACK IN TIME

In 1811 a man made a derogatory remark about Jesus Christ in a public school. Somebody filed suit against the man, and surprisingly, it reached the Supreme Court. The highest Court in the land concluded: "If you attack Jesus Christ, you attack Christianity, and if you attack Christianity, then you attack the government upon which this nation was built. Therefore, an attack on Jesus Christ is equivalent to an attack on the United States." That man was given a prison term and fined $500 for verbally attacking Jesus Christ. [47] If it were possible for our Founders to get in a time machine and fast-forward into today's culture, they would be astounded at how our laws and court rulings are the opposite of what was originally intended for the nation. Today, for example, it is no longer those who profane the name of Jesus Christ, but those who proclaim His name that are viewed as breaking the law. Cursing or taking God's name in vain is no big deal in most schools, but you let a student quote from the Bible, or wear a Christian T-shirt and he or she is the one reprimanded and censored for expressing their faith. Sadly, since the coup of our education system by activist judges and liberal elitists, two generations have now passed and many of today's school administrators and teachers are themselves clueless about America's Christian heritage due to the fact that they are now products of the same secularized system they work in.

The reality is this. The bible was the reason that schools were founded in our nation. One of earliest education laws in our country was passed in 1647 to combat illiteracy, but especially biblical illiteracy. The purpose of the school was to teach people to read and understand the Bible. [48] The 1690 Connecticut Illiteracy Law required all existing sates and incoming states to establish schools that will teach "religion, morality, and knowledge." The Bible served as the primary text in these schools. [49]

Attempting to remove any vestige of Christian influence from

America's schools is nothing new. We must remember that Satan's strategy is to capture the minds and hearts of our young people. He is the perpetrator behind it all. Back in the 1840's an attempt was made in Philadelphia to establish a school that would be free of the Bible and any Christian influence. As you may imagine, this ignited a legal battle that reached the Supreme Court. Read carefully this ruling from the highest Court in the Land: *"Why may not the Bible, and especially the New Testament, without note or comment, be read and taught as a Divine revelation in the school—Its general precepts expounded...and its glorious principles of morality inculcated?... Where can the purest principles of morality be learned so clearly or so perfectly as from the New Testament? Where are benevolence, the love of truth, sobriety, and industry, so powerfully and irresistibly inculcated as in the Sacred Volume?"*[50] *It is heartbreaking to see what we once were, and what we are today. Today's Justices have made abortion, same-sex marriage and the elimination of the Bible from our schools the law of the Land.*

America's first 100 colleges were for the purpose of training ministers. Noah Webster, as of Webster's Dictionary, was known as the "The Schoolmaster of America." He said, "The Christian religion... is one of the things in which all children under a free government ought to be instructed." [51] Dr. Benjamin Rush was recognized as "The Father of Public Schools under the Constitution." He was also known as "The Father of American Medicine," "The Father of American Psychiatry," and credited with assisting in helping begin the American Sunday School Movement. He was a founding member of America's first Bible Society. As an advocate for free public schools for all youth in America, this brilliant educator said, *"The only foundation for a useful education in a republic is to be laid in religion. Without this there can be no virtue, and without virtue there can be no liberty."*[52] On March 28, 1787, Dr. Rush proposed his plan for public education in America: *"Let the children who are sent to those schools be taught to read and write...and above all, let both sexes be carefully instructed in the principles and obligations of the Christian religion. This is the most essential part of education."*[53] In 1791 Dr. Rush wrote "A Defense of the Use of the Bible as a Schoolbook" in which he expounded five reasons for preferring the Bible as a textbook. Among those, he stated, *"The Bible contains more knowledge necessary to man in his present state than any other book in the world. Christianity is the only true and perfect religion; and that in proportion as mankind adopts its principles and obeys its precepts they will be wise and happy."*[54]

Webster and Rush were two of the most brilliant minds ever to have graced this nation and both were considered founders and forerunners of America's public education. Their passion for placing the Bible as the primary textbook in our schools and for infusing its truth into the youth of our nation did not go unnoticed in the formation of America's universities.[55] Consider the following rules in the charters of these prominent schools:

Harvard University

Mr. Harvard insisted that the enrolling students abide by this mandate: *"Let every student be plainly instructed and earnestly pressed to consider well the main end of his life and studies is to know God and Jesus Christ which is eternal life (John 17:3) and therefore to lay Christ in the bottom as the only foundation of all sound knowledge and learning. And seeing the Lord only giveth wisdom, let every one seriously set himself by prayer in secret to seek it of Him (Prov. 2:3). Every one shall so exercise himself in reading the Scriptures twice a day that he shall be ready to give such an account of his proficiency therein."* [56] The two mottos of Harvard University were "For the Glory of Christ" and "For Christ and the Church."[57]

Yale University

When classes began in 1701, Yale required that *"The Scriptures... morning and evening are to be read by the students at the times of prayer in the school....studiously endeavoring in the education of said students to promote the power and purity of religion."*[58] In 1720 Yale charged its students: *"Seeing God is the giver of all wisdom, every scholar besides private or secret prayer, wherein all we are bound to ask wisdom, shall be present morning and evening at public prayer in the hall at the accustomed hour."*[59] Then in 1743, and again in 1755, Yale instructed its students: *"Above all have an eye to the great end of all your studies, which is to obtain the clearest conceptions of Divine things and to lead you to a saving knowledge of God in his Son Jesus Christ."*[60]

Princeton University

Princeton required that *"Every student shall attend worship in the college hall morning and evening at the hours appointed and shall behave with gravity and reverence during the whole service. Every student shall attend public worship on the Sabbath…Besides the public exercises of religious worship on the Sabbath, there shall be assigned to each class certain exercises for their religious instruction suited to the age and standing of the pupils….and no student belongs to any class shall neglect them."* [61]

Columbia University

Originally founded as King's College in 1754, Columbia's admission requirements were straightforward: *"No candidate shall be admitted into the College….unless he shall be able to render into English…the Gospels from the Greek… It is also expected that all students attend public worship on Sundays."*[62]

Dartmouth University

Founded in 1754, its charter was succinct to its purpose: *"Dartmouth College is established for the education and instruction of youths….in reading, writing, and all part of learning which shall appear necessary and expedient for civilizing and Christianizing the children."*[63]

William & Mary

In 1692, William & Mary's charter states that the university was founded so that *"the youth may be piously enacted in good letters and manners and that the Christian faith may be propagated to the glory of Almighty God."*[64] A century later, William & Mary was still pursuing this goal, for in 1792 the requirements stated: "*The students shall attend prayers in chapel at the time appointed and there demean themselves with that decorum which the sacred duty of public worship requires.*[65]

Once again, the first 100 colleges reflected a similar Christ-centered purpose with the Bible being foundational to all academic pursuits. Many of our Founding Fathers were graduates of these Ivy League schools. So, let's compare our educational roots with where we are today.

Past: The Bible was the source of public schools in America which made the United States the most prosperous and most admired nation in history.

Present: The Bible has been removed from public schools, the Ten Commandments and prayer have been ruled as illegal, and now our prosperity has been replaced with bankruptcy. The United States is anything but admired in much of the world as we now lead the world in teenage pregnancies, juvenile homicides, suicides, and a host of other socially unacceptable behaviors.

Many refuse to make the connection, but I submit to you there is a correlation between banning the Bible, prayer, and the Ten Commandments from our classrooms in the 1960's until this present hour and the decline of our nation as reflected in the moral decadence, vulgarity, and profanity, and academic decline of today's schools. Righteousness exalts a nation, but sin is a reproach to a nation. God will not be mocked. He has magnified His Word above His name (Ps. 138:2). For our nation to officially legislate His Word from the minds and eyes of our children is a personal assault on the very character of almighty God. He will not, and has not, passively stood on the sidelines. We are reaping what we have sown. Thank God for those Christian students and Christian administrators who strive to make a difference for Christ in the confines of such an anti-God bureaucratic system. Also, thanks be to God for all the homeschoolers and private Christian schools that are standing in the gap, keeping high the standard, and shining as light in a culture that is staggering, stumbling, and groping in darkness.

Founding Father Patrick Henry

They tell us, sir, that we are weak...But when shall we be stronger? Will it be when we are totally disarmed, and when a British guard shall be stationed in every house?...Sir, we are not weak, if we make a proper use of the means which the God of nature hath placed in our power. Three million people, armed in the holy cause of liberty...are invincible by any force which our enemy can send against us. Besides, sir, we shall not fight our battles alone. There is a just God who presides over the destinies of nations, and who will raise up friends to fight our battles for us. The battle, sir, is not to the strong alone; it is to the vigilant, the active, the brave...Why stand we here idle?...I know not what course others may take; but as for me, give me liberty or give me death!" [1]

It cannot be emphasized too clearly and too often that this nation was founded, not be religionists, but by Christians; not by religion, but on the gospel of Jesus Christ." [2]

— Patrick Henry (1736-1799)
was the five-time Governor of Virginia,
helped write Virginia's Constitution, and was
Commander-in-Chief of the Virginia Militia

CHAPTER 6

How to Kill A Nation

Perhaps a better title for this chapter would be, "How to Steal a Nation." As an expansion of the previous remarks on education, I find it necessary to dig deeper as we uncover the hidden agenda of those who desire to transform America into something we barely recognize. Already, we are well along this path of transformation, but you are about to read some things that most likely will require time to process. Initially, you'll not want to believe it. In fact, much in this book is not easy to digest and the tendency is to shake the head in disbelief, or at best, display skepticism toward what is written. For these reasons, I have gone to great length to meticulously document my findings.

A huge part of the formula in transforming America is by transforming our schools. That has largely been done by transforming the learning environment from one of academics to one that propagates an agenda in which the teachers become social engineers or facilitators in programming the minds of our children. I am fully aware that there are exceptions, especially in smaller communities, but as one who speaks in schools of all size communities, I've been mildly surprised at how entrenched political correctness has found its way into the smallest and most rural of our towns. The NEA has done a thorough and masterful job in intimidating our school administrators to refrain from exposing our students to anything resembling Christianity. The same, however, cannot be said about Islam which seems to be looked upon more favorably as proof that we are tolerant and diverse toward those of other religious persuasions.

"You and Your Classmates Will Become Muslims!"

These were the words that appeared on a flier from a course in Islam taught at Excelsior School in Byron, California. The seventh graders were required to take a three-week course in Islam that mandated them to learn the tenets of the Muslim faith, wear a robe, and read verses from the Koran. Now get this, they had to memorize twenty-five Islamic terms and learn six Islamic phrases in Arabic, twenty Islamic proverbs, and the Five Pillars of Faith. In addition, they had to study ten key Islamic prophets and disciples. It gets worse. The students had to pick a Muslim name for themselves and go on a make-believe journey to Mecca. The handout read, *"From the beginning, you and your classmates will become Muslims."*

Can you imagine if a teacher tried to teach the Ten Commandments, explain the Gospels, require the students to memorize the Beatitudes, or re-enact the crucifixion and resurrection? That teacher would be suspended and most likely fired. Even mentioning the name of Jesus creates a firestorm, but in this classroom the students are taught that Islam is the true religion and they are instructed how to pray to Allah. This social studies/history book is entitled Across the Centuries and has been adopted by the California school system.[3] Historians have shown that Muhammad had multiple wives, including a ten-year-old girl. But, this course portrayed him as an extremely moral man who wanted a society of purity. When confronted with these concerns, Nancy Castor, the Byron middle school principal, stated "We do not endorse any religion. We just make the students aware."[4]

Valeria Moore was a concerned mother of a seventh grade daughter whom she claims was indoctrinated in the Islamic religion for over four months. This was over twenty years ago, but she recounts, "Upon arriving at Joseph Kerr Junior High School in Elk Grove, California one day, we were greeted by a huge banner on the front grounds of the school that read, "There is one God, Allah, and Muhammad is his prophet." She remarked, "What if we put up a sign that says, 'Jesus is Lord' for thirty minutes?" When she started reading her daughter's history book, she was astonished to find that America's history had been revised to show that our nation had been given birth through an Islamic heritage rather than through Judeo-Christian beginnings."[5]

Make no mistake. Political elitists have an agenda of transforming America into a socialistic nation and their political correctness agenda has found a welcome mat in our public schools. Of course, once our kids graduate from high school and arrive on our secular college campuses, the indoctrination only intensifies. Abby Nye is just one example. It was her first of four days of freshman orientation and she was not prepared for what she was about to hear. She described it as an indoctrination of moral relativism, tolerance, gay/lesbian/trans-gendered rights, and New Age spirituality. In addition, there were skits condoning, and actually encouraging, premarital sex, underage drinking, and the normality of homosexuality. They were advised that, "If you have sex when you're drunk, you have the right to press charges for rape."[6] As Abby later proceeded to her English class, she was in for another surprise. Looking at the required reading assignments, she would be mandated to read essays on "Why America Deserved the Terrorist Attacks of 9/11"; "Why We Should Listen to the Columbine Killers"; and "Why 'Under God' Should Be Removed from the Pledge of Allegiance."[7] This is not what you would expect from an English class. Furthermore, is this what our students and parents are paying for in thousands of dollars of student debt? Once again, none of this is coincidental. The opening days of orientation are designed to ridicule those who hold Christian beliefs and hopefully ostracize them or intimidate them into silence. Christianity and expressions of faith are a threat to the radical academic left.

Lest you think I am being biased in describing our professors of academia as leftists, consider the following survey conducted by Frank Luntz, a frequent guest on Fox News and respected researcher. One hundred fifty-one professors from Ivy League schools were surveyed with results showing that 84 percent voted for Al Gore in the 2012 election and only 9 percent voted for George W. Bush. When asked to name the best president of the past forty years, Bill Clinton was their top choice. When asked about party affiliation, only 3 percent chose Republican. [8] This sampling is a strong indicator that the faculties of our secular universities have few, if any, conservative representatives. Often a radically liberal perspective will be espoused in classrooms filled with young people who are still trying to determine what they believe and are like clay in the hands of professional social engineers who know exactly which buttons to push. As much as we may prefer to believe otherwise, our college campuses are feeding grounds for atheistic propaganda and socialistic brainwashing. This explains the popularity of 2016 socialist presidential candidate Bernie Sanders among students. Here was a 74-year-old self-avowed socialist who few analysts took seriously, but he began to defeat Hillary Clinton in state after state and was outraising her in campaign donations by millions. Students flocked to his rallies with frenzied enthusiasm. "Feel the Bern" became the slogan as he challenged the youth to begin a new revolution in transforming America. The only logical explanation for such magnetism lies in the reality that Sanders was a reflection of reinforcing what they had been taught in their university classrooms.

Thanks to the NEA and ACLU, a strong case can be made for the public school system doing more to undermine our freedoms, patriotism, and Christianity than any other institution.

GOVERNMENT-RUN SCHOOLS: A SPIRITUAL GRAND CANYON

The removal of the Ten Commandments, prayer, creationism, and America's Judeo-Christian heritage from our schools have all combined to create a spiritual void, a crevasse the size of the Grand Canyon. Of course, it is so much more than the omission of these cherished traditions and truths, but the increasingly hostile spirit toward anyone who identifies with Christianity or traditional family values. It is common knowledge that 70-85 percent of our young people will drop out of church upon graduating from high school. The assumption is that upon leaving home and arriving on the college campus, they have the spiritual life sucked out of them. However, Ken Ham, a prominent Christian statesman and founder of *Answers in Genesis* and the highly acclaimed *Creation Museum*, has another perspective and his research proves it.

We could offer a plethora of statistics, but let's break it down to a few summary statements based on Ham's research. Incidentally, he boldly claims to have hired the best researcher on the planet to document his findings. What we know is this: We are one generation away from the evaporation of the church as we know it and all the evidence proves that the church is bleeding profusely. Where Europe stands today spiritually, America will be tomorrow.

Rather than dropping out of church upon arriving to college, Ham surprisingly contends that 90 percent of them were lost in middle school and high school. In fact, 40 percent left the Church during elementary and middle school years. He says, "We are losing many more people by middle school and many more by high school than we will ever lose in college." [9] Surprised? You're not alone. Ham explains his research by offering this insight: "Students didn't begin doubting in college, they simply departed by college. Two-thirds of those who are sitting among us have already left in their hearts, and it will only take a couple years before their bodies are absent as well."[10] In other words, college campuses only allow our students to do physically what they've already done mentally and spiritually. And that is, disengage. While they sit in the pews or in their youth group with a glazed look in their eyes, mentally they've checked out.

It is one thing to know when our children are disengaging, but it is quite another to understand why they're doing it. Ready for this? One of the primary reasons was because of Sunday School, according to Hamm's research.[11] But here is the deeper reality. Ninety percent of children from church homes attend public/government schools where they are taught a biological, anthropological, geological, and astronomical history of the universe that totally contradicts the Bible's account of creation, the Flood, and the Tower of Babel.[12] This reality alone removes the most basic foundation of the Judeo-Christian heritage of our country. Though most of our Christian students may not openly admit it, here is the internal dialogue they're having with themselves: *"If I can't trust the Bible in the earthly things, why should I trust it in the spiritual things?"* Again, the bread crumbs lead to the classrooms of our government-run schools. Oh, to be sure, parents harbor the bulk of responsibility for not instilling a stronger biblical worldview. Yes, oftentimes the church has done a poor job in its discipleship of students. But the schools in America have our kids more hours of the day than any other institution.

WHERE IT ALL BEGAN

It is impossible to understand the decline of our educational system without tracing it back to the father of progressive education and then connecting the dots to this present hour. His name is John Dewey, an atheist and a socialist, whose goal was to transform the nation, including its economic system. For that to happen, Dewey knew it would be an arduous task, one requiring decades of time and patience. For you see, he understood that the most efficient way of accomplishing this mammoth vision would be to re-define values to children. So, his mission mandated that new textbooks be written and old ones be revised to reflect the socialist view.

Jo Ann McCauley is a former school teacher who spent six months in intensive research of the public school textbooks. She was astounded by what surfaced. I'll cut to the chase and provide this summary of her findings: "One of the methods used in bringing about changes in the child is a method developed by Dr. Sidney Simon, called *values clarification.* It is based upon the proposition that there are no moral absolutes, no right or wrong. Dr. Simon instructed the teachers that when a child comes to school, his values are in a state of confusion. And since the parents and the church have contributed to that confusion, the school must help the child clarify his own values. Simon taught that the creation of personal values should be left up to each student, not dictated by the church or his parents. Morals and values coming from parents or church are to be replaced with amoral, situational, godless values and morals. In the process, they are reshaping reality for the child. This method is designed to convince the child that he has the 'right' to develop his own personal values and morality, free from authority of any kind. The purpose is to instill within the child the belief that there is nothing particularly right or wrong, that everything is situational. And, when the child's values have been clarified by the school, and he has adopted the correct values, he will govern his life by a set of moral values at odds with those of his Christian parents." [13] This would seem to explain the epidemic of rebellion toward authority, whether it be toward parents, police, or teachers. If you were to ask most adults, they likely would agree, "Yes, I have observed a resistance and sometimes open defiance from teenagers toward authority figures in their lives." Most parents tend to think it's because of the media or their children's peers. Certainly, those are contributing factors, but many are oblivious that it could very well be the curriculum to which their kids are exposed. For this reason, I've often told youth pastors that they have the most challenging job on earth. Parents often expect these young pastors to work wonders with their children, but two to three hours per week at church compared with 40 to 60 hours of exposure from school and media puts youth pastors at a distinct disadvantage. When the messages received by our youth from these sources are often in conflict with their church, which message do you think our kids are most prone to embrace?

Let's get back to Dewey. To reiterate, Dewey's strategy for transforming America into a socialistic nation was to revolutionize the entire educational system. It was under his influence that our schools abandoned the basics of reading, writing, and rithmatic, the three R's. In Dewey's own words, he stated, "I believe that the true center of correlation on the school subjects is not science, not literature, nor history, nor geography, but the child's social activities." [14] Wow, he just said a mouthful. Even some of Dewey's disciples praised *illiteracy* as a way to more easily bring about the desired socialistic changes. [15] Chillingly, Dewey wrote in *Teacher Magazine* in 1933, "There is no God and there is no soul. Hence, there are no needs for the props of traditional religion. With dogma and creed excluded, the immutable truth is also dead and buried. There is no room for fixed, natural laws or moral absolutes." [16] Again, this is the father of today's modern educational system.

This man was a hard-core radical, not content to merely be critical of Christianity, but actually declared that the State would be god, the public schools would be the church, and the teachers would be the prophets. Once again, from his own pen came these words: "Every teacher should realize the dignity of his calling; that he is a social servant set apart for the maintenance of proper social order and the securing of the right social growth…In this way, the teacher is always a prophet of the true God and the usherer of the true kingdom of God."[17]

Dewey moved to Russia in the 1930's and was influential in incorporating his educational philosophy within the communist school system in Soviet Russia. He returned to America with praise for Lenin and Stalin who offered Soviet citizens free education, free medical care, and security in old age. Thus, he returned more determined than ever to transform America into one just like the Soviets. Let's allow him to speak for himself. In a 1929 book titled, *Impressions of Soviet Russian and the Revolutionary World*, Dewey gushed with praise for Russia's socialistic structure: "Russia is a revolution, involving a release of human powers on such an unprecedented scale that it is of incalculable significance not only for that country, but for the world...The people go about as if some mighty, oppressive load had been removed, as if they were newly awakened to the consciousness of released energy...There is an enormous constructive effort taking place in the creation of a new collective mentality; a new morality I should call it."[18]

If you think his assessment of Russia's educational system had no impact upon our present system, think again. After Dewey's repeated affirmations of Russia's system, the National Education Association in 1937 said, "The present capitalistic and nationalistic social system has been supplanted in but one place—Russia—and that change was effected by revolution. Hence the verdict of history would seem to indicate that we are likely to have to ***depend upon revolution for social change of an important and far-reaching character.*** (emphasis added)[19]

It should be clear by now that Dewey was determined to replicate the Soviet system here in the United States—educationally, politically, and spiritually. Yes, his antagonism toward Christianity and our free enterprise system are all a matter of record. Dr. Samuel Blumenfeld is considered a world-renown expert in the teaching of reading and the decline of literacy in our nation. He claims that the epidemic of mass functional illiteracy was brought about deliberately by an "educational Mafia" that kidnapped American public education in the late 1800's. Dr. Blumenfeld actually charges John Dewey with being the first one to formulate the notion that high literacy rates were an obstacle to socialism. [20]

Do you see the ramifications? American's decline in education has been orchestrated and engineered. Marlin Maddoux emphatically says, "The system has been carefully crafted to undermine Christianity, patriotism, and freedom. It is a diabolical plan to deconstruct the whole of Western civilization!" [21] This is how to steal, and ultimately, kill a nation.

USING CHILDREN AS GUINEA PIGS

How would you feel if you discovered your child was being subjected to behavior modification techniques for experimental research by the federal government and as the parent you were refused to view the test? Such was the case with Anita Hoge. Public schools in Pennsylvania were being used for psychological research to determine the children's values, beliefs, and attitudes, but then having them molded by behavior modification. The test was known as the Pennsylvania Educational Quality Assessment (EQA). When requesting to see the test, school officials repeatedly denied her access. Then, more parents became concerned. More determined than ever and suspicioning that something didn't seem right, the parents travelled to the state education agency in Harrisburg. No luck. Refusing to give up, they drove to Washington, D.C. and found what they were looking for. [22] Blown away by what they discovered, they uncovered a how-to-manual with a 1971 U.S. Office of Education contract number on it entitled *Training for Change Agents*; or seven volumes of 'change agent studies' commissioned by the U.S. Office of Education to the Rand Corporation in 1973-74. Behaviorist researchers had obtained grants from the U.S. Office of Education to explore ways to 'freeze' and 'unfreeze' values and 'to implement change.'[23] The test included 370 questions measuring the attitudes, values, beliefs, opinions, and home life of the children. There were only 30 questions on math and 30 on reading. This test was part of larger national test called the National Assessment of Educational Progress (NAEP).

Inquiring minds want to know, "What does any of this have to do with my child's academic achievement? How does such a test improve his scholastic standing on the continuum of knowledge and academic excellence?" The short answer is, it doesn't. Are you ready for this? Pennsylvania was a pilot state for developing this research and experimenting for the purpose of obtaining the desired result of behavioral change so that the children conform to the government's desired outcome and more of what the government wants the child to believe. Teachers would be the change agents. After years of tweaking, experimenting, researching, and spending untold thousands of tax-payer dollars, the government fine-tuned and completed this elaborate undertaking. The final touch was to come up with a name that would resonate with educators while also being accurately descriptive of this new approach to educating our youth. The system they created is now known as *Outcome-Based Education.* Sound familiar? It should because this is what's being used throughout the entire public education system in America. It's no wonder that millions of parents are confused about the goals of the educational establishment.

Bev Eakman was a high school teacher of English, literature, and debate for nine years. She co-founded the National Education Consortium and is the former editor and writer of the official newspaper of the National Aeronautics and Space Administration (NASA). She was the chief speech writer for the National Council for Better Education, also Chief Justice Warren E. Burger, and a writer for the United States Department of Justice. The recipient of numerous awards and appearing on over 700 nationwide radio/ TV talk shows, Eakman disclosed a seven-point list of the values teachers should try to instill in their students. This list was given to educators in North Carolina at an in-service workshop. They were:

- There is no right or wrong, only conditioned responses.
- The collective good is more important than the individual.
- Consensus is more important than principle.
- Flexibility is more important than accomplishment.
- Nothing is permanent except change.
- All ethics are situational; there are no moral absolutes.
- There are no perpetrators, only victims. [24]

Once again, there has been a huge paradigm shift in the approach to public education starting with John Dewey and trickling down to what we have today. Teachers are seen as change agents dispensing a curriculum carefully crafted by the government and designed to program the minds of our children with sophisticated behavioral modification techniques that have been tested and proven effective for producing the desired values and beliefs in this generation of young people. Frankly, it is understandable why many of our teachers give little thought to this subtle, evolving history and overall educational process since they themselves are a product of the very system described.

Hitler, Mao Tse-tung, and Stalin were the greatest murderers of the twentieth century and each was a socialist and a believer in Darwinian evolution. The path of socialism that much of America has embarked upon will destroy and wipe from memory the principles that made us the greatest nation in world history. Unless something changes, we may be staring at a totalitarian system equally as corrupt as Russia, yet more subtle in its implementation.

THE CLINTON'S INFLUENCE

In 1979, Governor Bill Clinton implemented an activist agenda designed to change the direction of the public schools in Arkansas. As part of his agenda, he founded the *Arkansas Governor's School* which took approximately 400 of the best and brightest juniors and seniors throughout the state and indoctrinated them in a six-week program of liberal, humanistic thinking. Out of the 400, a handful of exceptional students were identified who could be future political leaders. Mark Loury served as publicity director for the Governor's School. Here was his perspective: "They're bringing a political agenda in the guise of academic excellence—It was something that was well orchestrated, well organized. It was mind-bending and manipulative. And the faculty all knew that it was going on." [25] Hillary gave lectures at the school with prominent themes that uprooted traditional beliefs, promoted moral relativism, endorsed homosexuality, and derided the biblical foundations of America. One student said, "Hillary Clinton talked about converting the schools of America into something similar to the Governor's School." Well, guess what? The same techniques used in Bill Clinton's Arkansas Governor's School are being used in classrooms all over America. [26]

Mark Tucker, president of the National Center on Education and the Economy (NCEE) sent an 18-page letter to Hillary Clinton after Bill was elected president of the United States. In the letter, Tucker laid out the components of a master plan for the Clinton Administration to take over the entire U.S. educational system and would be the fulfillment of the dream of John Dewey. [27]

If this is the first time you've been exposed to such information, it is unsettling to say the least. Certainly, the traditional function of education has been to teach basic knowledge and skills such as reading, writing, math, science, and history. However, with Outcome Based Education, the primary purpose is no longer to impact academic knowledge. Thus, it should come as no surprise that our nation's test results are lower in comparison to other countries in the industrialized world. In fact, given what you've read so far, if we step back and take an objective look at the direction of our nation, the condition of our schools, our global standing in the world, the political landscape, the legislation and Supreme Court rulings, it all begins to make sense after analyzing the transformation that has occurred in our educational system and the radical liberalism taught in our universities. Indoctrination has occurred and is being played out on the stage of political correctness throughout every institution in America.

Professor Allen Quist taught political science at Bethany Lutheran College and served three terms in the Minnesota House of Representatives. This subject of the transformation of America's educational system was one that deeply concerned him. He began to investigate it for himself. Here is one small example of what he discovered. Of the textbook *We the People*, he says, "It is not really a study of American government at all. It is all about producing a radical transformation of American government so that we willingly give up our national sovereignty and freedom and succumb to a one-world government of tyranny instead. One-world government is the unifying theme and purpose of the new federal curriculum. The book is really propaganda. It is social engineering, not education. It is decidedly anti-American and anti-freedom and is designed to indoctrinate our citizens into being willing to give away our national sovereignty." [28]

UNDERMINING THE FAMILY

We know that the basic fundamental building block for our society is the family so if, indeed, liberal elitists are socially engineering the classrooms of America and programming the minds of our youth with a socialistic agenda, it would only make sense that part of the strategy would include undermining traditional family values. Dr. Paul Vitz was a professor of psychology at New York University and systematically examined ninety widely used elementary social studies texts, high school history texts, and elementary readers to see if such was the case. He was stunned by what he found. In forty social studies texts for grades one through four, religion was treated as old-fashioned and unimportant. In fact, Christianity was basically omitted from beyond the Colonial period of our history. Words like *marriage, wedding, husband, and wife* did not occur in the books. No explicit definition of family is given. There is not one reference to marriage as being foundational to the family. The texts included many feminist stories that openly derided traditional manhood. There was no doubt in Dr. Vitz's mind that the clear intention of the school textbooks was to change the definition of family and reprogram the minds of students.[29] Be mindful that this was well before the Supreme Court's ruling on same-sex marriage. The groundwork was being laid for such a transformation of the family.

WE'RE NOT BASHING TEACHERS

Attorney John Whitehead says, "When the kids are in school, the government considers itself their legal guardian!"[30] The public school principal becomes master over the child, while the parent is forced into a subordinate position in the relationship. Our loyalty to the system is so embedded into the American psyche that much of what has been written here will be looked upon as blasphemous. Understanding this, I've attempted to document these findings. We must understand that the examples shown in these last two chapters are not extreme nor are they isolated. I can relate to Dr. James Dobson's sentiments: "I've been very careful not to be negative to the public schools because there are many Christian teachers that are struggling mightily to do what's right there, and

I haven't wanted to put pressure of them. But given the fact that in every classroom in the state they're being taught homosexual propaganda and these other politically correct postmodern views, I think it's time to get our kids out."[31]

Again, be reminded that one of the largest segments of our population that sends its children to private schools is the demographic of public school teachers. Who better understands the sub-par performance and toxicity that often contaminates the minds of children? In the most subtle of ways, I fear that we have embraced an approach to educating the most impressionable among us, our children, by resorting to a posture of complacency while behind closed doors they are being subjected to the ridicule and criticism of the very Judeo-Christian values we are trying to promote in our homes.

I am fully aware that many public schoolteachers will be reading these words and prone to adamantly disagree. Please do not be angry with me. I am not undermining you, but rather have a deep admiration for those Christian teachers who see their schools as spiritual warzones and see themselves as God's missionaries. Indeed, you are light in darkness. Granted, our schools have much to offer in terms of facilities and extracurricular activities. But the heart of the issue is the curriculum and the indoctrination that is occurring. In other words, it's not about the teachers, but about the system itself. We've seen the liberalism of the NEA. We've noted the decadent anti-Christian, anti-American agenda of the father of modern education, John Dewey. We've observed example after example of textbooks and the documentation of inside perspectives from those who experienced firsthand the blatant opposition of traditional values. Bottom line is this: People who do not share our values control the curriculum with the primary aim of removing our values from society. The classroom is their laboratory for achieving such goals. Yes, there will be exceptions where children emerge from the system unscathed and stronger in their faith. But these are the exceptions, not the norm.

The statistics are there for everyone to see. We are losing this generation of young people. The battle for their hearts and minds will continue to be waged. Currently, we are losing the battle. Apart from a massive spiritual awakening, Christianity will be marginalized, considered to be culturally irrelevant, and resembling our European neighbors while church buildings become museums from a previous generation. It need not be this way. There is still hope. God has always chosen to work through a minority, but we can no longer capitulate to the culture. We must be change agents for a cause that exceeds ourselves, the very souls of our children.

However, given today's government-run schools, I'm reminded of the words of Jesus: "Whoever offends one of these little ones, it would be better for him if a millstone were hung around his neck, and he were drowned in the depth of the sea." (Matthew 18:6) We are drowning. Sadly, the life jacket has been banned, ruled illegal and unconstitutional.

President Andrew Jackson

"That book, Sir, is the Rock upon which our republic rests. Sir, I am in the hands of a merciful God. I have full confidence in his goodness and mercy....The Bible is true. I have tried to conform to its spirit as near as possible. Upon that sacred volume I rest my hope for eternal salvation, through the merits and blood of our blessed Lord and Savior, Jesus Christ." [1]

— Andrew Jackson (1767-1845)
was the 7th President of the United States of America and also a lawyer, U.S. Senator, and a judge.

Alexis de Tocqueville's View of the Koran

"I studied the Koran a great deal. I came away from that study with the conviction there have been few religions in the world as deadly to men as that of Mohammed. So far as I can see, it is the principle cause of the decadence so visible today in the Muslim world and, though less absurd than the polytheism of old, its social and political tendencies are in my opinion to be feared, and I therefore regard it as a form of decadence rather than a form of progress in relation to paganism itself."[2]

— Alexis de Tocqueville
is a French philosopher who toured the United States in 1831, but offered an objective perspective of Islam

CHAPTER 7

America's Terrorism Crisis Dangerous Lightning

A small group of jihadists led thirty Iraqi men, women, and children at gunpoint to what was soon to be the bloody death of each one. Dressed in black hoods, the cameraman yelled, "Allahu Akhbar!" (God is great) into the microphone and the rest of the jihadists responded with similar chants until they worked themselves into a frenzy and blended into one long, loud cheer. The first victim was a young woman, hopelessly staring into the camera with a look of utter despair. The camera zoomed in. As the shouting reached its peak, the terrorists beheaded her, but not with one swooping chop. Instead, it was by sawing through her neck with knives until she choked on her own blood. But the jihadists kept sawing, and sawing, and sawing. Finally, they pulled her head off, waved it to the camera, and then motioned for the next victim to come forward.

Even al-Qaeda leader Osama bin Laden rejected such depraved, brutal tactics. So, this terrorist organization known as Al-Qaeda in Iraq, or AQI, became the Islamic State of Iraq and Syria, ISIS. Never has one generation witnessed the wide-spread prevalence of terrorist attacks as what has occurred in this 21st century. While there is a multiplicity of terrorist groups, the overwhelming majority of Muslim descent, none is more brutal than ISIS. ISIS is stronger than any jihadist group in world history. It is also the richest terrorist group [3] and controls more firepower as well as territory than any jihadist organization in history. [4] ISIS has pledged to raise the black flag of jihad over the White House. [5] Each of these terrorist groups is motivated by the same hate, the same faith, and the same tactics. The common goal is the establishment of a global Islamic state and the spreading of terror is the means to bring such submission. [6] The atrocities for accomplishing such are almost too horrific to print, but to name a few:

- Shooting a baby in the face, in front of the baby's mother, as a warning against collaborating with American forces.
- Raping women and then telling them to redeem their honor they must blow themselves up as suicide bombers.
- Placing explosives in a boy's backpack and then detonating it while he attends a family wedding.
- Using mosques to ambush American soldiers.
- Playing on the compassion of American soldiers, they put bombs on handicapped children and physically impaired kids.
- A refugee woman said that placing decapitated heads in a row has become a trademark, trophy-style execution favored by ISIS militants. [7]

Are these a collection of psychopathic killers? No, these are radical Islamists, part of a religion in which they perceive themselves as agents of the coming apocalypse. They don't just believe that the End Times and the Day of Judgment are imminent—they believe they are charged with playing an active role in bringing these times about. While refraining from the technicalities and tenets of the Islam religion, suffice it to say that neither ISIS, nor any of the other terrorist organizations, are the JV Team that Obama declared them to be. Indeed, 1.6 billion Muslims regard the Koran as the perfect, immutable, unchangeable word of God. [8] Given that fact, when one reads the Quran we find more than 100 references to violence and the killing of infidels (anyone who does not accept the teaching of the Koran is an infidel). For example, Sura 2:216 says,

"Fighting is prescribed for you, and ye dislike it. But it is possible that ye dislike a thing which is good for you, and that ye love a thing which is bad for you. But Allah knoweth, and ye know not."

Sura 9:5 says, "Fight and slay the unbelievers wherever you find them, and seize them, beleaguer them, and lie in wait for them in every stratagem of war."

Sura 9:29: "Fight those who do not believe in Allah or the Last Day, nor hold that forbidden which hath been forbidden by Allah and his apostle, nor acknowledge the Religion of Truth (i.e. Islam), (even if they are people of the book), until they pay the tax with willing submission and feel themselves subdued."

Sura 4:89, 91: "Seize them and slay them wherever you find them."

If there is any doubt regarding these seemingly clear admonitions to wage jihad against anyone who does not embrace the Islamist religion, Ayatollah Khomeini declares: *"We are at war against infidels. Take this message with you, 'I ask all Islamic nations, and all Muslims, all Islamic armies, and all heads of Islamic states to join the Holy War. There are many enemies to be killed or destroyed. Jihad must triumph....Muslims have no alternative....to an armed Holy War against profane governments....Holy War means the conquest of all non-Muslim territories...It will be the duty of every able bodied adult male to volunteer for this war of conquest, the final aim of which is to put Koranic law in power from one end of the earth to the other."*[9]

Sheik Omar Abdel Rahman agrees: *"Muslims must kill the enemies of Allah, in every way and everywhere in order to liberate themselves from the grandchildren of the pigs and apes who are educated at the table of the Zionists, the Communists, and the Imperialists."*[10] His colleague, Sheik al-Tamimi did not mince words when he declared, *"There is fury everywhere....Islam is escalating and cannot be resisted. I pray Allah may tear apart America just as the Soviet Union was torn apart..."*[11]

So, if Islam is a loving, peaceful religion, you could never draw that conclusion by reading their own writings or by listening to their leaders. Instead, we find them killing innocent men, women, and children in the name of Islam and wear it as a badge of honor. The more you kill the more Allah is honored.

To be fair, within the Islamic faith there are liberals, moderates, conservatives, non-violent fundamentalists and violent fundamentalists. So, yes, it is important to distinguish between the majority of Muslims and those who are radical extremists. To lump all Muslims together as terrorists would be comparable to saying that all white Christian men in the United States are part of the Ku Klux Klan. The majority of Muslims do not see themselves in a holy war against America.

Yet, the terrorist group, Hamas, states in its charter that "Allah is its goal, the Prophet its model to be followed, the Koran its constitution, Jihad its way, and death for the sake of Allah its loftiest desire." [12]

THE INSIDE STRATEGY OF RADICAL ISLAMISTS

Fouad Hussein spent years working inside al-Qaeda's inner circle and eventually earned their trust. In so doing, he got them to open up about their plans. To his amazement, a 20-year timeline was disclosed which, thus far, radical Islamists have followed with great precision. Keep in mind, the unveiling of this strategy comes from the terrorist's inner circle and includes seven phases: [8]

Phase I: The Muslim Awakening (2000-2003)

Beginning with 9/11, this phase was aimed at provoking the West so that Americans and their allies would be easier targets.

Phase II: Opening Eyes (2003-2006)

A political effort to reawaken millions of followers of Islam and return them to the foundations of their faith would be accomplished through tactical battles in Iraq and Afghanistan. Terrorist bases of operation would be established in other Arabic states in which multitudes of Muslims would pledge allegiance to bin Laden.

Phase III: Arising and Standing Up (2007-2010)

Special priority would be placed on Syria, but also on neighboring Jordan, Turkey, and Israel, where secular and anti-Islamic governments reign.

Phase IV: (2010-2013)

Revolution begins to sweep the Middle East and the infidel governments, such as Egypt's, begin to fall. Attacks against the United States continue with special emphasis on cyberattacks to target America's economic power.

Phase V: (2013-2016)

The West will begin to lose much of its will to fight, allowing al-Qaeda and its allies to re-create the Caliphate for the first time in nine decades. Because Western resistance is so limited, the Caliphate will grow in strength and territory.

Phase VI: (2016-2019)

This will be the West's final, dying breath to confront the growing Islamic armies. The West will muster all of its technological capabilities to destroy the Caliphate and the many thousands of Muslims who have volunteered to fight on its behalf.

Phase VII: (2020)

The stunning victory will convince the many millions of Muslims who had remained on the fence to join the Islamic state. One and a half billion Muslims strong, the Caliphate will be the world's lone superpower.

It cannot be denied that the first five phases have been right on schedule.

Home-Grown Jihadists

Ahmed Omar Abu Ali moved to America when he was four years old and was high school valedictorian. On the outside he was friendly, bright, and successful. But on the inside, he was being radicalized. Although he entered the University of Maryland to study engineering, he later transferred to the University of Medina in Saudi Arabia to study Islamic law. Shortly thereafter, he embraced the views of Islamic jihadism and joined al Qaeda. With a full American citizenship, an American passport, and a respectable university student, after being trained in detonating explosives and forging documents Ali returned to America to assimilate into the community with the goal of unleashing weapons of mass destruction upon our nation. Thanks to the efficient work of Homeland Security, he was arrested and sentenced to thirty years in a maximum security federal prison.

While we applaud this result, it is especially disturbing that he graduated from the Islamic Saudi Academy (ISA) in Alexandria, Virginia, just across the Potomac River from the White House and the Capitol building, the epicenter of American democracy. This school's mission is to educate a new generation of Muslim young people capable of studying at American universities, working in American jobs, and influencing American society with the values of the Qur'an. It is a prestigious institution among Muslims, both in the U.S. and Saudi Arabia. In fact, the Saudi ambassador to the United States is chairman of the school's board of directors and Saudi students attend free. [13] Al Jazeera calls it "the largest institution teaching the Arabic language and Islamic education on the East Coast of the U.S." [14] Its most famous graduate was convicted of trying to assassinate the president and a Washington Post investigation found that ISA "used textbooks that compared Jews and Christians to apes and pigs, told eighth-graders that these groups are the enemies of the believers and diagrammed for high school students where to cut off the hands and feet of thieves."[15] Be reminded that 15 of the 19 terrorists who attacked us on 9/11 were Saudis. Former CIA director James Woolsey told a congressional committee that over 95 percent of Saudis between the ages of 25 and 41 had sympathy for Osama bin Laden.[16]

There are an estimated 1,200 mosques in the U.S., and between 50 and 80 percent are believed to be dominated by a theology of hatred and violence.[17] Between 1990 and 2000, the number of mosques in the United States increased 42 percent, and one in five mosques now run full-time elementary, middle, and secondary schools. So, a new generation of fully devoted Muslim leaders is being raised in our own backyard.[18] Mega-mosques are being built in major American cities. For example, the 48,000-square-foot Dearborn Mosque in Dearborn, Michigan is three stories high and is the largest Sunni mosque in the U.S. Were you aware that the $12-million Islamic Center of America, also in Dearborn, is the largest Arab American religious and cultural facility in North America?[19]

A publication was found in one of the U.S. mosque's containing these inflammatory words: "Muslims who convert out of Islam, of course, are apostates…and, under Saudi law, they are to be put to death." Sheik Bin Uthaimin is quoted: "Our doctrine states that if you accept any religion other than Islam, like Judaism or Christianity, which are not acceptable, you become an unbeliever. If you do not repent, you are an apostate and you should be killed because you have denied the Qur'an."[20]

So, let's summarize. We have Saudi state education here on American soil that teaches little children the virtues of jihad. High school curricula are replete with jihad indoctrination. One high school texts says, "To be true to Muslims, we must prepare and be ready for jihad in Allah's way. It is the duty of the citizen and the government. The military education is glued to faith and its meaning, and the duty to follow it."[21] To be clear, not all Muslim children who attend Islamic schools in the U.S. are being indoctrinated with violent jihadist theology. In fact, most of the 1.3 billion Muslims in the world are peaceful and pose no threat to the U.S. But here's the question, "How many Radicals are there in the United States?" In 2007, the Pew Research Center published the largest and most comprehensive study of Muslim American opinion ever done. The study involved 60,000 interviews with Muslim Americans and found that nearly seven in ten Muslims in America had a "somewhat unfavorable" or "very unfavorable" view of al Qaeda.[22] However, 5 percent of all Muslims in America admitted that they had a favorable view of al Qaeda. Moreover, nearly three in ten (27 percent) said they either didn't know or refused to answer the question about their view of al Qaeda. So, out of 2,350,000 Muslims, this means there are at least 117,500 Muslims inside the U.S. who liked Osama bin Laden and his colleagues and have a favorable view of their terrorist network. I assume they hold the same opinion for ISIS. If those who refused to answer the question were disguising their own support for al Qaeda, there could be another 600,000 or more Radical Muslims inside our country. Pew researchers pressed even further and asked the Muslims in the U.S. if they believed suicide bombings against civilian targets were ever justified. While 78 percent said no never, this leaves 22 percent who either favor suicide bombings or refused to answer the question. More specifically, the numbers from the survey played out like this: 23,500 Muslims in America believe suicide bombings against civilians are often justified; 164,500 Muslims in America believe suicide bombings against civilians are sometimes justified and 211,500 refused to answer the question.[23]

Gallup did a similar survey worldwide. I'll cut to the chase. Seven percent of Muslim respondents thought that the 9/11 attacks were completely justified and they view the United States unfavorably. Now 7 percent seems to be a small number, but when considering there are 1.3 billion Muslims in the world, this percent equates to 91 million people. So, yes it is comforting to know that the vast majority of the world's Muslims are peaceful people. But, it is discomforting to know that 91 million Muslims hate the United States and are radicalized. Incidentally, 91 million is three times the population of Canada, ten times the population of Sweden, and more than twelve times the population of Israel. If they formed their own country, they would represent the twelfth largest nation on the planet. So, this is no small thing. [24]

Obama Sending Mixed Signals

Soon after his election, you may recall that Obama traveled to Cairo Egypt and delivered his now-famous speech that under his leadership America was making a massive policy shift. So, we pulled out of Iraq despite pleas of "all the major Iraqi parties." [25] Then, as further evidence of America's new policy and staying true to his word, Obama stood in support of the Muslim Brotherhood government, despite its treaty violation with Israel and its persecution of Christians in Egypt. Unbelievably, even after the Brotherhood allowed jihadists to attack our American embassy and raise the black flag of jihad over our diplomatic facility, Obama still supported this terrorist organization.

Hassan al-Banna, the founder of the Muslim Brotherhood, wrote about the centrality of jihad: "Jihad is an obligation from Allah on every Muslim and cannot be ignored nor evaded. Allah has ascribed great importance to jihad and has made the reward of the martyrs and the fighters in His way a splendid one.....The verses of the Qur'an and the Sunnah of Muhammad are overflowing with all these noble ideals and they summon people in general to jihad, to warfare, to the armed forces, and all means of land and sea fighting." Why would an American president embrace such an entity?

And then there is Libya and the Benghazi debacle in which our American ambassador and three more brave Americans were killed. Just days earlier, we offered aid to the very jihadists who turned their anger on the United States by attacking our embassy. What went under-reported was the fact that Obama's administration refused to reinforce the embassy's security, even though it knew of the deteriorating situation, but Obama was concerned that it would anger the local Muslim population.

In the most recent conflict with Hamas, Israel needed the support of the United States, but instead, Obama's administration rebuked Israel and chose to advance the proposals that empowered Hamas's most staunch allies—Qatar and Turkey. In other words, the Obama administration rewarded Hamas for its terrorist violence.

You may recall the crisis in Iraq where tens of thousands of Christians faced an imminent massacre, but instead of intervening with force, we pinpricked a few insignificant sites which sent ISIS the message that they had nothing to fear from the United States. Equally as perplexing was the fact that the Kurds were the only group in the region willing to fight ISIS but we refused to provide them with the heavy weapons they needed. Again and again, President Obama appeased jihadists. [26]

Obama acknowledges that he has no strategy for fighting this plague of global terrorism, but he has made it clear that America will no longer be out in front as a world leader, but instead we will lead from behind. Such a strategy has proven counterproductive. The Washington Post reports that the inflow of foreign fighters to ISIS includes 130 from the U.S., 100 from Canada, 600 from Great Britain, 600 from Germany, 1,200 from France, 440 from Belgium, and hundreds more from other countries in our European alliances. [27]

The Worst Diplomatic Agreement in History

As though the aforementioned mixed signals from the Obama Administration were not enough to create uneasiness regarding our lax stance on terroristic aggression, the unthinkable occurred when Obama dispatched his Secretary of State, John Kerry, to negotiate what many have said is the worst agreement in U.S. diplomatic history. With whom did we negotiate? Iran, who is the world's foremost state sponsor of terrorism. This was a bombshell that sent shockwaves throughout the world, not the least of which was our allies. To be concise, the insanity of this deal can be reduced to four glaring concerns:

First, Tehran was able to keep all of its illicit nuclear facilities without destroying any of them. Thus, it can quickly expand its enrichment activities and rapidly shorten the nuclear timeline once the restrictions on uranium enrichment levels expire in 10 to 15 years.

Second, inspections on Iran's nuclear facilities can only occur with Iranian approval, giving them time to conceal any devious activities. Never mind Iran's long history of violating previous nuclear agreements. Kerry just says that we need to be focused on the future, not fixated on the past. In other words, let bygones be bygones.

Third, not the least of which, we allowed Tehran to recover approximately $150 billion in frozen assets that will boost its economy. That's right, Iran has the world's fourth-largest crude oil reserves and the second largest natural gas reserves, much of which have been untapped due to sanctions. Now, however, we gave them a signing bonus of $150 billion which is 25 times the annual budget of the Iranian Revolutionary Guard. [28] By relieving the sanctions, Iran's ability to sell more oil will bring $300-400 billion into the Iranian economy, which means that we are paying them to undermine our own policies and best interests throughout the region. Unbelievable! This only enhances its military capabilities, and support for networks of terrorist groups while putting our allies at great risk. Iran already has the largest missile arsenal in the Middle East. No doubt, this money will be used to fuel Islamist revolutionaries in Yemen and Bahrain which it already supports, and to prop up the Assad regime in Syria. Connecting the dots, as absurd as it sounds, this means that America is an accomplice or cooperating partner with the world's foremost state sponsor of terrorism!

Fourth, Israel's Prime Minister, Benjamin Netanyahu, travelled to the United States to address a joint session of Congress at the invitation of House Speaker John Boehner. In his own dignified manner, he eloquently presented the case against Iran and other dictatorial governments threatening Israel's safety. He basically begged us to stand with Israel. Obama snubbed him, refused to speak with him. Five days following Netanyahu's visit with Congress, a team of five Obama campaign operatives were sent to Israel for the purpose of leading an effort to defeat the Israeli Prime Minister in the upcoming national elections. Despite this unprecedented cutthroat move by an American president against our greatest ally in the Middle East, Netanyahu won a narrowly contested election. Israel's security in the region was already shaky, and now her greatest long-standing ally seems to be forming an alliance with her staunchest enemy, Iran itself. Indeed, Iran has provided thousands of increasingly long-range rockets to Hamas and the Palestinian Islamic Jihad in Gaza in addition to the estimated 100,000 rockets and missiles it has supplied to Hezbollah. [29] All of these regimes have called upon the Islamic world to annihilate Israel. Keep in mind that God has promised to curse those who curse Israel. Such negotiations put America at odds with God Himself. It is one thing to have a rogue nation as our enemy, but it is another to have almighty God Himself opposing our nation. What is more disturbing is that crowds of radical Islamists gathered in the streets of Tehran lifting signs and chanting, "Death to America" all while the negotiations were being conducted.

We know for a fact that Iran computer hackers have already targeted U.S. banks, NASDAQ, defense contractors, major U.S. military installations, San Diego's Navy Marine Corps Intranet, and critical infrastructure. [30] We also know that Iran conducted sophisticated computer espionage in the fall of 2015 through a series of cyberattacks against State Department officials. [31] Frankly, our president's ideological worldview, along with his own Islamic roots, seemingly prevents him from objectively assessing Iran's threat to the security of our nation. If someone wanted to write the playbook for "How to Destroy America," Obama could not have written the script any better. Treating Iran like a normal country, despite the regime's longstanding, radical Islamist ideology, its ongoing attempts to export revolution, its decades of hatred for America, its global leadership of sponsoring terrorism, and its unabashed efforts to destroy Israel, defies political sanity, contradicts the ethics of diplomacy, and is a betrayal of the presidential oath of keeping America's security as the top priority. It is no wonder that many are calling this the worst agreement in U.S. diplomatic history. But, as columnist Charles Krauthammer says, "Obama will get his "legacy." Kerry will get his Nobel Prize. And Iran will get the bomb." [32]

Sharia Law in America?

Muslims are using our own Constitution against us in pointing to their right to utilize their own Islamic Tribunal Court as mandated by their religion. So, in February 2015, the North Texas Islamic Tribunal in Irving, Texas had established itself as a sharia court. The Irving City Council responded by passing a resolution officially recognizing the U.S. Constitution as the law of the land. And yet it passed by a narrow 5-4 vote. Why would four out of nine council members vote in favor of Sharia law? Apparently, they were more afraid of appearing politically correct than they were committed to preserving the integrity of America's laws. [8] If such an issue was closely debated in the conservative Bible-belt of Irving, Texas, one only wonders the outcome if such were to occur in a more liberal state with more liberal council members.

Yet, the naivete' of the Obama administration continues to amaze. State Department spokeswoman Marie Harf, said, "We can't kill our way out of this war. We need to go after the root causes that lead people to join these groups, whether it is lack of opportunity for jobs....We can help them build their economies so they can have job opportunities for these people." [8] She can't be serious! To think that Muslim poverty is threatening our national security is laughable. I mean, come on, I know that Obama said he did not have a strategy for fighting terrorism, but creating a jobs program for terrorists is beyond the pale. Terrorists aren't attacking us because we said something to offend them or because they're out of work. They are attacking us because they are motivated by an ideology that urges them to kill in the name of their God who insists that martyrdom will be rewarded with heavenly pleasures.

A FACT HARD TO BELIEVE

According to the FBI, 94 percent of terrorist attacks carried out in the United States from 1980 to 2005 were by non-Muslims. This means that an American terrorist suspect is over nine times more likely to be a non-Muslim than a Muslim. According to this same report, there were more Jewish acts of terrorism in the United States than Islamic. [33] Therefore, critics contend that in the name of objectivity, just as we cannot blame the entire religion of Judaism or Christianity for the violent actions of those carrying out crimes under the names of these religions, there is no justifiable grounds to blame Muslims for terrorism. Furthermore, there have been over one thousand terrorist attacks in Europe in the past five years with less than 2 percent instigated by Muslims.[34]

Sympathizers of Muslims are quick to point out that five of the past twelve Nobel Peace Prize winners have been Muslims.[35] A study carried out by the University of North Carolina showed that less than .0002 percent of Americans killed since 9/11 were killed by Muslims.[36] U.S. News and World Report confirmed these findings by stating that "Of the more than 300 American deaths from political violence and mass shootings since 9/11, only 33 have come at the hands of Muslim-Americans.[37] Charles Kurzman, Professor of Sociology at the University of North Carolina claims that Islamic terrorism "doesn't even count for 1 percent of the 180,000 murders in the U.S. since 9/11."[38] Another group conducted an extensive review of the 2,400 terrorist attacks on U.S. soil between 1970 and 2012. Only 60 were carried out by Muslims which equaled 2.5 percent.[39]

You're probably scratching or shaking your head in disbelief. To be fair and balanced, this aspect of terrorism needed mentioning. So, does this negate everything this chapter has espoused? Does this minimize the threat of Islamic terrorism in America? Has the media been biased in its reporting and are Republicans over-reacting by demanding that we identify the terrorists by their name, Islamist extremists?

The answer to each of these is "no." Let's be clear. Never in our lifetime has there been terrorist group like ISIS. Never in our lifetime have so many terrorist groups, all of which are Islamists, made clear declarations of their intent to attack and destroy America. Never have we seen the brutality of beheadings as performed by radical Islamists. Never have we seen the prevalence of suicide bombings such as carried out by Islamist extremists. Never have we fought in an unconventional war of combatting an ideology rather than tanks and missiles. Throw in the fact that Islam's "holy" book advocates the killing of infidels, and given the fact that the worst attack on American soil was organized and perpetrated by Islamist extremists, we are justified in being vigilant and wary toward those of Muslim descent. This is not being racially prejudice or unjustifiably profiling. This is the real world and life in the 21st century.

Whether in Europe, Asia, or the Middle East, aspiring powers are flexing their muscles because they clearly see a superpower in decline. They ignore Washington's dictates and our politician's words are empty rhetoric. Russia refuses to withdraw its aggression into the Ukraine. China refuses to abandon its base-building endeavors in the South China Sea. Saudi Arabia refused to endorse the U.S.-brokered nuclear deal with Iran. ISIS refuses to capitulate in the face of U.S. airpower. The world's nations see our broken economy, our political scandals, our moral freefall, and they know it's just a matter of time before total collapse occurs. Like a lion waiting in the shadows ready to pounce on his prey, America is vulnerable without God's hedge. Our only hope is to cry out in repentance by restoring righteousness in our nation. The process begins in the house of God, that is, the churches throughout the Land whose complacency and hypocrisy have been an indictment on the very Gospel we claim to represent.

Founding Father John Jay

"Providence has given to our people the choice of their rulers, and it is the duty, as well as the privilege and interest in our Christian nation, to select and prefer Christians for their rulers." [1]

— John Jay (1745-1829)
was the first Chief Justice of the United States Supreme Court, appointed by President George Washington. A Founding Father, he served as the President of the Continental Congress and was very instrumental in the ratification of the Constitution. He also served as Governor of New York.

CHAPTER 8

Obama: A President Without A Precedent

Bursting onto the political scene in 2004 as the keynote speaker at the Democrat National Convention and then following up with his election as a first term senator in 2005, Barack Hussein Obama was well on his way to carving a path to the White House in 2008. The populace knew little about the man. A strange name for an American president and an even stranger political ideology, few pundits gave him a shot at being elected, especially given the fact that he was running against the other half of the well-oiled, well-funded Clinton campaign machine, Hillary herself. To the surprise of many, this young orator began captivating the imagination of millions. Forget about town halls, he was packing out coliseums and stadiums with frenzied enthusiasm, unlike anything ever witnessed in American politics. Upon winning the Democrat nomination, conservatives began researching his birth certificate, his roots, his education, his associations, his ideology, and his voting record. Running under the mantra of "Hope & Change," it resonated with the majority of the nation, though many were completely oblivious as to the meaning of "change." He promised to transform the nation, but again, most did not understand what such a transformation would look like. He also promised the most transparent administration in history, but now we all know what a joke that was. Conservative talk shows warned their viewing and listening audiences that, if elected, Obama would be the most inexperienced, radical, and liberal president in U.S. history. Despite such warnings, the nation embraced this suave, articulate, well-dressed, charismatic family man as the first African American president and what many would describe as "the coolest." Underneath the exterior, however, resides a dark and dangerous political agenda unlike anything that American politics has ever seen. Out of the view from most Americans was his disturbing background of associations with communists, including Frank Marshall Davis, and terrorists such as William Ayers, and his longstanding pastor as an anti-American racist. Obama was indoctrinated with an Islamist education in Indonesia and a hard-core Marxist orientation in college. Even in his book, *Dreams from My Father*, he states that while in college he was attracted to Marxist professors. Thanks to the mainstream media, his subversive background was largely ignored. Indeed, you will see in the following pages that he is the president without a precedent. You must draw your own conclusions, but it is an undeniable claim that no sitting president has elicited such widespread questions and concerns regarding his hatred for the very nation he was elected to lead. It was not long into his presidency that many were shell-shocked by his sympathy for our enemies and his incompetent ideology that led him on an "apology tour" throughout the Middle East and Europe. Consequently, the morale of our military personnel plummeted as evidenced by reports that more active-duty U.S. soldiers have been dying by suicide than in combat.[2] Yes, America is undergoing Obama's promised fundamental transformation of the nation, that of replacing our constitutional limited-government, free enterprise system with a socialist, wealth-redistributionist system run by an all-powerful government. Such radical change cannot be accomplished if Americans are calm, content, and relatively happy. Thus, Obama has followed his mentor, Saul Alinsky's leftist *Rules for Radicals*. Supporting this claim, Rush Limbaugh says, "The more chaos there is, the more requirement there is for him to step in and control the chaos."[3] Best-selling author, David Limbaugh, says Obama's leftist agenda is "solely dedicated to manufacturing issues to keep the nation in a constant state of uproar, angst, and disharmony."[4]

Before even completing his first year in office, Obama's Department of Homeland Security issued a report warning about the threat of militant, violent extremists. And just who were these horrible people? According to the report, they were pro-lifers, NRA supporters, thosc who were opposed to illegal immigration and government debt. [6] I'm not making this stuff up. Tea Party affiliates were particularly implicated which occurred again with the IRS scandals that targeted such conservative groups. Of course, if further clues were needed regarding whom we'd just elected into the White House, look no further than the headline that appeared on *Newsweek's* cover just three weeks after Obama's inauguration in January 2009 proclaiming, "WE ARE ALL SOCIALISTS NOW." [6] Another clue was his coldness toward Israel's Benjamin Netanyahu, refusing to meet with this great American friend and statesman when he traveled to Washington after accepting an invitation to address Congress. Unbelievably, Obama's campaign team actually set up shop in Tel Aviv attempting to defeat the Jewish state's prime minister and long-standing American ally.

Compounding the questions surrounding his oath to keep America safe was his *annual* habit of releasing tens of thousands of *illegal criminal* aliens back into the nation's neighborhoods. We're talking about thousands who entered our country illegally, committed criminal acts of violence such as murder, rape, and assault, convicted by our courts, but then he sanctioned the release of such individuals, including thirty thousand in 2014. Of the 36,000 released in 2013, 193 were homicide convictions. Even more disturbing is the release of 151 terrorists from Guantanamo Bay prison, 75% considered to be high-risk. That is, they are likely to pose a threat to the U.S. and its allies. [7] Among those released in January 2016, was Abu Bakr Ibn Muhammad al-Ahdal, an al Qaeda member who was described as a willing terrorist against the U.S. Another was Muhammad Salih Husayn al-Shaykh, a man who pledged to kill as many Americans as possible. These are just two examples. [8]

Nothing reveals the character and ideology of a person more than his associates. Obama's appointees are the clearest litmus test of our president's radicalism. Anita Dunn, his White House communications director, claimed that the mass-murdering Chinese communist leader Mao Tse-Tung was one of her "favorite political philosophers." [9] And how can we forget Van Jones, the admitted communist who, in earlier years, founded the communist group STORM (Standing Together to Organize a Revolutionary Movement). [10] If you're thinking, "Wait a minute, terms like communist, Marxist or socialist are not making the news, so who's the one being extreme here?" I understand those sentiments. Such terms are too radical for most Americans to embrace so they've been carefully replaced and couched in more palatable language such as, *economic justice, fairness, redistribution, progressivism, spreading the wealth around, and everyone's fair share."* However, the dangerous ideological heartbeat of Marxism and socialism are pounding underneath those innocent-sounding terms. But I digress, so let's get back to a sampling of Obama's appointees.

APPOINTEES REFLECTING OBAMA'S RADICALISM

- **Arif Alikhan**, Assistant Secretary for the Office of Policy Development, was responsible for derailing the LAPD's efforts to monitor activities within the city's Muslim community where numerous radical mosques and madrassas were known to exist. [11]

- **Ron Bloom**, Senior Counselor to the President for Manufacturing Policy, asserts that "the free market is nonsense." Now, this is the guy advising the President for manufacturing policy. He said, "We kind of agree with Mao, that political power comes largely from the barrel of a gun." [12]

- **Carol Browner**, Assistant to the President for Energy and Climate Change, formerly served as a "commissioner" of the

Socialist International, the umbrella group for 170 "social democratic, socialist and labor parties in 55 countries. The Socialist International's "organizing document" cites capitalism as the cause of "devastating crises," "mass unemployment," imperialist expansion," and "colonial exploitation" worldwide. [13]

- **James Cole**, Deputy Attorney General, contended that prosecutions related to terrorism should be adjudicated in civilian courts rather than military tribunals. He legally represented Prince Naif Bin Abdulaziz Al Saud, who headed the terror-aligned Al Haramain Islamic Foundation with 13 branches of the Foundation having ties to al Qaeda.
- **Rahm Emanue**l, Chief of Staff, who said regarding the economic recession, "You never want a serious crisis to go to waste—and what I mean by that is it's an opportunity to do things that you think you could not do before."
- **Charles Freeman**, nominated for Chair of the National Intelligence Council, was quoted as saying that America had provoked Islamic terrorism by failing to put an end to "the brutal oppression of the Palestinians by an Israeli occupation that is about to mark its fortieth anniversary and shows no sign of ending." He withdrew his nomination.
- **Eric Holder**, Attorney General, who has sought to try Islamic terrorists in civilian courts rather than military tribunals, and has filed suit against several states that had passed laws designed to stem the flow of illegal immigration. He wants to make it easier for illegal aliens to vote, which is also ACORN's goal.
- **John Holdren**, Assistant to the President for Science and Technology, views capitalism as a harmful economic system and once called for a "massive campaign to de-develop the United States in order to conserve energy and facilitate growth in underdeveloped countries. [14] This guy is off the charts,

even for a leftist. In the event of an overpopulation crisis, he supports laws requiring compulsory abortion, government confiscation of new born babies, and believes the government should dictate family size. [15]

- **Dawn Johnsen**, Assistant Attorney General to the Office of Legal Counsel, believes that nominees for the federal judiciary should automatically be disqualified from consideration if they subscribe to the concept of Constitutional originalism as opposed to the notion that the Constitution is a malleable "living document." [16] She is the former legal director for the National Abortion Rights Action League that opposes any restrictions on abortion for any reason, at any time of pregnancy, even late term abortions. [17]
- **Harold Koh**, Legal Advisor to the U.S. State Department, believes that the world's problems are too complex and deep-rooted for any single country to address. Therefore, he is an advocate for a one-world government. Koh believes Muslim law—Sharia law—should be applied to some disputes in U.S. courts. His views are in contradiction to the constitution he swore to uphold, but he is in charge of all legal issues for the U.S. State Department.
- **Eliseo Medina**, National Latino Advisory Council, served as an Honorary Chairman of the Democratic Socialists of America.
- ***Cecilia Munoz**, Director of the Domestic Policy Council, calls for immigration reform that would create a clear path to citizenship for illegal immigrants, and describes organized opposition to this agenda as a "wave of hate." She is the nation's foremost advocate for granting amnesty to millions of illegals.
- **Susan Rice**, Ambassador to the United Nations, contends that terrorism is primarily "a threat borne of both oppression and deprivation." In the aftermath of the deadly September 11,

2012 attacks on the U.S. consulate in Benghazi, Rice went on five separate news program and falsely stated that the attacks were a "spontaneous reaction" to an obscure Internet video that was critical of the Prophet Mohammed. Afterwards, it was learned that the American consulate in Benghazi had been attacked and threatened at least 13 times before the deadly September 11 attack.

- **Ellen Tauscher**, Undersecretary of State for Arms Control and International Security, believes that in order to discourage aggressive dictators from developing nuclear weapons, the United States should disarm itself of its own nuclear stockpiles.[18]
- **Mark Lloyd**, Chief Diversity Officer, Federal Communications Commission, plans to shut down conservative talk radio. He says, "It should be clear by now that my focus here is not freedom of speech or the press."[17]
- **David Ogden**, Deputy Attorney General, is a big pornography defender. He believes that public libraries should be free-speech zones in which school children have the right to access anything they want on school computers. He believes there is a constitutional right to possess child porn.
- **Elena Kagan**, Solicitor General, who was confirmed as the fourth woman to sit on the United States Supreme Court. A lesbian, she had no judicial or appellate experience. Amazingly, she was never even a judge or argued before the Supreme Court!
- **Arne Duncan**, Secretary, Department of Education, was the CEO of Chicago's public schools. Needless to say, the Duncan era for public education in Chicago was horrendous with pathetic graduation rates, and failures in reading and math proficiencies. He was effective, however, in promoting the homosexual lifestyle to these students.
- **Kevin Jennings**, Assistant Deputy Secretary for the

Department of Education, is the founder of the Gay Lesbian and Straight Education Network (GLSEN), a group dedicated to promoting the homosexual agenda to school children as young as five.

- **Rosa Brooks**, Under-Secretary of Defense for Policy, called President Bush "our torturer in chief" and compared Bush's anti-terrorist policies to Hitler's policies. She is now in charge of deciding defense policy.
- **David Axelrod**, Political Advisor, has a long history of working for socialist candidates. His mother wrote for a New York City tabloid called *PM Magazine*, which often promoted the Communist Party line.
- **Preeta Bansal**, General Counsel and Senior Policy Advisor, Office of Management & Budget, advises Obama in selecting federal judges. She believes in a "living Constitution" and works to eliminate the "original intent" concept.
- **Melody Barnes**, Domestic Policy Council, believes in unrestricted abortions for any reason at any time of pregnancy. [18]

Look, I understand this stuff is a bit monotonous, not exactly a good bedtime read. But I went through this litany of appointees (again, just a small sampling) to dislodge the refusal in believing that Obama could not be this extreme. We've never seen a president this extreme, so it is admittedly hard to wrap our brains around such radicalism from an American Commander-in-Chief. Frankly, the fact that he was elected twice says more about America's culture than it does about the Obama himself. The reality is, difficult as it may be to believe, a large number of Obama appointees hate America's Christian heritage and the American Constitution. Many of these extremists were quietly indoctrinated in our liberal universities, sitting under radical Marxist professors, and were shielded from being scrutinized and properly vetted. Obama ran as a hip moderate, a reformer, and someone who would fight the corruption in Washington. Like a beautiful gag gift, neatly packaged under the Christmas tree, the recipient can hardly contain his excitement until....until he unwraps the decorative paper and discovers the contents on the inside do not match the exterior on the outside. The more the American public unravels the wrapping paper surrounding the Obama presidency, the more it realizes the gift inside was anything but a gift. Many have buyer's remorse.

MUSLIM APPOINTEES

What you are about to read is disturbing, not merely because the names are hard to pronounce, nor because these individuals are separated from the mainstream Protestantism and Catholicism to which we are accustomed. Rather, Obama has placed these Muslims in high-ranking positions with alleged ties to terrorist organizations. You read that correctly. It feels strange even writing this. Like you, I am stunned, angered, and deeply saddened that so many Islamist sympathizers are influencing our government at the highest levels. Unless I'm missing something, this appears to be treason and a violation of their oath of office. Yet, Obama and senior officials are complicit with these appointments, all of which raises serious questions regarding their own allegiance to the American people whom they serve, not to mention the Constitution as our supreme rule of law. Again, this is not inspirational reading, so I will refrain from a detailed description of each individual's link to a radicalized ideology, but the abbreviated sketch provided is enough to alter your blood pressure.

Arif Alikhan, Assistant Secretary for Policy Development for the U.S. Department of Homeland Security, was responsible for derailing the LAPD's plan to monitor potential terrorist activities within the Los Angeles Muslim community where many radical mosques were known to have provided aid to the 9/11 hijackers. He was born in Damascus, Syria.[19] Oh, and by the way, he is a devout Sunni Muslim who has participated in a Muslim Public Affairs Council fundraiser, an organization that openly advocates Sharia Law with the intention of overthrowing the U.S. government. Any normal thinking American has to wonder, "Why would devout Muslims be appointed to Homeland Security positions when it was devout Muslims who flew planes into U.S. buildings?"

Mohammed Elibiary, Homeland Security Adviser, is an Islamic cleric and an invited guest speaker to honor the late Ayatollah Khomeini. He was reportedly given access to highly sensitive data containing hundreds of thousands of intelligence reports, including the names on terrorist watch lists and sensitive FBI reports.

Rashad Hussain, Special Envoy to the Organization of the Islamic Conference, participated in the American Muslim Council's 11th annual convention, an organization headed by the Muslim Brotherhood leader Abdurahman Alamoudi.[20]

Salam al-Marayati, Obama adviser, is the founder of the Muslim Public Affairs Council which defends Muslim extremist violence. He is a sympathizer with Hamas and Hezbollah. He says, "Yesterday's terrorists in the Middle East are today's leaders. The PLO is the number one example of this...The PLO 35 years ago was considered a terrorist organization, nobody should deal with them...But they became the people in authority, in Palestine, today. So Hamas today, the way it's being viewed, is exactly how the PLO was viewed 30 years ago. And, in fact, even Hamas in terms of its social and educational operations is doing exactly what the PLO was doing 35 years ago, as well as its quote unquote military operations." This is the guy Obama's administration handpicked to represent the U.S. government at the annual Organization for Security and Cooperation in Europe human-rights conference. Makes you feel safe and secure knowing that he's advising our president on domestic and foreign policy, doesn't it?

Imam Mohamed Magid, Obama's Sharia Czar from the Islamic Society of North America and named to his Department of Homeland Security in 2011. He persuaded DHS to erase from its curriculum any suggestion that Muslim terrorism draws its inspiration from the laws and doctrines of Islam.

Eboo Patel, Advisory Council on Faith-Based Neighborhood Partnerships, refers to revolutionary communist Van Jones as an "American patriot" and one of "the true giants of history." Patel says, "I actually grew up in the same hometown that Bill Ayers did and was taught the same myths about America, a land of freedom and equality and justice." [20] He's the grandson of Muslim Brotherhood's founder, Siraj Wahhaj, who was named as a co-conspirator in the 1993 World Trade Center bombing. Who in their right mind would consider this man to be an outstanding candidate to serve as an advisor for Faith-Based Neighborhood Partnerships? He allegedly advocates the Islamic takeover of America under the banner of Sharia Law.

John Brennan, CIA Director, is a devout converted Muslim with reported strong ties to the Muslim Brotherhood. [21]

Valerie Jarrett, Senior White House Advisor, is the daughter-in-law of Vernon Jarrett, a Chicago Communist, according to FBI files.

Huma Abedin, Deputy Chief of Staff to Secretary of State Hillary Clinton, has family ties to the Muslim Brotherhood. Huma's mother, Saleha Abedin, is deeply involved with the Muslim Brotherhood. Her brother, Hassan, is on the board of the Oxford Centre for Islamic Studies (OCIS), the same board on which notorious Muslim Brotherhood leader Sheikh Youssef Qaradawi serves. [22]

Lois Lerner, IRS Director, has been implicated in providing material support to Malik Obama, the President's half-brother.

Malik is known to be an active member of the Muslim Brotherhood. In order to grant Malik special privilege, she used an alias and a private email server to complete the act. In other words, she knew what she was doing was treason and attempting to cover it up. Of course, she implicated her own guilt by refusing to answer questions regarding the IRS scandal of targeting conservative groups, something that was long suspected but now proven to be true.

Okay, you get the point. Other devout Muslims serving in the Obama White House include Ali Abunimah, Azizah Al-Hibri, Tariq Abdullah Khalid Al-Mansour, Salam Al-Marayati, Mazen Asbahi, Minha Husaini, Ingrid Mattson, Dalia Mogahed, Edward Said, Kareem Shora, and Nawar Shora.[23]

Given this glaring number of devout Muslims selected by our President, one can only wonder if Obama himself is a secret Muslim, especially since he was educated in Muslim schools during his formative years. A common thread that weaves its way through many of these names is the direct or indirect link to the Muslim Brotherhood. The Brotherhood's mission states that "Muslims must understand that their work in America is a kind of grand Jihad in eliminating and destroying the Western civilization from within and 'sabotaging' its miserable house by their hand…so that… God's religion (Islam) is made victorious over all other religions." Take note of the word "within." This is a "stealth jihad" that incrementally gains influence over the culture. These appointments should have raised red flags all over the place. Somebody is asleep at the wheel. Where is Congress? Where is the Justice Department? The nails are being hammered into America's coffin and our elected leaders are making a mockery of our Constitution by their silence. This is Obama's playbook on how to transform a nation. We can only pray for a President who surrounds himself with competent godly men and women whose hearts hunger for righteousness and who have a holy fear of God. Indeed, righteousness exalts a nation, but sin is a reproach or shame to any people.

NOW CONSIDER TRUMP'S CABINET

As of this writing President-Elect Donald J. Trump has yet to be sworn into office but has been decisive and swift in his cabinet choices thus far. In fact, the completion of his cabinet is on track to be the fastest ever, but then again, who's counting? It's not the time frame but the character, caliber, and quality of nominees that brings encouragement to the evangelical community throughout the nation. For years Christians have been praying for godly men and women to occupy positions of leadership within the Washington Beltway. Now, even though his cabinet selections are far from being filled, already Trump has appointed more Christians to high positions within his cabinet than any President in recent memory, more than Bush who attempted to implement faith-based initiatives and even more than Reagan who rode to office on the influence of the Moral Majority.

Most encouraging is the fact that these individuals do not appear to be Christian in name only. On the surface all indications are that they walk their talk. These individuals have boldly spoken of their faith, written about Jesus, and actively served Him in their churches as well as the public sector. Reading through this partial list of nine cabinet members, one cannot help but make the contrasting comparison with the previous list whom Obama appointed.

Mike Pence, Vice-President: From day one Pence has unashamedly declared his faith in Jesus Christ. "My Christian faith is at the heart of who I am. I'm a Christian, a conservative, and a Republican, in that order." [24] Pence says, "We need Jesus more than ever right now." [25] Although he grew up as an altar boy in the Catholic Church, it was at a Christian music festival when he was in college that Pence says, "I gave my life to Jesus Christ. My Christian faith is at the very heart of who I am. I try and spend a little time on my knees every day." His stance on abortion "proceeds out of the belief, that ancient principle…where God says before you were formed in the womb, I knew you." [26]

Ben Carson, Department of Housing and Urban Development: Dr. Carson, a world-renown surgeon, is a creationist who describes his conversion to Christ as a teenager by saying that he fell to his knees in bathroom and prayed, "Lord, you have to help me because I can't fix this." [27] Carson was raised in poverty by a mother who could not read. Carson says, "I would describe myself first of all as a Christian—Evangelical in the sense that I believe we have a responsibility to proclaim the Gospel and show other people why we live the way that we do and hopefully that will affect their lives. I think that's a very important component of what we do." [28] After being diagnosed with cancer, his reaction was one of taking it to God in prayer. I said, "Lord, if it's time for me to go, You know what is best. I don't want to go, but if it's time, that's fine. I trust You." [29]

Reince Preibus, Chief of Staff: Priebus is a lifelong member of the Greek Orthodox Church but also maintains dual participation at Grace Church in Racine, Wisconsin where he started a Bible study and prayer group for young married couples. [30] On the official Republican website, writing as chairman of the GOP during Easter, Priebus said, "We celebrate the resurrection of Christ and the love of God in providing a savior. Just as the first Christians praised God at the sight of the empty tomb, we too praise our good and merciful God today for His victory over the grave. Christ's sacrificial work provides an example for us all, and we join with the Psalmist in saying, 'You make known to me the path of life.' Easter is a time for the celebration of new life, and I pray we will all draw on that new hope throughout the year." [31]

Nikki Haley, Ambassador to the United Nations: An immigrant from India, Haley describes her conversion to Christ (after she was married) as "having a profound impact on my daily life and I look to Him for guidance with every decision I make. God has blessed my family in so many ways, and my faith in the Lord gives me great strength on a daily basis. Being a Christian is not about words but about living for Christ every day."[32]

Tom Price, Secretary of Health and Human Services: A medical doctor himself, Dr. Price has not only proposed to dismantle the Affordable Care Act, commonly known as Obama Care, but has written a replacement plan for it. As for his faith, he's a Presbyterian who aligns himself with conservative evangelicals. He's opposed to same-sex marriage, federal funding for abortion, and federal requirements that insurance plans cover contraception with no co-pay.[33]

Betsy DeVos, Secretary of Education: Betsy is the daughter-in-law of Richard DeVos. She was raised in the Reformed Christian church, attended Christian schools including a Christian Calvinist college. She also sent her own children to Christian schools and is a member of the Mars Hill Bible Church in Grand Rapids, Michigan. She has been an advocate for school choice and vouchers for years, but all of her political activism "is an outgrowth of my Christian faith and an effort to advance God's Kingdom. I want to impact our culture in ways that are not the traditional funding-the-Christian-organization-route, but by changing the way we approach things—in this case, the system of education in the country."[34]

Scott Pruitt, Environmental Protection Agency: Pruitt was Oklahoma's attorney general and a committed Southern Baptist. He served as a deacon at First Baptist Church in Broken Arrow, Oklahoma and is also a trustee for Southern Baptist Theological Seminary. He says, "A Christian worldview means that God has answers to our problems. And part of our responsibility is to convey to those in society that the answers that he has, as represented in Scripture, are important and should be followed."[35] As you might suspect, he opposes marriage equality, transgender bathroom access, and abortion.

Rick Perry, Secretary of Energy: The former governor of Texas is well known for his Christian stance. In 2009 he was quoted as saying that non-Christians will be condemned to hell, called evolution "a theory out there" and advocated teaching creationism in the classrooms of our public schools. He also compared homosexuality to alcoholism and said that it is a disorder that can be treated. Then, in 2011 he held a Christian national prayer rally in which 30,000 attended. He called America "a nation in crisis." He further sparked controversy by saying, "There's something wrong in a country where gays can serve in the military but our kids can't openly celebrate Christmas." [36] Yes, this man is bold, godly, and not of the politically-correct variety.

Ken Blackwell, Trump's Domestic Policy Advisor: Blackwell is senior fellow at the Family Research Council and is responsible for the domestic side of Trump's transition team. He served as Cincinnati's mayor and Ohio's secretary of state. He was instrumental in consolidating evangelical support by organizing the "religious advisory council" and desires to surround Trump with wise leaders. Blackwell's convictions are strong, as are the aforementioned men and women. Regarding homosexuality, he calls it a transgression against God's law and supports conversion therapy for gays. [37]

Jeff Sessions, Attorney General: Growing up as a child Sessions was active in the Boy Scouts and Camden Methodist Church. He graduated from a Methodist-affiliated college and is a Sunday School teacher at Ashland Place United Methodist Church in Mobile, Alabama. [30]

Rex Tillerson, Secretary of State: Tillerson is also described as a devout Christian who attends church weekly and teaches a Bible study. [29]

Mike Pompeo, Director of the CIA: He attends Eastminster Presbyterian Church where he serves as a deacon and teaches Sunday School to fifth-graders. [38]

Elaine Chao, Secretary of Transportation: Don't let the name throw you. She's the first Asian-American to hold a cabinet-level position but she is also the wife of Senate Majority Leader Mitch McConnell. McConnell is a Southern Baptist and in 2016 he spoke with CBN's David Brody about his faith. However, little has been said about Chao's commitment to Christ, but it may be assumed that she aligns with these mentioned. [30]

Kellyanne Conway, Trump's Campaign Manager: Conway is the first woman in U.S. history to lead a successful presidential campaign. Her resume and backstory is most interesting, but in the context of her Christian commitment, little has been written. Suffice it to say that she grew up as a Catholic and continues practicing her faith. She believes that walking the walk is what's most important. Obviously, her political convictions align themselves with conservative evangelicals. The firmness of her religious beliefs was seen when she refused to appear on Bill Maher's show because of his atheistic ridicule of Christians. [38]

In addition to these Christian appointees to Trump's cabinet we know that Governor Mike Huckabee, an openly avowed evangelical Christian, was offered a cabinet position but declined the invitation because "it was not a good fit," according to Huckabee. Also, my pastor (Dr. Johnny Hunt) announced this past Sunday that Georgia's former governor, Sonny Perdue, had been vetted and was being seriously considered as Trump's Secretary of Agriculture. For years, Governor Perdue was a member of First Baptist Woodstock (where I attend) and actually taught a Bible study class of young married couples. The point is simply this. The Trump Administration is, and has, made an intentional effort of reaching out to competent, conservative individuals, many of whom are strong in their Christian faith and whose walk with God has been exemplary by their active service to their local churches. For those of us who have prayed for God's intervention in behalf of our nation, these appointments are viewed as a Divine activity by the unseen sovereign Hand of God in answer to the prayers of His people throughout the Land.

Trump has promised to eliminate The Johnson Amendment of 1954 that prohibits churches from endorsing political candidates. If his Christian appointments to high positions in his cabinet are any indication, the window of opportunity for spiritual awakening throughout the land has seldom seen a better climate. Again, the contrast between this incoming administration and the one we've just experienced with Obama is the difference between two polar opposite ideologies or worldviews. Those of us in the evangelical world are convinced that God is answering our prayers and has chosen to intervene in the midst of our crises.

Obama & Abortion

Multiple presidents have opposed the pro-life stance held by conservatives, but once again Obama is a president without precedent when it comes to his liberal views. In July 2006 he voted against a bill stipulating that the parents of minor girls who get out-of-state abortions must be notified of their daughters' action. Now that his daughters are "of age" I doubt he would vote the same today. In March 2008 he voted against a bill prohibiting minors from crossing state lines to gain access to abortion services. The same month, he voted "No" on defining an unborn child as a human being eligible for the State Children's Health Insurance Program. [39]

On July 17, 2007, Obama declared: "The first thing I'd do as President is sign the Freedom of Choice Act." This bill would have terminated all state restrictions on government funding for abortions. It would have invalidated state laws that protected medical personnel from losing their jobs if they refused to participate in abortion procedures. In 2000, Obama voted against a bill that would have ended state funding for partial-birth abortion, a procedure where the abortionist maneuvers the baby into a breech (feet first) delivery position and permits the baby's entire body to exit the birth canal except for its head. Then, scissors are used to puncture the baby's brain and kill it while the head is still inside the mother. Our president approved state funding for such a barbaric, murderous act. [40] I fear that we, the American people, have hands stained with their innocent blood by electing such a man to office.

OBAMA'S HISTORIC FIRSTS

- First President to violate the War Powers Act, unilaterally executing American Military Operations in Libya without informing Congress in the required time period. [40]
- First President to refuse to tell the public what he did for eight hours after being informed that a U.S. Ambassador was facing imminent death during a terror attack and then lie about the reason for the Ambassador's death by blaming it on an Internet video rather than what he knew to be the case. [40]
- First President to have his Attorney General held in criminal contempt of Congress for his efforts to cover up Operation Fast and Furious that killed over 300 individuals and then claim Executive Privilege to shield the AG. [40]
- First President to use the IRS to unfairly target political enemies. [41]
- First President to issue unlawful recess appointments over a long weekend—while the U.S. Senate remained in session (against the advice of his own Justice Department). [42]
- First President to order a secret amnesty program that stopped the deportations of illegal immigrants across the U.S., including those with criminal convictions. [43]

- First President to sue states for enforcing voter ID requirements, which were previously ruled legal by the U.S. Supreme Court. [44]
- First President to arbitrarily declare an existing law unconstitutional and refuse to enforce it (Defense of Marriage Act) [45]
- First President to increase surveillance of American citizens under the Patriot Act by 1,000 percent in four years. [46]
- First President to demand a company hand over $20 billion to one of his political appointees. (BP Oil Spill Relief Fund) [47]
- First President to have a law signed by an "auto-pen" without being present. [48]
- First President to announce an enemies list, including his opponents' campaign donors, and then have them punished by using government instrumentalities. [49]
- First President to send 80 percent of a $16 billion program (green energy) to his campaign contributors, leaving only 20% to those who did not contribute. [50]
- First President to propose an Executive Order demanding companies disclose their political contributions to bid on government contracts. [51]
- First President to leak confidential IRS tax records to groups aligned politically with him for partisan advantage. [52]
- First President to use the EPA to punish political enemies and reward political allies. [53]
- First President to have his Administration fund an organization tied to the cop-killing terrorist group, the Weather Underground. [54]
- First President to move America past the dependency tipping point in which 51% of households now pay no income taxes. [55]

- First President to increase food stamp spending by more than 100% in less than four years. [56]
- First President to spend a trillion dollars on "shovel-ready-jobs" and later admit there was no such thing. [57]
- First President to threaten insurance companies after they publicly spoke out on how Obamacare caused their rate increases. [58]
- First President whose economic policies have the number of Americans on disability exceeding the population of New York. [59]
- First President to sue states for enforcing immigration laws passed by Congress. [60]
- First President to see America lose its status as the world's largest economy. [61]
- First President to redistribute $26.5 billion of the taxpayers' funds to his union supporters in the UAW. [62]
- First President to threaten an auto company (Ford) after it publicly mocked bailouts of GM and Chrysler. [63]
- First President to attempt to bully a major manufacturing company into not opening a factory in a Right-to-Work state (Boeing's facility in South Carolina). [64]
- First President to be held in contempt of court for illegally obstructing oil drilling in the Gulf of Mexico. [65]
- First President to lie repeatedly to the American people about the murder of a U.S. Ambassador and three other diplomatic personnel for purely political reasons, rewriting a "talking points" memo no fewer than a dozen times to avoid referencing a pre-planned terror attack. [66]
- First President to openly defy a congressional order not to

share sensitive nuclear defense secrets with the Russian government.[67]

- First President to leak highly classified military and intelligence secrets to Hollywood in order to promote a movie that could help his re-election campaign.[68]
- First President to send $200 million to a terrorist organization (Hamas) after Congress had explicitly frozen the money for fear it would fund attacks against civilians.[69]
- First President to golf 122 times in his first four-and-a- half years in office.[70]
- First President to preside over a cut to the credit rating of the United States government.[71]
- First President to unlawfully seize telephone records of more than 100 reporters to intimidate and/or bully them.[72]
- First President to send millions in taxpayer dollars to his wife's former employer.[72]
- First President to add more to the National Debt than ALL the previous Presidents before him.[72]
- First President to take 17 vacations in his first term, stretching over 74 days.[73]

Obama's Black-Robed Appointees

In recent years it has become increasingly apparent that one of the most significant roles of a President is his appointments to the judicial benches throughout the Land. There was a time when our judges were objective, non-biased, strict original constructionists in their interpretation of the Constitution. As we've seen, however, activist judges are legislating from the bench and exerting more power than was ever intended by our Founders. Judges today have issued rulings that years ago would have been unthinkable, same-sex marriage just to name one. The standard for such rulings is no longer based on precedents or an original intent perspective of the Constitution, but rather in the belief that the Constitution is a living document and must be interpreted in light of the changing culture. This dangerous, liberal mindset renders our Constitution as irrelevant, just a piece of paper that's seen its better days.

As of 2014, Obama had placed four judges on the D.C. court which shifted its composition to seven Democratic appointees and four Republicans. [74] But it's not just D.C; it is also in federal courts around the country, 280 to be exact, which represents a third of the federal judiciary! When Obama took office, Republican appointees controlled ten of the thirteen circuit courts of appeals; Democratic appointees now constitute a majority in nine circuits. [75] But here is the sad, yet significant reality. Federal judges have life tenure, so all of Obama's judges will continue serving long after he leaves office. So, the Obama fingerprint and liberal policies will be perpetuated for years, perhaps decades.

Obama stated, "When I came into office, I think there was one openly gay judge who had been appointed. We've appointed ten." Regarding his legal legacy, it centers on gay rights. When asked to name the best Supreme Court decision of his tenure, it was neither the Affordable Care Act in 2012 nor the defeat of the Defense of Marriage Act a year later. Instead, it was the legalization of same-sex marriage throughout the nation. [75]

HOW COULD THIS HAVE HAPPENED?

Obviously, millions of Americans believe that Obama is the greatest president in modern history. Obama himself believes this. He touts himself as having saved the nation from another Great Depression and takes no responsibility for America teetering on the brink of total economic collapse. He sees nothing wrong with giving the greatest sponsor of terrorism, Iran, billions of dollars in a deal that gives the Iranians nuclear capability even while chanting, "Death to America!" It's futile to continue this tirade, but I never cease to be amazed at how respectable Americans can look at the same political and economic landscape, and arrive at polar opposite conclusions. It's the difference between a biblical worldview and one that is secular.

As for Obama, his ideological path has been unfolding since childhood, but the mainstream media stumbled all over itself with infatuation while Hollywood, academia, and the African American community sat mesmerized by his swagger. Conservative talk radio and a few Fox News anchors tried to warn the public of his radical views, but beyond that, few were sounding the alarm. Therefore, his background, education, family history, and all the rest went largely undetected and under-reported.

In Obama's book, *Dreams from My Father*, he writes "It was my father's image, the black man, son of Africa, that I'd packed all the attributes I sought in myself." [76] The book is about how Obama created his own identity and defined his core values by taking his father's dreams and making them his own. So, where his father failed in carrying out the dream, the son would succeed. That being said, we cannot understand our President without understanding his father and the dreams he had. His father had four wives and was a chronic alcoholic and wife-abuser. Barack Sr., a self-described socialist, was vehemently opposed to U.S. foreign policy and U.S. defense spending. President Obama confided to journalist David Mendell, "Every man is trying to live up to his father's expectations or make up for his mistakes. In my case, both things might be true." [77] Dinesh D'Souza, in his book Obama's America, writes "Never before has America had a president tutored and mentored by a Communist and part-time pornographer; by a "professor of terror" who advocated armed resistance against America and her allies; by a socialist so radical that he was ejected by the foreign socialist government he served in; by an incendiary theologian whose philosophy can be summed up in the phrase "God damn America"; and by a former terrorist who, like Osama Bin Laden, attempted to blow up the Pentagon and other symbols of American power. Obama didn't accidentally encounter them; he sought them out."[78]

Like me, you've probably wondered, "Is our President a socialist? Is he a closet Muslim working in co-op with terrorists? Or is he just outright incompetent?" If he's a socialist, this would explain his economic policy, but not his foreign policy. If he's a secret Muslim, this would explain his foreign policy, but not his domestic and social policies. If he's naively incompetent, this discounts his intelligence entirely. However, there is another explanation that makes total sense. He is an anti-colonialist just like his father. Anti-colonialism is the doctrine that rich countries of the West got rich by invading, occupying and looting the poor countries of Asia, Africa, and South America.

Keep in mind, our President is committed to the dream of his father, an anti-colonialist. In 1965, Obama Sr. published an article in the *East Africa Journal* stating his objective: "We need....to eliminate power structures that have been built through excessive accumulation so that not only a few individuals shall control a vast magnitude of resources as is the case now." To achieve this goal, he proposes the use of state power to take over large parts of the private sector and taxing the rich with rates up to 100![79] You may recall that Obama's re-election centered on attacking the rich, the millionaires and billionaires.

Let's listen again to the words of D'Souza, research scholar from Stanford University and former White House domestic policy analyst: "He (Obama) is doing what he does because he has objectives quite different than fostering economic growth; he intends to use the rod of government control to tame exploitative capitalists and severely regulate the private sector; he wants to strengthen Iran and Syria's roles in the Middle East while diminishing that of the United States; and he cares more about reducing America's nuclear arsenal than about preventing Iran from getting a nuclear bomb."[80] This falls in line with the anti-colonialism philosophy.

Okay, let's review. Obama Sr. recommended limitless tax rates on the rich and for the state to use its power to control and dominate the institutions of the private sector. Obama frequently talks about people being forced to pay their "fair share" in taxes. And then, the private sector is made up of big corporations, insurance companies, pharmaceutical companies, oil companies, automobile companies, and so on. Obama Sr. proposed that the government seize control of these industries and turn them from private profit-making entities into regulated arms of the state. Bingo! Look at the banking crisis. Look at the takeover of healthcare, General Motors, and other financial institutions. Let's not forget that health care reform was pushed through without one Republican vote. Furthermore, the education sector is already under government control. This is the anti-colonial objective and this is the dream of his father. No, it is not what is in America's best interest and no, it does nothing to stimulate our economy. What it does do is punish the rich and make big corporations pay for their misdeeds. Anti-colonialism views them as greedy, selfish exploiters who must be punished for what they have done to the rest of the world. If America collapses as a result, so be it. If America ceases to be a global superpower, Obama is willing to lead us down this path. He is that committed to his father's dream.....or perhaps he is that hungry for his father's love and approval, which he never received. Like it or not, we have all now been impacted by his radical worldview and find ourselves out on the limb of a twisted family tree.

Daniel Webster's Warning to America

"If we abide by the principles taught in the Bible, our country will go on prospering; but if we and our posterity neglect its instructions and authority, no man can tell how sudden a catastrophe may overwhelm us and bury all our glory in profound obscurity.

Whatever makes men good Christians, makes them good citizens. Let us not forget the religious character of our origin. Our fathers were brought hither by their high veneration for the Christian religion. They journeyed by its light, and labored in its hope.

If religious books are not widely circulated among the masses in this country, I do not know what is going to become of us as a nation. If truth be not diffused, error will be; If God and His Word are not known and received, the devil and his works will gain the ascendancy; If the evangelical volume does not reach every hamlet, the pages of a corrupt and licentious literature will; If the power of the Gospel is not felt throughout the length and breadth of the land, anarchy and misrule, degradation and misery, corruption and darkness will reign without mitigation or end."[1]

— Daniel Webster (1782-1852)
served as a U.S. Congressman, a U.S. Senator, and as the Secretary of State for three different Presidents

CHAPTER 9

The American Family Crisis Tsunami Alert

Tony Evans, Senior Pastor of Oak Cliff Bible Fellowship in Dallas, Texas, says, "If you want to know what is wrong with a nation, I will take you to the states; and if you want to know what is wrong with the states, I will take you to the cities; if you want to know what is wrong in the cities, I take you to the local communities; and if you want to know what is wrong in the communities, I take you to the family!" He's right on. The epicenter for most of the nation's problems can be either directly or indirectly traced back to the homes of its citizens. The culture around us has radically changed, but it is because the homes within the culture have radically changed, and that's because the mindset of the families living in those homes has radically changed.

These are unprecedented times. We are living in the midst of a revolution that is redefining life as we've known it. Right and wrong are being redefined. Marriage has been redefined. A moral shift of magnanimous proportion has, and is, occurring within our nation that is leaving our children confused and questioning the long-standing traditions of their parents and pastors. I received a call today from a pastor with concerns about a student in his youth group who is dating a transgender girlfriend. The young man is the son of a prominent, dedicated family in the church. This teenager has challenged the pastor's stance on biblical sexual identity. While such a conversation would have been unthinkable a few years ago, it is reflective how this revolution is transforming and contaminating the minds of the upcoming generation. Make no mistake, every dimension of our lives will be impacted and those who refuse to accommodate its demands will pay a price. Lines in the sand are being drawn. There is no middle ground.

What at one time was considered perversion and immoral is now being celebrated as morally good.

Many churches will capitulate to the cultural norms by abdicating their responsibility of upholding the moral standards espoused in Scripture. The seismic shift within the American family has left no segment of our congregations untouched, but in this postmodern age of tolerance and diversity there is an eerie silence in most pulpits when it comes to addressing the family dynamic from a biblical perspective. This is unfortunate because a large percentage of church members gather on Sunday mornings with their families fractured, divorces being contemplated, ongoing affairs, pornography addictions, stress from blended siblings, and child support payments from previous marriages tearing apart the family finances. Yet, due to the delicate, sensitive nature of these issues, large numbers of pastors refuse to address them with Bible in hand for fear of someone being offended. Indeed, the moral authority of the Church has been largely neutralized by the pervasiveness of moral relativism taught in our schools and practiced in our society and the Church, by in large, has caved. John Whitehead, President of Rutherford Institute, says, "Major religious institutions have virtually little to no moral or spiritual impact on American society." [2] What a sad indictment upon the Church in America! The following pages will highlight just how far into the cultural abyss the family has fallen. I fear that we in the Church are too busy with our own agendas, noble as they may be, and operating on frenzied schedules that have us stressed to the max with little margin in our own lives, that the greater issues confronting our children are somehow flying under the radar while we sleepwalk our way through this social revolution that poses as the most serious threat to our religious liberties in American history.

THE WORLD LEADER WE DON'T WANT TO BE

The family unit as the basic building block of our society has collapsed. History tells us that not far behind will be the nation itself caving under the weight of insurmountable pressures and problems of its own making. While committing national suicide, it's as though we turn a blind eye and deaf ear to the following facts:

- America has the highest divorce rate in the world. [3]
- America has the highest percentage of one person households in the world. [4]
- The United States has the highest teen pregnancy rate in the entire world, more than twice as high as Canada, more than three times as high as France and more than seven times as high as Japan. [5]
- The United States has the highest child abuse death rate in the industrialized world. [6]
- The United States has the highest rate of child poverty in the world. [7]
- The United States leads the industrialized world in fatherless homes. [8]
- America has the highest incarceration rate and the largest total prison population in the entire world. [9]
- The United States leads the world in murders. [10]
- The United States leads the world in total crime. [11]

- The United States is the world leader in producing pornography.[12]
- The United States leads the world in illegal drug use.[13]

Of the ten above stated facts, the one that is the greatest contributor to the rest is fatherless homes. In fact, fatherless homes are the curse of this generation and the contributing factor in most of our nation's moral concerns. It is perplexing as to why our government and churches have not taken a greater lead in attempting to remedy this epidemic. Contrarily, some of our government programs, such as the welfare system, actually reward immorality and financial irresponsibility by offering assistance with paying bills, buying groceries, and providing housing which only contributes to dead-beat dads. Again, culturally speaking, there is no "right and wrong," "moral or immoral," so we're supposed to be tolerant lest someone be offended or classify us as judgmental. Thus, the pulpits, schools, and government become accomplices in accelerating our moral freefall. As the English statesman, Edmund Burke, said, "The only thing necessary for evil to triumph is for good people to do nothing." However, if anything should compel us to action, the following should serve as a wake-up call. Perhaps you have read or heard some of this before, but the cumulative effect of seeing the far-reaching impact that divorce and the absence of a father has upon our nation is breathtaking.

FATHERLESS HOMES: THE CURSE OF OUR GENERATION

- Children from single-parent homes are twice as likely to repeat a grade in school and more than twice as likely to be suspended or expelled from school.[14]
- Young men from these homes are twice as likely to end up in jail as those who come from traditional two-parent families.[15]

- Children without a dad at home are seven times as likely to be delinquent and almost twice as likely to have pulled a knife or a gun on someone in the past year. [16]
- Gang involvement is twice as high. [17]
- 90 percent of the increase in violent crime between 1973 and 1995 was committed by those born out of wedlock and raised in a single-parent home. [18]
- The annual average income of a traditional family is $101,000, but of a single-mother family it is $35,000. [19]
- Children from divorced homes experience lower scores in school, higher absenteeism, and a dropout rate of 31 percent, compared to only 13 percent for children from intact homes. [20]
- Children who have experienced a divorce are 50 percent more likely to develop health problems. [21]
- Children of divorce suffer higher rates of depression, addiction, and arrest. [22]
- Thirty-three percent of girls of divorced parents become teen mothers, compared with only 11 percent of girls from intact homes. [23]
- The adult children of divorce are 89 percent more likely to divorce than those raised in intact families. [24]
- The lifespan for children of divorce averages five years less than those who grew up in intact families. [25]
- Nearly all of the increase in child poverty since the 1970s can be attributed to family breakdown. [26] In fact, children from fatherless homes are six times more likely to live in poverty. [27] An unbelievable one in three kids in America lives in poverty. [28]
- Children of single-parent homes are more than twice as likely to commit suicide. [29]

- Divorce is the leading cause of childhood depression. [30]
- 75% of adolescent patients at chemical abuse centers are from single-parent families. [31]
- 70% of teenage pregnancies are single-parent children. [32]
- 63% of youth suicides are single-parent children. [33]
- 75% of juveniles in youth correction facilities are from single-parent families [34]

My apologies to those who have gone through the trauma of a broken home and may interpret these stats as uncompassionate or harsh. This is the very reason that many preachers never address this. It's too delicate and sensitive. It is high risk rhetoric which, undoubtedly, will be offensive and cause many to become defensive in justifying their current circumstances with such lines as, "But, you don't know my situation. Besides, who are you to judge?" Let's not go there. Yes, life is unfair. Yes, the psychological skin has been burned. Yes, the wound is deep. Yes, you may have been a victim of horrendous circumstances. Yes, yes, yes, but facts are facts and to deny these facts is to perpetuate the problem and forfeit the opportunity of perhaps preventing someone else from making the same mistake. When I was a child, many parents of that generation stayed together and toughed it out for the sake of the children. Today, we've bought into the lie that children are resilient and do not need a dad in the house. Feminists have done much to convince the culture that men are not necessary. Now having the benefit of decades observing, researching, and gathering all the statistical data necessary, study after study has concluded that children need two parents in the home. Oh, to be sure, we can all point to exceptions....but they are just that, exceptions. Certainly, the Bible is the supreme authority on this subject, but if further evidence is needed, the comments from these foremost experts will be found helpful:

In a landmark study, psychologist Judith W. Wallerstein was among the first to bring the impact of divorce upon children to the forefront. Dr. Wallerstein and another colleague recruited 60 families with 131 children who were products of divorce and followed them for ten years and then did a follow-up after twenty-five years. Wallerstein died in 2012 at the age of 90, but listen to the wisdom of her decades of research: "Twelve to eighteen months after the divorce we found family after family still in crisis, their wounds wide open. Their symptoms were worse than they had been immediately after the divorce. After five years, 37% of the children had gone downhill: It would be hard to find any other group of children—except, perhaps, the victims of a natural disaster—who suffered such a rate of sudden serious psychological problems. After 10 years, 41% of the children of divorce were worried, underachieving, self-depreciating and sometimes angry young men and women. By ages 19-23, 66% of the female children of divorce found that they were more haunted and scarred by the divorce in their earlier lives than either they or the researchers had realized. Forty percent of the boys were found to be floundering in their lives. Divorce was the single most important cause of enduring pain and anomie in their lives. The young people told us time and again how much they needed family structure. An alarming number of teenagers felt abandoned, physically and emotionally."[35]

James Q. Wilson, considered to be one of the world's brightest and most well-respected social scientists, says: "Almost everyone—a few retrograde scholars excepted—agrees that children in mother-only homes suffer harmful consequences: the best studies show that these youngsters are more likely than those in mother/father families to be suspended from school, have emotional problems, become delinquent, suffer from abuse and take drugs."[36]

The Center for Law and Social Policy (CLASP) found: "Most researchers now agree that…studies support the notion that, on average, children do best when raised by their two married biological parents. Research indicates that, on average, children who grow up in families with both their biological parents in a low-conflict marriage are better off in a number of ways than children who grow up in single, step, or cohabiting-parent households."[37]

Child Trends concludes: "An extensive body of research tells us that children do best when they grow up with both biological parents in a low-conflict marriage."[38]

A diverse team of family scholars working collectively from the Universities of Texas, Virginia, Minnesota, Chicago, Maryland, Washington, UC Berkeley, and Rutgers University reported that children who live with their own married parents:

- Live longer, healthier lives both physically and mentally
- Do better in school
- Are more likely to graduate and attend college.
- Less likely to live in poverty.
- Less likely to be in trouble with the law.
- Less likely to drink or do drugs.
- Less likely to be violent or sexually active.
- Less likely to be victims of sexual or physical violence.
- More likely to have a successful marriage when they are older.[39]

Sociologist Paul Amato, in a study published by Princeton University and the Brookings Institute, explains: "Compared with children who grow up in stable, two-parent families, children born outside marriage reach adulthood with less education, earn less income, have lower occupational status, are more likely to be idle (that is, not employed and not in school), are more likely to have a non-marital birth (among daughters), have more troubled marriages, experience higher rates of divorce, and report more symptoms of depression....Research clearly demonstrates that children growing up with two continuously married parents are less likely than other children to experience a wide range of cognitive, emotional, and social problems, not only during childhood, but also in adulthood."[40]

Finally, Sara McLanahan of Princeton University, one of the world's leading scholars on how the family dynamic impacts a child's well-being, explains from her extensive investigations: "If we were asked to design a system for making sure that children's basic needs were met, we would probably come up with something quite similar to the two-parent family ideal. Such a design, in theory, would not only ensure that children had access to the time and money of two adults, it would provide a system of checks and balances that promote quality parenting. The fact that both adults have a biological connection to the child would increase the likelihood that the parents would identify with the child and be willing to sacrifice for that child and it would reduce the likelihood that either parent would abuse the child."[41]

Cumulatively speaking, these "experts" have many decades of experience and they each arrived at the same conclusion. They had no biased presuppositions. They are social scientists who objectively and extensively studied this issue and concluded that it's not even a close call: "Children do better emotionally, psychologically, mentally, physically, academically, domestically, professionally, socially, and financially when raised in a healthy marriage with a father and a mother. No surprise, this is precisely what the Bible teaches. Yet, the social and moral fabric of America is being ripped apart by liberal elitists determined to transform the nation into a socialistic model, unrecognizable from anything we've known in the past. Sadly, our children have been the innocent victims of this social experiment and now trying to parent their own children without a role model or point of reference to draw from.

Statistically speaking, "If the United States enjoyed the same level of family stability today as it did in 1960, the nation would have 750,000 fewer children repeating grades, 1.2 million fewer school suspensions, approximately 500,000 fewer acts of teenage delinquency, about 600,000 fewer kids receiving therapy, and approximately 70,000 fewer suicide attempts every year."[42]

THAT WAS THEN, THIS IS NOW!

America was founded upon Judeo-Christian beliefs which said, "There is a God." Today, the existence of God and morality are matters of personal opinion and has little relevance to our social problems. Traditionally, Americans believed that man is a spiritual being who stands in need of a relationship with God to fulfill his purpose in life. Today, man is the product of evolution, a highly evolved animal. Traditionally, there were universal, moral principles providing us with a compass of absolute right and wrong. Today, there is no absolute truth. All standards and values are relative. Traditionally, the nuclear family was the cornerstone and fundamental building block of society, a sacred institution that was to be protected from sexual immorality. Today, the family is seen as a product of evolution with many possible forms as a social organization. Traditionally, the nation looked to God for our dependency and to solve those problems exceeding our own capacity. Today, technology, social sciences, and the role of the state in social engineering have replaced God. We've transitioned from a theistic-centered culture to a secularized, humanistic one.

To demonstrate just how decadent we've become and how dramatic the moral shift of the nation is, consider the fact that in the "not-so-distant" past, Americans viewed homosexuality, illegitimate childbirth, divorce, and premarital sex to be immoral, wrong, unacceptable. Today, however, 58 percent view homosexuality, 67 percent view illegitimate childbirth, 69 percent view divorce, and

66 percent view premarital sex as all being moral.[43] Alarmingly, as recent as 2008 the majority of Americans would have been on the traditional side of this moral equation.[44] This reveals how quickly a culture can radically change. Yes, that was then and this is now.

In this so-called age of enlightenment, we're groping in darkness. John Whitehead, President of the Rutherford Institute, offers an astute observation in stating that when family structures break down, people tend to look to mega-structures, such as the state, for help. The public costs of family breakdown exceeds $112 billion a year as federal, state, and local governments spend more money on police, prisons, welfare, and court costs, trying to pick up the pieces of broken families.[45] Another author concurred: "The marriage bond is the fundamental connecting link in Christian society. Break it, and you will have to go back to the overwhelming dominance of the State."[46] Is this not precisely what we are seeing today? The State, Big Brother, has stepped in to replace the role of the father. Need money? The State offers welfare. Need groceries? The State offers food stamps. Need housing? The State offers public housing. Need medical attention? The State offers Medicaid. So, who needs a father when the State is the "Big Daddy" filling the domestic void? In fact, who needs God? Two-thirds of American adults and four-fifths of born-again Christians are concerned about the moral condition of the nation. Another three-quarters of all Americans are worried about the future of our nation, as well they should be.[47] But it's one thing to worry and be concerned, it's another thing to take action. There is a leadership vacuum in America, and we need a Moses, a Joshua, a Josiah, a national voice of moral authority around which the nation can rally. Seemingly, the only thing the population knows to do is look to the political system as the savior. But, the root of the nation's problems is not political, but moral and spiritual.

Nevertheless, the government is now performing the tasks

formerly done by the nuclear family and hard as it may be to believe, it has not happened by accident. Dating back to the "Father of Modern Education," John Dewey's Marxist vision for America is unfolding before our eyes. Indeed, Soviet historian Mikhail Heller stated that one of the first things Lenin did when he came to power in the Soviet Union was to institute a no-fault divorce policy. Lenin and Stalin both understood that to maintain control of the people it would be necessary to completely destroy the family. [48]

WHEN FAMILIES SUFFER, CITIES SUFFER

It's no secret that America's cities are in big trouble. Many are bankrupt. Crime is rampant. The inner cities are war zones. The five cities listed below are merely a microcosm of much of the nation.

Baltimore

Ready for this? Only 16% of 15-17year old teens in Baltimore have been raised in an intact, married family. This is a crisis on steroids. Again, the breadcrumbs lead to the breakdown of marriage in the inner city. [49] Studies showed that these teenagers are facing poorer health and hardships than those in the economically distressed areas of Johannesburg, South Africa; Ibadan, Nigeria; Shanghai, China, and New Delhi, India.

Chicago

The epidemic of gun violence in Chicago is staggering. By the end of the third quarter of 2015, 2,300 had been wounded. [50] The city began 2016 with the bloodiest start in two decades. [51]

In a brief span of time, 82 were killed and the president declared the city to be a warzone. The National Guard was called in to restore order. Alarmingly, in June 2012, more Chicago residents had been killed—228-- than the number of U.S. troops killed in Afghanistan—144. [52] Nearly half of Chicago's 20-24 year olds are unemployed which only feeds the crimes involving violence and drugs. In eight of the city's neighborhoods, unemployment reaches 66%.[53] Guess what's missing? The fathers.

Detroit

With a graduation rate of only 38%, an unemployment rate of over 17%, and known as the nation's murder capital, it is no surprise that Detroit is the poster child for ailing cities.[54] Median annual household income in Detroit is $25,193 (2011) which is half of what the rest of the nation is earning ($50,502).[55] The number of families living in poverty is three times that of the national rate. One in five children lives in poverty in the U.S., but in Detroit it is a staggering 57%.[56] With 78,000 homes abandoned and 40 percent of the city's street lights not working, Detroit increasingly resembles a ghost town. Only a third of the city's ambulances are operational and if you call the police in Detroit, be prepared to wait. The average response time is about an hour.[57]

Atlanta

Homeless youth, a graduation rate of 44%, and one of the leading cities in America for crime place Atlanta in the same gene pool as other cities in crisis.[58]

Cleveland

The FBI Crime Report ranks Cleveland as the fifth most dangerous city in the nation.[59] Unbelievably, more than half of the kids in Cleveland are victims of poverty and are under-nourished. The poverty rate is the second highest in the nation.[60]

While these cities have been highlighted, it needs to be noted that the same could just as easily been said about St. Louis, Memphis, Oakland, Modesto, Wilmington, Buffalo, Miami, or New Orleans and many more. Incidentally, it is undeniable that America's cities are liberal while the rest of the country is mostly conservative. Of all the major cities in America, the only ones that went Republican in the 2012 presidential election were Phoenix, Oklahoma City,

Fort Worth, and Salt Lake City.[61] I only mention this to draw attention to the correlation between urban decay throughout the cities of our nation and the liberal policies that have contributed to it.

More Troubling Statistics

- For the first time in our history, more than a million public school students are homeless.[62]
- An all-time low 44.2 percent of Americans in the 25 to 34 year old age bracket are married.[63]
- More than half of all couples cohabit before getting married.[64]
- For women under the age of 30, more than half of all babies are born out of wedlock.[65] For the overall nation, 48 percent are born to a mother who is not married.[66]
- One out of every three children lives in a home without a father.[67]
- 42 percent of all single mothers are on food stamps.[68]
- 50 percent of all children will be on food stamps before reaching the age of 18.[69]
- Only 51 percent of all American adults are currently married.[70]
- 72 percent of black children are born out of wedlock with no father in the home.[71]
- In New York, 69 percent of black pregnancies end in abortion.[72]
- High school graduation for blacks is only 69 percent.[73]
- In an increasing number of states, there are more deaths than births.[74]
- The nation's marriage rate is the lowest since 1920.[75]

- Of all births to teenage mothers, more than 80 percent of the mothers were unmarried.[76]
- 60 percent of men and 40 percent of women will have an affair at some point in their marriage.[77]
- 45-55% of married women and 50-60% of married men engage in extramarital sex at some time during their relationship.[78]
- 57 percent of men and 54 percent of women admit to committing infidelity in their marriages.[79]
- AIDS is the leading killer of Americans between the ages of 25 and 44.[80]
- One in two sexually active young people will get an STD by the age of 25.[81]

The statistics continue infinitum. The moral fiber of our nation has unraveled and only almighty God can bring the healing so desperately needed. America, as a whole, has violated God's moral law, repudiated His Word, mocked His Name, defied His commands, rejected His existence, and flaunted its rebellion not unlike Sodom & Gomorrah. What is especially deeply disturbing is that Barna Group documented that "Of more than 70 other moral behaviors we study, when we compare Christians to non-Christians we rarely find substantial differences."[82] This is a sad commentary on the Christianity community and should serve as a clarion wake-up call to the American Church.

SAME SEX MARRIAGE

A brief perusal of defining moments in American history reveals the values of the nation at that time. When reflecting on the darkest days of our past, there was the Dred Scott Decision in 1857 which ruled that of people of African descent and held as slaves were not protected under the Constitution and could never be citizens of the

United States. There was Roe v. Wade in 1973 in which abortion, the killing of an unborn child while in the mother's womb, was the woman's right to choose and continues to be legal in all fifty states. Apart from the Court's rulings, such dark moments as the stock market crash in 1929, the terrorist attack on 9/11 of 2001, the bombing of Pearl Harbor on December 7, 1941 will forever go down in the annals of history as unforgettable dark days in our nation. But ranking at the top of America's darkest moments, along with the Court's ruling on abortion in 1973, would be Obergefell v. Hodges on June 26, 2015 in which the Court handed down a landmark decision giving same-sex couples the Constitutional right to marry. The ruling grants homosexuals the same legal rights and benefits as married heterosexual couples nationwide.

Let's be clear, however. This ruling was anything but a dark day for most Americans. Indeed, the Obama Administration lit up the White House in rainbow colors celebrating a long-awaited victory for which he campaigned. It was a narrow 5-4 decision. In his dissent, Justice Antonin Scalia called the decision "a threat to American democracy." [83]

Chief Justice John Roberts echoed, "This decision has nothing to do with the Constitution." [84] Who would have ever thought we would witness such a day when nine black-robed justices, actually five to be precise, would redefine the institution of marriage that had been the cornerstone of civilization for two millennia. This redefinition renders marriage as a genderless institution meaning that more kids will grow up without their own mother and father in a life-long commitment. James Dobson, Focus on the Family founder, says that "Gay marriage signals the fall of Western Civilization. I do not recall a time when the institutions of marriage and the family have faced such peril, or when the forces arrayed against them were more formidable or determined. Barring a miracle, the family that has existed since antiquity will likely crumble, presaging the fall of Western civilization itself."[85] Stating that God will destroy America because of the same-sex marriage ruling, citing Sodom and Gomorrah as examples, Pat Robertson said, "There's never been a civilization ever in history that has embraced homosexuality and turned away from traditional fidelity, traditional marriage, traditional child-rearing, and has survived. There isn't one single civilization that has survived that openly embraced homosexuality."[86] Conservative politician Pat Buchanan chimed in, "If the tenets of the 'gay-rights' movement are true, the Torah and New Testament are wrong. Christianity has been wrong since the time of St. Paul, Aquinas, and Augustine and the moral edifice by which men in the West have lived for 2,000 years was built on bigotry, prejudice and lies. Was it?"[87] Dobson went on record as saying, "…allowing same-sex marriage in the United States would lead to group marriage, marriage between daddies and little girls, or marriage between a man and his donkey."[88] Franklin Graham boldly declared, "With all due respect to the Court, it did not define marriage, and therefore is not entitled to redefine it. I pray God will spare America from His judgment, though, by our actions as a nation, we give Him less and less reason to do so."[89]

Justice Samuel Alito, another of the four dissenters, challenged the Court's rationale with some thought-provoking questions for which the Court offered no explanation: "If equality requires redefining marriage to include same-sex couple, what else does "equality" require? If the fundamental right to marry is simply about consenting adult romance and caregiving, what limits could the state ever place on it? What about a group consisting of two men and two women applying for a marriage license? Would there be any ground for denying them a license? How about siblings who want to get married?" Justice Roberts agreed by saying, "Every argument the court made to redefine marriage to include same-sex couples could be used to redefine it to include multi-person relationships."[89]

The ramifications of this historic ruling are mind-boggling, not the least of which concerns our children. The best protectors of unborn children are a strong marriage culture. The redefinition of marriage insists that there are no differences between the marital union of husband and wife and the union of two people of the same sex, even though a same-sex couple cannot conceive a child naturally. Let's be clear, nothing in the Constitution justifies what the Supreme Court did. It is unconscionable to think that a majority of five liberal justices could impose on the American people its judgment about how marriage should be defined, defying two thousand years of tradition. These judges were not elected and have no accountability, but they usurped the opinion of the American people about what marriage is and replaced it with their own opinion—without any constitutional basis whatsoever. Think of the arrogance in this ruling. These five men are saying that the marriage policy the United States has followed for all its history is now prohibited by the Constitution. Now, they're saying, "We know better." Justice Roberts nailed it by saying, "The right of the majority's decision has no basis in the Constitution or this Court's precedent. The Court invalidates the marriage laws of more than half the States and orders the transformation of a social institution that has formed the basis of human society for millennia. Just who do we think we are?"[90]

It should be noted that all nine Supreme Court justices are graduates of Yale or Harvard Law schools with four of the nine from New York City. Eight of them grew up in east and West Coast States. Not a single Southwesterner, not a genuine Westerner, and not even a Protestant of any denomination much less an evangelical Christian on the Court. With these facts in mind, Justice Scalia said, "To allow the policy question of same-sex marriage to be considered and resolved by a select, patrician, highly unrepresentative panel of nine is to violate a principle even more fundamental than no taxation without representation: no social transformation without representation."[91]

Justice Alito brings to the narrative another question concerning many Christians. He says, "I see dark days ahead. I assume that those who cling to old beliefs will be able to whisper their thoughts in the recesses of their homes, but if they repeat those views in public, they will risk being labeled as bigot and treated as such by governments, employers, and schools. By imposing its own views on the entire country, the majority facilitates the marginalization of the many Americans who have traditional ideas." [92] This is the question for many preachers who stand for the biblical definition of marriage. Will our right to dissent be protected? Will our right to speak and act in accord with what Americans have always believed about marriage be tolerated?

An amicus brief filed in the *Obergefell* (same-sex marriage) case by over one hundred scholars of marriage—their disciplines included sociology, psychology, economics, history, philosophy, literature, political science, pediatrics and family law—points out that where marriage has been redefined, the institution of marriage has been damaged, and this damage affects the children of heterosexuals. [93] The scholars predict there will be as many as nine hundred thousand more aborted babies and six hundred thousand more fatherless children. [94]

ELEVEN CONSEQUENCES OF THE COURT'S MONUMENTAL RULING

(1) The entire edifice of family law was wiped away by the wave of a judicial wand.

(2) Archbishop Sean P. O'Malley and other leaders of Catholic Charities of Boston announced that the agency will end its adoption work rather than comply with state law requiring homosexual adoption of children. [95] The same can be said of other religious agencies where parents will be precluded from using those agencies to place their children in families who share their values.

(3) Preaching against homosexuality and counseling of homosexuals will likely be prohibited. Get ready. Preachers will be monitored by atheist and liberal groups to ensure that there are no sermons stating that homosexuality is sin.

(4) Churches and other religious organizations will lose their Federal Income Tax Exemption. Criminal penalties, such as fines and imprisonment, may even be imposed on church leaders who refuse to compromise their biblical convictions. It is only a matter of time.

(5) The Court's ruling leaves open the door for three women or three men to marry or a brother and sister getting married to each other.

(6) eople of faith will be driven from public office because this ruling forces state officials to participate in wedding ceremonies which are sinful for Orthodox Jews, conservative Catholics, or Evangelical Christians.

(7) Television and other media outlets will become more pro-homosexual making it increasingly difficult to raise children in a debased culture where Gay Pride Parades flaunt nudity and other repulsive behavior designed to shock straight people.

(8) More businesses will be the target of lawsuits such as bakers, photographers, florists, and others that refuse to promote same-sex marriage because it violates their religious and moral values. No doubt, the courts will rule that gays are being discriminated against and those businesses will be forced to comply or close their doors.

(9) Every licensed professional will be required to bow down to the idol of "non-discrimination," or be cast out of his profession. While tolerating the immorality of gay marriage, the homosexual activists will not tolerate other views.

(10) The Court's ruling undermines the created male-female order. Nature itself reveals that God fashioned the male penis and

the female vulva/vagina as complementary sex organs. The Court displaced the Word of God, most likely invoking God's judgment.

(11) We only need to go back to the ancient Greeks, the behaviors of Babylon, Egypt and Rome, all of which were condemned in Scripture. Legitimizing homosexuality is an attempt to turn Western culture back to pagan behaviors. Those cultures did not survive. Nor will we.

John Adams warned, "Our Constitution is made only for a moral and religious people. It is wholly inadequate to the government of any other." [96] For Adams, it was unthinkable to assume that the Supreme Court justices themselves would lack the moral sanity and religious moorings to rule in a manner contradictory to God's Word. Yet, the very men who are charged with the responsibility of upholding our Constitution chose to ignore it along with two thousand years of civilized history and six thousand years of biblical authority. While sitting in their chambers, these Ivy League justices have enough brain power to put most of us to shame, but they lacked the wisdom of God to exercise proper judgment. So, it is not a deficiency of their intellect, but a cavernous void of common sense, and more importantly, wisdom that comes from only God Himself. Choices have consequences....and this one choice made by five men in behalf of three hundred million Americans may have very well been the tipping point for God's ultimate judgment upon our Land. God help us!

MacArthur's Profound Observation of History

History fails to record a single precedent in which nations subject to moral decay have not passed into political and economic decline. There has been either a spiritual awakening to overcome the moral lapse, or a progressive deterioration leading to ultimate national disaster."[1]

— Douglas MacArthur (1880-1964)
served as the Supreme Commander of Allied Forces in the Pacific during World War II.

CHAPTER 10

America's Morality Crisis Solar Eclipse

America possesses great wealth, but cannot control its streets. We have the greatest military the planet has ever seen, but cannot control the gangs or violence in our schools. Our cities are overrun with racial strife. Incurable diseases are raging out of control. Political corruption is at an all-time high. Judicial activism is rampant throughout the Land. The nation's economy is teetering on total collapse. Terrorism has paralyzed the nation with fear. Educational performance, when compared to other industrialized nations, is pathetic. Friends and neighbors are abandoning God and departing from the faith. And in the midst of it all, record setting floods, fires, tornadoes, and ice storms are occurring with increasing frequency. Embarrassing as it is, visitors from Third World nations are at greater risks in the streets of America than in their own underdeveloped homelands. Everywhere we turn there is decline, there is a crisis. But nowhere is the crisis and decline more evident than in the nation's morality. Indeed, the unraveling of our moral fiber is at the heart of all other crises.

We are in a state of national emergency and cannot afford to look the other way any longer. Politically, economically, culturally, socially, and morally, our nation has been reshaped. What we are seeing are warning signs from a loving God who is striving to turn the heart of the nation back to Himself. We have lost our moral compass and only the Church can point the way back. "Why is that?" you may ask. General Douglas MacArthur said it like this:

"History fails to record a single precedent in which nations subject to moral decay have not passed into political and economic decline. There has either been a spiritual awakening to overcome the moral lapse or a progressive deterioration leading to ultimate national disaster." [2] MacArthur defines this critical crossroads by saying, "What seems to be the problem is not the problem." The problem is not the economy. The problem is the moral decay that underlies the economic decline. He claims there has never been a nation in all of history that has succumbed to moral decay without declining politically and economically. But then he violates the political correctness of our day by factoring in the necessity of spiritual awakening without which there will be catastrophic consequences. Why the connection between moral decay and spiritual awakening? Here it is. What are our laws based upon? Answer: Morality. From where do morals originate? Answer: Theology. From where does theology originate? Answer: The Bible. To whom has the Bible been entrusted? Answer: The Church. What is the Church's purpose? Answer: To be salt and light in the culture. Salt is a preservative that keeps things from decaying. Thus, a thriving, evangelistically-minded, healthy, vibrant Church is the greatest safe-guard from a culture's moral decay. When connecting the dots or tracing the bread crumbs, it all leads back to the doorstep of the Church. Thus, the answer to our national dilemma is not the White House, but God's house!

The fact that America leads the world in practically every immoral category only places the spotlight on the anemic condition of a declining Church that has lost its way and is failing to fulfill its purpose. The citizenry of our nation is desperately looking for answers and seeking hope for a future that appears hopeless. Millions are concluding that materialism has failed us. The police have failed us. Politicians have failed us. Schools have failed us. The economy has failed us. Our courts have failed us. The one place they should be able to look for hope is to the Church and the message it proclaims, but sadly, all too often it has also failed us. More on this in the next chapter.

With too much to live with and too little to live for, millions have given up hope. Oh, they know something is wrong and with each election cycle the hope that a political savior will rescue us from impending disaster increases with optimism only to be disappointed once again. Suffice it to say, unless we regain the moral authority upon which America was founded, that is, a return to godly principles, then we face imminent disaster. It's that simple. But here lies the challenge. Decades of wrong turns place us in a dark wilderness with no clue how to get out. Historical revisionists have rewritten our history to the extent that millions have no recollection of where we began. We continue moving forward with a misplaced value system that only leads to further despair. Somehow, someway, somewhere, there must be a collective voice crying in the wilderness declaring that it is our own departure from God that holds us captive. America's past greatness is in direct correlation with our adherence to the Founding principles of our forefathers. Those principles can easily be uncovered with minimal research and it becomes undeniably clear that their intent was to create a country that is one nation under God guided by His Word (the Bible) and with an unapologetic commitment to the Gospel of Jesus Christ.

Here are just two out of hundreds of examples that could be given: The first regards hundreds of court rulings in which the Bible was referenced and cited in the decisions. But here's the kicker. If a defendant was sentenced to death by a jury, federal or state level, it was common for the judge to deliver a salvation message to the defendant in the courtroom. [3] Second, political scientists from the University of Houston wanted to know where our Founders came up with the idea for our form of government. So, they undertook a seemingly insurmountable challenge of about ten years researching fifteen thousand documents. To their surprise, 94 percent of all quotes were based on the Bible and 34 percent were direct citations, making it by far the single most cited source throughout the fifteen thousand documents.[4]

For those who are products of our government-run schools, this probably comes as a surprise. For we have abandoned our Christian heritage and removed all references to God in American history textbooks so the last two generations have not the foggiest idea how or why our nation was begun. The simple fact remains; we cannot expect to maintain our historical greatness by removing the very foundation upon which that greatness was built. Yet, we have done just that, and to try and repair what appears to be unrepairable is the monumental challenge facing us.

This is not a time for compromise nor is it a time for a spineless Christianity. I speak to our preachers now. Before moving outside the walls of our churches, which by way, is sorely needed, we must first sound the alarm to our congregations. The current state of decline rests with us. Remember? "If My people…." So, judgment begins first at the house of God. We must repent for leaving our first love. When God's people get right, then God's Hand of mercy is activated. This will require brokenness over our own sin. It will require boldness, transparency, and courage to address the issues that we've intentionally avoided. Each person sitting in our congregations must take responsibility for ungodly choices. This is part of the restoration process. No, it is not easy but we're at a stage of the disease where there are no easy remedies. The medicine prescribed is harsh and hard to swallow. There may be fallout. But when we look at Ezra, Jeremiah, Moses, and all the other prophets who stood at a similar place in their history, we have little alternative if we hope to survive. It would be good for denominational leaders to come together, designate specific Sundays and map out a plan so that we're all on the same page in calling the Christian community to prayer, fasting, and repentance. To their credit, the leadership within the Southern Baptist Convention has done this on at least two occasions in Dallas and Atlanta, but the magnitude of such action must transcend denominational lines.

Two thirds of Americans reject the notion of absolute truth. [5] That is, sixty-six percent do not believe there is any objective standard by which to judge right from wrong. There was a time in the not-so-distant past when the Christian Church was the culture's guardian for what is right and what is appropriate or righteous. But today, there has been a fundamental shift where the Church finds itself on the wrong side of morality, at least from the culture's perspective. Those who embrace biblical truth, especially on issues such as homosexuality and co-habitation, are viewed as intolerant, bigots, and repressive nuisances to society. Traditional values are relics from the past and anyone who believes otherwise may experience some degree of persecution, assuming that he or she openly stands for Truth.

Moral relativism, the ideology of the day, claims that morality and truth are relative, so "What may be right for you may not be right for me. What may be wrong for you may not be wrong for me. You have your god, I have my god. You have your truth, I have my truth. Besides, who are you to judge? There is no objective standard for right and wrong." This is the philosophy now dominating the nation. Each person becomes a god unto himself. Each does what is right in his/her own eyes. Since laws are based upon truth and moral standards, the laws become unenforceable because "No one can force their idea of right and wrong on me." Another example is when someone says, "I just can't see how one opinion is right, and the rest are wrong." This pluralistic attitude contends that all views have equal value, even if they contradict one another. Everyone must be tolerant so that no one gets offended. This is the recipe for anarchy and the dismantling of a civilization. That being said, the catastrophic consequences from this historic departure are ripping us apart and writing our own obituary.

A SNAPSHOT INTO THE HEARTS OF AMERICANS

Most discerning people know that America has changed significantly in a relatively short period of time. It's inconceivable how anyone could conclude otherwise. The following statistics will confirm those suspicions. In an extensive survey taken by the Barna Group, here is the proportion of American adults who believe the following specific behaviors are morally acceptable:

- 69 percent — Getting a divorce
- 67 percent — an unmarried woman having a baby
- 66 percent — a sexual relationship between an unmarried man and woman
- 63 percent — enjoying sexual thoughts or fantasies about someone you are not married to
- 63 percent — living with someone of the opposite sex without being married
- 58 percent — gay or lesbian relations
- 44 percent — using profanity
- 43 percent — looking at pornography
- 42 percent — having an abortion
- 34 percent — getting drunk
- 32 percent — sex between teenagers
- 19 percent — committing suicide [6]

Earlier, it was noted that only 34 percent believe in the existence of absolute truth, but in a separate survey, when asked where this truth can be found, it was discovered that only one out of ten American adults believe in absolute moral truth as found in the Bible. [7] The above statistics are a mere outgrowth of this skewed moral compass. So, what do you suppose is the determining factor when making moral choices? Four out of ten adults say, "If it *feels* right." When half of the population claims that belief in God is not necessary to be moral, then man becomes the center of his own universe believing that some internal spark of humanistic divinity will guide his feelings. [8] Emotions fluctuate and given the biblical doctrine of original sin, anyone depending on their feelings for moral guidance is inviting heartache and a life in disarray. So, today instead of asking "Is it right?" a large percentage of Americans are merely asking, "How do I feel about it?" Giving in to feelings without restraint is a false liberation, and something most would acknowledge. On the other hand, yielding to the voice of God as expressed, for example, in the Ten Commandments, becomes an imposition on "how we feel." You see, implicit in every commandment is a selfish feeling that needs to be restrained. "Thou shalt not steal," or "Thou shalt not lust for thy neighbor's wife" or "Thou shalt not envy thy neighbor's property," all require bringing one's feelings under a higher authority than themselves, something most refuse to do. Yet, it sounds so appealing, doesn't it? After all, what could be better than doing what feels good and feeling wonderful about oneself while doing it? However, the human heart is desperately wicked and sin is deceitful. All of us are morally weak in and of ourselves, and we each need the indwelling Spirit of God to empower us to a life that is pleasing to our Creator. The human heart is depraved, regardless of how good a person may be, and it will be a poor guide in navigating one's journey through life.

PRESIDENTS FOR EVANGELISM

But given this lax attitude toward moral issues which the Bible clearly describes as sinful, and understanding that sin always has deadly or destructive consequences, it is completely understandable why the nation is in such decline. Today's leaders and the attitude of the populace are in stark contrast to yesteryear when President Zachary Taylor affirmed, "A free government cannot exist without religion and morals, and there cannot be morals without religion, nor religion without the Bible." [9] Or what about President Teddy Roosevelt's strong language: "The teachings of the Bible are so interwoven and entwined with our whole civic and social life, that it would be literally— I do not mean figuratively, I mean literally— impossible for us to figure to ourselves what that life would be if these teaching were removed. We would lose almost all the standards by which we now judge both public and private morals; all the standards toward which we, with more or less resolution, strive to raise ourselves." [10]

Former Supreme Court Justice John McLean affirmed the same: "The morality of the bible must continue to be the basis of our government. There is no other foundation for free institutions." [11] In a unanimous 1844 decision, the US Supreme Court minced no words by boldly declaring, "Where can the purest principles of morality be learned so clearly or so perfectly as from the New Testament?" [12] Even the American Medical Association adopted its original code of medical ethics in 1847 by acknowledging that religion and morality were the foundation of medical principles. [13] But what about the following American presidents who "pushed" for Congress to further the Gospel throughout the land.

- In 1795, President Washington approved a grant of $1,000 to build a church for the Oneida Indians.

- In 1796, an act was passed by Congress under President Washington regulating the land given to the Society of United

Brethren for "propagating the gospel among the heathen." The act was extended under Presidents Adams and Jefferson.

- In 1803, Congress and President Jefferson approved a grant of $100 for seven years to a Roman Catholic priest to evangelize the Kaskaskia Indians, and $300 to help build them a church.
- In 1825, President John Quincy Adams, in a treaty with the Osage Indians, dedicated federal lands to a "missionary establishment" engaged in "teaching, civilizing, and improving said Indians."
- In 1833, Congress and President Jackson approved a grant of $3,700 to build a church for the Kickapoo Indians.
- In 1838, President Van Buren, along with Congress, approved funds to help build a church for the Oneida Indians. [14]

That was then, and this is now. The secularization of America, the rejection of biblical truth, and an anemic, compromising Church all combine to create a recipe for disaster, the kind we are now witnessing. The sad commentary on the Christian community of which I am an active part, is that more than 70 moral behaviors were studied and the Barna Group found little differences between Christians and non-Christians. [15] Perhaps this is partially attributed to liberal theology, partially to conservatives compromising, partially due to a fear of man rather than a fear of God when it comes to preaching truth, partially due to rampant biblical illiteracy, or partially because of a complacent, lukewarm Church that has left its first love. But, I think it is largely due to the fact that, according to Barna's research among evangelical Christians, 54 percent do not believe in absolute truth. [16] So, when you throw that into the pot and stir it all up, there's enough blame to go around and each of us bears a fair share of it. But this is no time for finger-pointing. Anything less than massive spiritual awakening birthed from the heart of God, infused into the heart of men and women, burned into the soul of His preachers, manifested within His Church, penetrating the darkness of our neighborhoods and local communities, and then like wildfires, spread throughout the nation touching every city until making its way into the halls of Congress and the Oval Office itself. It's happened before. It can happen again.

DOES A MAJORITY MAKE IT RIGHT?

If only 10 percent believe in the existence of absolute truth and if the majority of Christians likewise reject the notion, then how can the overwhelming majority of Americans be wrong? What is the problem with moral relativism? Frankly, a lot. Let's look at the inconsistencies. Those who disagree with legislating morality are saying, "It is not moral to impose morals. That is, they are trying to impose their own moral position by saying that morals should not be imposed on everyone. It is self-defeating. These same people do not want to eliminate all moral standards, only the ones they prefer and then replace the rest with their own. So, the essence and basis of laws involve morality. The question is, "Whose morality is the right one to impose?"

After all, without moral standards anarchy prevails. We don't allow consenting adults to steal, rape, or murder because innocent people would be hurt. Most everyone agrees that we need laws against rape, murder, theft, and child abuse. So, it's ludicrous for these moral relativists to say they do not want morals imposed on others when they actually advocate imposing their own morals on everyone. So, all laws impose morals on others. It is impossible not to legislate morality.

Here's the real kicker. Relativists claim there is no absolute truth. Well, if there is no absolute truth, then such a claim cannot be absolutely true. Again, it is self-defeating. Thus, the relativist is saying, "I am absolutely sure there are no absolutes." "Right and wrong" only make sense if there is a standard that defines right and wrong. To believe in relativism is to argue that there is no moral difference between Billy Graham and Hitler, between love and hate, or life and murder. People don't create truth, they find it. So, absolutes are absolutes only because they are the final standard by which everything else is measured. That standard for 200 years in America's history was the Bible, God's Word. Today, the vast majority pick and choose what they want to believe, but refuse to embrace it as the divine authoritative, inspired, inerrant Word that it is.

We have plenty to repent, not the least of which is our attitude toward abortion. Forty percent of Christians want to see abortion protected and continued, [17] and 65 percent of abortions (650,000 annually) are performed on professing Christians [18] with 250,000 each year on born-again Christians. [19] This alone causes one to ask, "How many Christians live together prior to marriage?" Increasingly, this is becoming a huge issue in the Church. *USA Today* published the result of a national survey in which 76 percent of 18-31 year-old American couples consider cohabitation to be acceptable. [20] Charisma News also claims that 65 percent of singles, many of whom identify themselves as "Christians", now live together before marriage. [21] No, we do not desire to be legalistic and yes we want the culture to know what we are for more than what we are against. No, we do not want to reduce the perception of Christianity as restrictive rules and regulations, but there is a moral standard to uphold. Followers of Jesus are called to be holy as He is holy. Admittedly, it's a high standard and one that will only ultimately be attained in Heaven, but the silence of our pulpits on the moral issues that are ripping apart families and the nation at large, is inexcusable. Look, as I've reviewed and proof-read what's been written thus far, some of the language I've chosen to use may sound a bit extreme…excessive…. over-the-top….alarmist….exaggerated. Granted, such words as "collapse," "destruction" or "imminent disaster," may be examples but they were carefully weighed before putting ink to the paper. So, here's another one. We are not simply traveling a dangerous path, but a cataclysmic one that is placing America's future in jeopardy, even to the point of no return. There, how's that sound? I have a hunch that a few years ago, such language would have seemed offensive, but times have changed haven't they?

Our Congress doesn't seem to get it. Their actions say so. However, we cannot make this claim for all congressmen. Several truly do understand the times we're in. One congressman confided to a friend, "This city doesn't get it. If we don't make major changes—and I mean sweeping reform—really quickly, I'm not sure how much longer as a nation we can actually survive." His apocalyptic tone continued, "I've never seen it worse than it is right now. And most of Congress is absolutely asleep. They're arguing over cosmetic changes but few people around here seem to realize just how much trouble we're really in."[22] Perhaps this is what President Trump meant when he declared, "We're going to drain the swamp."

It is easy to be armchair quarterbacks and say, "Why don't Americans just stand up and demand that our political leaders return to the nation's founding principles, but here's the predicament in that proposal. It's like asking a drug addict just to quit using drugs. Americans have become so dependent on the government to take care of them, that giving up the security and benefits promised by politicians in lieu of cutting government spending and taking personal responsibility is just too high of a price to pay. "Why don't congressmen and senators stop supporting policies that expand the debt and dependency?" you ask. Again, that's like asking a drug dealer to stop selling drugs. This is the dilemma we find ourselves in. Case in point is Bernie Sanders. This 74 year old is an admitted socialist who ran for president and promised free college tuition and many of other freebies. He gave Hillary Clinton, who was supposed to be a shoo-in, a run for her money, down to the wire. Just a few years ago his candidacy would have been one big joke, but now the tables are turned.

Incidentally, youth without objective standards of truth are 48 percent more likely to cheat on an exam, twice as likely to get drunk, three times as likely to use illegal drugs, and six times more likely to attempt suicide.[22] So, let's take a panoramic view of today's most pressing moral issues and the impact they're having on the nation.

SEXUAL ISSUES

Illegitimate Births

The New York Times reports that for women under age thirty, most births now occur outside of marriage.[23] *The Times* also reported, "Among mothers of all ages, a majority—59 percent in 2009—are married when they have children. Nearly two-thirds of children in the United States are born to mothers under thirty. The article noted a clear and devastating correlation between out-of-wedlock births and pathologies of all kinds— ranging from children falling into poverty, failing to graduate from school, being arrested for crimes, or suffering from emotional and behavioral problems.[24]

Half of all children will live in a single parent family at some point in their childhood.[25] The statistics for these kids are horrendous and heart-breaking. Everything from suicide to drugs and crime, not to mention psychological problems will plague these children throughout life and most will pass on this cycle of dysfunction to their children only to be perpetuated by their children as well. Illegitimate births often produce fatherless homes, so statistically their backs are against the wall.

- 63% of youth suicides
- 90% of runaway children
- 85% of behavior disorders
- 71% of high school dropouts
- 80% of rapists

- 71% of teenage pregnancies
- 90% of adolescent arsonists

All come from fatherless homes![26]

Furthermore, those without a dad can expect the following:

- Over half will live in poverty
- Daughters are 53% more likely to marry as teenagers
- They are 111% more likely to have children as teenagers
- They are 164% more likely to dissolve their own marriages.[27]

Lawrence Tone, a noted Princeton University family historian, says "The scale of marital breakdowns in the West since 1960 has no historical precedent that I know of. There has been nothing like it for the last 2,000 years, and probably longer."[28]

Pornography

Porn generates more revenue than ABC, NBC, and CBS combined with some 70 million Americans finding it morally acceptable.[29] The porn industry is larger than Microsoft, Google, Amazon, eBay, Yahoo!, Apple, Netflix, and EarthLink all *combined!*[30] Porn's revenues total more than all professional sports teams combined![31] In a Department of Justice study, it is reported that the porn industry targets 12-17 year-old boys to ensure they become regular consumers and lifetime addicts.[32] The average age of Internet exposure to pornography is 11 years old.[33] Comcast made $50 million one year on porn programming and approximately 30 percent of all pay-per-view revenue is generated by pornography.[34] Half of all hotel guests order pornographic pay-per-view movies which accounts for 80 percent of in-room entertainment revenue.[35] Porn sites are visited three times more often than Google, Yahoo! and MSN Search combined.[36] Sixty-six percent of all men between the ages of 18 and 34 view pornography every month.[37] Especially disturbing is the fact that America produces 89 percent of all the porn on the planet. [38] With porn being such a booming business it should come as no surprise (but it still does) that every 30 minutes a new pornographic video is created in the United States. [39] Every second, 30,000 people are viewing porn. [40] Other studies show that 85 percent of young men and nearly half of young women watch porn at least once a month, while 1 in 8 online searches and 1 in 5 mobile searches are for porn. [41] I suspect this helps account for the fact that one-in-thirteen teen girls report participating in group sex and the average age is 15 years old. [42]

When the erotic novel *Fifty Shades of Grey* hit the theaters, it sold 45 million in the United States and the opening weekend exceeded that of the previous record-holder for February releases, *The Passion of the Christ.* [43]

"Yes, but that's non-Christian men," I hear someone saying. Think again. A survey taken at a Promise Keepers event revealed that over 50 percent of the men in attendance were involved with porn after one week of attending the event. That was 20 years ago. [44] Today, fifty percent of Christian men and 20 percent of Christian women say they are addicted to pornography and the most popular day of the week for viewing porn is Sunday. [45] Josh McDowell's research revealed that 78.8 percent of all men that attend evangelical churches watch pornography. He says that 67 percent of all divorces are directly related to pornography. Even more alarming is McDowell's opinion that 80 percent of youth pastors view pornography. [46] Various studies have shown that on any given Sunday morning, 50 percent of the men sitting in the congregation are addicted to porn. A survey conducted by Christianity Today found that "at least 50 percent of Christian pastors are struggling with pornography."

The Barna Group uncovered similar findings. That is, 77 percent of Christian men, ages 18-30, view porn monthly and 36 percent view it daily. [47]

In the spring of 2000, Zogby International asked more than a thousand U.S. adults whether they had ever visited a porn site. Only 1 in 5 had done so. Among born-again Christians, 18 percent had gone to such sites. Most recently, the Barna Group examined porn use and found that 64 percent of men and 20 percent of women viewed porn at least monthly. For Christian men, it is 55 percent. Keep in mind that only 16 years ago one out of every five men had ever gone to a porn site, but now one-third of men under 30 do so on a daily basis. [48]

We can see that the stats are "off the charts" and it's understandable why many are now declaring porn to be the leading addiction in the church. Here is what's really at stake in all of these statistics regarding the sexual sins of America. Anthropologist J.D. Unwin conducted an extensive study on the 86 different societies throughout human history and found that the one common denominator leading to their destruction was sexual immorality. He said, "Sexual fidelity was the single most important predictor of a society's ascendancy. In human records there is no instance of a society retaining its energy after a completely new generation has inherited a tradition which does not insist on prenuptial and postnuptial continence." Unwin was not a Christian and such findings perplexed him and said that he had no explanation for such irrefutable data. [49] Take a moment to process what you've just read. Sexual activity outside the divine parameters of marriage is not some innocent, harmless, recreational activity that has no repercussions. On the contrary, the consequences are enormous, both for an individual and for the nation as a whole.

Homosexuality

Despite what the media and liberal groups would have us believe, the homosexual population in our nation is much less than is commonly reported. The 1990 US Census Bureau found less than 1 percent of the population to be homosexual. In 1991, the University of Chicago conducted an extensive nationwide survey and found that about 1.7 percent of the population is homosexual. [50] Then in 1994, the American Sex Survey, the most exhaustive piece of work done to date about people's sexual orientation, found that 2.7 percent of the population was homosexual men and 1.3 percent was homosexual women. [51] Granted, we're going back in time by 20-plus years but the point remains that the numbers regarding the "gay" population in America have been greatly inflated. Nevertheless, their influence in Washington with lobbyists and the politically correct crowd is quite substantial.

In the brief space we have here, I want to make it perfectly clear that God loves the homosexual as much as He loves anyone. Homosexuality, however, is defined in Scripture as sin. There is no gray area here. It is called an abomination. Strong language to be sure, but I'm not the author of it. As Christians, we are to reach out to all people groups with no prejudice or respect of orientation. The Christian community has fallen short in this arena. For that, I am deeply saddened. Now, we have come to the place where it is classified as "hate speech" to preach what the Bible says about the subject. The homosexual community wants the nation to view their lifestyle as normal and healthy. And when seeing respectable celebrities, professional men and women, and even clergy who identify with the gay community, then it seems to validate their claim. But here is what we're not being told:

- 78 percent of male homosexuals have or have had a sexually transmitted disease. [52]
- Male homosexuals are about 1,000 times more likely to acquire HIV/AIDS than the general population. [53]
- By the gay community's own reports, 24 percent of homosexual males reported having up to 100 partners in their lifetime. [54]

- 30 percent of 20-year-old gay men will be HIV positive or dead from the AIDS virus by the age of 30.[55]
- The average age of death for HIV-infected men is 39, while the average age of death of homosexual men from all other causes is just 42.[56]
- Only 2 percent of homosexual men will ever reach old age (defined as age 65 and older). Even when AIDS is not present, fewer than 12 percent of homosexual men will ever reach old age.[57]
- Domestic violence occurs at a rate twice that of heterosexual couples.[58]
- 43 percent of white male homosexuals estimate having had sex with 500 or more different partners, while 28 percent reported more than 1,000 sexual partners. 79 percent admitted that at least half of their partners were strangers![59]
- In a study conducted by Centers for Disease Control and Prevention (CDC), they found that 1,100 sexual partners is average for gay men while some reported as many as 22,000 partners in their lifetime.[60]
- In a study of 156 homosexual couples, they discovered that not a single couple living together more than five years was able to sustain a monogamous relationship.[61]
- The average duration of a homosexual relationship is between 9 and 27 months.[62]
- More than half of all people diagnosed with AIDS in the United States, and as many as 56 percent of new HIV infections, are homosexual males.[63]

It's called the homosexual lifestyle, but it would better be described as the homosexual death-style. In Genesis 18-19 we find the first biblical account of homosexual activity and Jesus refers to it in Matthew 11:23-24 as an example of receiving God's judgment. Jude 7 also provides Sodom and Gomorrah as examples of God's punishment. The Levitical Law lists various things that are in violation of God's character and moral law. Among them is homosexual intercourse. Leviticus 18 warns that to practice such sin will defile the land and destroy a civilization. Again, in Leviticus 20 we find a lengthy list of sexual sins that are not only prohibited, but deserving of the death penalty. Romans 1 and 1 Corinthians 6 affirms God's disapproval of such a lifestyle. If you are reading this and happen to be a homosexual or have friends and family who have embraced this orientation, please do not assume that I am being judgmental. It is challenging for ink and pen to convey the love and kindness that is in my heart toward those who are held captive by this sin. It is deceptive and destructive. God does not condemn homosexual practice any more than heterosexual sin. Sex outside of marriage, living together before marriage, and lusting with the eyes in pornography are all equally as sinful. There is hope and there is help. First Corinthians 6:11 says, "And that is what some of you were." God had delivered some of the Corinthians believers from this very lifestyle. And so He can today.

Same-Sex Marriage

This issue was addressed in an earlier chapter on the family, so a few cogent statements here should suffice. The understanding of marriage that has been central to Judaism and Christianity and has been the cornerstone of civilizations throughout human history has now been redefined by the highest Court in the Land. Out of 195 countries in the world, America is one of only 21 nations to legalize same-sex marriage. While liberals applaud this fact as a great accomplishment and an example for the rest of the world to follow, the displeasure of a holy God should be our greatest concern. Unlike those who prefer a "living Constitution" that changes with the times, God's standards have not, will not, and do not change.

Then, to further compound our immorality, we have governors approving legislation for transgender bathrooms and President Obama requiring that public schools implement such policy or their federal funding will be reduced or removed. It only serves as further confirmation that we are witnessing a revolution unlike anything in the nation's history. The secularization of our culture has created a moral chasm that will transform future generations and present unprecedented challenges for the Church. We have yet to see how this redefinition of marriage and transformation of the family will play out. But be assured, the floodgates have been legally opened and an immoral tsunami will sweep through the country leaving no family untouched. These moral revolutionaries will see to it. The Church will be challenged by the culture to abandon everything Christianity has taught for two thousand years.

The Court minimized the definition of marriage as merely an intensive loving emotional bond. With that definition, it was not a difficult leap to legitimize same-sex marriage. However, this skewed definition was not only a departure from traditional marriage but opened the door for polygamy and all kinds of sexual relationships. If marriage is no longer defined as a monogamous union between a man and a woman, then what prevents brother and sister from marrying or from marrying your pet dog? Again, the Church will be strongly challenged to embrace the politically correct message of demonstrating understanding and compassion by compromising its historic stand on the timeless, inerrant principles of God's Word. To show compassion at the expense of truth is to betray the very truth we claim to represent. Truth is inherently compassionate, but Satan, the god of this world, will twist it to sound reasonable and more palatable.

We could address rape, abortion, incest, sex abuse, adultery, and a host of other sexually-related sins, but space is simply too limited. Likewise, I am refraining from discussing a plethora of other moral issues such as school violence, murders, thefts, burglaries, white collar crimes, incarceration stats, and so forth. However, there is one other category of immorality that deserves a platform, that of drugs and addiction.

Drugs

According to the most recent study by the federal Department of Health and Human Services, more than 24 million Americans use illegal drugs.[64] The breakdown includes:

- 1.5 million cocaine users aged 12 and up, plus 1.3 million using hallucinogens, another 595,000 using methamphetamine, and 681,000 using heroin.
- 9.9 million Americans aged 12 or older reported driving under the influence of illicit drugs during the past year.
- 1,647 people use cocaine every day for the first time, 463 use heroin every day for the first time, 395 daily use methamphetamines for the first time, every day 2,058 start using ecstasy for the first time, and 4,110 new people start using illegally obtained psychotherapeutics every day.
- In 2013, one-quarter of all Americans aged 12 and up participated in binge drinking, about 60 million people. ("Binge drinking" means having five or more drinks on the same occasion on at least one day in the 30 days prior to the survey.)
- Heavy drinking was reported in 16.5 million people 12 and older. ("Heavy drinking" means binge drinking on at least five days in the past 30 days.)
- Among young adults aged 21-25, the rate of binge drinking is 43.3 percent, and the rate of heavy drinking is 14.4 percent.
- In an average year, 30 million Americans drive drunk and 10 million drive impaired by illicit drugs.[65]

- There is an overdose death every 19 minutes and prescription drug abuse is the fastest growing drug problem in the nation.[66]
- For every overdose death, nine persons are admitted for substance abuse treatment and 35 visit emergency rooms for treatment.[67]
- More than 70 million are taking mind-altering drugs and another 60 million have an alcohol problem. That's at least 130 million who are trying to get through life by chemically altering their minds. Given our population of 320 million, that's an astonishing number.[68]

The aforementioned statistics are a lot to take in one sitting. At the risk of sounding redundant, unless there is a massive invasion of God's Spirit via His Church in America, the moral landscape of our nation will only get darker and the greatest nation ever to exist will find its place in the annals of history along with other great empires that faded into oblivion. We are now in the twilight of our existence with a few flickering stars in the flag, but the light that must shine the brightest is that found in the Church, the body of Christ. To that Light, we now give our attention. Read on.

Grant's View of How the Bible Shaped America

"Hold fast to the Bible as the sheet anchor of your liberties; write its precept in your hearts, and practice them in your lives. To the influence of this Book are we indebted for all the progress made in true civilization, and to this Book must we look as our guide in the future....

I believe in the Holy Scriptures, and whoso lives by them will be benefitted thereby. Men may differ as to the interpretation, which is human, but the Scriptures are man's best guide...I did not go riding yesterday, although invited and permitted by my physicians, because it was the Lord's day, and because I felt that if a relapse should set in, the people who are praying for me would feel that I was not helping their faith by riding out on Sunday...."[1]

— Ulysses S. Grant (1822-1885)
was the 18th President of the United States of America and Commander-In-Chief for the Union during the Civil War.

CHAPTER 11

The Crisis in The American Church

After wading through the statistical sewage of America's perilous condition, you may feel like taking a hot shower, running to hide, or hibernate under the covers of your bed. Indeed, our nation has entered into its own version of the dark ages, albeit many continue to try and ignore the signs despite bells ringing, alarms sounding, and the lights on the dashboard flashing before us. The question you may be asking is, "Have we passed the point of no return? Is there still hope?" No, and yes. I will expound in a later chapter, but let's be clear, the Church should be, and is, our light in dark times. The message embodied by the Church, the Gospel of Jesus Christ, is our greatest hope. Jesus described the Church as salt, a preservative that keeps things from decaying. The problem today is that we've lost our saltiness and the challenge is to also get the salt out of the shaker so that it penetrates our communities.

The rhetoric of the historic 2016 election was unlike anything we had seen and the character assassinations were at an all-time high. Emotions were passionate from both sides of the aisle as Americans once again placed their hope in a White House occupant to work miracles. But the focus is misplaced and needs transferring from the White House to God's House. Unfortunately, when a person off the street walks into the average church today, he may be appalled by what he finds. A Director of Missions from one of our major cities confided that upon visiting dozens of the churches throughout the area, he was shocked at the shallow, unbiblical sermons. As we will see, his experience is no exception.

I live in what has been called the buckle of the Bible Belt. Churches are everywhere in metro Atlanta, but less than 20 percent of the population attends on any given Sunday. So, the Bible Belt has basically disappeared in terms of church participation. And in the midst of a culture that is shifting, the temptation for the Church is to shift with it in order to maintain relevance. Certainly, we cannot afford to be culturally irrelevant but neither should we compromise the message, water down the Word to make it more palatable, or draw the false conclusion that contemporary music, elimination of choirs and organs, or the addition of praise bands will be the cure-all. Reducing the sermon to 20 minutes and streamlining the service to fit into an hour certainly accommodates the preference of most attendees, but confining the Spirit of God to move within such structure is often counterproductive. But, so long as people don't miss the opening kickoff on TV or are not too late for the restaurant by noon, then no one rocks the boat and complaints are kept at a minimum. Occasionally, we hear talk about "reclaiming America" which seems to imply going back to the way it used to be. First, we need to reclaim the families on our own church roles, we need to reclaim our youth that are being assaulted from every side, we need to reclaim our senior adults who are as confused as anyone by the changes in the culture, we need to reclaim our young couples who demonstrate sporadic attendance and nominal commitment due to the stresses of children, work, and sports leagues. Hey, we even need to reclaim our pastors, 70 percent of whom are discouraged or depressed. In short, the Church itself is on life support and needs resuscitating. The church must get healthy. And for that to happen, the leadership will need a clear vision from God and the backbone of biblical prophets to withstand the onslaught of criticism that most likely will occur.

Doing something radical such as fasting for days, eliminating the Sunday morning sermon in lieu of leading the congregation in a solemn assembly of prayer, eliminating programs that have seen their better days, and so forth. Anything short of a surge of the Holy Spirit's anointing that produces the manifest power and presence of Almighty God in our midst is only religious activity and spiritual rhetoric, something that is already too prevalent.

Large Oak trees or Redwood trees that are centuries old can appear to be in good health because they have a long, silent dying process. But, internal disease will rot the trees within and then external forces from without will cause the trees to collapse. This describes too many of our churches today, as evidenced with 4,000 closing their doors every year compared to just over 1,000 new church starts. [2] Looking for a church home may be compared to a prospective homeowner who is about to purchase a house. He and his family do the walk-through and they love every facet of the house. The floor plan is ideal, the amenities are exquisite, the lawn is lush and the landscape is manicured. It has great curb appeal and the window treatments, along with the 60-inch TV are being thrown in as extra incentives. Everything on the outside appears to be the house of their dreams. The only remaining detail is the required termite inspection which, to the family's dismay, revealed extensive deterioration. The foundation is rotting from termite activity hidden from the naked eye. Now, that obviously is not the news those prospective homeowners want to hear but they are very grateful to be informed about the status of what they had assumed was to be their dream house. Similarly, when looking at the evangelical landscape from the outside, all appears to be intact. Mega churches are in every major city and spinoffs from these churches have produced satellite sites as well. There is no shortage of facilities equipped with high tech sound boards, amphitheater-style seating, strobe lights, and all the innovation necessary to stay current with the culture. With multi-million dollar budgets the mega churches can hire the finest musicians to perform for worship that rivals anything the secular culture has to offer. Adopting a "Come as you are" approach, the norm today sees congregants attending with shorts, a t-shirt, and flip-flops while the church leadership wears jeans and polos insuring that no one feels "out of place." In fact, it's the "coat & tie" crowd that's now the exception. Yet, despite outward appearances, all the statistics indicate that termites are inconspicuously creating massive decline in churches throughout the land. I'll break the narrative down into bullet points which make it somewhat easier to identify.

- Every year, 2.7 million church members fall into inactivity and from 1990 to 2000 the combined membership of all Protestant denominations in the U.S. declined by 5 million members while that population itself increased by 24 million. [3]
- In 1900 there was a ratio of 27 churches per 10,000 people whereas today there 11 churches per 10,000 people in America. There's a projected need of 38,000 new churches to keep up the population growth. [4]
- Other than China and India, the United States has the highest unchurched population in the world. [5]
- Half of all churches in the U.S. did not add any new members in the last two years. [6]
- Only 18 percent of Americans "frequently" attend church and that figure is expected to drop to 15 percent by 2025 and only 12 percent by 2050. [7]
- A staggering 34 percent of millennials (1981-1989) do not affiliate with any religion, according to the Pew Research Center's Religious Landscape Survey. [8]
- Of those unaffiliated, 31 percent describe themselves as atheists or agnostics. [9]

- According to a study done by LifeWay Research, membership in Southern Baptist churches will fall nearly 50 percent by the year 2050. [10]
- Barna Group reports that 60 percent of all Christians between the ages of 15 and 29 are no longer involved in any church. [11]
- Barna Group found that less than 1 percent of all Americans between the ages of 18 and 23 hold a biblical worldview. [12] Defining a biblical worldview, the participants in the survey must agree with the following six statements:

  Believing that absolute moral truth exists.

  Believing that the Bible is completely accurate in all of the principles it teaches.

  Believing that Satan is considered to be a real being or force, not merely symbolic.

  Believing that a person cannot earn their way into Heaven by trying to be good or by doing good works.

  Believing that Jesus Christ lived a sinless life on earth.

  Believing that God is the all-knowing, all-powerful creator of the world who still rules the universe today.

- Again, less than 1 percent agreed with all of those statements.
- 52 percent of all American Christians believe that some non-Christian faiths can lead to eternal life. [13]
- In the past decade, more people in the U.S. have become churchless than live in Australia or Canada. [14]
- 23 of 25 major evangelical denominations, including the Southern Baptist Convention, are experiencing decline. [15]
- 34,000 missionaries from other nations were sent to the United States in 2010. [16]

- The United States receives more missionaries than any country in the world, confirming how other nations view America as morally corrupt and spiritually bankrupt. [17]
- Barna research shows that Protestant churches spend 88% of its ministry dollars on adults while 40 percent of attendees in a typical week are children. [18]

WHAT ABOUT SOUTHERN BAPTISTS?

The following is by no means an attempt to throw Southern Baptists "under the bus." This is the denomination of which I am affiliated and have been all of my life. I was saved, baptized, and called to preach in a Southern Baptist church. So why separate them from the rest of the church culture in America? The reason is because historically Southern Baptists have carried the evangelical mantle and been the pace-setter among other denominations for baptisms. After all, we are the largest Protestant denomination in the world, so the perception may be that while the Church as a whole in America is in decline, the same would not hold true for the largest mission-minded denomination on the planet. Sadly, that is not the case.

- Of the approximately 38,000 churches reporting, 17,400 of them recorded no baptisms in the 12-to-17-year-old category and 23,500 churches reported baptizing one or less. [19]
- In 2012, 60 percent of the more than 46,000 churches in the Southern Baptist Convention (SBC) reported no youth (12-17 year olds) baptisms and 80 percent reported one or less baptisms among young adults (ages 18 to 29). [20]
- 75 percent of Southern Baptist children raised in our churches have not been won to Christ by age 19. [21]
- For the past two decades, at least 70 percent of Southern Baptist churches are plateaued or in decline. [22]

- In 2014, the SBC experienced the lowest number of baptisms since 1947, reflecting a decline in 8 of the last 10 years.[23] This is in spite of the fact that we have 10 million more members, 1,700 more churches, and the population of America has more than doubled during that time. Conclusion: We're doing less with more.
- Southern Baptist churches lost 200,000 members in 2014, the largest one-year decline since 1881….in spite of the total number of SBC congregations increasing for 15 consecutive years.[24]

To say that Christianity in America is receding would be an understatement. Just as the cultural landscape in the nation has transformed into something hardly recognizable, so it is with the church landscape. You may be old enough to recall the Moral Majority back in the '70's, but today's America is neither moral nor in the majority. Rather, we have shifted into a post-Christian age in which evangelical believers comprise only 7 to 9 percent of the population. This translates into 22 to 28 million, but we're losing 2.6 million of those each decade.[25] Incidentally, these stats were not randomly accessed nor were they "rough" estimates but they were confirmed in four separate independent studies by some of the most reputable firms: (1) Dr. Christian Smith, Professor of Sociology at Notre Dame (2) David T. Olson, American Church Research Project (3) Barna Group (4) Christine Wicker, Award-winning religion reporter.

As an example of how quickly this shift has occurred, consider that in 1996 sixty-eight percent of Americans opposed gay marriage, but today the majority not only favors it, but the courts have legalized it.[26] If we continue our present trajectory and if anyone wants to know what America will look like in the next three decades, we need look no further than our neighbors in Europe where only 2.5 percent of the population is attending Bible-based churches. [27] A spiritual plague has killed the next generation of European believers and the same is happening here. We do not have the luxury of ignoring these trends because we are now one generation away from the church, as we've known it, completely evaporating into museums of a previous generation and a feint memory of what it once was. Again, where Europe is today spiritually, America will be tomorrow unless fundamental changes are made and problems confronted and addressed.

SENIOR ADULTS ARE DISAPPEARING

This may, on the surface, appear not to be case. After all, stand in the back of most of our churches and you'll observe a sea of gray, or blue, depending on your perspective. While that may be true, there are fewer of them today than last Sunday because 1,000 of them are dying every day. [28] Over the next twelve years, this faithful, older generation will no longer be with us. Ramifications for the church are huge because 50 percent of all donations come from this Builders generation. [29] This means that total giving for many of our churches will decrease by as much as 50 percent. Even if the economy recovers and the stock market is booming, it will have no impact on this reality. Some projections actually predict that giving may drop by as much as 70 percent within the next twenty-five to thirty years. [30] This is a silent crisis that few are talking about but it will be here sooner than later. The consequences will be devastating as pastors will be forced to resign or transition to bi-vocational work. Seminary professors and other church staff will be laid off. Church properties will be foreclosed. Ministries will be eliminated.

Prior to the Great Recession of 2008, going back to 2000, tithing decreased by 62 percent [31] and in 2004 the church reached its lowest level of giving since 1961, even lower (in percentage) than the worst years of the Great Depression. [32]

One may be prone to think that such decline in giving can be replaced by reaching more of the younger generation. That would be nice, but those over the age of 75 give four times as much as 25-to-44-year-olds. [33] Research found that while 17 percent of Christians say they tithe, only 3 percent actually do. [34] Of course, as people age, physical limitations prevent them from volunteering or serving in the ministries for which they are most passionate. So, while this is occurring at the older end of the chronological continuum, something equally as alarming is occurring on the youthful end.

YOUNG ADULTS ARE LEAVING!

An unbelievable 260,000 evangelical young adults walk away from Christianity every year. [35] Reputable studies from Josh McDowell, George Barna, LifeWay Research and other secular researchers all agree on this one thing. That is, 70 to 80 percent of evangelicals in their twenties are leaving the faith. [36] Staying out late on Saturday nights and sleeping in on Sunday mornings is the norm for this age group. We often assume that those who leave will eventually return, but again, research indicates otherwise. For every three young evangelicals who leave, two do not return. [37] Simply stated, millions are silently walking out the back door and secretly deciding, "I'll never go to church again." According to the Barna Group, "American teens are displaying the lowest levels of participation in prayer, reading religious resources….and being involved in witness to peers since Barna began surveying teenagers." [38] We are losing about seven out of every ten evangelical teens. [39] Moving into the 18-to-29 year-olds, there are twice as many atheists as evangelicals. [40] So, at this critical time in American history when the nation most needs the Church, the Church finds itself facing perhaps its greatest crisis since the birth of our nation.

AN INCONVENIENT TRUTH..... THAT WE'D RATHER NOT HEAR

Ken Ham, president and founder of Answers in Genesis and the Creation Museum, was also disturbed by the information you've read and the statistical data regarding the church's decline, so much so that he enlisted a leading researcher to uncover what's really happening. I suppose we could say that he engaged in spiritual forensics. The long-held assumption within the church has been that we are losing our students once they go to college. In other words, they leave the security of their parents, the accountability of their church, and begin to explore life on the campus and all it has to offer. Fraternities, sororities, and liberal professors become the "easy out" as for why our once "committed" youth no longer attend church. Ham's research, however, blows that theory out of the water. He found that 90 percent of them were lost in middle school and high school. In fact, 40 percent are leaving the Church during elementary and middle school years! By the time they got to college, they were already gone. [41] To think that we are losing more people by middle school and high school than we will ever lose in college is, well, unthinkable! They were disengaging while still sitting in the pews. They were preparing their "getaway" while faithfully attending youth groups. The college campus only provided them an opportunity to do *physically* what they had already done *mentally and spiritually.*

If, indeed, this is a true and accurate interpretation of the "forensic" data, the logical follow-up question is, "Why?" What are the components leading to such departure from the faith? Is the church doing something wrong? Are the families responsible? What responsibility do the students themselves share? Well, brace yourself and swallow hard because Ham investigated the effects of Sunday School, the kinds of kids leaving the Church, and the reasons the Church has lost its relevance to the culture. The results were shocking.

Are you sitting down? You'll not want to believe it. His conclusion was that Sunday School is actually more likely to be detrimental to the spiritual and moral health of our children. It sounds like heresy doesn't it? The initial reaction is to completely discount it as bogus, but here is why such an emphatic statement could be made:

Students who *regularly* attend Sunday School are actually……

- More likely NOT to believe that all the accounts/stories in the Bible are true/accurate.
- More likely to doubt the Bible because it was written by men.
- More likely to doubt the Bible because it was not translated correctly.
- More likely to defend premarital sex.
- More likely to accept that gay marriage and abortion should be legal.
- Much more likely to believe that God used evolution to change one kind of animal into another.
- More likely NOT to believe the earth is less than 10,000 years old.
- Much more likely to question the Bible because they believe the earth is not less than 10,000 years old.
- More likely to doubt the bible because of the secular dates of billions of years for the age of the earth.
- More likely to have heard a pastor/Sunday school teacher teach that Christians could believe in millions/billions of years.
- More likely to question the earth is young and the days of creation are 24 hours each.
- More likely to believe that dinosaurs died out before people were on the planet.

- More likely to view the Church as hypocritical.
- Much more likely to have become anti-church through the years.
- More likely to believe that good people don't need to go to church. [42]

To reiterate once again, this was no quack researcher. Probing questions and statistical analysis by top researchers came to the conclusion that Sunday school is one of the reasons why we are losing our children before they ever get to college. Can we all say, "Wake-up call?"

Sunday school didn't do anything to help them develop a Christian worldview. In fact, it clearly harmed the spiritual growth of the kids. [43] Those are not my words, but Ken Ham's. To further substantiate this claim, notice the response to the following questions:

"Do you believe that God used evolution to change one kind of animal into another?" 27.2% of those attending Sunday school answered "yes." Only **18.8%** of those who do not attend Sunday school believed in this type of evolution. [44]

"Do you believe that premarital sex is wrong?" 40.8% of those attending Sunday school answered "yes." **47.7%** of those not attending Sunday school answered "yes." [45]

"Do you feel good people don't need to go to church?" 39.3% of those attending Sunday school answered "yes." **28.9%** of non-attenders answered "yes." [46]

"Do you feel the Church is relevant to your needs today?" 46.4% of Sunday school attenders answered "no." **39.6%** of non-attenders answered "no." [47]

"Do you believe that you have become anti-church through the years?" 39.1% of Sunday school attenders answered "yes." **26.9%** of non-attenders said "yes." [48]

From these responses, whatever Sunday schools are doing, it is apparently a statistical failure. In all fairness, there are exceptions, but that's the problem, they are exceptions. You may be prone to think that this research was done in liberal to moderate churches. Quite the contrary. These results come from the most dedicated, conservative, Scripture-affirming churches in America. That's what makes this so disturbing. The tendency seems to be to blame this epidemic of departure on those who have left. We accuse them of being insincere, uncommitted, lazy, indifferent, and on it goes. Certainly, nobody "forced" them to leave, but before casting stones, it would do us well to first get the log out of our own eye and re-examine what we should be doing differently.

Here is Ham's contention, and who can argue with him? Ninety percent of children coming from Christian homes attend public/government-run schools. [49] There they are taught a biological, anthropological, geological, and astronomical history of the universe that totally contradicts the Bible's account of creation, the Flood, and the Tower of Babel. At the crux of the issue is the authority of God's Word. The events of Genesis are foundational to the gospel. When Jesus was explaining the doctrine of marriage in Matthew 19:4-7, He quoted from the Genesis account. The heart of the gospel is dependent upon the Genesis account of the Fall of man, the doctrine of original sin. Ultimately, every single biblical doctrine is directly or indirectly founded in the account given in Genesis 1-11. So, to undermine this history or to reinterpret it by claiming it as myth or symbolic is to undermine the rest of the Bible and to assault the gospel itself.

To teach our children that God's Word is true regarding the Resurrection and the miracles of Jesus, but then tell them they can reinterpret the Genesis account on the basis of secularism's teaching about millions of years of evolution, is to undermine biblical authority. In reality, we have made man the authority over God's

Word. For in essence we are saying, "You can take God's Word as written in certain places, but not at the beginning in Genesis." Are we not teaching our children that man can reinterpret God's Word according to what the majority in the culture might believe? As Ham contends, it is this loss of biblical authority that has opened the door to the epidemic we are now experiencing in the Church. When the structure of a Christian worldview collapses, it is replaced with moral relativism until ultimately, the entire Bible is rejected. [50] Indeed, 2 Corinthians 11:3 warns us that Satan will use the same attack on us that he did on Eve: *"But I am afraid that, as the serpent deceived Eve by his craftiness, your minds will be led astray from the simplicity and purity of devotion to Christ."* The same question Satan used in the Garden, he is using today among our youth. That is, "Has God not said?"

Only one out of every four adults has a high level of trust in our religious institutions. [51] In fact, according to Gallup there is not a single institution, whether it is our military, the Presidency, public schools, the Supreme Court, our banks, or Congress in which even half of the nation has confidence. This erosion of confidence in our most basic of institutions has been replaced with cynicism, anger, skepticism, and lethargy. Were you aware there is a barometer that tracks the overall trust of core institutions across nations? In the most recent surveys done in twenty-three nations, the United States ranked fourteenth in institutional confidence. [52] This placed us among the group of nations labeled as most distrusted. Sixty percent of the public have little faith in the media and admit that they cannot depend on the media to give them the straight scoop. [53] Even pastors don't trust other pastors in their own denominations. Furthermore, the laity within the denominations do not trust their pastors. Given the epidemic of moral scandals that have touched virtually every community and made headlines in the media, such distrust is understandable. Perhaps it also helps explain why the typical household donates less than 3 percent of its income to the Church. [54]

When Americans were asked about their most important goals in life, their responses had little to do with God or faith. Instead, the attention revolved around personal accomplishments and possessions as indicated below:

A Composite View of American's Priorities

Maintaining good health	20%
Getting a better job	15%
Being a good parent	10%
Taking care of family	8%
Surviving life's challenges	7%
Being a better Christian	6%
Experiencing greater happiness	5%
Reducing debt	5%
Making more money	4%
Self-improvement	4%
Having a better relationship with God	2%
Going to heaven	2%
Having a good marriage	1%
Serving others	1% [55]

These stats make more sense when considering that only 4 percent of American adults and just 10 percent of born-again Christians possess a biblical worldview. [56] Amazingly, Barna's research also found that less than half of all Protestant pastors possess a biblical worldview. [57]

THE SILVER LINING

Two-thirds of American adults and four-fifths of born-again Christians are concerned about the moral condition of the nation. The overwhelming majority of all Americans are worried about the future of the nation. Two out of three are discouraged by the direction the country is moving. [58] On the other hand, three-quarters of all born-again adults say they would like to know how Christianity relates to current issues they are facing in life. [59] Here's the takeaway. Americans are looking at the cultural landscape, the political landscape, the moral landscape, the religious landscape, and the economic landscape and are wondering, "Is there any hope?" This internal nagging is a strong indicator of an openness for truth and purpose. Most Americans have the remnants of a Christian heritage and there is a residual carryover within their souls that knows not only is something wrong, but they know at the core of their being what is right. When God's people witness, share the Gospel, and when His preachers prophetically proclaim a strong message of Truth in love, all under the anointing of His Spirit, then a spiritual rumbling can occur throughout the Land. This, in no way is approaching our perilous times with rose-tinted glasses of naivety. Rather, we cannot ignore the increasing hostility and defiant posture toward Christ-followers in America. Marriage has been redefined, religious freedoms are being restricted, government intervention looms over us, the IRS is monitoring those churches that dare to speak the truth and is ready to criminalize such as "hate speech." Divorce is winked upon, adultery is swept under the rug, four thousand babies are killed in the womb every day, an unelected judiciary legislates from the bench by creating laws that violate biblical principles, and celebrities are worshiped while Jesus Christ is devalued. The biblical worldview is mocked as being antiquated and alternative worldviews are exalted. This is the America we now live in. But in the face of it all, this is no time to call a retreat. This is a time for leaders to stand boldly for righteousness. We cannot expect our congregations to do so if the example does not begin within its own leadership.

We frequently hear critics arguing that the church is too political. Consequently, many pastors shy away from anything that may be perceived as controversial despite the Bible's clear position on the issues. We have a generation of preachers who are man-pleasers, but this must change. In the days of our Founders, preachers boldly addressed the moral issues of their day. They unapologetically reproved politicians who were in violation of the Bible. I am not advocating stirring up a hornet's nest or having a martyr complex, but we must exert biblical influence on the public policies and moral climate of our day. The silence within the pulpits of our land harbors partial blame for the mess we're in. Isaiah 59:19 says, *"When the enemy comes in like a flood, the Spirit of the Lord will raise up a standard against him."* The statistics contained in these previous two chapters expose the fact that those who sit in our pews on Sundays are confused about what the Bible says on the moral issues of our day. Could it be the reason that the majority have an unbiblical worldview is because preachers are preaching something other than the Bible? Our silence is an indictment on the high calling we've received from God. When the culture is inundated with the sewer of immorality to the point that we have a pandemic of perversions that threaten our very survival, and when study after study reveals little difference between the moral standards of a secular culture and that of our church members..... for today's preacher to be silent, in my estimation, is a betrayal to the integrity of His calling. Our silence is being interpreted by our congregations as condoning, and is leaving them confused at a time when they need moral clarity and a spiritual mentor more than ever. But as it stands now, the Church in America is influenced by society more than influencing society itself.

Ironically, in America there are more Bibles, more churches, more Christian bookstores, more Christian schools, more Christian radio and television ministries than anywhere on the globe. Yet, despite being surrounded by Christian influences, our nation leads the world in practically every immoral category. As stated earlier, this only magnifies the anemic condition of the American Church. There was a day when the Church served as the moral conscience of the nation. We may never regain that day, but neither must we resign ourselves to a fatalistic attitude that says, "Oh well, whatever happens, happens." Nor should we use the sovereignty of God as an excuse for our inactivity or indifference. Before doing anything, we must first humble ourselves, pray, seek God's face and turn from our wicked ways....and then, as preachers, call our people to do the same.

The Connection Between Christianity and Constitutional Freedom

""In my opinion, the present constitution is the standard to which we are to cling. Under its banner bona fide must we combat our political foes, rejecting all changes but through the channel itself provided for amendments. By these general views of the subject have my reflections been guided. I now offer you the outline of the plan they have suggested. Let an association be formed to be denominated "The Christian Constitutional Society," its object to be first: The support of the Christian religion. Second: The support of the United States."[1]

— Alexander Hamilton (1757-1804)
was a signer of the Constitution and known as the "Ratifier of the Constitution." He authored 51 of the 85 Federalist Papers and was the first Secretary of the Treasury and founder of the New York Post.

Hamilton's Personal Commitment to Christianity

"I have carefully examined the evidences of the Christian religion, and if I was sitting as a juror upon its authenticity I would unhesitatingly give my verdict in its favor. I can prove its truth as clearly as any proposition ever submitted to the mind of man. I have a tend reliance on the mercy of the Almighty, through the merits of the Lord Jesus Christ. I am a sinner. I look to Him for mercy."[2]

CHAPTER 12

Are We Rome?

The greatest civilizations from the beginning of history have an average lifespan of 200 years during which time they have all passed through a progressive cycle:

1. From bondage to spiritual faith;
2. From spiritual faith to great courage;
3. From courage to liberty;
4. From liberty to abundance;
5. From abundance to complacency;
6. From complacency to apathy;
7. From apathy to dependence;
8. From dependence back into bondage. [3]

Knowing that every civilization in world history has followed this pattern, one cannot help but ask, "Where is America in this life cycle?" Most likely we are at number 7, between apathy and dependence. However, with at least forty percent of the nation dependent upon the government, a strong case can be made that we have reached the final stage in the survival cycle. If we hope to avoid the inevitable fall of America, the only option is to recognize the historic path we are following, place into government wise leaders who understand the times in which we are living, and most importantly, spiritual leaders who will call the body of Christ to prayer, fasting, and repentance. Desperate times call for desperate measures. The final nail is about to be hammered into America's coffin. We've been writing our own obituary. The stench of death's decaying odor is all around us. We need not die by suicide. Yet, the spiritual darkness that hovers over our Land, the inability to discern right from wrong, and the rampant corruption within our own government are only three symptoms of our moral freefall. As we approached the election of 2016, I read a comment from a concerned citizen asking , "Is this what we have to choose from? A compulsive liar who is under criminal investigation for putting our national security in jeopardy and a profane, narcissistic adulterer and bully who has had over 3,000 lawsuits filed against him. Do you mean to tell me that out of 300 million people, these are best candidates we could put forth? We're voting for children on both sides of the aisle." Sadly, these were not the best candidates. The Republicans had a slate of seventeen competent candidates, most of whom were strong men and women of character. Many were outspoken Christians with a strong sense of right and wrong. Collectively, they were considered to be the strongest lineup of presidential candidates that Republicans had offered the American people in all of its history. Frankly, it was an amazing field whose credentials were off the charts. Yet, the American people chose for their nominee the one with the weakest character, the most checkered past, the most inexperienced in the world of politics, and the most moderate in many of his positions. Yes, at this pivotal moment in American history, the nominee of choice clearly exposed the harsh reality that character, strong morals, core conservative principles were no longer the criteria for selecting an American president. The election of 2016 was unlike any other and the consensus of many is that the American people deserved better. One seminary president, along with another highly influential denominational leader, stated that for the first time ever they were being forced to do something they never dreamed would happen. That is, they could not in clear conscience vote for either candidate due to their immoral positions and choices. Keep in mind, this was a public panel discussion held during the Southern Baptist Convention, the world's largest Protestant denomination. The auditorium erupted with applause upon hearing those statements. Personally, I was stunned and was further reminded of the defining moments in which we are living. Realizing that the next President would most likely nominate four Supreme Court justices and knowing that Trump had already submitted an outstanding list of conservative nominees whom he would recommend, this alone was enough to tilt the scales in his favor for me. A no-vote-at-all, in my way of thinking, was a yes-vote for Hillary. Too much was at stake in this defining moment not to vote. Those evangelicals who refused to participate in the electoral process because it violated their conscience, I can appreciate their stance while also respectfully disagreeing with it. I will not be held accountable for their conscience, but I would have difficulty in living with my conscience knowing that my non-vote was instrumental in putting a rank liberal in the White House and influencing the next 40 years of Supreme Court legislative activism. No, Trump was not my first choice, nor my second, nor my third. But, I had to align with the ABC group, Anybody But Clinton.

While this may sound a bit too impassioned, the Democrat Party is not the same Party of our grandparents. Their platform and ideology is toxic, dangerous, and diabolically opposed to the principles of God's Word. Their language is couched in friendly terms that mean something entirely different than what the average voter is thinking. And yes, the Republican Party has its own issues, but if America does not have strong leadership to right the ship, then the nation's best days are behind her. The die is cast and we are in a severe state of protracted decline. If you have read the previous chapters, then you know this is not some baseless conjecture. The facts speak for themselves. Whether it is job creation, poverty, morals, technological advances, economic sustainability, personal safety, infrastructure condition, homelessness, family stability, foreclosures, crime, violence, unemployment, mass shootings, you name it. America is in the lower rung of industrialized nations.

Who Are the Nation's Heroes?

Another reflection of a nation's value system is its heroes. The people's choice of heroes says something about the people themselves, just as the presidential nominees make a statement about the nation's value system. History tells us that in the last stages of decadence and decline, an empire's heroes tends to be celebrities....... sports stars, singers, actors, and musicians. And so it is today in America. It makes no difference how immoral the lifestyle of the musician, how foul the language of the lyrics, or how vulgar the sexual references, millions are emotionally attached to their musician of choice. The same comparisons can be made with sports stars and actors.

Sir John Bagot Glubb's Perspective

Sir John Bagot Glubb (1897-1987) was an honored British General and historian. He wrote about the collapsed empires from the past. In his 1987 book *The Fate of Empires and the Search for Survival,* he described the factors that were paramount to Rome's collapse. He notes that the average age of empires since the time of ancient Assyria (859-612 B.C.) is 250 years. Only two other empires made it to 267 years. America, as of this writing, is 240 years old, and the signs of decline are all around us. Glubb cites the following factors in Rome's collapse. **First, there was sexual immorality, an aversion to marriage in favor of "living together" and an increased divorce rate that all combined to undermine family stability.** [4] Contained within this context was the prevalence of abortion and homosexuality. Indeed, America is a mirror of ancient Rome's moral bankruptcy. **Second, an unusual number of foreign immigrants settled in Rome's capital and**

major cities, creating not only diversity, but divisiveness as well. [5] Need we say more? With 42 million immigrants along with 12 million illegals living in our states, America reflects Rome in this regard. **Third, irresponsible pleasure-seeking and pessimism increased among the people and their leaders.** [6] Poll after poll reveals that the overwhelming majority of Americans believe America is headed in the wrong direction and Congressional approval ratings are at all-time lows. Pessimism is through the roof. **Fourth, Rome had 1.2 million people in A.D. 170 and to keep the masses content, the government provided food to about half of its non-slave population.** [7] Based on these four indicators we can easily say, "Yes, we are Rome." To believe that America will avoid the fate of other great empires is to do so to our own peril. The philosopher George Santayana once said, "Those who cannot remember the past are condemned to repeat it." [8] Therefore, we must remember....

Dr. Carl Wilson's Perspective

Historian Carl Wilson, in his book *Our Dance Has Turned to Death*, gives another perspective on the comparisons between the fall of the Roman Empire and where America stands today.

(1) Men ceased to lead their families in worship. Their view of God transitioned into a more naturalistic, mechanical approach. [9]

(2) Men began to selfishly neglect their wives and children to pursue material wealth. Materialism dominated their thoughts. [10]

(3) Men changed their sexual values, committing adultery with lower class women and getting involved with homosexuality. [11]

(4) Women abandoned their domestic duties at home and began to seek status and wealth outside the home. Finding their

identity outside the home, women placed an emphasis on sex outside of marriage, more for pleasure than for conceiving children.[12]

(5) Divorce became rampant and culturally acceptable.[13]

(6) This decrease in birthrate produced an older population with less ability to defend itself, thus making the nation more vulnerable to its enemies.[14]

(7) Finally, unbelief in God, diminished parental authority, and the erosion of moral principles affected the economy and government. It was this internal weakness and fragmentation that ultimately destroyed the nation.[15]

Much could be written on each of these points, but why repeat the obvious. In Paul's letter to the Church in Rome, we read about the nation's spiritual decline. He mentions idolatry, ingratitude, unnatural sexual desires, and then anarchy. The final stage is judgment from God Himself. In Rome, the value of human life was low and sex trafficking abounded. Today, we have proof of Planned Parenthood selling aborted babies' butchered body parts to the highest bidders. The devaluing of human life in America is at an all-time low. In the Romans One passage, the Apostle clearly delineates the seriousness of a nation embracing homosexuality, even to the extent of invoking God's judgment. Yet, America falls on the opposite side of the ledger as indicated when the Supreme Court handed down its ruling on the legalization of same-sex marriage. The White House, primed and ready for the Court's official pronouncement, turned on the floodlights using rainbow colors representing GLBT's mantra. The White House's action and the Supreme Court's ruling were in open defiance of God's moral standards for a society and only served to accelerate our demise and gave further reason for God to unleash harsh judgment upon our beloved Land. Indeed, we find ourselves living in the perfect storm as all the components from vanishing Empires of the past now make their imprint upon the U.S.A. If God judged Sodom and Gomorrah, how can He not do so upon America?

Dr. Carl Zimmerman's Perspective

In 1947, Harvard sociologist and historian Dr. Carl Zimmerman studied the deterioration and disintegration of various cultures and published them in his book *Family and Civilization.* As with the previous historians mentioned in this book, Zimmerman found a definite and common pattern that led to the fall of every great nation, empire, and civilization. It is nothing less than remarkable that the very same patterns appear in every single case. The eight common elements of every civilization, as gleaned by Zimmerman, are as follows:

(1) Marriage lost its sacredness and divorce became common. [16]

(2) The traditional meaning of marriage was lost as alternate forms and new definitions of marriage arose. Traditional marriage vows were replaced by individual marriage contracts.

(3) Women lost interest in child bearing and mothering, preferring to pursue power and influence.

(4) Public disrespect for parental authority increased.

(5) Juvenile delinquency, promiscuity, and rebellion accelerated.

(6) Adultery increased throughout the nation.

(7) Those in traditional marriages refused to accept family responsibilities.

(8) Increased tolerance for all kinds of sexual perversions, especially homosexuality, became common and acceptable. [17]

Sir Edward Gibbons Perspective

In 1788, Sir Edward Gibbons was England's most eminent historian of the 18th century. He published the most comprehensive history of the Roman Empire ever compiled. His masterpiece, *The History of the Decline and Fall of the Roman Empire*, encompasses several volumes, but for the sake of brevity, here are the five causes Gibbons gives for the collapse of the Roman civilization:

(1) **The undermining of the dignity and sanctity of the home.**

(2) **Higher and higher taxes**

(3) **A mad craze for pleasure with sports becoming more exciting and brutal.**

(4) **The building of great armaments when the real enemy is within.**

(5) **The decay of religion with faith fading into mere form and losing the power to guide the people.** [18]

Arnold Toynbee's Perspective

Historian Arnold Toynbee (1869-1975) wrote a classic analysis on the rise and fall of civilizations. In his 12-volume work, *A Study of History*, he examines 21 great civilizations. The only one still standing is the United States of America. In particular, Toynbee points out the parallels between Rome and America.

(1) Financial difficulty contributed to the fall of Rome with military spending being the largest item in the imperial budget. Of course, America has also relied on massive debt to finance much of its expenditures. America has spent itself into bankruptcy and has earned the reputation as the world's largest debtor nation.

(2) As already stated, Toynbee's assessment with Rome's decline

of the family agrees with that of other historians. Abortion and adultery were common practices within the Roman Empire. Honesty and noble character disappeared and sexual immorality became rampant.

(3) Rome assumed that their empire would always continue. That it was too big to fail.[19]

(4) Interestingly, in its latter days Rome lost control of its borders. Although the city had 13 miles of high walls that were 40 feet in height, Rome hired barbarians to sustain their military efforts, not unlike America hiring companies and outsourcing our military efforts.[20]

Further Parallels with Rome's Collapse

(1) Decline in Morals and Family Values. There were 32,000 prostitutes in Rome. Roman emperors became notorious for wasting money on lavish parties. The most popular amusement was watching the gladiatorial combats in the colosseum and also watching lions devour Christians to the applause of the crowd.

(2) Political Corruption. It became Rome's practice of selling the throne to the highest bidder. In a span of 100 years, Rome had 37 different emperors, 25 of whom were removed from office by assassination. This contributed to Rome's overall decline.

(3) The Decline in Public Health. Many of the wealthy had water brought to their homes through lead pipes, but instead of the water being purified, there was actually lead poisoning which spread disease. The consumption of alcohol was also a big problem throughout the Empire.

(4) Unemployment. Unable to compete with the lower prices of larger estates, many farmers lost or sold their farms which created high unemployment. At one time, the emperor was importing grain to feed more than 100,000 citizens in Rome alone.

(5) **Inflation.** Once the Romans stopped conquering new lands, the flow of gold into the Roman economy decreased. Their currency became less valuable. Eventually, even their salaries had to be paid in food and clothing. Taxes were collected in fruits and vegetables. Skyrocketing inflation resulted and put a strain on the economy.

(6) **Urban Decay.** To be sure, the wealthy Romans lived in luxury with homes furnished with marble floors, intricate tiles, and customized glass windows. However, most Romans lived in the small, smelly rooms of apartment buildings. At one time there were 44,000 apartment houses within the city walls of Rome. Anyone who could not pay the rent was forced to live on the crime-infested streets. This contributed to urban decay.

(7) **Inferior Technology.** The scientific achievements of the Romans were limited almost entirely to engineering and public services. To be sure, they built marvelous roads and bridges. They established the first system of medicine for the benefit of the poor. Yet, they failed to invent many new machines to keep up the production of goods more efficiently. As a result, they could not provide enough goods for their growing population and ceased to adapt their technology to the changing times.

(8) **Military Spending.** In order to defend their borders, Rome's budget was drained by its military which left little surplus for public housing or for maintaining its infrastructure, such as roads and aqueducts. Thus, many lost the desire to defend the Empire. This became such a problem that Rome began hiring soldiers from the unemployed city mobs and

even from foreign counties. Not only was such an army unreliable, but also extremely expensive to maintain. The emperors were forced to raise taxes which led to increased inflation.

(9) **The Final Blow.** Rome's borders were left open and the enemy began crossing over. Roads and bridges were left in disrepair and fields were left untilled. Pirates and bandits made travel unsafe. Cities could not be maintained. Trade and business began to disappear. The Empire could no longer sustain itself. Thus, the fall of the Roman Empire. [21]

There is an overlap with each historian's perspective, but such duplication only serves to further validate where America stands in light of the same historical paths these once-great nations traveled. Such redundancy is not intended to bore you, the reader, but rather to emphasize the consistency of some of the greatest historians, all of whom are giving America a wake-up call. Statistical data and extensive commentary could be given for each historian's fatal factors which would shed further light on America's plight, but I chose to refrain from stating the obvious and allow you to draw your own conclusions.

Six Requirements for Government Leaders

Scripture has much to say about the qualifications necessary for effective leadership. From God's vantage point, character matters. Unfortunately, such is not the case with most voters today. The Book of Proverbs offers timely advice for the leaders who serve our nation:

(1) **Righteousness**—"When the righteous are in authority, the people rejoice; but when a wicked man rules, the people groan." (Proverbs 29:2) There has been a lot of groaning the last several years. "It is an abomination for kings to commit

wickedness: for the throne is established by righteousness." (Proverbs 16:12)

(2) **Wisdom**—"I, wisdom, dwell with prudence, and find our knowledge and discretion....by me kings reign, and rulers decree justice. By me princes rule, and nobles, all the judges of the earth." (Proverbs 8:12-16)

(3) **Honesty**—"Excellent speech is not becoming to a fool, much less lying lips to a prince." (Proverbs 17:7)

(4) **Separation from bad influences**—-"Take away the dross from silver, and it will go to the silversmith for jewelry. Take away the wicked from before the king, and his throne will be established in righteousness." (Proverbs 25:4-5)

(5) **Personal Purity**—"Do not give your strength to women, nor your ways to that which destroys kings." (Proverbs 31:3)

(6) **Protection of the weak and the defenseless**—"Open your mouth for the speechless, in the cause of all who are appointed to die. Open your mouth, judge righteously, and plead the cause of the poor and needy."

This is How Low We've Sunk

As I look at these essential character traits for national leadership, and then I look at the political corruption, the devious lying, the numerous scandals, the greed, and deception that citizens have endured from those whom we elected, it is little wonder that confidence in our government is at an all-time low. When Hillary Clinton and Donald Trump faced off in the 2016 presidential election, it was the first time that I can remember when neither candidate was considered trustworthy or honest by the majority of voters. This is how low we've sunk. When comparing our Obama, Clinton, and Trump, all would be disqualified by God's standards.

When George Washington was sworn into office, he kissed the Bible that was used. Then he held a two-hour worship service in the Congressional Hall. [22] Today, Obama is more likely to kiss the Koran than the Bible. Judge Roy Moore was fired from his position on the state Supreme Court for keeping a monument of the Ten Commandments in the entry way to a state building. That's how far removed we are from the Faith of our Founders. In 1776, 11 of the 13 colonies required a person to make a profession of faith in Christ before he could run for political office. [23] Today, if a politician speaks openly about Jesus it is to his detriment and is considered intolerant and politically incorrect. That's how far we've fallen. In 1777, Congress voted to spend $300,000 to distribute Bibles in every classroom in America as part of the curriculum. [24] In fact, 197 of the first 200 colleges were founded by churches. [25] It was a requirement to have a theological degree before obtaining a law degree because laws are based on the nature of God. [26] Today, the Bible is banned from our schools and illegal to be read in the classroom. That's how low we've sunk. Proverbs 14:34 says, "Righteousness exalts a nation, but sin is a reproach to any people." "Reproach" means to be brought low. Nations that once respected us, now mock us. The Muslim world wants Americans out of their countries because we bring in ungodliness via movies and pornography. Missionaries in foreign lands hear comments such as, "Why are you Americans here in our country evangelizing us? Why don't you go back home and evangelize your own people?" Ungodly means "without God." We've taken God out of the classrooms, the Ten Commandments off the walls, nativity scenes out of the public square, and the name of Jesus out of commencement speeches so that incrementally God has been removed from the national landscape and anything resembling Christian values is censured. We are no longer one nation under God, but a nation "without God," ungodly. Oh, certainly there are more churches in America than anywhere in the world, but the Church is mostly asleep or complacent at best. So, the nation at large ignores the Church as an irrelevant institution. We've been secularized. President Ronald Reagan said, "If America ever forgets that we are one nation under God, we will be one nation gone under." [27]

I saw a T-shirt with a cross on the back and Romans 1:16 which says, "I am not ashamed of the gospel of Christ, for it is the power of God to salvation for everyone who believes." On the front of the shirt it said, "This shirt is illegal in 51 countries." Think about that. There are 51 countries in the world today where I could be imprisoned or even killed for wearing a shirt with the image of a cross or with the words of Scripture printed on it. Yet, if a child today wore such a shirt to school, he or she would be forced to change clothes due to the offensive nature of the message. In today's politically-correct environment, everything is about tolerance.

SIGNS OF DECLINE

(1) America's child poverty levels are worse than in any developed country, including Greece, Lithuania, and Estonia.

(2) Median adult wealth in the U.S. (39,000) is 27th globally, putting us behind Cyprus, Taiwan, and Ireland.

(3) America ranks #12 behind Israel, Sweden, and Australia when it comes to "life satisfaction."

(4) America's per capita wealth, health, and education are mediocre when compared with other industrialized nations.

(5) The U.S. military is overstretched, we are ill-prepared technologically, and at-risk economically.

(6) Median wealth per adult ranks 27th out of 27 high-income countries. While we may feel like global leaders, the reality is that per capita income in the U.S. has remained unchanged since 2000.

(7) Educationally, the U.S. ranks 16th out of 23 countries. The U.S. ranked near the bottom in skills survey, 16th in adult literacy, and 21st in adult numeracy out of 23, and 14th in problem-solving.

(8) Health-wise, the U.S. citizens rank below many other wealthy countries. For every 100,000 births in the U.S., 18.5 women die. Saudi Arabia and Canada have half that maternal death rate.

(9) The U.S. ranks 36th out of 162 countries in people living below poverty. Officially, 45.3 million people are impoverished. The U.S. is 34th out of 35 nations surveyed when it comes to children living in poverty. Only Romania was lower. Children in all of Europe, Canada, Australia, New Zealand, and Japan fare much better.

(10) The U.S. has the highest income inequality in the world.

(11) America has more prison incarcerations than anywhere in the world. Only China comes close.

(12) The U.S. is ranked 17th out of 175 countries for corruption.

(13) The U.S. is 20th out of 178 nations for stability.

(14) Utilizing 52 economic indicators, the U.S. ranked 16th out of 133 countries for social progress.

(15) The U.S. is a world leader in divorce, abortions, teen pregnancies, illegal drugs, pornography consumption, and a host of other socially unacceptable behaviors. [28]

The above does not bode well for the health and future of our beloved nation, especially when seeing the parallels with the fallen Roman Empire. We are living on borrowed time. Thankfully, there are many books sounding the alarm, so we must "rally the troops" and collectively pray for wisdom in how to proceed from here. Courage, boldness, and wisdom from God Himself will be essential requirements. As you will see in an upcoming chapter, persecution looms on the horizon for those of us who strive to let our voices be heard. Historian Will Durant said, "There is no significant example in history, before our time, of a society successfully maintaining moral life without the aid of religion."[29]

So, where will the future take us? Perhaps we will be consumed by internal moral decay and collapse from our massive debt. Perhaps we will be unable to fund our military and we'll be overtaken by an enemy. Perhaps a terrorist attack will wreak havoc on our economy and create a massive blackout by attacking our electrical grid. Perhaps we will elect incompetent leaders who take us over the cliff in their blind, foolish ways. Yet, better still, another scenario is this: Christians throughout the nation begin huddling in home prayer groups; churches open their doors during the daytime for the Christian community to come and pray; pastors begin to call their congregations to repentance and become burdened for spiritual awakening; Christian businessmen send a message to their communities by placing signage on the doors that they are closed for a specified hour to pray for the country; Christian city councilmen, school board members, local mayors, Christian athletes, high school students begin to make a difference in their own circles of influence; letters to the editor begin to call people to prayer. The list is endless. You are limited only by your imagination Come on, Church! Let's rise up in this defining moment of American history. It is not too late. Politics and government are not the answer. The explosive, transforming, resurrection power of Jesus Christ is America's only Hope.

As a Foreigner, Tocqueville's Immediate Observation of America

"Upon my arrival in the United States the religious aspect of the country was the first thing that struck my attention. In France I had almost always seen the spirit of religion and the spirit of freedom marching in opposite directions. But in America I found they were intimately united and that they reigned in common over the same country...Religion in America...must be regarded as the foremost of the political institutions of that country; for if it does not impart a taste for freedom, it facilitates the use of it.

In the United States the sovereign authority is religious... There is no country in the whole world where the Christian religion retains a greater influence over the souls of men than in America, and there can be no greater proof of its unity and of its conformity to human nature than that its influence is powerfully felt over the most enlightened and free nation of the earth. The safeguard of morality is religion, and the morality is the best security of law as well as the surest pledge of freedom." [1]

— Alexis de Tocqueville (1805-1859)
was a French philosopher who toured America in 1831 observing people and institutions. His "Democracy in America" is described as the most comprehensive analysis of the relationship between character and society in America that has ever been written.

CHAPTER 13

The Coming Persecution

Cultural changes are sweeping America unlike anything we have witnessed in our lifetime. Such epic changes are engulfing the nation like a tsunami and anyone in the path of this massive tidal wave should either be fully prepared for what is coming or else be swept away by the mighty torrent. Irrevocable trends have been put into motion that are seemingly irreversible. For well over 200 years Christians in America lived in a persecution-free society thanks to a Constitution that esteems freedom of religion and freedom of speech. However, such is rapidly changing as hostility toward Christianity escalates. Those who dislike America and all she has stood for are determined to transform the nation into a socialistic society, but if such is to be realized, then Christianity must be silenced and its influence eliminated. Powerful lobbyists, influential politicians, activist judges, a liberal media, and government-run schools have been working in concert to accomplish this objective. These powerbrokers will stop at nothing short of achieving their goal of supplanting the nation's Christian heritage with its own secularized agenda. This covert operation has been going on for decades but has been so strategically subtle and incrementally deceptive that with the exception of a few protests no one seems to have noticed. Older generations, however, have a perspective that more easily recognizes the radical changes that have occurred. As Christians are increasingly forced to be silent or leave the public square, our faith will be tested in ways we never imagined. In particular, the legalization of same-sex marriage has ramifications for the Church that will make homosexuality a lightning rod issue for years to come. Preaching what the Bible teaches on sexual morality will be viewed as hate speech and runs the risk of being misunderstood and publicly vilified.

A Pew Research study shows a "marked increase" in hostility toward religion since 2009. [2] We have seen this to be the case for owners of bakeries, florists, and photography studios who refused to compromise their deeply-held biblical beliefs when "forced" to decide if they would be compliant participants in serving for same-sex weddings. This avalanche is just beginning. Like a criminal hiding in the dark shadows behind a tree just waiting for the appropriate time to lurch onto an unsuspecting jogger, this special interest group now has the law on its side and the persecution awaiting Christians via lawsuits will be unprecedented. For Christians, this is the new normal and we can forget about longing for the good ole days. To be sure, America's foundational legal system was based upon God's moral law, and while the words of the Constitution have not changed, its' interpretation has.

As an example of how rapidly this seismic shift in morals has occurred, consider that a Gallup poll in March of 1996 showed 27 percent approving of same-sex marriages while 68 percent opposed. By July of 2014, 55 percent approved of same-sex marriages and 42 percent opposed. For a few decades now, evangelical voters have found a home in the Republican Party due to its strong stance on moral issues that reflect biblical, traditional family values. However, we now see Republican Party leaders beginning to waffle and broadening the tent by asking, "How can we attract the next generation of voters if we refuse to support the issues that young people embrace?" A Pew Research Poll shows a 39 percentage point difference between younger Republicans and older Republicans with the young favoring gay marriage. [3] Thus, it would seem that the Republican Party will gradually begin to resemble the Democrats in an effort to gain favor with the voters. Sadly, many churches have adopted the same thinking by compromising what the Bible says in order to accommodate the cultural values of the day. So, as Christians we can expect the thermostat of persecution to turn up the heat. At times, the temperature may seem unbearable. But let's also remember that New Testament Christianity thrived in the most hostile environments and some of our New Testament books were penned from prison while enduring the persecution of Christianity.

PERSECUTION IN THE MAKING

It is common knowledge that public schools have become spiritual warzones and the intensity on this battlefield seems to only be increasing. What is especially strange is that any vestige of Christianity is viewed as inappropriate, unconstitutional and should be immediately removed. Along with such action, a void has been created, thus requiring something else with which to replace it. That "something" is secular humanism. Charles F. Potter, founder of the First Humanist Society of New York, wrote these words: "Education is a most powerful ally of Humanism, and every American public school is a school of Humanism. What can the theistic Sunday schools, meeting for an hour once a week, and teaching only a fraction of the children, do to stem the tide of a five-day program of humanistic teaching." [4] Incidentally, the Humanist Manifesto refers to humanism as a religion. Even the United States Supreme Court recognized secular humanism as a religion. [5] So, the Court banished any appearance of Christianity in our schools while substituting another religion in its place. Since we now know the ambition of this secular religion is to indoctrinate our children with the goal of transforming America into an atheistic state, let's take a brief look at only a fraction of the Court's rulings to gain a better understanding of the degree of hostility that exists toward Christianity in our culture.

(1) We all know about the Supreme Court's outlawing prayer

in our public schools, but you are probably not as familiar with Wallace v. Jaffree that banned a moment of silence at the beginning of the school day if that moment of silence was used for prayer. Will somebody please help me to understand how a moment of silence violates the law or how such a time could possibly constitute the endorsement of religion? [6]

(2) In DeKalb County, Alabama the Court ruled that any prayers spoken "aloud in the classroom, over the public address system, or as part of the program at school-related assemblies and sporting events, or at a graduation ceremony" were prohibited—even if the school did not endorse them. To show what a serious offense this was, the Court appointed an attorney to serve as a prayer monitor to oversee the school to make sure the order was carried out. "Are you serious?" Over a period of eight months alone the court-appointed prayer policeman pocketed $62,000. [7] If this occurred in Communist China, Russia, North Korea, it would come as no surprise. But to have a Court-appointed prayer policeman in an American school to ensure that prayers are not being verbalized among the students is just one more example of hatred toward anything associated with Christianity.

(3) The ante was upped in West Virginia when a judge not only outlawed student-led graduation prayer at St. Albans High School but he ordered the offending school system to pay $23,000 in legal fees to the eighteen-year-old atheist who brought the suit. [8] I frequently speak in school assemblies, but there are many invitations not extended even though the principal has my manuscript, a stack of endorsements, and my own word not to violate church/state guidelines. It is rulings like this one in West Virginia that has school

administrators paranoid that some atheistic student or parent will file such a suit just because I happen to be a preacher.

(4) It's not just high schools, but this heavy-handed judicial activism trickles down to our elementary kids, even our kindergartners. A Vermont kindergartner was forbidden to tell his classmates that God is not dead because such talk was not allowed at school. [9] School administration officials at a Kentucky public school told a student he was not permitted to pray or even mention God at school. [10] A teacher in an elementary school in Florida overheard two of her students talking about their faith in Jesus and rebuked them, not for talking in class, but for talking about Christ in class. She ordered them not to discuss Jesus at school. [11] A principal at a Denver elementary school removed a teacher's personal Bible from his desk where he kept it to read during silent time. School officials did not want the Bible to be in the sight of the students. [12]

(5) Of course, Christmas has not escaped the scrooge of the Courts. In Frederick County, Maryland, a school employee was barred from distributing Christmas cards with a Christian message. A fourth grader in Ephrata, Pennsylvania, was forbidden from handing out religious Christmas cards to his classmates. [13] A school district in California has forbidden teachers from uttering the word "Christmas" in class and instructed them not to wear Christmas jewelry. [14] Pattison Elementary School in Katy, Texas not only banned the singing of Christmas songs, but threatened grade reductions for students who refused to participate in singing songs of other faiths. [15] It gets even crazier. Officials in St. Paul, Minnesota ordered that a few red poinsettias be removed from the Ramsey

County Courthouse because those particular flowers could be associated with Christmas and might offend certain people. White ones were permitted, not red. [16] Then, in Eugene, Oregon Christmas trees were banned from public places because they are associated with a religious holiday. [17] The Madison, Wisconsin school board banned student recitation of the Pledge of Allegiance in public schools and prohibited students from singing the national anthem. "Why?" you ask. The board said the words "under God" in the pledge were offensive to some and many opposed the militaristic themes in the "Star-Spangled Banner." [18]

(6) If you graduated from high school a few decades ago, then you're probably oblivious to the historical revisionism in American History textbooks. I recall reviewing a public school history text and compared it with a homeschool American History textbook. No kidding, it was as if they were describing two different countries. As mentioned earlier, "God, Jesus, Bible," or any semblance of Christianity is intentionally omitted from the textbooks of our public schools even though the Bible and Christianity were the primary instruments in forming the foundation of our country. America's Christian heritage is undisputed by any credible historian, but by selectively eliminating the very reason for America's existence imparts to our children a distorted view of why and how our nation was formed. In examining sixty widely used social studies textbooks used by 87 percent of public schools, not one mentioned the spirituality of the Pilgrims. [19] One book had thirty pages on the Pilgrims, including the first Thanksgiving. But there was not a single reference to religion. Another textbook described the Pilgrims as "people who make long trips." It is common for these books to treat Thanksgiving without

explaining to whom the Pilgrims gave thanks. Many public schools now portray Thanksgiving as a multicultural harvest feast in which American colonists gave thanks to Indians. [20] One high school American history textbook devotes six lines to George Washington, but six and a half pages to Marilyn Monroe. [21]

(7) It is significant to note that the National Education Association has supported and endorsed every Democratic presidential candidate since 1972. It's safe to say that academia frowns upon the Christian worldview and spares no opportunity to assault it.

(8) Utilizing the zoning laws of respective cities, establishing Christian churches or even holding home Bible studies can be forbidden. This is becoming more and more prevalent as any denomination wanting to plant a church or any church wanting to go through an extensive building program can testify. In Portland, Oregon, Sunnyside Centenary United Methodist Church was ordered that its attendance should be limited to seventy people and was even further restricted for Wednesday night Bible studies and other uses of its church facilities. [22] In Marietta, Georgia, only a few miles from where I live, Art and Norma Ellison regularly hosted prayer meetings at their home on Friday evenings for six to eight people. Despite the fact that most of those attending parked in the driveway, the City and Planning Department sent a letter to the couple informing them they were violating the zoning code by operating a church in a residential neighborhood and gave them ten days to discontinue their meetings. The same occurred in Onalaska, Wisconsin where Richard and Audrey Gilmore hosted a Bible study for five college students. [23] Once again, the same occurred in Denver, Colorado along with many

other cities throughout the nation.[24] In Phoenix, a man was hosting a Bible study in his home which was an apparent violation of the city zoning laws. He was sentenced to 60 days in jail, three years of probation, and fined $12,180.[25]

(10) As extreme as some of these examples may seem, they are not isolated incidents. But this one is perhaps the worst of all. The family of a preacher's wife in Colorado wanted to engrave the name Jesus on their deceased mother's tombstone. Her final wish was to have her cemetery marker engraved with the ichthus symbol and the word Jesus written inside the fish. City officials said that the name of Jesus would offend people. Keep in mind, this was a cemetery. Unbelievable![26]

(11) One of the most prolific examples of discrimination against Christians in recent years occurred when Democratic lawmakers in more than six major cities called for a ban on Chick-fil-A's expansion efforts. What was their crime? Truett Cathy, the founder of Chick-fil-A, along with his sons, is a strong Christian who believes that marriage is a union between one man and one woman. Yet, this family-owned business does not wear Christianity on its cuff and does not make it a practice to preach the Gospel to its customers. Nevertheless, their Christian values are well known and the family certainly does not shy away from its pro-life, pro-family values when asked about their faith. In Washington, D.C. Chick-fil-A was accused of peddling "hate chicken." In Philadelphia the family was called homophobic. Chicago's mayor, Rahm Emanuel, said, "Chick-fil-A's values are not Chicago values. They disrespect our fellow neighbors, residents, and family members." Alderman Joe Moreno said, "Because of this man's ignorance, I will now be denying Chick-fil-A's permit to open a restaurant."[27] This should serve as a wake-up call to Christians everywhere because it

brings into focus the ultimate goal of sanitizing the public square of anyone who holds to a biblical view of morality. It's not about tolerance, but forced acceptance.

(12) Similar stories are rampant throughout the country, such as Frank Turek who was fired from Cisco over his religious view that marriage should be between a man and a woman. Likewise, a Cargill Foods employee was fired for having a sign on his private vehicle supporting traditional marriage. And on it goes.[28] It's safe to say the goal of gay activists is to intimidate people into silence.

(13) A spokesman for the Gideons claims that "In most countries we are allowed to go into public schools and give Bibles to students. But we can't do it here in America."[29] Sadly, until just recently, public schools in Russia welcomed the Gideons. Public schools in the United States banish them.

(14) Our military has become a politically-correct warzone. In recent years, Christian prayers have been banned at the funeral services for veterans at Houston's National Cemetery. Evangelical leaders like Franklin Graham, Tony Perkins, and Lt. General Boykin were banned from speaking at military events. A war-games scenario at Fort Leavenworth identified evangelical Christians as potential threats. At Ft. Campbell, Kentucky a lieutenant colonel e-mailed his three dozen subordinates to be on the lookout for domestic hate groups. Among the groups the Army listed were the Family Research Council and the American Family Association, both credible, reputable Christian organizations. Alongside them were the Ku Klux Klan and Neo-Nazi groups.[30] I suppose the conclusion is if you're a Christian who believes in the Bible, then you're profiled and on a watch list. We saw an example of this when the IRS targeted Christian ministries and pro-life groups—all deemed as enemies of

the Obama administration. The Billy Graham Evangelistic Association and Samaritan's Purse ran a full-page ad supporting North Carolina's marriage amendment. The ad said, "Vote for biblical values this November 6, and pray with me (Billy Graham) that America will remain one nation under God." Not long after running the ad, both ministries were audited by the IRS. The message being sent was, "If you mess with the Obama administration, you will suffer the consequences." [31]

(15) Putting this persecution within the military in its proper perspective, listen to the words of Coast Guard Rear Admiral William Lee: "The problem that men and women like me face in uniform who are in senior leadership positions is that the higher you are, the more vulnerable you are to being taken down. You get in the cross hairs of those people who lay in wait outside the gate, waiting to take us to task for expressing our faith." Lee proceeded to tell the story of one of his young soldiers who tried to commit suicide. "When I looked at that young man and heard his story, the rules say, 'Send him to the chaplain.' My heart said, 'Give this man a Bible." However, to do so would be in violation of policy. Even so much as whispering, "Here is the answer; take it home; I'll talk about it if you want to." That would be considered crossing the line. The Obama administration endorsed military reprimands for any soldier who keeps a Bible on his desk. [32]

The US Army directed troops to remove a Bible inscription that a vendor etched into the serial numbers of weapon scopes. They received a directive to turn in their scopes so the bible references could be removed. The verses appeared at the end of the scope serial numbers, reading JN8:12 and 2COR4:6. After the letters and numbers were scraped off, soldiers were directed to apply black paint to ensure the verses were totally covered.[33] I find it very sad to know that we have soldiers going into combat fighting for our freedom and are disallowed to see a verse of Scripture on their weapon that may serve as a source of hope and comfort. This is political correctness run amuck. These guys (and gals) put on a uniform to defend our freedom, not the least of which is freedom of religion, but yet they are stripped of their own freedom to practice the very freedom for which they are fighting.

Two Baptist chaplains were forced out of a Veterans chaplain training program after they refused orders to stop quoting the Bible and to stop praying in the name of Jesus.[34] Correct me for being so simple-minded, but I thought that's what chaplains were supposed to do. If a chaplain is not allowed to use the Bible or pray over patients, then what purpose do they serve?

JUDICIAL ACTIVISM: THE STRONG ARM OF PERSECUTION

The United States was founded on the right of the people as a whole, through democratic processes and their elected representatives, to decide the most important issues facing the nation. This fundamental, founding principle which has distinguished America from the rest of the world has now changed. We could see it coming. For example, in the 2000 decision Boy Scouts of America et al. v. Dale, the Supreme Court came within one vote of declaring that people have a constitutional right to engage in homosexual conduct, even though the Constitution says nothing about homosexual conduct. As a private organization, the Boy Scouts had an official position against homosexual relationships, and forcing them to hire a homosexual scoutmaster would be in violation of that message. Had the Court ruled against the Scouts, it would have set a legal precedent that could be used against any Christian ministry that opens its doors to the public.

Yet, it came within one vote of doing just that.

The more important question is this: Were we, the citizens of this nation, given the right to vote on this all-important issue? No. Did the representatives of the people in state legislatures vote to approve such a requirement? No. Yet, four justices thought they had the right to impose their beliefs on the entire nation. The ramifications for the church would have been huge. It should be noted that since this 2000 ruling, the winds of political correctness have blown stronger and liberalism's tentacles have extended even further into the heart of the culture so that the Boy Scouts in 2013 reversed their long-standing policy by openly admitting gay boys into their organization. No doubt, the threats of law suits and seeing how the Court was leaning to the left created undue pressure upon the Scouts to cave to the pressure.

In 2003 Massachusetts' Judicial Supreme Court decided by a 4-3 majority to allow same-sex couples the right to marry.[35] Again, did the citizens of Massachusetts or their representatives decide this question? No. The primary author of Massachusetts' constitution was none other than John Adams, one of our Founding Fathers. He, and any of the other original Founding Fathers, would have considered such to have been unconstitutional and yet, the US Supreme Court continues to invent "constitutional rights" that previous justices never dreamed of doing.

Then, in 2009 Iowa's Supreme Court followed suit with Massachusetts in allowing same-sex marriage contending that limiting marriage to one man and one woman was unconstitu tional.[36] There was not a word in the Iowa constitution about same-sex marriage, but the idea of limiting marriage to one man and one woman was inconsistent with the judges' new ideas of what the Iowa constitution should say. The original meaning of the constitution did not matter. All that mattered was the liberal opinions of the judges who imposed their standards on the rest of the state. Thus, an entire state's understanding of marriage was transformed in the blink of an eye. Do you see where this is headed? We could see this train coming down the track and preparing the way for 2015's monumental ruling on same-sex marriage. It was just a matter of time.

Again, the ramifications are far-reaching and could fill an entire book. The point is, those who once considered homosexuality to be destructive to society now find themselves on the other side of the debate. It has now become morally wrong for us to express our opposing viewpoint. Now, we must raise our children in a manner that is consistent with the law of the land and adheres to their viewpoint....or else. Once again, the US Constitution says nothing about giving homosexuals special rights, but the Supreme Court supposedly discovered it in the Constitution. The question should be asked, "Did the authors of our Constitution ever intend that traditional moral values should be excluded as a basis for the laws? I mean, where does the Constitution say anything about guaranteeing homosexuals to be a special class with special protections under the law? It simply does not.

The Court's ruling on same-sex marriage was decided, not by the people of the United States, but by the Court. And, there is nothing that any citizen can do to change it. Wayne Grudem, Research Professor of Theology and Biblical Studies at Phoenix Seminary, says, "What happens if the citizens of the nation decide that they want to change the laws that have been created by the Supreme Court? What if citizens decide they do not think that abortion should be allowed at every point during a woman's pregnancy or that they want to allow an opening prayer at a high school graduation ceremony or before a high school football game? The simple fact is that the citizens of the United States have absolutely no power to overcome these rulings. It would not matter if the Congress itself and all fifty state legislatures passed laws restricting a woman's right to have an abortion in certain circumstances. It would not matter, because the Supreme Court has ruled that such laws are not constitutional. The people of the nation are no longer allowed to make the decision for themselves. The Supreme Court makes such decisions for the people, and all the people are able to do is submit to that decision."[37]

DON'T MISS THIS!

It is imperative that you carefully read this section because it sheds light and insight on why America has changed and what has been the strategy of liberalism. You see, after Roe v. Wade liberal politicians began to realize that their goals for transforming America could be accomplished much quicker and easier by going through the courts than trying to persuade the people and their representatives to approve the changes. Therefore, instead of acting as a "check and balance" against the Supreme Court, elected officials concluded that they would uphold the Court's judicial activism by simply appointing other judges at the lower courts (district and appeals). So, liberal Presidents would appoint justices who would promote judicial activism for the purpose of imposing their convictions on the whole nation. Here's a case in point. Remember Robert Bork? He was President Reagan's nomination as a Supreme Court justice in 1987. I'll refrain from a review of his resume', but suffice it to say that at the time of his nomination he was considered the most qualified and able constitutional scholar in the United States. But, the liberals realized that if he was nominated then a majority of the Supreme Court would most likely overturn Roe v. Wade. Bork's nomination, after strong opposition from liberals, was defeated 58-42. Justice Anthony Kennedy was his replacement. That single vote in the US Senate changed the course of history in the United States. If for no other reason, this is why Christians should vote in Presidential elections. I hear evangelicals say they refused to vote for either candidate in the 2016 election simply because neither reflected a biblical morality. Yet, Donald Trump submitted a list of Supreme Court nominees whom he would approve if elected and each one met the "smell" test by conservatives in Washington. If three or four Supreme Court justices are likely to be vacated in the next few years, why would any Christian sit at home on Election Day?

Despite the fact that it is unconstitutional for the Supreme Court to have any legislative or executive power, this is precisely what has happened. And if the popular culture can persuade judges to abandon the idea of an original understanding of the constitution, then those judges are likely going to reflect the liberal culture. This is what happened with abortion. You see, herein lies the real battle. Is our Constitution to be interpreted as a living document that accommodates the cultural times in which it lives, or should it be interpreted on the basis of the original meaning of the law at the time it was written? Democrats, as a rule, believe that it changes with the times. Republicans are mostly originalists. This is why many say that the control of the judicial system is the single most important issue for the future of the United States.

Are you following the bread crumbs? People want to know, "What is wrong with our nation? Why have we moved so far away from traditional moral values?" Quite simply, the Supreme Court, instead of sending such decisions for the people to vote and decide, has heavy-handedly imposed its own opinion on the American people and made it the law of the Land. Huge decisions such as abortion, same-sex marriage, the removal of religion from public events and public places, the removal of teaching absolute moral standards in our schools, the removal of mentioning God or Jesus in our history textbooks, the undermining of sexual morality through mild restraints on pornography. The list goes on. Keep in mind, these people are unelected, unaccountable, and irreplaceable until they die or resign.

CHIEF JUSTICE JOHN ROBERTS ON THE COURT'S SAME-SEX RULING

In the Court's 5-4 ruling, Chief Justice Roberts was among the dissenters. There is no better example of judicial activism than this recent ruling. You and I were not in the Courtroom, but we need to hear the Chief Justice's perspective because he did not mince words and seemed to have a clear understanding of just how historic this ruling was and what it would mean for the future of our nation. Here are some excerpts:

"Just who do we think we are? This Court is not a legislature. Whether same-sex marriage is a good idea should be of no concern to us. Under the Constitution, judges have power to say what the law is, not what it should be. The people who ratified the Constitution authorized courts to exercise "neither force nor will but merely judgment.....The truth is that today's decision rests on nothing more than the majority's own conviction that same-sex couples should be allowed to marry because they want to, and that 'it would disparage their choices and diminish their personhood to deny them this right.' Whatever force that belief may have as a matter of moral philosophy, it has no more basis in the Constitution than did the naked policy preferences adopted in Lochner......Although the policy arguments for extending marriage to same-sex-couples may be compelling, the legal arguments for requiring such an extension are not. A State's decision to maintain the meaning of marriage that has persisted in every culture throughout human history can hardly be called irrational. The majority's decision is an act of will, not legal judgment. The right it announces has no basis in the Constitution or this Court's precedent. The Constitution itself says nothing about marriage, and the Framers thereby entrusted the States with the whole subject of the domestic relations of husband and wife.....As a judge, I find the majority's position indefensible as a matter of constitutional law.....The premises supporting the concept of marriage are so fundamental that they rarely require articulation. The human race must procreate to survive. Procreation occurs through sexual relations between a man and a woman. When sexual relations result in the conception of a child, that child's prospects are generally better if the mother and father stay together rather than going their separate ways. Therefore, for the good of children and society, sexual relations that can lead to procreation should occur only between a man and a woman committed to a lasting bond……From the standpoint of history and tradition, a leap from opposite-sex marriage to same-sex marriage is much greater than one from a two-person union to plural unions, which have deep roots in some cultures around the world. If the majority is willing to take the big leap, it is hard to see how it can say no to the shorter one. It is striking how much of the majority's reasoning would apply with equal force to the claim of a fundamental right to plural marriage….Those who founded our country would not recognize the majority's conception of the judicial role. They after all risked their lives and fortunes for the precious right to govern themselves. They would never have imagined yielding that right on a question of social policy to unaccountable and unelected judges. And they certainly would not have been satisfied by a system empowering judges to override policy judgments so long as they do so after a quite extensive discussion…..If you are among the many Americans—of whatever sexual orientation—who favor expanding same-sex marriage, by all means celebrate today's decision. But do not celebrate the Constitution. It had nothing to do with it."[38]

What does judicial activism have to do with the persecution of Christians? Everything. Look at the rulings cited earlier. Activist judges interpret the Constitution as a living document which means cultural trends ultimately determine right and wrong by the Court. The Christian's voice, beliefs, and lifestyle will be muzzled or at least confined to the four walls of a church building. Grudem says, "The one practical way that individual

Christians can influence this issue is by voting. Every Christian citizen who votes helps one side or the other on this issue every election." Then, he gets bolder in expressing his true political colors. "If Democrats are elected to the US Senate, they will tend to perpetuate the system of activist judges. If Democrats are elected to the US House or to state offices, some of them will advance to positions in the US Senate or to the Presidency. At the state level, Democratic governors will appoint justices who follow these activist tendencies, and Democrats in state legislatures will generally support this trend as well. Therefore voting for Republican candidates for state and national position is the best way—in fact, the only way known to me—to bring about a change and break the rule of unaccountable judges over our society. I believe this is the most important issue facing the nation, for it will decide who will rule the nation." [39] As of now, it appears we are being ruled by nine unelected, unaccountable lifetime justices.

UP WITH ISLAM, DOWN WITH CHRISTIANITY

The FBI has purged its anti-terrorism training documents of any material deemed "offensive" to Muslims. [40] Erwin Lutzer, former pastor of Moody Bible Church in Chicago, says that we have a stealth jihad in America. He claims that "We are very naïve as Americans if we judge Islam by its more tolerant American version. If you really want to understand Islam, you have to go to Egypt and see what the Christians are enduring there. You have to go to Saudi Arabia, Iran, Iraq—this is really Islam and what the religion is once it begins to take over a country." [41] Yet President Obama never missed an opportunity to promote what he perceived to be Islamic contributions to the United States. He once said that Ramadan reminds us that Islam is part of the fabric of our nation. He said, "Islam has contributed to the character of our country and Muslim Americans, and their good works, have helped to build our nation." [42]

In 2011, the President watered down the meaning of Christmas in his weekly address to the nation. He told Americans to remember a spirit of service—whatever they believe. "Servicc to others—that's what this season is all about. For my family and millions of Americans, that's what Christmas is all about. So, whatever you believe, wherever you're from, let's remember the spirit of service that connects us all this season—as Americans. Each of us can do our part to serve our communities and our country, not just today, but every day." That's pathetic, Mr. President! What a cop-out for someone who claims to be a Christian. I know some would object by saying, "Steve, give him some slack. He's the president of all Americans, not just Christian Americans." Well, let's go back to Reagan. Go back to our Founders. Even go back to George W. Bush in 2007 when he explained the celebration of Easter to the American people: He said, "The resurrection of Jesus Christ is the most important event of the Christian faith…On this powerful day, let us join together and give thanks to the Almighty for the glory of His grace." He followed that the next year by declaring, ""The Resurrection of Jesus Christ reminds people around the world of the presence of a faithful God who offers a love more powerful than death. Easter commemorates our Savior's triumph over sin, and we take joy in spending this special time with family and friends and reflection on the many blessings that fill our lives. During this season of renewal, let us come together and give thanks to the Almighty who made us in His image and redeemed us in His love." [43]

Frank Page, former president of the Southern Baptist Convention and current chairman of the Executive Committee, issues this word of warning: "A biblical worldview will not be tolerated in the twenty-first century. There will be active and open persecution because of the biblical worldview of churches. When you have national leaders who say that Baptists and other evangelicals are guilty of hate speech because of our recitation of simple scripture, then you are going to see the alienation and active persecution of churches in the United States. I'm not a conspiracy theorist, but I do believe the day is coming when churches will see outright persecution as well as a continued pattern of harassment and marginalization in this culture. Churches better gear up and realize that day is coming."[44]

Being a bold Christian in today's culture is not for wimps. We need Christian patriots who will rise to the occasion. Storm clouds are brewing, the winds are blowing, and our liberties are being assaulted with increasing frequency. But why are we surprised. We can expect to be persecuted for our views. Rejection comes with the territory for standing on God's Truth.

It's time for pastors to cease from pacifying church members, to refrain from censoring sermons so as not to offend anyone, and to simply preach the Word of God undiluted and uncompromised. If church members leave, so be it. If controversy arises, that's too bad but let's not water down God's truth to accommodate man's agenda. The fear of God is more important than the fear of man. Pleasing God is more important than pleasing man. Yes, there will be a price to pay, but God's reputation is of greater significance than man's. Regardless of how dark or how hot it gets, we cannot afford to be intimidated, bullied, or silenced. To succumb sends a message to our members…and be assured, they are watching.

Rarely, if ever, have we found ourselves in such perilous times. What if the government requires churches to perform same-sex marriages or lose their tax-exempt status? What if the government requires churches and religious organizations to hire transgendered staff? Such persecution in the future is not only possible, but likely. Yes, it would be nice if large crowds rise up to protest and protect us. Yes, it would be nice if family and friends rallied behind us. But, like the Apostle Paul sitting in prison, they all may abandon us. I'm not an alarmist, but a realist. It is time to seek the Lord and draw near to Him. And when those in authority demand that we stop preaching the Truth, may the boldness of Peter and John be reflected in our witness by saying, "We ought to obey God rather than men" (Acts 5:29). The Gospel of Jesus Christ will not, and cannot, be chained or harnessed.

Columbus Credits God for Leading Him to Discover America

"I prayed to the most merciful Lord about my heart's great desire, and He gave me the spirit and the intelligence for the task; seafaring, astronomy, geometry, arithmetic, skill in drafting spherical maps and placing correctly the cities, rivers, mountains and ports. I also studied cosmology, history, chronology, and philosophy. It was the Lord who put into my mind (I could feel His hand upon me) the fact that it would be possible to sail from here to the Indies. All who heard of my project rejected it with laughter, ridiculing me. There is no question that the inspiration was from the Holy Spirit, because he comforted me with rays of marvelous illumination from the Holy Scriptures, a strong and clear testimony from the 44 books of the Old Testament, from the four Gospels, and from the 23 Epistles of the blessed Apostles, encouraging me continually to press forward, and without ceasing for a moment they now encourage me to make haste. Our Lord Jesus desired to perform a very obvious miracle in the voyage to the Indies, to comfort me and the whole people of God. For the execution of the journey to the Indies I did not make use of intelligence, mathematics or maps. It is simply the fulfillment of what Isaiah had prophesied. All this is what I desire to write down for you in the book. No one should fear to undertake any task in the name of our Savior, if it is just and if the intention is purely for His holy service. The working out of all things has been assigned to each person by our Lord, but it all happens according to His sovereign will even though He gives advice."[1]

— Christopher Columbus (1451-1506)
is credited with discovering America

CHAPTER 14

Expressions of God's Judgment (Part 1)

The next five chapters delineate various ways in which God carries out His judgment on nations. The severity of His judgment is in proportion to the seriousness of the sin itself. His judgment may range from of an economic collapse, an invasion from foreign powers, natural disasters, or acts of terror. To the casual observer, such incidents appear to be random and merely an unfortunate series of coincidences. However, the true and living God of Scripture who rules and reigns over the nations is orchestrating the events of history and filtering it all through His sovereign Hand which will ultimately culminate in the return of Jesus Christ for the establishment of His earthly Kingdom. He is an on-time God with nothing catching Him off-guard. Indeed, He is the One who has the hairs on our heads numbered and who sees every sparrow fall to the ground. Never this side of eternity will we fully understand the ways of our Lord for we are told that His thoughts are not our thoughts and His ways are not our ways. Yet, in the midst of this mysterious dimension of His Divine Plan, staying true to the holiness of His nature, He necessarily and lovingly chastens His children. Such chastisement also extends to nations, particularly those to whom much has been given in terms of His blessing, such as the Christian heritage that America has enjoyed.

My family and I have just returned from vacationing in Boston. What a city! We fell in love with the area, but seeing the history of this great city was another reminder of our nation's rich heritage. In the midst of the towering skyscrapers was the Old North Church where Paul Revere warned, "The British are coming! The British are coming!" In the heart of downtown Boston were the grave sites of Benjamin Franklin, Paul Revere, Samuel Adams, John Winthrop, John Hancock, Patrick Henry, and others of our Founding Fathers. These men paid the ultimate sacrifice for our freedom and the overwhelming majority of our Founders were committed Christians who pointed America toward the flawless principles of God's Word. To this day, we continue to enjoy many of the residual blessings of our Christian beginnings. The closest parallel to America is Israel herself, for indeed our Founders looked to what God said to Israel in the infancy of her existence and attempted to implement similar biblical principles to ensure the success of our nation. Clearly, our Founders understood that it is righteousness that exalts a nation and it is sin that brings it to shame. History certainly validates that God rewarded their efforts by elevating the United States of America as the greatest nation in world history. Our Founders clearly understood, however, that a departure from these founding principles would invoke the displeasure of God and lead to the nation's decline. They warned of this repeatedly in their writings.

What you will read in this "judgment" section of the book are warnings from God that Israel failed to heed and, thus, paid the consequences. Like Israel, God is getting our attention with warning after warning. But in prideful defiance, America looks the other way and persists in pursuing the path to destruction. Surely, we can agree that God has been exceedingly merciful and gracious. It is nothing less than remarkable that our nation still stands. He has held back our enemies. But, now are economy is hemorrhaging, natural disasters are intensifying, calamites are increasingly frequent. In short, God is turning up the heat. The case can be made that no nation in history has rejected God's truth and fallen out of favor with God more quickly than America. And now, we shall see what this means for our nation.

LESSONS FROM AMOS

We are living in momentous times, not unlike the days of Amos. It was a time of prosperity and pleasure, but to its detriment the nation rebelled against the Source of its blessing, God Himself. With today's technology, there's the opportunity of sinning more frequently but make no mistake, human nature has not changed. The same apathy and disregard for God that Israel displayed, America has done the same to a degree unparalleled in history. The very Bible that was once extolled and revered, is now assaulted and defamed. We stand without excuse because in the book of Amos, and throughout the Bible, we have one account after another of Israel choosing the very path we have embarked upon. What makes God's judgment all the more sobering is the fact that Israel was His "chosen nation." He had delivered them from slavery in Egypt. He provided for them in their wilderness years. He had entered into a covenant with them at Mount Sinai. He had given them His laws. In ways that were nothing less than miraculous, God expressed His blessing upon this, His special nation.

But all of that was about to change. Oh, His love for the nation remained equally as strong, but like a parent disciplining a rebellious child, God's holiness could not remain passive. On the outside, all appeared well. Israel sang God's praises. They were elegantly clothed, politically and militarily influential, displaying an abundance of food, luxurious homes, and the best entertainment the culture could supply. Yet, underneath this veneer was a cancer of moral decay that was destroying the nation, but strangely enough, no one seemed to notice. Except God! So, God raised up His prophet, Amos, to become His mouthpiece.

Amos was a shepherd from Tekoa (1:1; 7:14, 15), ten miles south of Jerusalem. Oddly enough, Amos was from the southern kingdom of Judah, but delivered his message to the northern kingdom of Israel. As you can imagine, this did not gain him favor with his audience. Furthermore, he was a layman, not a professional prophet, but called by God nonetheless. Like that of the other prophets, his message was discomforting and not seeker-friendly. He did not placate to the political correctness of his day. When he says that "God has sworn by His holiness" (4:2) he is reminding his audience that the attribute of God's justice is being activated. That is to say, the nation must brace itself because punishment is coming. Even more intriguing is the fact that he is making this bold proclamation at Bethel where the temple was located. These folks were faithful in their religious customs, they tithed, they offered sacrifices, and they gave various offerings. Amos was not impressed, nor was God. Amos goes so far to say that their form of worship was actually idolatry because they were imposing their way upon God's prescribed way. One can only imagine the glares and stares that he received. No doubt, he would have much preferred the sheep field. Although he was out of his comfort zone, to his credit, he stayed the course and preached what God put upon his heart.

One of the things God said in Amos 3:15, *"I will destroy the winter house along with the summer house; the houses of ivory shall perish, and the great houses shall have an end,"* says the Lord." This, of course, speaks of the wealth within the nation. Although many owned multiple houses, they were blinded by their riches while ignoring the oppressions that were being inflicted on the poor. Perhaps I am making more of this than necessary, but last week I visited Newport, Rhode Island, known for its mansions from a previous era in American history. Breathtakingly beautiful, no expense was spared in the construction of these massive edifices. Especially interesting was the fact that these homes were not the primary residences of their owners. They were summer homes worth untold millions of dollars with furnishings fit for a king. Now this is just one small town in our nation and is not intended as a criticism for anyone who can afford a second residence. It is simply a reminder that like Israel, we are a nation satiated with materialism and indulging the flesh with extravagance beyond description.

Wealth in itself was not the sin of Israel, but the manner by which such wealth was obtained. Exploiting the poor and using the courts to their own advantage, they were guilty of everything from bribery to obstruction of justice to unfair taxation, and slandering their critics. We are told, *"They hate the one who rebukes in the gate, and they abhor the one who speaks uprightly. Therefore, because you tread down the poor and take grain taxes from him, though you have built houses of hewn stone, yet you shall not dwell in them....For I know your manifold transgressions and your mighty sins: Afflicting the just and taking bribes; diverting the poor from justice at the gate. Therefore the prudent keep silent at that time, for it is an evil time."* (Amos 5:10-13) Furthermore, their religious observances were despicable to God. Listen to the Lord's disdain: *"I hate, I despise your feast days, and I do not savor your sacred assemblies. Though you offer Me burnt offerings and your grain offerings, I will not accept them, Nor will I regard your fattened peace offerings. Take away from Me the noise of your songs, for I will not hear the melody of your stringed instruments..."* (5:21-24)

Amos is speaking to a nation held in the grips of moral decay. He is shouting to the people, mincing no words, but offering a stinging rebuke for their complacency, rebellion, and forgetting the God who had once blessed them. Since the nation refused to heed the prophet's warning, God was left with no other option but to inflict righteous judgment. God proceeds to tell them He is fed up with their self-righteous, self-indulging, immoral lifestyle: *Behold I am weighed down by you, as a cart full of sheaves is weighed down. Therefore flight shall perish from the swift, the strong shall not strengthen his power, nor shall the mighty deliver himself; He shall not stand who handles the bow, the swift of foot shall not escape, nor shall he who rides a horse deliver himself. The most courageous men of might shall flee naked in that day," says the Lord."* (2:13-16) In simple terms, God is thundering His warning that "Despite your wealth, your military, your power, your wisdom, your technology, there is no one able to stand against the judgment I am about to bring." Let us not forget that the goal in all of this is repentance. The good news for us is that we still have time to repent. There is still hope for spiritual awakening. While merciful warning signs are being dispensed on our nation, it is our responsibility to respond to them. Furthermore, God's preachers must help our congregations understand and interpret the times in which we live.

THE LION IS ROARING!

Interestingly, Amos means "burden-bearer" implying that proclaiming such harsh denunciations year after year was a heavy burden for the prophet to shoulder. On more than one occasion he depicts God as a roaring lion. He says, *"The Lord roars from Zion (1:2)* and in chapter 3, verse 8 he once again declares that *"A lion has roared! Who will not fear? The Lord God has spoken!"* A lion roars when it is about to pounce on its prey. Like a clap of thunder, God is shouting his warning to Israel once again that a storm is approaching. The Lion of Judah is about to pounce! Anyone within hearing distance of a lion's roar knows to run for cover. Even hearing the roar of a lion conveys the nearness of judgment. The roar is a warning. There is time to escape. For America, the Lion is roaring. The question is, "Are we listening? Do we recognize the roar?" Perhaps the more fundamental question is, "How was the 'roaring of the Lion' finding expression for Israel?"

For starters, God withheld rain from the nation (4:7) so that severe drought occurred. Also locusts devoured their gardens and vineyards which, of course, impacted their economy (4:9). No doubt, there were those who assumed they were simply victims of a bad weather pattern or an unexplainable infestation of insects that was plaguing the nation. But verse 7 reads, "I withheld rain from you." Verse 9 says, "I blasted you with blight and mildew." God steps up and takes full responsibility for these calamities. You can read the text for yourself and see that God repeatedly sends one plague after another upon the nation, but the reoccurring phrase *"Yet you have not returned to Me,"* appears. We see it is verses, 6, 8, 9, 10, and 11. Such repetition is just another reminder of God's merciful desire not to punish, but to forgive.

God raises the question, *"Can two walk together, unless they are agreed? Will a lion roar in the forest when he has no prey?"* (3:3-4) This is the language of two people walking together in a covenant relationship. They meet, they date, and they proceed through life in a covenant marriage. But here the two are parting ways. No longer do they have anything in common. While reconciliation is always God's desire, there comes a time when repentance is no longer an option. A nation can reach the point of no return. God's warnings are not endless and His mercy will not always strive with man. His wrath is a last resort. That's why He issues one warning after another, year after year. However, such grace cannot be presumed upon. And Amos is telling Israel that it is too late.

FORTY YEARS OF WARNINGS.....

For four decades the prophet warned the people of impending judgment, and the ultimate death blow seems to correspond in severity with the seriousness of their calloused heart. In 3:10 we are told, "They do not know to do right." The population had lost all discernment between right and wrong. The next verse reads, *"Therefore, thus says the Lord God: An adversary shall be all around the land; He shall sap your strength from you, and your palaces shall be plundered."* And who shall be this adversary? In what form will this adversary appear? *"But, behold, I will raise up a nation against you, O house of Israel," says the Lord God of hosts; And they will afflict you...."* (6:14)

We dare not miss the application. While the nation was busy making money, and hypocritically practicing their religion, God was capturing their attention with famines, floods, droughts, blights, locusts, and epidemics, much of what we see in America now. Here it is, before our very eyes. Yet, I fear that we are prone to theologically explain it away or shrug our shoulders with the same indifference of the Israelites in Amos' day. I have articles in my files of blight disease, insects destroying thousands of acres, historic floods, historic droughts, historic wildfires, mudslides, snowfall, you name it. They have inundated our nation in recent years. We are experiencing record-setting natural disasters, but no one dares to call it what it is. With hardened hearts, we have a way of explaining everything in natural terms. It's just nature running its course. Finally, in Amos 4:12, as if the Lord has issued his final warning, we find the chilling words, *"Prepare to meet your God!"*

The ramifications for Israel lay in the fact that God was going to use Assyria, a wicked nation, as His ultimate instrument of judgment upon the Land. Floods had not worked. Drought had not worked. Pestilence had not worked. Disease had not worked. So, now the nation would be annihilated by a foreign power. God had actually become Israel's adversary. As seen in the previous chapters, America's moral compass is skewed, our military is depleted, our economy is in the tank, our educational system is distressed, our churches are weak and in decline, our families are fragmented with divorce, adultery, and pornography while our children are silently suffering and our streets are rampant with crime and gang-related activity. On top of this, we have an activist judiciary determined to transform America into something unrecognizable with the legalization of same-sex marriage being just one example. There is no doubt that we have activated the judgment of God.

It is no small thing when God declares war on the very religious system that prevailed within the nation. He says, *"In the day I punish Israel for their transgressions, I will also visit destruction on the altars of Bethel; and the horns of the altar shall be cut off and fall to the ground."* Even those who went to church every week were blinded to their sin. When describing the nation's ills, the church-going population never made the connection that they were a big part of the problem. When 2 Chronicles 7:14 is quoted, I often remind congregations that God is not calling the Supreme Court, Congress, or the ACLU to repentance. This verse is issuing the challenge for God's people to pray, humble themselves, seek His face, and turn from their wicked ways. Judgment must first begin at the house of God, but often the people stare listlessly as if the problem remains "out there" somewhere. Misguidedly, we still believe the change that needs to occur is in the White House while God is calling for change in His House. Many were encouraged by the results of 2016's Presidential election. My brother-in-law said recently, "The sky seems bluer, the grass seems greener, and the sun seems brighter. Everybody I meet seems to have a renewed hope for America." While I am not disparaging such optimism, a word of caution must be offered. That is, the source of America's problems is not, and never has been, political. Furthermore, America was just as sinful the day after the election as the day before. Once again, as important as the political landscape is, the fundamental problem lies in God's House, not the White House. More on this in a subsequent chapter.

In Amos 4:-1-4 the prophet refers to women as "Cows of Bashan," not exactly a flattering term. In fact, it was quite demeaning. He describes them as a bunch of well-fed cows who are just following the herd, content with an animalistic existence. This symbolic language reflects a self-focused value system with beauty and body being the primary concern. Some commentators refer to this language as a reference to women assuming leadership within the nation. That is, when a nation degenerates, the leaders who should be the trend-setters and standard-bearers are the women instead of the men. Yet, becoming animalistic in their mindset, their outlook is exclusively carnally-driven. When visiting New York City recently, young women were parading themselves on the busy sidewalks of Times Square, completely topless and wearing only a thong. Body paint covered their breasts and they were accosting passersby enticing them for a picture. The same is true in Vegas. Perhaps it is true for other cities, but it seems we have lost all sense of decency.

A FAMINE IN THE LAND

In 8:11 Amos warns the nation beginning with the word, "behold," another way of saying, "Listen up! Pay attention!" What follows is the description of a famine, but of a different sort. Rather than a physical famine, what he describes is a spiritual famine in which God no longer will be speaking to them or they will no longer be able to hear Him when He does speak. Regardless, it is a day when spiritual barrenness results from either preachers not preaching God's Word or the people simply refusing to attend and listen, or yet perhaps a combination of the two. Please note that the famine is caused by God Himself as an expression of His wrath. Verse 11 says, "I will send a famine in the Land." God promises to stop speaking to them or even when He does speak, they will not be able to hear His voice. Incidentally, the judgments pronounced by Amos are progressive in nature. That is, each one gets a little more severe. With this famine for God's Word being the last judgment, it is the most devastating blow to the nation. This explains much about our nation. When people turn their ears from the Divine Moral Compass of God's Word, there is moral degradation and decadence of every kind. When God's people turn their hearts from obeying God's Word, the result is powerless churches.

Are we not living in such day? The overwhelming majority of churches close their doors on Sunday evenings, and why is that? The people have spoken with their feet by refusing to attend, so pastors conclude that the best stewardship of their time can be spent elsewhere than investing 15-20 hours of sermon preparation for a spattering faithful few who show up. On the other hand, seldom is God's Word being preached without compromise. Most are tickling the ears, soft-peddling the Gospel, watering down Divine Truth, and inserting comedy, profanity or any tactic designed to capture attention for a 20-minute sermonette. We have theater seats, staging with strobe lights, and crowds gathered with coffee in hand while embracing an entertainment mindset that is ready for the show to begin. Hey, I am not opposed to utilizing the best technology, the most comfortable settings, or the highest standards of talent available in order to make the worship experience the most positive, uplifting event of the week. However, it is all too easy to displace the centrality of the proclamation of God's Word with a performance mentality that centers on music, drama, and other items that may be "attention-getters" but fail to give God's Word its proper respect. After all, God has magnified His Word above all His Name (Psa. 138:2) and when we assemble for worship we dare not substitute it or relegate it to a lesser place of prominence. I attend one of the great churches in America, First Baptist of Woodstock, Georgia, a congregation of about 7,000 in attendance. Our 9:30 service has a large orchestra that electrifies the atmosphere with vibrant praise music. Our choir permeates the auditorium with its unified voices of praise that reflects the radiance of His glory. Different praise teams from week to week are packed with talented musicians, many of whom could audition for Broadway. With such abundant talent, it would be easy to supplant God's Word with forty-five minutes of music and 20 minutes of sermon. But no, we sing two sets of worship songs, special music, and then

40-45 minutes allotted for the sermon. God's Word is the focus! Such, however, is not the case in most of our churches. Thus, the service is often designed to draw the crowds, having entertained them with performance-driven worship, in hopes that they will return. Call it seeker-friendly or whatever, but there is a famine for the Word of God in today's culture.

Other churches are liturgical with a coldness and deadness that comes more closely to resembling a funeral service for a dead corpse than the celebration of a risen Savior. Multitudes in our society are disillusioned with the hypocrisy, staleness, and shallowness of the service. They leave the same as they came. People want to feel good. They want to be entertained. They do not want to be challenged or confronted with sin or straight Bible-preaching. Guys like me are out of step with the times. We're called "old school," and dinosaurs who preach too long and too hard. Never do I want to be obnoxious, offensive, or unkind. Yet, truth by its very nature can often be offensive, but when spoken in love and authoritatively under the Spirit's anointing, conviction falls and life-change occurs.

The Hebrew word Amos uses for "hearing" is the word "shama" which means to listen intelligently. Thus, the Jewish people were hearing the words of the prophets, but they weren't taking action with their obedience. Again, this is where the American Church is today. Throughout the book of Hebrews, we find the admonition "Today, if you hear My voice, harden not your hearts." To hear God's Word without obeying God's Word produces a hardened heart. The same sun that melts the ice hardens the clay. For decades the American Church has sat under the Word, but suppressed the Truth by refusing to obey. The result is a spiritual callousness that manifests itself in complacency. This, to me, helps explains the prevalent lethargy characterizing so many of our churches.

IT'S A STRANGE DAY

Perhaps "unsettling" or "disturbing" would be better descriptions for the modern church's approach to ministry. Many preachers refuse to preach on hell, immorality, or repentance. Others approach the pulpit with the motivation of insuring that the congregation will exit the building feeling good and happy. By the thousands, many sit in our congregations who are living in adultery, enslaved to sexual sin, addicted to chemical substances, idolizing money, and worshiping sports. Knowing they should be better and do better, many walk through the doors of our churches hoping to hear a Word from God. Instead, the pulpits are silent for fear of being offensive or sounding judgmental or worse yet, losing members that results in declining numbers.

To counter such risk, many play it safe by resorting to positive thinking sermons, a pop psychology approach that talks about being successful, healthy and wealthy. Television preachers offering prayer cloths for purchase or selling water for healing or soliciting money for a "prophetic" word over their lives, is an embarrassment for those of us in vocational ministry. The lack of discernment and gullibility of people is sickening, but it is symptomatic of the famine.

One of the great preachers of the twentieth century, Martyn Lloyd-Jones, observed this decline in preaching by saying that if you had visited London a hundred years ago, your problem would have been which of the great preachers to go and listen to. He said, "There were a great many of them, and the problem was which of them to select. But today the position is entirely different. There is no problem at all. Is there *any* preacher that you want to go and listen to, who is worth your time to go and listen to? There is a scarcity of preachers because, it seems to me, people no longer believe in preaching as they once did." [2] Another man said that he had been preaching for years and was considered to be a good preacher. But no one wanted a good preacher. They wanted singers and quiet men to give a few words verse-by-verse. They wanted to hear soft sermons, but did not want preaching. In fact, he was criticized for bold preaching and was actually dismissed from some churches for preaching so passionately. His name was John Wesley. George Whitefield could say the same.[3] Our day is no different.

Once again, let's be clear. The famine described is not due to a lack of opportunity to hear God's Word. My goodness, we have small churches, mega-churches, and everything in-between. We have emotionally-charged charismatic churches, cold-liturgical churches, and everything in-between. Likewise, we have Bibles in all shapes and sizes. Bibles for teens, Bibles for women, Bibles for men, Bibles for veterans, Bibles on eschatology, Bibles on apologetics, a Bible for practically every demographic group imaginable. Furthermore, we have more preachers than any country in the world, but what we don't have are congregations that choose to obey. Nor do we have auditoriums overflowing with capacity crowds. This issue was addressed in a previous chapter so I'll refrain from being repetitious other than to mention that Barna Research finds only 7% of professing Christians live by a Biblical worldview. That is, 93% of professing Christians do not base their lives, their habits, or their relationships on what the Bible says. Quite simply, they do not see the world through the eyes of Scripture.[4] This, too, reflects a famine of hearing God's Word.

Biblical Illiteracy Abounds

"Just how bad is it?" you may ask. You decide. In an article by Al Mohler, president of Southern Baptist Theological Seminary in Louisville, Kentucky, fewer than half of all adults can name the four Gospels. Barna Research reports that 60 percent of Americans cannot name five of the Ten Commandments. Multiple surveys indicate that 82 percent of Americans believe that "God helps those who help themselves," is a Bible verse. What is even more disturbing is that 81 percent of born-again Christians do as well. A majority of adults think the Bible teaches that the most important purpose in life is taking care of one's family. Fifty percent of graduating high school students thought Sodom and Gomorrah were husband and wife. In another poll, an embarrassing number of respondents indicated that the Sermon on the Mount was preached by Billy Graham. [5] Is it any wonder that we find ourselves in our present condition? Youth pastors are expected to draw crowds of students, retain their attention, and produce Christ-honoring disciples. Easier said than done. Everyone is distracted these days, pastors included. We're all busy, too busy for our own good and our own growth. Here's the reality: We will not live higher than our beliefs. We live in a dumbed-down society with dumbed-down beliefs that have created dumb citizens unable to discern right from wrong.

Yet, 25 million copies of the Bible are sold in the United States annually with nine out of 10 homes owning a Bible. Despite this fact, only 16 percent of churchgoers read the bible daily and 25 percent of churchgoers don't read the Bible at all. About 50 percent of those sitting in our congregations read their Bible once or twice per month, if that much. [6] In another study, LifeWay research found that 45 percent of those who regularly attend church read the Bible more than once a week. [7] This means that 55 percent fail to do so. With the average American owning three Bibles and translations galore available, we stand without excuse. To say that we are a biblically illiterate nation is not an overstatement nor is it misrepresenting the facts to say that our churches are likewise biblically illiterate. A George Barna study found that the majority of professing Christians do not believe in the existence of Satan or the Holy Spirit. Twenty-two percent believe that Jesus sinned while he was on earth. [8]

Before closing out this chapter, let us not forget that despite having more churches, more Bibles, more preachers, more Christian schools, more Christian bookstores, and more Christian media, America is in the midst of a famine for the Word of God. Such famine is obviously not due to a lack of opportunity, but an unwillingness to hear and respond in obedience. As the Lord said of Israel, we have become a stiff-necked generation. In Amos' day, the Lord was the instigator of such judgment. For us, when observing the abundance of biblical resources available, but then seeing the decline in our churches, their powerless influence in society, and all the statistical data that reinforces the accusations of hypocrisy(i.e. little difference in the moral standards of unbelievers versus that of professing Christians), one is led to conclude that God's judgment has fallen upon our nation with a similar famine for the Word as in the day of Amos.

Noah Webster's View on Education and Freedom

"Education is useless without the Bible. The Bible was America's basic text book in all fields. The Christian religion, in its purity, is the basis or rather the source of all genuine freedom in government. Almost all the civil liberty now enjoyed in the world owes its origin to the principles of the Christian religion... The religion which has introduced civil liberty is the religion of Christ and His apostles....The moral principles and precepts contained in the Scriptures ought to form the basis of all of our civil constitutions and laws." [1]

Noah Webster's View on Elections and Politics

"If the citizens neglect their duty and place unprincipled men in office, the government will soon be corrupted; laws will be made not for the public good so much as for the selfish or local purposes; Corrupt or incompetent men will be appointed to execute the laws; the public revenues will be squandered on unworthy men; and the rights of the citizens will be violated or disregarded. If a republican government fails to secure public prosperity and happiness, it must be because the citizens neglect the divine commands, and elect bad men to make and administer the laws."[2]

— Noah Webster (1758-1843)
known as the "Schoolmaster of the Nation," compiled the American Dictionary of the English Language. He was elected for nine terms to Connecticut's General Assembly and three terms to Massachusetts' Legislature

CHAPTER 15

Expressions of God's Judgment (Part 2)

Seldom do Americans perceive God as having anything to do with presidential elections. But in Isaiah 3:4 we read, *"I will give children to be their princes, and babes shall rule over them."* The backdrop for this passage sees an influx of pagans influencing Judah to abandon its religious heritage of worshipping the true and living God. Though wealthy and militarily powerful, the nation had begun worshiping the false gods of surrounding nations that had migrated into the country. Abandoning her religious heritage was no small thing because God had made it clear in Exodus 20:3-4: *"You shall have no other gods before Me. You shall not make for yourself a carved image—any likeness of anything that is in heaven above, or that is in the earth beneath, or that is in the water under the earth; you shall not bow down to them nor serve them. For I, the Lord your God, am a jealous God, visiting the iniquity of the fathers upon the children to the third and fourth generations of those who hate Me, but showing mercy to thousands, to those who love Me and keep My commandments."* Perhaps nothing activates the wrath of God any quicker than for a person or nation to abandon the worship of Almighty God with some cheap man-made substitution. An idol is anything that holds top priority in our lives, the place reserved only for God, be it money, hobbies, pleasure, sports, or self. From Genesis to Revelation, we see that He is a jealous God and will have no rivals. After all, He alone is our Creator, our Redeemer, and the Giver of every good and perfect gift. Thus, He alone is worthy of our allegiance. And certainly, America has been the recipient of His blessings, all traceable to our reverence for His

Word and our devotion to Jesus Christ as shown by the writings of our Founding Fathers and evidenced by the first 100 universities begun for the purpose of training ministers in His Gospel.

Yet, when Judah departed from the God of her Fathers, she did so to her own demise. God replaced stable, strong leadership with "children and babes." Such description is not intended as a reference to age, but to a lack of experience and wisdom. It is apparent, therefore, that God sometimes judges a nation by removing wise leadership, causing the nation to suffer the dire consequences. In other words, those who govern the nation will not be qualified to do so. Rather, they will display incompetence, selfishness, and greediness, the very characteristics of young children and babies. Thus, God gives the nation the leadership it deserves instead of what it needs.

Obama, in my opinion, fell into this category. Considered by a majority of Americans to be the worst president since World War II, [3] this man's transgressions against our nation are too numerable to list. But here is a brief sampling of just a few grievances. There was the time when He declared that America is not a Christian nation nor is it an exceptional nation any more than "the Brits believe in British exceptionalism and the Greeks believe in Greek exceptionalism." [4] From the cancellation of placing U.S. defensive missiles in Poland to major reductions of America's nuclear arsenal, his negative influence on our military will long remain after he leaves office. US retreats in Iraq and Afghanistan were proven to be abysmal failures; unprecedented reductions of our nation's military has made us vulnerable unlike anything seen in modern history; the purging of our military's most effective military officers was unconscionable, not to mention admitting to the world that his Libyan philosophy was to lead from behind; he erased red lines in Syria after making empty threats over Assad's use of chemical weapons against its citizens, another global embarrassment. Who will ever forget the Benghazi scandal in which his administration ignored our diplomats' plea for help, resulting in their deaths, including Ambassador Stevens and then lying about the attack by saying it was the result of a video; he enabled Russian aggression in the Ukraine; his ineptitude in understanding the imminent threat of terrorism, calling ISIS the JV Squad, then his reluctance to defeat them or even to identify the enemy as Islamic extremist terrorism has been baffling to the nation; his betrayal of Israel and open disdain for Benjamin Netanyahu by refusing to meet with him during his trip to Washington was shameful. Yet, Obama's disdain for Netanyahu was so deep that he actually sent an envoy to Israel for the purpose of preventing his re-election His international leadership has been disastrous and America's global respect has declined immensely.

On the domestic front, his leadership has been equally as inept. His $800 billion stimulus bill was accompanied by the government take-over of two of the nation's big three automobile companies. The mishandling of the stimulus spending is well-documented. The infamous takeover of healthcare, commonly known as "Obamacare," was based upon lie after lie promising the American people a reduction in costs and if you like your physician you can keep your physician, none of which were true. Hundreds of thousands of dollars were wasted just trying to create a functional website for Obamacare. This healthcare legislation was passed without one Republican vote and has been a nightmare for insurance companies and physicians alike. Race relations under Obama are worse than they have been in over 40 years. [5]

IS OBAMA A MUSLIM?

This is a question many have raised only because of his unrestrained sentiments for the Muslim faith. For example, Obama has praised the moon god, Allah, and hosted a celebratory dinner to open the month of Ramadan held in the state dining room while refusing to attend the 100th anniversary of the Boy Scouts, perceived to be a Christian organization. He once refused to attend the National Day of Prayer, claiming it to be offensive to non-Christians. Yet, he has no problem offending Christians by showing his reverence for Islam in bowing down to Saudi Arabia's king Abdullah and describing the Muslim call to prayer as "one of the prettiest sounds on the Earth." [6] He has stated that he would side with the Muslims if the political winds shifted and gives credit to the Quran as directing his life. [7] Most disturbing were his executive orders to remove references of "Islamic terrorist" from all US military and law enforcement counter-terrorism training manuals while at the same time compiling a list of Americans whom he and his administration considered to be potential terrorists. Included in the list were bible-believing Christians. During his first presidential campaign, he had a Freudian slip when he told interviewer George Stephanopoulos, "You're absolutely right that John McCain has not talked about my Muslim faith…." These are only small samplings of his admiration for Islam while at the same time repeatedly denigrating Christianity.

GIVING US WHAT WE DESERVE

Throughout Scripture God sets up kings and takes down kings to serve His purpose. Man is not in control, God is. One of the final judgments God exerts on a nation is by giving them the leaders they deserve which hastens their destruction. In the next chapter, I will explain why I believe that God has given America over to its own desires, but a part of this "giving up" a nation is reflected in the leadership the country has elected. Never was this more apparent than in the 2016 presidential election. On the Republican side of the ticket, the primaries saw 17 candidates vying for the top spot. By far, it was the most competent and godly group of candidates in recent memory, perhaps ever. Though representing various denominations, those who spoke openly about their faith in Christ or trust in God included Ted Cruz, Ben Carson, Marco Rubio, Mike Huckabee, Rick Santorum, Rick Perry, Bobby Jindal, John Kasich, and Scott Walker. While the other candidates were not opposed to Christianity, these nine had strong credentials as evangelical Christians even though their denominational affiliation may have appeared otherwise. With the exception of Carson, the political track record of these men was remarkable. Each one could point to an undeniably impressive resume. Yet, the candidate the nation overwhelmingly chose was Donald Trump, a man with no political experience. His brash style, profane language, bullyish name-calling and off-the-cuff statements that appeared emotionally impulsive and often retaliatory, won him more votes than any Republican candidate in history. Trump was perceived as a narcissistic egomaniac. But his victory signaled a shift among Republican voters. There was a time when experienced, competent, and strong Christian leadership would have endeared itself to the American people. But Americans were "fed up" with the empty rhetoric, the do-nothing congress, and the broken promises of past Republican candidates. The electorate was disgusted with establishment politics. They wanted an outsider, someone to shake things up and get things done. Commitment to Christ, political experience, and moral standards were no longer major considerations.

However, while Trump's victory surpassed any Republican primary in history, all was not well within the Party. His insulting comments, such as the face of Carly Fiorina and Heidi Cruz did not set well with many. Giving the candidate's names such as Lyin' Ted, Little Marco, or Low Energy Jeb was common throughout his campaign. So, when the Republicans marched into Cleveland for its national convention, it did so as a divided Party. Many of its leaders boycotted the Convention by refusing to attend, including the Bush Family, John McCain, Lindsey Graham, and most notably, John Kasich. As the sitting governor of Ohio, it was only common courtesy and political etiquette to welcome the delegates to the great state of Ohio. But no, Kasich chose to distance himself by not even attending, a glaring failure and talking point throughout the week. But, an even greater headline was that of Ted Cruz who, surprisingly, was given a place on the program as one of the keynote speakers. Being Trump's stiffest opposition during the primaries, news analysts were wondering if he would endorse Trump. After all, this was the national Convention; one designed to let bygones be bygones, and unify the Party to defeat Hillary. But no. When it became apparent during his speech that an endorsement was not forthcoming, the crowd literally booed him off the platform. The next morning in a town hall press conference, he dug in deeper and said, "I don't make it a practice of supporting someone who defames my wife and my father." The night of Cruz' speech was designed to be Mike Pence's night, Trump's choice for his running mate. But the Cruz debacle overshadowed everyone and multiple commentators, including Charles Krauthammer, believe that Cruz committed political suicide. Trump tried picking up the pieces with an outstanding final speech, but the damage had been done. Republicans left Cleveland just as divided as they had arrived.

On the other side of the aisle, the only two candidates the Dems could put forth were Hillary Clinton and Bernie Sanders. Sanders was/is a self-avowed socialist who called for political revolution in America and has no church affiliation. Yet, in state after state Sanders' campaign was raising more money and gaining more votes as students rallied to his cause, perhaps because his platform proposed a free college education paid for by the government.

Clinton, on the other hand, was trying to run a campaign while also appearing before Congressional Investigative committees, FBI interrogations, and a feeding frenzy of news reporters regarding classified security breaches during her tenure as Secretary of State.

In short, she was staring prison time in the face while running for the highest office in the Land, a first in American history. A House panel, led by South Carolina Congressman Trey Gowdy, grilled FBI Director James Comey on his recommendation not to prosecute Clinton. Here is a brief excerpt of Gowdy's interrogation of Director Comey:

Gowdy: Secretary Clinton said there was nothing marked classified on her e-mails sent or received. Was that true?

Comey: That's not true. There were a small number of portion markings on I think three of the documents.

Gowdy:: Secretary Clinton said, "I did not e-mail any classified information to anyone. On my e-mail there was no classified material." Is that true?

Comey: There was classified information e-mailed.

Gowdy: Secretary Clinton used one device, was that true?

Comey: She used multiple devices during the four years of her term as Secretary of State.

Gowdy: Secretary Clinton said all work-related e-mails were returned to the State Department. Was that true?

Comey: No. We found work-related e-mails, thousands that were not returned.

Gowdy: Secretary Clinton said neither she nor anyone else deleted work-related e-mails from her personal account.

Comey: We found traces of work-related e-mails in—on devices or in space. Whether they were deleted or when a server was changed out, something happened to them, there's no doubt that the work-related e-mails were removed electronically from the system.

Gowdy: Secretary Clinton said her lawyers read every one of the e-mails and were overly inclusive. Did her lawyers read the e-mail content individually?

Comey: No

Since criminal prosecution has to do with evidence of intent and consciousness of guilt, Gowdy proceeded to methodically and systematically rip Clinton by saying to Director Comey, "Two days ago, Director, you said a reasonable person in her position should have known a private email was no place to send and receive classified information. You're right. An average person does know not to do that. This is no average person. This is a former First Lady, a former United States senator, and a former Secretary of State that the president now contends is the most competent, qualified person to be president since Thomas Jefferson. He didn't say that in '08 but says it now. She affirmatively rejected efforts to give her a state.gov account, kept the private emails for almost two years and only turned them over to Congress because we found out she had a private email account. So you have a rogue email system set up before she took the oath of office, thousands of what we now know to be classified emails, some of which were classified at the time. One of her more frequent email comrades was hacked and you don't know whether or not she was. And this scheme took place over a long period of time and results in the destruction of public records and yet you say there is insufficient evidence of intent. You say she was extremely careless, but not intentionally so. My time is out but this is really important. You mentioned there's no precedent for criminal prosecution. My fear is there still isn't. There's nothing to keep a future Secretary of State or President from this exact same email scheme or their staff. And my real fear is this, what the chairman touched upon, this double track justice system that is rightly or wrongly perceived in this country. That if you are a private in the Army and email yourself classified information you will be kicked out. But if you are Hillary Clinton, and you seek a promotion to Commander-in-Chief, you will not be. So what I hope you can do today is help the average person, the reasonable person you made reference to, the reasonable person understand why she appears to be treated differently than the rest of us would be." [7] Indeed, the message received by Americans is that Hillary Clinton was given preferential treatment and only reinforces the belief that Washington politics is corrupt. Without question, the entire email scandal and all that surrounded it led millions to conclude that her actions went beyond incompetence and a lack of good judgment. Rather, millions of Americans were convinced that she was an extension of political corruption with the Beltway and voters marched to their precincts to express their displeasure. Thus, Trump capitalized on his "Drain the Swamp" mantra.

The point in re-visiting this investigation is that Clinton repeatedly looked the cameras and American people in the eye and lied again, and again, and again. This is what the FBI Director clearly confirmed. Amazingly, in a subsequent interview with Chris Wallace on Fox News, with a transcript of the Comey interview in his hands, Wallace called her out on the lies that Director Comey clearly stated, but she had the audacity to look him squarely in the eyes with a straight face and say the following: "Chris, that's not what I heard Director Comey say, and I thank you for giving me the opportunity to, in my view, clarify. Director Comey said that my answers were truthful, and what I've said is consistent with what I told the American people..." [8] I find this appalling and an insult to the intelligence of the American people. There must be a psychological term for a person who lies so much that they actually believe they're telling the truth even when being shown the transcript of repeated contradictions with the truth. I call it "delusional." Yet, despite her devious, deceptive lies, she won the Democratic primary as their candidate for President of the United States. Granted, only 37 percent of people believed that she was honest and trustworthy, "But let's make her our President nevertheless."[9] One commentator's assessment was, "The American people know that she's a liar and untrustworthy. That's not the issue. What's important is, they don't care." Both Trump and Clinton's nomination for President speak volumes about the moral shift in the American culture. Furthermore, in 2008 Mitt Romney ran against Obama, a freshman senator who had been a community organizer. The economy was in shambles, the beginnings of The Great Recession. Romney should have won easily, but again, conservatives were blinded to this shift in American culture. It is apparent that no longer is it the most qualified, the most moral, or the most experienced candidate that guarantees a run for the presidency. At one time, character mattered. Today, as part of God's judgment, it appears that we are getting what we deserve.

Under his watch, Obama has accumulated more debt than all of the prior US presidents combined. [10] Other countries own half of all outstanding US debt, including China, not exactly an ally. As stated in a previous chapter, our military has been decimated under Obama's watch. Our military leaders have decried Obama's reduction of military weapons and personnel, warning him that our national security is being put at risk.

America, founded on Judeo-Christian principles, has turned its back on God and our death spiral has only accelerated as we continue to defy the warning signs God is giving us. The removal of prayer from public schools, the eradication of the Ten Commandments from schools and courthouses, the banning of valedictorian speeches that mention God, the persecution of Christians in the military, the killing of 58 million unborn babies while still in the mother's womb, and the legalization of homosexual marriages have all combined to push us down the slope of moral depravity. Arrogance, rebellion, blasphemy, and abomination are words that quickly come to mind. Just as there will be degrees of punishment in hell, some sins are considered worse than others, contrary to what we often hear. It seems that both historically and biblically, whenever a nation embraces homosexuality as an acceptable alternative lifestyle and, of all things, sanctions same-sex marriage, that nation is in its final stages of moral corruption and destruction. Only God knows if we have gone beyond the point of no return.

One of the most perplexing negotiated deals in American history, one that is regarded as the most catastrophic in our nation's history, occurred when Obama's Secretary of State John Kerry was dispatched to Iran to cut the deal. Bear in mind that Iran is the world's leading sponsor of terrorism and known for its constant chanting "Death to America" and "Death to Israel," even while the deal was being negotiated! The deal actually calls for the United States to defend Iran against any attacks from an outside country, including Israel. We may never know all the details, but it is reported that we agreed to remove sanctions and compensate Iran, a nation committed to our destruction, $150 billion not to develop a nuclear weapon for ten years. After this deadline is met, Iran may move forward with its nuclear program. Think about that. Bankrupt as we are, we paid $150 billion for this hater of America to use those funds against us. Perhaps I am missing something, but this is naiveté' on steroids.

Equally as disturbing is the fact that the Obama Administration repeatedly leaked classified information regarding Israel and actually stopped weapons shipment to Israel while it was taking on thousands of incoming missiles from Hamas terrorists. When Obama found out that Israel had asked the Defense Department for shipments of Hellfire missiles, he personally stepped in and blocked the shipments. [11] When God promises in Genesis 12:3 to bless those who bless Israel and curse those who curse Israel, such treatment of Israel by the Obama Administration has jeopardized America's national security. Historically, America's greatest line of defense has been our allied relationship with Israel. But today, thanks to Obama's radical agenda, Islamists take precedence over Israel. At least, that's the perception. In Zechariah 2:8, the Lord warns, "....he who touches you (Israel) touches the apple of His eye." This is language that should bring grave concern to every God-fearing American. While our government diplomats sat at the negotiating table with the world's leading sponsor of terrorism, Iranians were chanting obscenities outside the negotiating halls with "Death to America!" Having violated 20 previous international treaties, what could possibly convince US officials of their trustworthiness now?

During a 2004 interview, Chicago Sun Times reporter Cathleen Falsani, asked then State Senator Barack Obama "What is sin?" His reply was revealing when he defined sin as "Being out of alignment with my values." What are those values? According to his record as a senator, he voted against protecting babies who survived abortion in favor of leaving them to die. [12] In fact, he voted against the Born Alive Infant Protection Act four times. On his third day in office he repealed the pro-life "Mexico City Policy" that had prevented groups performing and promoting abortion from receiving U.S. foreign aid funds. Under Obama Planned Parenthood, the largest abortion provider in America, taxpayer funding jumped from 33 percent to nearly 50 percent with an annual investment of $487 million going to Planned Parenthood. When he told the nation's largest baby-killing organization that "You have a president who is right there with you," he wasn't kidding. He actually refused to sign an emergency budget that put funding the military at risk until Planned Parenthood funding was included in the budget. [13] Do I need to remind the reader of the Planned Parenthood executive who was secretly recorded describing the barbaric procedure of crushing the baby's organs and then another executive was negotiating compensation for the baby's body parts?

Given this horrific practice and given the fact that our own president stamped his approval on such, the words of Psalm 106:35-42 are particularly pertinent: *"But they mingled with the Gentiles and learned their works. They served their idols, which became a snare to them. They even sacrificed their sons and their daughters to demons, and shed innocent blood, the blood of their sons and daughters, whom they sacrificed to the idols of Canaan; and the land was polluted with blood. Thus they were defiled by their own works, and played the harlot by their own deeds.* ***Therefore the wrath of the Lord was kindled against His people, so that He abhorred His own inheritance. And He gave them into the hand of the Gentiles, and those who hated them ruled over them. Their enemies also oppressed them, and they were brought into subjection under their hand."*** It will soon be fifty years since the historic and horrific ruling by our Supreme Court to legalize the killing of unborn babies within the wombs of their mothers, but I fear that we've become inoculated to the hatred God has for this sinful action, but it does not require a seminary degree to understand the high regard our Creator has for the sanctity of life.

Each is entitled to his or her own opinion. Understandably, there will be disagreements, but what we do know is that God's judgments are real, his methods are varied, and one that Scripture clearly identifies is that of giving a rebellious nation rulers that accelerates its destruction. This chapter closes with reminders from some gleanings in the book of Daniel:

"He removes kings and raises up kings. . . ." (2:21)

". . . you know that the Most High rules in the kingdom of men, and gives it to whomever He chooses." (4:25)

". . . until you know that the Most High rules in the kingdom of men, and gives it to whomever He chooses." (4:31)

". . . till he knew that the Most High God rules in the kingdom of men, and appoints over it whomever He chooses." (5:21)

Repetition in Scripture is one way God has of making His point. God still rules in the kingdom of men, and He still removes and raises up rulers, according to His choosing. Let us pray for His mercy in giving us the leader we need, not what we deserve.

At the time of this writing, in all fairness to President-elect Trump, his cabinet selections have been stellar, his Supreme Court nominee is a conservative originalist similar to Scalia, several evangelical Christians sit on his cabinet, and he has kept billions of dollars from leaving our country by providing incentives to corporations even before being sworn in as President. The stock market reached historic highs at least seventeen times since Trump's election. So, I will sit back with the rest of the nation and observe from afar, but faithfully pray for Donald J. Trump and his administration. As of now, he has made good on his campaign promises and deserves the full support of the American people, especially those who "held their nose" and voted for him. He has his hands full in correcting the many political potholes produced from eight long years of leading from behind.

Winthrop's Motivation in Coming to America

"Whereas we all came to these parts of America with the same end and aim, namely, to advance the kingdom of our Lord Jesus Christ, and to enjoy the liberties of the Gospel thereof with purities and peace, and for preserving and propagating the truth and liberties of the gospel. I will ever walk humbly before my God, and meekly, mildly, and gently towards all men…to give myself—my life, my wits, my health, my wealth—to the service of my God and Savior.."[1]

— John Winthrop (1588-1649)
was the founder and first Governor of Massachusetts and elected twelve times

CHAPTER 16

Expressions of God's Judgment (Part 3)

The inability or unwillingness of a nation to hear God's Word along with God giving that nation incompetent leadership are two of the most severe expressions of God's judgment imaginable. For America, by every appearance the evidence seems to validate this very claim. Yet, there is a third expression of God's judgment which results in a spinoff of several other judgments, not unlike a tornado producing smaller funnel clouds or the strong winds from a hurricane creating other catastrophic weather conditions such as hail, tornadoes, and flooding. This expression of divine retribution is none other than God removing His hedge of protection from our nation.

THE DOCTRINE OF HEDGES

In Job 1:10, God placed a hedge of protection around Job which Satan was unable to penetrate. Ecclesiastes 10:8 says, "Whoever breaks through a hedge or wall will be bitten by a serpent." That is to say when the hedge is removed Satan moves in to kill, steal, and destroy. The Hebrew word for "hedge" actually means "a wall." In biblical times a hedge was a defensive wall built around a city and comprised of stones. Inside these stones were poisonous serpents. When the hedge was broken, the serpents would strike innocent victims. So, God had placed a spiritual hedge around Job and all of his family and possessions so that Satan could not touch him without God's permission.

The same was true of ancient Israel. In Isaiah 5:1-5, God refers to Israel as a vineyard, but because of her rebellion there was no fruit. So, God said, "I'll take down the hedge." As a result, Israel was trampled by her enemies. The passage reads like this: *"Now let me sing to my Well-beloved. A song of my Beloved regarding His vineyard: My well-beloved has a vineyard on a very fruitful hill. (He's referring to Israel as a vine or vineyard) He dug it up and cleared out its stones, and planted it with the choicest vine. He built a tower in its midst, and also made a winepress in it; so He expected it to bring forth good grapes, but it brought forth wild grapes. And now, O inhabitants of Jerusalem and men of Judah, Judge between Me and My vineyard. I will take away its hedge, and it shall be burned."*

God is saying, "I created the nation of Israel, I planted them, I prospered them, I blessed them, I did all I could for them. I even placed a hedge of protection around them. But when I came to get My fruit, instead of a sweet cluster of grapes, the fruit was rotten, wild, and worthless." Because of the nation's disobedient and defiant attitude toward God, God declared to Israel, "I am removing the hedge that I placed around you." The parallels for America should be obvious. From the infancy of our nation until the past few decades, America has enjoyed God's protective hedge and unparalleled blessings. For ancient Israel, her first line of defense was not weapons or diplomacy, but God Himself. The same has been true for America. Today, however, we are in grave danger as the divine hedge that once protected us is now removed.

In Scripture, the words "hedge, shield, and wall" are synonymous. These words are interchangeable and they speak of God's covering. God was Job's shield and was untouchable by any enemy. God's presence surrounded him like a wall. To Abraham, God said "I am a hedge and wall about you on all sides—you have nothing to fear from any enemy." (Genesis 15:1) When the Bible says the hedge is removed, it actually means the presence of the Lord leaves. So, the hedge is a metaphor for spiritual protection. Yet, we have declared war on God.

Have you ever wondered why our nation has been so blessed? Why were we exalted as the greatest nation in world history? One reason, "Righteousness exalts a nation, but sin is a reproach to any people." Why is it that for over two hundred years pestilence, terror, and wars that reached the shores of other nations, never reached ours? Why is it that other nations have looked to us to lend them food and to send them aid in times of international crisis? Why do millions of immigrants flee their countries and come to America with the hope of seeing their dreams fulfilled? Quite simply, no other nation had a Christian beginning such as America. No other nation in history was founded on biblical principles like America. This is not fabrication, imagination, or speculation. This is a fact of history, but one that has been expunged from our textbooks so the vast majority of Americans, even our school teachers who are products of government-run schools, are often oblivious to this reality. Our Pilgrim forefathers wrote the Mayflower Compact while crossing the waters to come this Land and in their own words they said, "The purpose for coming to these shores is for the glory of God and the propagation of the Gospel of our Lord and Savior, Jesus Christ." History is replete with examples of how God's protective hedge has been upon us.

Sadly, today we have told God that there is no room for Him in our nation. With a clinched fist toward Heaven, we've told Him to remove His hedge. "When did we say that?" you might ask. Through our actions we have told Him "Take Your prayers, take Your Commandments, take Your Word, take your Name, take creation, take the pledge, take Christmas, take anything that resembles Christianity and remove it from our sight and the hearing of our children's schools, take the name of Jesus and just go back to Heaven and leave us alone! Remove them all from the laws of our land. We can make it on our own." By our actions, that is precisely the message we have sent to God. So, we've expelled God from our schools and our government. He's now impeaching America by removing His hedge of protection. This means we are left to our own devices, our own counsels, and our own wisdom for the future of our Land. We are vulnerable to our enemies as never before. There are many ramifications and applications that can be traced to God removing His hedge of protection, but I'm convinced that terrorist attacks, the influx of illegal immigrants by the millions, and many of today's natural disasters are the result of our blatant and collective rebellion toward the God of our Fathers and His displeasure has reached a tipping point. The protective hedge that America has known throughout most of its history is no longer present. Look around. The signs of decline are everywhere.

I believe 9/11 may very well be an example of what we're describing. There is a risk of being misunderstood here, so let me be very clear. God did not cause 9/11 and God did not initiate 9/11, but once the hedge is removed, we are vulnerable to satanic attack. Forty-nine people died in Orlando in the worst mass shooting of our nation's history and the worst terrorist attack since 9/11. These and other random mass killings are becoming so prevalent, unlike anything we've ever witnessed, that it causes us to wonder, "What in the world is going on?" Scripture teaches the judgment of abandonment. The wickedness of turning our backs on the God who has been the Source of our heritage and blessing has invoked His anger. Think about it. Leading the world in immorality and exporting it throughout the planet has made us the moral polluter of the planet. We have terrorized our teachers into believing they will lose their jobs if they even mention Jesus to their students. We have mandated the teaching of atheistic evolution while prohibiting the truth of creationism. The cumulative effect of the Supreme Court's godless rulings has activated the wrath of God. Please hear me out, for I know this sounds like a fear-mongering extremist whose opinions are alarmist at best and radical at worst. Such a position is unpopular and not one that I ravish myself. I much prefer being more mellow, polite, kind, and diplomatic when discussing these issues. But I simply cannot escape the parallels of God's judgment in Scripture with what is happening to our nation. I fully believe there is a strong correlation, one that cannot be ignored.

WHEN GOD REMOVES HIS HEDGE OF PROTECTION

Romans 1 is especially relevant for our nation today as it reflects upon how and why God's wrath is revealed upon a nation. For convenience sake, here is the stated text followed by some observations that apply to the times in which we live.

"For the wrath of God is revealed from heaven against all ungodliness and unrighteousness of men, who suppress the truth in unrighteousness, because what may be known of God is manifest in them, for God has shown it to them. For since the creation of the world His invisible attributes are clearly seen, being understood by the things that are made, even His eternal power and Godhead, so that they are without excuse, because, although they knew God, they did not glorify Him as God, nor were thankful, but became futile in their thoughts, and their foolish hearts were darkened. Professing to be wise, they became fools, and changed the glory of the incorruptible God into an image made like corruptible man—and birds and four-footed animals and creeping things.

Therefore ***God also gave them up*** *to uncleanness, in the lusts of their hearts, to dishonor their bodies among themselves, who exchanged the truth of God for the lie, and worshiped and served the creature rather than the Creator who is blessed forever. Amen.*

For this reason ***God gave them up*** *to vile passions. For even their women exchanged the natural use for what is against nature. Likewise* *also the men, leaving the natural use of the woman, burned in their lust for one another, men with men committing what is shameful, and receiving in themselves the penalty of their error which was due.*

And even as they did not like to retain God in their knowledge, ***God gave them over*** *to a debased mind, to do those things which are not fitting; being filled with all unrighteousness, sexual immorality, wickedness, covetousness, maliciousness; full of envy, murder, strife, deceit, evil-mindedness; they are whisperers, backbiters, haters of God, violent, proud, boasters, inventors of evil things, disobedient to parents, undiscerning, untrustworthy, unloving, unforgiving, unmerciful; who, knowing the righteous judgment of God, that those who practice such things are deserving of death, not only do the same but also approve of those who practice them." (Romans 1:18-32)*

The passage begins by telling us that God's wrath is being revealed from heaven upon the earth. Let's walk through the first few verses by asking three questions. First, why is God's wrath being revealed? Verse 18 clearly says, "Because His Truth is being suppressed in unrighteousness." That is, God's righteous Truth throughout the nation is being smothered by unrighteous lies. It is being held down, restrained with unrighteous motives. Need we expound on this? We have already documented such heinous acts that antagonize, intimidate, and eliminate God's Law throughout the Land.

Despite this cultural restraint upon God's Truth, we see in verse 20 that creation itself bears witness to His power and existence. It is fascinating that "His invisible attributes are clearly seen." The invisible is clearly seen? Yes, by those things that are created, even His eternal power and Godhead." Indeed, "the heavens declare the glory of God and the firmament shows forth His handiwork." So, we see evidence or proof for the existence of God and the power of God through creation. That is, through the beauty of a sunrise or sunset, through the majesty of the mountains, through the vastness of the oceans we see a reflection of the power and existence of God. There is a design to the universe; therefore, there must be a Designer behind it. Verse 20 tells us that this reality is clearly seen. We're told that the rejection of God's Truth produces a confused mind and a darkened heart (v. 21). Likewise, as God's Truth continues to find resistance and rejection in America, spiritual darkness becomes more pronounced.

For example, I recall during the 2008 Democratic National Convention that the mention of God was left out of the party platform and it created enough unrest that the decision was made to reinstate God into its political platform. This was on national television and when the chairman brought the motion to the floor for a vote to reinstate God into the party platform, there was a resounding "NO!" from the delegates on the Convention floor. I remember being stunned because this was a vivid picture and representation of the nation's attitude toward God.

So, in contrast to man's profession to be wise, a nation of fools was produced (v. 22). The next observation lies in how God's wrath is expressed. The answer is found by the three statements, "God gave them up, God gave them up, and God gave them over." This is an example of God abandoning a nation. It is a heart-stopping picture of God backing off and removing His protective hedge from a nation. You see, there comes a place in the mind of God where this "Do your own thing" mentality or "If it feels good, do it" philosophy so pervasively permeates the culture to where holy God backs off and says, "America, you want to do your own thing? You're so bent on pursuing your agenda with disregard for My Word and My character? Well, go ahead and do it." Thus, God removes His protective Hand from the nation which is reflected in corrupt leadership, corrupt education, and corrupt legislation. Truth becomes relative and the citizens do what is right in their own eyes. But the first expression of God's wrath in this passage is found in sexual immorality. Impurity, pornography, and adultery are rampant. Verse 24 simply reads, *"God gave them up to uncleanness (moral impurity), in the lusts of their hearts, to dishonor their bodies among themselves."*

The second expression of God's wrath is another step down the ladder of degradation. Verse 26 describes it by saying, *"God gave them up to vile passions."* It's a reference to gross affections, immoral desires, and a perversion of God's design for loving relationships. And what might that be? *"For even their women exchanged the natural use for what is against nature. Likewise also the men, leaving the natural use of the woman, burned in their lust for one another, men with men committing what is shameful and receiving in themselves the penalty of their error which was due."* This is not gay-bashing or homophobia. God loves the homosexual as much as He loves anyone. He has their best interests at heart. I'll refrain from citing the statistics surrounding the homosexual lifestyle, but if interested you may go to my book, *Truth Decay*. In these brief verses, we have four statements regarding the homosexual lifestyle. (1) It is unnatural for a man to burn in lust toward another man or for a woman to burn in lust toward another woman. (2) It is shameful. (3) It is in error to the Truth. (4) Whenever a nation embraces or endorses homosexuality as an acceptable alternative lifestyle, there is a penalty to be paid. This is not being judgmental, but simply repeating what the Bible says.

It is important to note that homosexuality was not the CAUSE of God's judgment, but rather it was the CONSEQUENCE of God's judgment. Put another way, the Bible does not say that God gave them up BECAUSE of homosexuality or sexual impurity. Instead, it says that God gave up TO homosexuality, TO sexual immorality." This is a huge distinction, for it lets us know that sexual immorality, and more specifically, homosexuality, were instruments of God's judgment and expressions of God's wrath upon the nation. Therefore, when God removes His protective hedge from the nation, sexual immorality and homosexuality become more prevalent. According to Scripture, it is evidence of His displeasure. So, what we saw in the Court's 2015 ruling on same-sex marriage is Romans 1 being played out. The Washington elite and liberals interpreted the ruling as evidence of a nation that is tolerant and open to diversity, but in reality it was evidence of a holy God turning His back, giving us up, and removing His protective hedge.

The final step down this ladder of degradation is found in verse 28: *"God gave them over to a debased mind"* and you can read the text to see the things that a darkened mind produces. I am especially struck by these: haters of God (the hostility today toward Christianity), inventors of evil things, disobedient to parents, undiscerning (the inability to identity truth from error, right from wrong) untrustworthy (attitudes toward politicians), and on the list goes.

Before leaving Romans 1, let's go back to the primary reason for God's wrath, the suppression of His Truth. Today, we silence Truth speakers. We hate the light. We run to the darkness. Remember, they exchanged the Truth of God for the lie. And so it is today. Moral relativism is the ideology of our day which says, "What's right for you may not be right for me. What's wrong for you may not be wrong for me. You have your truth, I have my truth. You have your God, I have my God. Besides, who are you to judge? There is no objective standard by which to judge right from wrong." The overwhelming majority of Americans subscribe to this way of thinking, even within the Christian community. So, if the Bible is not the standard by which we judge right from wrong, then what becomes the standard? Man himself. One person's opinion is no better than the other. Man becomes a little god unto himself. Remember Romans 1, worshipping the creature more than the Creator. Romans 1 is a snapshot of the nation in which we are now living.

GOD GIVES UP ISRAEL

The Romans passage is not the only place we find the terminology, "God gave them up" or "God gave them over." Interestingly, we find it throughout the Old Testament in God's dealings with Israel. The parallels between America and Israel are interesting in that both nations have the God of Scripture as its object of worship. Jehovah God was the cornerstone of both nations. Therefore, if we can see how God dealt with Israel during similar times of her history, perhaps we gain insight as to what God is doing with America. Check out the following five passages as a sampling of how God repeatedly withdrew His protection from Israel.

PSALM 78:58-62

"For they provoked Him to anger with their high places, and moved Him to jealousy with their carved images. When God heard this, He was furious, and greatly abhorred Israel, so that He forsook the tabernacle of Shiloh, the tent He had placed among men, and delivered His strength into captivity, and His glory into the enemy's hand. ***He also gave His people over*** *to the sword, and was furious with His inheritance."*

Twice in these brief verses we see that God "was furious." Like Israel, in our multicultural, pluralistic nation we have pursued false gods and adopted all religions as co-equal.

PSALM 81: 9-14

"There shall be no foreign god among you; nor shall you worship any foreign god. I am the Lord your God, who brought you out of

the land of Egypt; open your mouth wide, and I will fill it. But My people would not heed My voice, and Israel would have none of Me. ***So I gave them*** *over to their own stubborn heart, to walk in their own counsels. Oh, that My people would listen to Me, that Israel would walk in My ways! I would soon subdue their enemies, and turn My hand against their adversaries."*

We can practically hear the heart of God bleeding as He pleads, "Oh, that My people would listen to Me." Sounds simple enough, right? If we would only listen to God, look at what He promises. "Soon I would subdue your enemies. Soon I would turn My hand against your adversaries." Though spoken to Israel, I believe He would honor the nation that embraces His Word in obedience. If our adversary is a bad economy, if it is terrorism, or whatever is afflicting the nation, God would intervene if only we repented of our sin and obeyed His Word. Because of Israel's idolatry, God gave the nation over to its own counsels. Today, we have Ivy League economists and Rhodes scholars having roundtable discussions on how to solve the nation's ills. By factoring out the wisdom of God, we do so to our own demise.

PSALM 106:35-42

"But they mingled with the Gentiles and learned their works; they served their idols, which became a snare to them. They even sacrificed their sons and their daughters to demons, and shed innocent blood, the blood of their sons and daughters, whom they sacrificed to the idols of Canaan; and the land was polluted with blood. Thus, they were defiled by their own works, and played the harlot by their own deeds. Therefore the wrath of the Lord was kindled against His people, so that He abhorred His own inheritance. ***And He gave them*** *into the hand of the Gentiles, and those who hated them ruled over them. Their enemies also oppressed them, and they were brought into subjection under their hand."*

Foreigners had inhabited Israel and brought their own false gods with them. God warned Israel not to engage in such idolatry, but not only did the Israelites engage their minds by learning about these false religions, but actively participated by sacrificing their sons and daughters to demons. The Bible vividly depicts it by saying "The land was polluted with the blood of their sons and daughters." Did God sit passively in Heaven doing nothing about it? Was God idle and indifferent to such atrocities? No, verse 40 says, "Therefore, the wrath of the Lord was kindled against His people." We cannot read this without applying it to abortion. Just as Israel shed the innocent blood of her children, so we have done the same by killing 58 million unborn, defenseless babies through abortion. Just as with Israel, I do not believe God has been indifferent. And how did His wrath find expression? By delivering Israel into the hand of a foreign power. He says, "Those who hated them ruled over them. Their enemies oppressed them. And they were brought into subjection under their hand."

Think about the trillion dollars owed to China. Think about our dependency on Middle East countries for our energy supply. What if Iran chose to close the Strait of Hormuz? If China called in our debt, if Middle East countries shut down the flow of oil to America, we could easily be oppressed and brought into subjection under their hand, just like Israel was. This is only one application.

NEHEMIAH 9: 29-30

"And (You) testified against them, that You might bring them back to Your law. Yet they acted proudly, and did not heed Your commandments, But sinned against Your judgments, which if a man does, he shall live by them. And they shrugged their shoulders, stiffened their necks, and would not hear. Yet for many years You had patience with them, and testified against them by Your Spirit in Your

prophets. Yet they would not listen; ***Therefore, You gave them*** *into the hand of the peoples of the lands."*

God tried calling the nation back to His law, but notice their response to His judgments. They acted proudly, shrugged their shoulders, and stiffened their necks. Here we see arrogance, indifference, and obstinacy. Yet, despite their prideful, complacent, obstinate attitude, for many years God had patience with them. Rather than destroying the nation, God's patience was reflected by lovingly raising up prophets who preached powerfully under His Spirit's anointing. Still, the Israelites refused to hear, so God resorted to His final judgment by removing His protective hedge and giving the nation into the hands of a foreign power.

1 KINGS 14: 9-10, 16

"...you have done more evil than all who were before you, for you have gone and made for yourself other gods and molded images to provoke Me to anger, and have cast Me behind your back—therefore behold! I will bring disaster on the house of Jeroboam....And ***He will give Israel up*** *because of the sins of Jeroboam, who sinned and who made Israel sin."*

Once again we find idolatry at the heart of Israel's rebellion, but this time the idolatry is led by Israel's king, Jeroboam. God's indictment upon him is that he was guilty of more evil than all the kings who reigned before him. This certainly reveals that God is watching and keeping a record of the nation's leader. God's anger is activated by the actions of Jeroboam because the king had literally cast God behind his back as one would throw out garbage. "Behold!" signifies "Listen up! Attention! Warning!" Not only does God specify Jeroboam as the target for disaster, but the nation itself experiences the removal of God's protective hedge all because of the sins of the nation's leader.

RECOGNIZING GOD'S JUDGMENT

The purpose of these five chapters is to awaken our awareness of God's judgment and understand that what the world defines as one thing, God has an entirely different definition. Here are just a few examples:

- Homosexuality is not our problem. The hedge has been removed. ***"...who exchanged the truth of God for the lie.... For this reason God gave them up to vile passions. For even their women exchanged the natural use for what is against nature. Likewise also the men, leaving the natural use of the woman, burned in their lust for one another, men with men committing what is shameful..."*** **(Romans 1:25-26)**
- Random shootings and rampant crime are not our problem. The hedge has been removed. ***"For I set all men, everyone, against his neighbor."*** **(Zechariah 8:10)**
- Bad laws are not our problem. They are signs of God's judgment and the removal of His protective hedge. ***"because they had not executed My judgments, but had despised My statutes, profaned My Sabbaths, and their eyes were fixed on their fathers' idols. Therefore I also gave them up to statutes that were not good, and judgments by which they could not live."*** **(Ezekiel 20:24-25)**
- Incompetent leadership is not our problem. The hedge has been removed. ***"I will give children to be their princes, and babes shall rule over them."*** **(Isaiah 3:4)**
- The fact that women, radical feminists in particular, are being elevated to positions of power is not our problem. The hedge has been removed.
- Gay Pride Parades are not the problem. The hedge has been removed. ***"The look on their countenance witnesses against them, and they declare their sin as Sodom; They do not***

hide it. Woe to their soul! They have brought evil upon themselves." **(Isaiah 3:9)**

- Venereal diseases are not our problem. The hedge has been removed. ***"....burned in their lust for one another.... committing what is shameful, and receiving in themselves the penalty of their error which was due."*** **(Romans 1:27)**
- The fact that Congress, the Department of Justice, or the FBI did not deal justly in prosecuting the guilty (i.e. Hillary Clinton's email scandal, IRS scandal targeting conservatives, The Benghazi attack, Operation Fast and Furious, Obamacare, abuse of Executive order, Solyndra, just to name a few of dozens in recent years) is not our problem. The hedge has been removed. "He who justifies the wicked, and he who condemns the just, both of them alike are an abomination to the Lord." (Proverbs 17:15) ***"The earth is given into the hand of the wicked. He covers the faces of its judges."*** **(Job 9:24)**
- The fact that there is a famine for the hearing of God's Word and pervasive complacency in the face of strong preaching is not our problem. It is symptomatic of God's judgment. The hedge has been removed. ***"They have blown the trumpet and made everyone ready, but no one goes to battle; For My wrath is on all their multitude."*** **(Ezekiel 7:14)**

SO, WHAT IS OUR PROBLEM?

Isaiah 63:10 nails it. *"But they rebelled and grieved His Holy Spirit; So He turned Himself against them as an enemy, and He fought against them."* Not only is God America's greatest hope; He may also be our greatest threat. We often quote Romans 8:31 that says, *"If God be for us, who can be against us?"* But if God be against us, it matters not who is for us.

God is not waiting for the ACLU, the NOW, the NEA, or the Supreme Court to repent. Rather, God looks upon His Church and is looking for His people to repent. While the eyes of America are on the White House, the eyes of Jesus are on God's House. What we face as a nation is not whether you fall under the banner of an elephant or a donkey. The question is, "Do you align with the Lion of Judah?" Regardless of who sits in the Oval Office, we know who sits on the Throne!

FROM GLORY TO SHAME!

It seems only fitting that we conclude this chapter with a passage from Hosea 4. Verse 1 opens by saying, *"For the Lord brings a charge against the inhabitants of the land: 'There is no truth or mercy or knowledge of God in the land. By swearing and lying, killing and stealing and committing adultery, they break all restraint, with bloodshed upon bloodshed. Therefore the land will mourn."* Kind of sounds like our land, doesn't it. But then, check out verse 6: "My people are destroyed for lack of knowledge. Because you have rejected knowledge....Because you have forgotten the law of your God, I also will forget your children."

God is getting in Israel's face and leveling His indictment upon them. You see, the Israelites were looking around at their "once-blessed" nation and it was obvious that they were in decline. The signs of deterioration were all around them. The nation was being destroyed, so they wanted to know why. God, therefore, raises up His prophet Hosea to offer an explanation. He says, "There are two reasons you're being destroyed. First, you lack knowledge of Me and My law. "Not only do you not know Me as you once did, but you have actually rejected Me." The second reason for your destruction is that *"You have forgotten the law of your God."* Israel had spiritual amnesia. In America, we have also forgotten God's law and have become a nation of biblical illiterates. In addition, our churches all too often display a form of godliness, but reject the power that comes from being godly. Our knowledge of the Lord and His Word is embarrassing. But here is the startling declaration the Lord makes. *"Because you have forgotten the law of your God, I also will forget your children."*

This is an astounding pronouncement. Let's be clear. Our children are not forgotten in the sense that God no longer loves them, but the fact that this generation of young people seems so far from the heart, the intent, and the plan of God for their lives reflects this verse. America today is a leader among the industrialized world in child poverty, juvenile homicides, teenage pregnancies, teenage suicides, and fatherless homes.

The final nail in the coffin is hammered out in the next verse: *"I will change their glory into shame."* It would be all too easy to give a litany of examples of how this has happened in our beloved nation. Suffice it to say that our global respect has declined immensely as America now leads the world in crime, pornography, divorce, abortion, teenage pregnancies, juvenile homicides, and illegal drugs. We cannot expect to maintain our civilization with 12-year-olds having babies, 15-year-olds killing each other, 17-year-olds dying of AIDS and 18-year-olds ending up with diplomas they can't even read. Our glory has been changed to shame. Sadly, we don't even know how to blush! Psalm 9:17 reminds us, *"The wicked shall be turned into hell and all nations that forget God."* Spiritual amnesia of this magnitude can only be conquered by a massive spiritual awakening that begins within the Christian community as our pulpits become aflame with the anointed proclamation of God's Word, described by Jeremiah as a fire: *"His Word was in my heart like a burning fire shut up in my bones; I was weary of holding it back, and I could not."* May this generation of preachers refuse to hold back the fire that is burning in our souls, for it must find expression if we are to be true to the high calling we've received from God. Like Jeremiah, the weeping prophet, it will not be a popular message, but it is the only hope for calling God's people to repentance and the only remedy for the much-needed healing of our beloved nation.

Dr. Robert Jeffress, pastor of First Baptist Church in Dallas, Texas and an avid supporter of Trump from the beginning, declares that he may be the most faith-friendly president in modern American politics. With his Religious Advisory Board comprised of the best of America's spiritual leaders, his Supreme Court and Cabinet appointments, his follow-through on repealing federal funding for abortions along with other campaign promises, this president may very well be a mighty instrument in the hand of a sovereign God to usher in the political reformation that has been long overdue in our nation.

Anne Graham Lotz, Billy Graham's daughter, says "I see what happened in this election as being a tremendous movement of God in answer to prayer. I believe God has put Trump in office because the Bible says that God puts the leaders in charge. He can put bad leaders in charge and He can put good leaders in charge. He has put Mr. Trump in charge." [2] I agree. Thus far, he is proving himself to be a good leader, one who is deserving of our prayers and support. Perhaps we are seeing this human vessel, flaws and all, be an instrument in God's hand and proving once again that "as the heavens are higher than the earth, so are My ways higher than your ways, and My thoughts than your thoughts." (Isa. 55:9)

John Witherspoon's Strong Convictions

"God grant that in America true religion and civil liberty may be inseparable and that the unjust attempts to destroy the one, may in the issue tend to the support and establishment of both. He is the best friend to American liberty, who is most sincere and active in promoting true and undefiled religion, and who sets himself with the greatest firmness to bear down profanity and immorality of every kind. Whoever is an avowed enemy of God, I scruple not (do not hesitate) to call him an enemy of his country."[1]

— John Witherspoon (1723-1794)
a signer of the Declaration of Independence and
President of Princeton University.

CHAPTER 17

Expressions of God's Judgment (Part 4)

Natural Disasters, Terrorism and More

The relationship of natural disasters with God's judgment requires a few preliminary observations, always bearing in mind that Scripture is the Source of our authority. God forbid that I, or anyone else for that matter, should attempt to speak where Scripture is silent or that we should pretend to know the mind and purpose of God in specific disasters. Admittedly, this subject is beyond my mental paygrade, but it is crucial to our discussion on the question, "Is God Judging America Today?" I would hope by now we can agree that, indeed, He is. The more pertinent question is, "How is His judgment being expressed?"

Most assuredly, some of our questions surrounding this issue will remain a mystery, for *"His thoughts are not our thoughts and His ways are not our ways."* (Isa. 55:8-9) Balancing the love of God and the justice/holiness of God can sometimes be challenging. Those with the spiritual gift of mercy will sometimes perceive the treatment of judgment as too harsh and want to defend God's loving nature. Striking a balance is always the goal, but since the subject before us is God's judgment, there will understandably be critics who disagree with the premise set forth. Again, difficult as it may be, let's remove our emotions, our past experiences, and even our theological upbringing by allowing God's Word to have the final say on this highly volatile subject.

OBSERVATION # 1

Scripture teaches that God is sovereign ruler of the universe, Maker of Heaven and earth, but also Sustainer of our planet. While we live in a sinful, fallen world, and while meteorologists may point to weather patterns that cause such forces of nature, God is the ultimate source. Job 37:12 says, *"From the chamber of the south comes the whirlwind, and cold from the scattering winds of the north. By the breath of God ice is given, and the broad waters are frozen. Also with moisture He saturates the thick clouds; He scatters His bright clouds; And they swirl about, being turned by His guidance, that they may do whatever He commands them on the face of the whole earth.* ***He causes it to come, whether for correction, or for His land, or for mercy.****"* God is not the author of suffering, but allows it to accomplish His purpose. So, whether God initiates a storm or permits the storm, it did not escape His attention or His power to prevent it. Thus, He either causes the disaster or He permits it, but rest assured God is in control.

OBSERVATION # 2

At the very heart of God's nature is love in its highest and purest of form. God is love (1 John 4:6). God does not take pleasure in the death of the wicked (Ez. 18:23). *"Though He causes grief, yet He will show compassion according to the multitude of His mercies. For He does not afflict willingly, nor grieve the children of men."* (Lam 3:32) So, while God does not delight in expressing righteous indignation or unleashing His wrath against sin, even then there is a loving purpose beyond what we can fathom.

OBSERVATION # 3

Any student of the bible must acknowledge that God does judge the earth today, but where it gets "sticky" is in attempting to define the reasons for the judgment. What I mean is this. In Scripture, there were prophetic warnings that first called for people to repent before judgment came. By doing so, the people were able to make a connection between their sin and the judgment. Repentance is what God is looking for, making it all the more imperative for today's preacher to warn the nation and Church of what God's judgment looks like and the Scriptural reasons why He often expressed such judgments.

OBSERVATION # 4

God's judgments are always fair, even when we do not understand them. When a tornado destroys a town or a hurricane wipes out an entire area, the question of "why" always arises. Innocent people are killed and godly lives are disrupted. It rains on both the just and the unjust. Perhaps the churches will be strengthened; perhaps thousands will turn to Christ; perhaps people are taken to heaven that otherwise would have faced an even more disastrous future. We simply do not know. Questions abound, answers are few. Like Job, a man who lost his ten children, health, houses, livestock, financial portfolio, yet in the midst of it all he exclaimed, "Though He slay me, yet will I trust Him." (Job 13: 15) Thrown in the fiery furnace for their godly stand in refusing to participate in the idolatry of their day, the three Hebrew children spoke saying, "*....our God whom we serve is able to deliver us from the burning fiery furnace, and He will deliver us from your hand, O king. But if not, let it be known to you, O king, that we do not serve your gods, nor will we worship the gold image which you have set up.*" (Dan. 3:17-18) Faithfulness in the midst of fiery circumstances is what honors God and often there is no logical explanation for what is happening around us. Remember, at the time of his suffering, God never explained to Job why such was happening.

OBSERVATION # 5

Let us be unmistakably clear that throughout Scripture God used every conceivable natural disaster as an expression of His judgment toward sinful practices. Here are just a few examples:

Earthquakes

"You will be punished by the Lord of hosts with thunder and earthquake and great noise, with storm and tempest and the flame of devouring fire." (Isa. 29:6)

Tornadoes and Hail

"Therefore thus says the Lord God: 'I will cause a stormy wind to break forth in My fury; and there shall be a flooding rain in My anger, and great hailstones in fury to consume it." (Ez. 13:13)

"The Lord has His way in the whirlwind and in the storm, and the clouds are the dust of His feet." (Nah. 1:3)

"....the Lord cast down large hailstones from heaven on them as far as Azekah, and they died. There were more who died from the hailstones than the children of Israel killed with the sword." (Joshua 10:11)

Hurricanes

"He commands and raises the stormy wind, which lifts up the waves of the sea. They mount up to the heavens, they go down again to the depths; their soul melts because of trouble. They reel to and fro, and stagger like a drunken man, and are at their wits end. Then they cry out to the Lord in their trouble, and he brings them out of their distresses. He calms the storm, so that its waves are still." (Ps. 107:25-29)

"Then the Lord sent a great wind on the sea, and there was a mighty tempest on the sea, so that the ship was about to be broken up." (Jonah 1:4)

Floods

"With an overflowing flood He will make an utter end of its place, and darkness will pursue His enemies." (Nahum 1:8)

"Behold, the Lord has a mighty and strong one, like a tempest of hail and a destroying storm, like a flood of mighty waters overflowing, who will bring them down to the earth with His hand." (Isa. 28:2)

Wildfires

"Behold, I will kindle a fire in you, and it shall devour every green tree and every dry tree in you; the blazing flame shall not be quenched, and all faces from the south to the north shall be scorched by it. All flesh shall see that I, the Lord, have kindled it; it shall not be quenched." (Ez. 20: 47-48)

"But I will punish you according to the fruit of your doings," says the Lord; I will kindle a fire in its forest, and it shall devour all things around it." (Jer. 21:14)

Famine and Drought

"Do not rejoice, all you of Philistia...I will kill your roots with famine…" (Isa. 14:29-30)

"Also I gave you cleanness of teeth in all your cities, and lack of bread in all your places; Yet you have not returned to Me," Says the Lord. I also withheld rain from you, when there were still three months to the harvest. I made it rain on one city, I withheld rain from another city. One part was rained upon, and where it did not rain the part withered. So two or three cities wandered to another city to drink water, but there were not satisfied; Yet you have not returned to Me," Says the Lord." (Amos 4:6-8)

Volcanoes

"For behold, the Lord is coming out of His place; He will come down and tread on the high places of the earth. The mountains will melt under Him, and the valleys will split like wax before the fire, like

waters poured down a steep place. All this is for the transgression of Jacob and for the sins of the house of Israel." (Micah 1:3-5)

The aforementioned disasters are only a small sampling and by no means are intended to innumerate the breadth of natural disasters in Scripture that are attributed to God. We know that God judged the Egyptians and the Pharaoh in Exodus with various "natural" disasters. He did the same with Sodom and Gomorrah, Ananias and Sapphira, and the list continues.

OBSERVATION # 6

Creation is decaying and we're reminded in Romans 8:19 that "creation eagerly waits for the revealing of the sons of God." Simply put, when those of us who are born again receive our glorified bodies at the return of Christ, then creation itself will be renewed and freed from the sentence of the curse it has been under since the day sin entered the world in the Garden of Eden. But even now, we must be reminded that God is Lord of all creation. "I form the light and create darkness, I make peace and create calamity; I, the Lord, do all these things." (Isa. 45:7)

The Objection to God Expressing His Judgment Today

There is no shortage of theologians who object to the notion of God expressing judgment upon nations, people, or cities today. One objection is that God's wrath was poured out on Jesus, so there is no need for further acts of judgment against the human race. God is no longer using natural disasters or storms to punish us. I believe this is a naïve view of Scripture and is confusing the judicial wrath of God for the eternal punishment of our sin with the chastisement/anger of God in calling a people to repentance. There is simply no Scriptural support for this position.

The more practical objection and one that is quite "thorny" to answer is "Why God? What did we do to deserve such a disaster? What is God saying through it?" Is it the abortion clinic in the nation or the Wall Street scandals or the expulsion of God from our schools? With whom is God displeased? When natural disasters hit in the Bible, God did not leave His people to guess why. Amos 3:7 says, "Surely the Lord God does nothing unless He reveals His secret to His servants the prophets." Objectors say, "a punishment without a known reason accomplishes nothing." In the Bible, when God brought punishment to a people, there was a pattern. That is, when engaged in blatant wickedness, they received a clear prophetic call to repentance, given an opportunity to escape, but then judgment came in the absence of repentance. So, if large natural disasters upon a nation are a message from God, then what do local storms say? Yes, it is difficult to use weather in gauging God's displeasure with a region or nation.

Furthermore, if natural disasters are God's means of expressing His judgment, then why wouldn't Vegas or Washington, D.C be the first? After all, just about everything imaginable that opposes God occurs in these cities. So, the real issue is not whether God does use natural disasters, but knowing when such disasters are direct judgments of God and what is God saying through those judgments?

I believe God still uses natural disasters as a means of His judgment and I believe that He is presently bringing various forces of nature against America. The dilemma presented is in applying this conclusion once it has been made. Admittedly, it is here that much caution must be exercised. While I understand those who disagree and can appreciate their sentiments in refusing to tread into the tall weeds of such discussion, I acknowledge having insufficient answers to these legitimate questions. However, I know of no serious student of the Bible who would disagree that

God still uses natural disasters to speak in today's world. It is the forewarning and interpretation of His message that seems to be most problematic. However, let us be reminded that God is not obligated to explain Himself to anyone. He is God almighty. If He did not explain Himself to Job, a man who feared God, shunned evil, was blameless in his conduct (Job 1:1), and yet encountered "unbelievable" natural disasters, then we ought not so readily dismiss the natural disasters pummeling America today. It is clear to me that God is calling the nation to turn to Him and for His Church to return to Him through the various disasters that are now occurring with increasing regularity. Here are just a few headlines from recent years. Truthfully, in researching this I was astounded by the increasing frequency and intensity of such disasters. Every page of this book could have been filled with one disaster after another from the past two years alone, but it's my hope that what you are about to read is sufficient proof that these disasters go beyond the realm of coincidence. They are not from Mother Nature, but Father God speaking through the storms.

HEADLINES FROM RECENT NATURAL DISASTERS

- **"West Virginia Flood Was 'One In A Thousand Year' Event"** [2]
- **"West Virgina's Worst Flooding In A Century"** [3]
- **"South Carolina Flood Called 1000-Year Flood"** [4]
- **"Missouri's Flood Called A '500-Year' Flood And Worst Natural Disaster In History"** [5]
- **"Historic Rainfall And Flooding Continues In Missouri, Winter Storm Adds To The Mix"** [6]
- **"Worst Rains In 1,000 Years"** [7]

- **"The Mississippi River Is About To Have A Record Flood Completely Out Of Season"** [8]
- **"Record-Breaking Floods Sweep Through St. Louis Area"** [9]
- **"More Storms Loom As Record Rain Floods North Texas"** [10]
- **"Historic Winter Flood Along Mississippi River Sets Record"** [11]
- **"Texas & Oklahoma Set All-Time Record Wet Month; Other May Rain Records Shattered In Arkansas, Nebraska"** [12]
- **"Record Flooding Hits U.S. Midwest"** [13]
- **"2015 Has Been A Year Of Record-Breaking U.S.Weather Events"** [14]
- **"2015 Worst US Wildfire Year On Record"** [15]
- **"California Drought Is Worst In 500 Years—Study"** [16]
- **"New England Record Snow Tracker: Boston Breaks All Time Seasonal Snow Record In 2014-2015"** [17]
- **"California Wildfires Evacuee: 'It Was Raining Fire From The Sky"** [18]
- **"Extreme Tornado Outbreaks Have Become More Common, Says Study"** [19]
- **"Drought Among The Worst In Texas In Past 500 Years"** [20]
- **"2011 Was Texas' Driest Year On Record"** [21]
- **"California's Worst Drought In History: The Breakdown"** [22]
- **"U.S. Droughts Will Be The Worst In 1,000 Years"** [23]
- **"Drought Covers One-Third Of U.S. Counties, The Largest Agricultural Disaster Area Ever Declared"** [24]
- **"California Drought Of 2012-2014 Is The Worst In 1,200 Years: Study"** [25]

- **"U.S. Drought Biggest Since 1956, Climate Agency Says"** [26]
- **"De Blasio: This Is One Of The Worst Snowstorms In New York City History"** [27]
- **"The Historic Tornadoes Of April 2011"** [28]
- **"Historic Tornado Outbreak"** [29]
- **"Record-Breaking 2011 Tornado Season"** [30]
- **"Help Still Needed After Record-Breaking Year For Disasters"** [31]
- **"Record-Breaking Flooding Bombards Missouri As Disasters Pound America"** [32]
- **"Record-Breaking Year Of Natural Catastrophes Changing How Homeowners Plan For Disasters"** [33]
- **"2015 Has Been A Year Of Record-Breaking U.S. Weather Events"** [34]
- **"Hurricanes Likely To Get Stronger And More Frequent: Study"** [35]

THE WORST TORNADOES IN U.S. HISTORY

Out of the top ten tornadoes in America's history, six of them have occurred since 1992. They are as listed:

#8 May 24-26, 2011, 158 twisters, $7.3 billion in damages, 402 injured.

#7 February 5-6, 2008, 92 twisters, $2.8 billion in damages, 505 injured.

#6 May 22, 2011, 54 twisters, $1.5 billion in damages, 1,225 injured.

#5 May 3, 1999, 71 twisters, $1.5 billion in damages, 825 injured.

#4 November 21-23, 1992, 103 twisters, $713 million in damages, 661 injured.

#1 April 26-28, 2011, 337 twisters, $11.2 billion in damages, 3,621 injured.[36]

THE WORST HURRICANES IN U.S. HISTORY

Out of the 15 most destructive hurricanes in American history, five of them have occurred since 2001:

- Katrina in 2005—-1,200 deaths and $108 billion in damages.
- Sandy in 2012—285 deaths and $71.4 billion in damages.
- Ike in 2008—195 deaths and $29.5 billion in damages.
- Irene in 2011—56 deaths and $7.3 billion in damages.
- Alison in 2001—41 deaths and $5 billion in damages.[37]

THE WORST YEARS FOR FOREST FIRES IN U.S. HISTORY

- 2000—-Northern New Mexico, a loss of 47,000 acres and threatened the Los Alamos National Laboratory. Also in the western U.S. there was a loss of 7.2 million acres, more than double the ten-year average!
- 2002—In the western U.S. Colorado had its worst wildfire in history, destroying 137,760 acres. Arizona lost over 500,000 acres, the worst in its history.[38]
- 2003—In southern California 15 fires burned 800,000 acres destroying 3,640 homes. The fire in San Diego burned 200,000 acres, the largest in California's history.[39]

- 2004—Wildfires in Alaska burned more than 6 million acres, the worst in the state's history.[40]
- 2006—More than 200 wildfires in a 24-hour period killed 10,000 cattle and horses, burned 191,000 acres. More than 3.7 million acres were burned in 2006.[41]
- 2007—Again in southern California, 500,000 acres were burned and over 500,000 people were evacuated.[42] Idaho also encountered its worst wildfire since 1910.[43]
- 2008—Two thousand fires burned in the summer in California alone.[44]
- 2010—In Colorado, one of the state's most damaging fires in history destroyed 6,181 acres.[45]
- 2011—Three separate fires in Texas created the worst conflagration in Texas history, destroying more than 32,000 acres and 1,700 homes.[46] There were 31,453 wildfires in Texas this year, making it the worst in state history.[47] Also, the largest single fire ever to strike the lower 48 states consumed 538,049 acres at a cost of $109 million.[48]
- 2012—In Colorado, a dozen wildfires burned simultaneously consuming more than 244,000 acres, giving the state its worst year of wildfires in history. New Mexico also suffered its worst fire in history, destroying 297,845 acres.[49]
- 2013—Arizona experienced the worst single loss of firefighters since the 2001, 9/11 terrorist attacks. California also encountered its third largest wildfire in history, destroying 257,314 acres.[50]
- 2014—-The largest wildfire in Washington State's history occurred, burning 250,000 acres.[51]
- 2015—Another state of emergency was declared in California as three major fires raged simultaneously, burning over 283,000 acres.[52]

EXCERPTS FROM A REPORTER'S PERSPECTIVE

I don't want to belabor this point, but it is important that we feel the impact of these storms and try to grasp the media's coverage of such disasters. So, here are a few excerpts:

"More than half of all U.S. counties have been designated disaster zones, the Department of Agriculture reports. Nearly three-quarters of the nation's cattle acreage is now inside a drought-stricken area, as is about two-thirds of the country's hay acreage, the agency reported."[53]

"America smashed the record for billion-dollar weather disasters this year with a deadly dozen, and counting. With an almost biblical onslaught of twisters, floods, snow, drought, heat and wildfires, the U.S. in 2011 has seen more weather catastrophes that caused at least $1 billion in damage than it did in all of the 1980's, even after the dollar figures from back then are adjusted for inflation.[54]

"Earthquakes, heat waves, floods, volcanoes, super typhoons, blizzards, landslides and droughts killed a quarter million people in 2010—the deadliest year in more than a generation. In the United States, FEMA declared a record number of major disasters in 2010, 79 as of December 14. The average year has been 34."[55]

"Unprecedented triple-digit heat and devastating drought. Deadly tornadoes leveling towns. Massive rivers overflowing. A Billion-dollar blizzard. And now, unusual hurricane-caused flooding in Vermont. If what's falling from the sky isn't enough, the ground shook in places that normally seem stable: Colorado and the entire East Coast. Arizona and New Mexico have broken records for wildfires. What's happening, say experts, is mostly random chance or bad luck."[56]

"Scorching heat and the worst drought in nearly a half-century are threatening to send food prices up. The drought is now affecting 88 percent of the corn crop, a staple of processed foods and animal feed as

well as the nation's leading farm export. 2012 is the hottest year ever recorded in the United States."[57]

"There has never been a time in recent history when we have seen so many natural disasters compressed into such a short period of time. So exactly what is going on here? Is something causing all of this or is this all one big coincidence? Last year, over 2,000 earthquakes struck southern California in just one week. Sadly, all of these natural disasters are coming at a time when the economy is coming apart at the seams."[58]

"One climate expert said, "our world is seemingly going crazy right now and nothing is stable anymore. The earth is shaking, natural disasters are becoming worse, the economy is falling apart and America appears to be coming apart at the seams. Unfortunately, I believe that things are going to become even more unstable in the months and years ahead."[59]

"Floods, tornadoes, earthquakes, tsunamis and other geological phenomena have left a trail of destruction during the first half of 2011. In the South, 14 states are now baking in blast-furnace conditions—from Arizona, which is battling the largest wildfire in its history, to Florida, where fires have burned some 200,000 acres so far. Already this year, some 40,000 wildfires have torched over 5.8 million acres nationwide."[60]

HOW DO WE INTERPRET SUCH WEATHER PATTERNS?

Take a moment to process the staggering costs both monetarily and in lives lost, then consider the fact that these are the worst natural disasters in the nation's history and most have occurred since the year 2000. Bear in mind, our records go back into the 1800's. Headline after headline contains the words, "Worst Ever," "Historic," "Record-Breaking," and even speak about the devastating impact of the storms in catastrophic terms of 500 years, 1,000 years, and 1,200 years. And, they range from floods, to snow storms, to hurricanes, to tornadoes, and to wildfires. They extend into every season of the year and are not confined to any region of the nation. It is worth mentioning that these disasters were not intended to represent an exhaustive list, but only enough for a point of emphasis. To attribute these phenomena as a cosmic coincidence or to global warming, or any such meteorological explanation is to trivialize it and factor God out of the equation. Incidentally, even insurance companies describe these events as "acts of God." Again, peering through the lens of Scripture, I am persuaded that the unseen Hand of a Sovereign God is capturing our attention and turning our eyes heavenward desiring to produce a humble spirit that embraces Jesus as Lord.

Frankly, I believe this is further evidence of God removing His protective hedge from the nation. As a result, Satan, who is the Prince of the power of the air (Eph. 2:2), unleashes more of his power to kill, steal, and destroy (Jn. 10:10). God is not initiating it. He is not causing it. But it seems that our nation's wickedness and hostility toward His Word, have invoked such judgment that God has done what He repeatedly did in Scripture. That is, He has stepped back at our insistence, removed His protective hand that rested upon America for two centuries, and given us over to our own desires. A consequence of the divine hedge being removed has affected the weather patterns of the nation. Again, this is only an opinion, but one that seems to find substantiation in God's Word.

It is worth noting that out of 1,100 Christians surveyed, 52 percent felt strongly that increasing disasters in the United States are a result of God's judgment on our national immorality. Thirty percent of believers emphatically believed that increased natural disasters should not be attributed to the wrath of God, but man's misuse of the ecosystem. One man said, "God will not punish the just with the unjust. The natural disasters are natural results of man's unwise acts. Man does things scientifically that confuses nature, and then disaster strikes." Another said, "God is love, never hate. God created nature and allowed nature to evolve; so I can't see a loving God using beauty He created to punish mankind! It just would not make sense. Only humankind abuses nature." The remaining 18 percent were unsure about whether the increasing natural disasters are an act of God. [61] The mixed reactions come as no surprise. On the contrary, it is somewhat surprising that the majority interpret the natural disasters as God sending a message to the United States.

CONSIDER AMERICA'S WICKEDNESS

Because of my deep love for this country and because of the patriotism that flows through my veins, it is painful to acknowledge where we stand today. We see the news and read the papers, but it is only a fraction of what has become so pervasive throughout our Land and now ingrained into our thinking. Euthanasia, murder, the daily killing of 4,000 innocent babies, homosexuality, divorce, sexual immorality, half of all babies born out of wedlock in some parts of the country, adultery, gambling, drugs, alcohol, pornography, greed, lust, false prophets, murder, violence, crime, the removal of God, the Bible, prayer from schools. The Pentagon now salutes gays in the military and our Defense Department hosts its own gay pride event. We daily export our anti-God perversions throughout the world. No nation has had a Christian beginning like America. Just like Israel, we've been given the Lord, the Law, and a land, but also like Israel, we have defied the Lord, defiled the land, and denied His Law. The overwhelming majority of Americans deny that the Bible contains absolute truth, and this is even true for a majority of church attenders. We have politicians encouraging us to surrender in the war on terror by negotiating with terrorists which we did with Iran. Others are calling for surrender to the war on drugs by legalizing them. So we did in

Colorado with marijuana. Still others say we should surrender in being so strict on sexual promiscuity, so we distribute condoms to our youth and condone living together without being married, which now a majority do. We grew weary in fighting the cultural war on the sanctity of marriage, so now same-sex marriage has been given equal status and anyone who disagrees is looked down upon. We've grown skeptical about our economic system of capitalism so now we are traveling the path toward socialism as evidenced with Bernie Sanders getting almost 50 percent of the votes in the 2016 Democratic primary. We owe $20 trillion, most of it to foreign nations.

When Israel was guilty of such sins, He took away her glory. Let's be clear. America has met the criteria God requires to bring down His judgment and we are now witnessing our downfall. The greater the sins of a nation, the greater His punishment will be. Given the relentless disasters of the recent past, it is only fitting to ask, "Is God sending a message?" God has continued to bless us, undeserving as we are. Yet, He is patiently calling us to repentance with a patience that has its limits. Learning from Israel's failure to heed God's warnings, we find ourselves on a parallel track.

Henry Blackaby expressed his view by saying, "Each time God sends hurricanes, floods, or other calamities He is speaking to His people. Many of the pastors never connected 9-11 with God's warning to people in America—that He's beginning to remove the hedge of protection from America because of the sin of God's people. But God's people never make the connection with their sin."[62]

Let us conclude this chapter with a poignant word from the legendary, late Dr. Adrian Rogers. "We say America is # 1. And we're right! We're # 1 in homosexuality, radical feminism, divorce, destruction of family values, abortion, political correctness, occult humanistic new age religion, and more! That's America—the home of the immorally free and brave! In our public school systems, prayer is out, policemen are in. Bibles are out, values clarification is in. The Ten Commandments are out, rape, armed robbery, murder, and bombs are in. Creation is out, evolution is in. Corporal punishment is out, disrespect and rebellion are in. Traditional values are out, unwed motherhood is in. Abstinence is out, condoms and abortion are in. Learning is out, social engineering is in. Happy days are out, Gothic fashion, gangster rap, heavy rock, heavy metal is in. Praise is out, blasphemy is in."

As it relates to this chapter, Dr. Rogers continues: "There's a bombing on one channel, a tornado ripping through the heartland on another, and a murderous killing spree on a third! Why is this? Because the hedge is down. In the mid 1980's the Midwest and California suffered the worst drought in history. Then record rains in both of these areas caused severe flooding soon thereafter. In 1989 Hurricane Hugo struck Charleston, South Carolina, doing immense damage. After Hugo, a powerful earthquake rocked San Francisco. In 1992, seven of the most powerful earthquakes in the world were centered in California, including the most powerful in the world—a 7.6 magnitude. Hurricane Andrew, one of the most destructive hurricanes to rock the Gulf Coast, hit southern Florida. The worst rioting since the Civil War took place in Los Angeles. A number of tornadoes devastated the American heartland. And a record-breaking forest fire swept through the west—devastating thousands of acres in California. In 1993 record storms slammed the East Coast, and then the worst terrorist attack in American history struck New York City. California was again hit with record wildfires. And soon after, we began hearing about mass killings and serial killings in America. And then in 1994 the coldest temperatures ever recorded hit the Midwest and the East. The cold was so intense that the wind-chill hit nearly 90 degrees below in some states. Is God doing all of these things? No! The hedge is down." [63]

Dr. Roger died in 2005. Thus, his observations regarding natural disasters were mostly from the 1980's and 1990's. Since then, the disasters he mentioned have only increased with greater frequency and intensity. It does appear that America has reached a perilous tipping point. One can only muse, "How much longer, O God, will you have mercy upon us before utter destruction is our lot?"

Ben Franklin's Assessment of Christianity

"History will afford frequent opportunities of showing the necessity of a public religion...and the excellency of the Christian religion above all others, ancient or modern. A Bible and a newspaper in every house, a good school in every district—all studied and appreciated as they merit—are the principle of virtue, morality, and civil liberty." [1]

— Benjamin Franklin (1706-1790)
was an American statesman, scientist, and philosopher. He helped draft the Declaration of Independence, helped found the University of Pennsylvania, organized the first postal system, was governor of Pennsylvania, and had many inventions to his credit, including bi-focal glasses.

CHAPTER 18

Expressions of God's Judgment (Part 5)

The Prophets

The America we love is sick, and we all know it. As we have seen in the preceding chapters, the blessings that made America great have been withdrawn. The America we knew has changed because the values of Americans have changed. Whether it is abortion, same-sex marriage, drugs, or co-habitation, you name it and we've legalized it. And if we haven't legalized it, the American populace has at least turned an eye, winked at it, and mentally embraced the cultural battle cry of tolerance and diversity that says, "To each his own." Admittedly, it's messy and risky to witness for Jesus or to raise the standard of morality in our communities by representing Truth without being perceived as a moral policeman who appears puritanically arrogant. I am not alluding to parading down Main Street with placards and signs that plaster our displeasure while shouting John 3:16 in unison. No, there is a kind, gracious, and diplomatic way of lovingly pointing our friends and loved ones to the One who has come to seek and save the lost. We all need rescuing from ourselves and from our sin. Apart from Jesus, there's a spiritual vacuum that creates the awareness of something missing. Most people are clueless as to what it is. They only know they are unfulfilled. The Saturday night party provided a little social stimulation, the hit of weed or line of coke induced a temporary buzz, or the concert and sports outing provided a momentary high, but the next morning the face in the mirror is the same. So is the emptiness. Bouncing from job to job offers little relief. Purchasing new toys is cool, until the new wears off. You get the picture. Everyone has their own pursuit of what seems to be the answer to a meaningful life. And to be sure, power, significance, status, pleasure—-all these things serve as temporary anesthetics, but God has set eternity in our hearts (Ecc. 3:11) and anything less than Jesus Christ will leave a person searching for something more. Much of what we are seeing today is a lost nation stumbling and staggering in spiritual darkness groping for something that truly satisfies. America is awash in debauchery and decadence, all of which are symptoms of a nation desperately striving to fill the void within. Anything less than the Gospel of Jesus Christ will leave them searching for something more. And thus, we have the mission of the Church which, at this moment, is sorely dropping the ball.

America finds its place in history today very similarly to where Israel found itself time and again. Therefore, by seeing how God warned Israel and chose to implement His judgments upon the land, we can recognize the birth pangs of the same judgments being duplicated in America and strive to avoid them.

The Old Testament contains a mountain of judgments with God pronouncing His displeasure upon Israel and executing various methods in expressing a holy anger designed to produce a spirit of repentance in drawing the nation back to Himself. Of course, this cycle of judgment and repentance occurs throughout the book of Judges. In fact, it seems that every prophetic book of the Old Testament has a theme of affirming God's covenant relationship with Israel despite Israel's rebellious nature, but then God's prophets warning the nation of impending judgment unless the people demonstrated remorse over their sin. The underlying theme of the prophetic books often point to the centrality of Christ and the anticipation of the establishment of His Messianic Kingdom as the ultimate prophetic fulfillment. That being said, God brought Israel into existence to reflect His glory and His character to the surrounding idolatrous nations of the world, pointing them to the One True and Living God. Yet, God's chosen nation failed miserably in this missionary enterprise. With the prophets serving as His mouthpiece, the nation's sins were exposed followed by warnings of judgment in the event they chose not to repent. The following is a brief overview of some of these prophetic themes.

THE PROPHET'S MESSAGE

JOEL

2:12—- *"Now, therefore, says the Lord, 'Turn to Me with all your heart, with fasting, with weeping, and with mourning."* With a plague of locusts serving as a backdrop, Joel is warning of future devastation unless repentance is evidenced.

JONAH

3:10— *"Then God saw their works, that they turned from their evil way; and God relented from the disaster that He had said He would bring upon them, and He did not do it."* Jonah's message was one of warning to Nineveh, a hateful, terroristic people, but clearly demonstrating that God loves people of all ethnicities. The reluctant prophet had to overcome his preconceived understanding of this dimension of God's nature, secretly desiring to see Him destroy the Ninevites, Israel's nemesis of terror.

AMOS

6:1— *"Woe to you who are at ease in Zion, and trust in Mount Samaria..."* As the earliest prophet to Israel, Amos sets the tone for future prophets, condemning immorality, warning of coming judgment and pleading with them to return to God and obtain mercy.

HOSEA

11:8—*"How can I give you up, Ephraim? How can I hand you over, Israel? ...My heart churns within Me; My sympathy is stirred."* God's love and faithfulness in the face of Israel's constant unfaithfulness is the theme of Hosea's message. While God is just and holy, Hosea conveys the sadness and loving weariness of God's nature in drawing her back unto Himself.

ISAIAH

40:25—*"To whom then will you liken Me, or to whom shall I be equal?" says the Holy One."* Again, it is a theme of God's holiness, warning of coming judgment, call to repentance, and the blessing of future messianic predictions.

MICAH

6:8—*"He has shown you, O man, what is good; and what does the Lord require of you but to do justly, to love mercy, and to walk humbly with your God."* Predictions of God's judgment are contained in this book due to the moral consequences of the nation's departure from God.

NAHUM

1:14—*"The Lord has given a command concerning you: Your name shall be perpetuated no longer. Out of the house of your gods I will cut off the carved image and the molded image. I will dig your grave, for you are vile."* Unlike Jonah's message that was intended to produce repentance within the Ninevites, Nahum's condemnation of Nineveh is a judgment of finality, a death sentence due to their blatant idolatry and immorality.

ZEPHANIAH

1:14—*"The great day of the Lord is near; it is near and hastens quickly."* While a faithful remnant survives, the prophet predicts God's judgment upon Jerusalem and in the coming of the Day of the Lord, Judah will not be exempt from such judgment.

JEREMIAH

18:6-8—*"O house of Israel, can I not do with you as this potter?"* says the Lord. *"Look, as the clay is in the potter's hand, so are you in My hand, O house of Israel! The instant I speak concerning a nation and concerning a kingdom, to pluck up, to pull down, and to destroy it, if that nation against whom I have spoken turns from its evil, I will relent of the disaster that I thought to bring upon it."* Warnings from the prophet are unheeded and Jerusalem falls. Known as the weeping prophet, Jeremiah persists in the assignment God entrusted to him by proclaiming a very unpopular message.

HABAKKUK

2:3b—*"Though it tarries, wait for it; because it will surely come, it will not tarry."* Concerned about the injustice surrounding the nation, God tells Habakkuk that He intends to use the Babylonians, a wicked nation, as His instrument of judgment upon Judah.

OBADIAH

4—*"'Though you ascend as high as the eagle, and though you set your nest among the stars, from there I will bring you down,' says the Lord."* By taking pride in the security of their mountains, Obadiah denounces the arrogance of the Edomites by predicting total annihilation of the Edomite nation.

EZEKIEL

43:2—*"And behold, the glory of the God of Israel came from the way of the east. His voice was like the sound of many waters; and the earth shone with His glory."* Writing before the final destruction of Jerusalem, Ezekiel's theme is that judgment follows sin. Terrifying visions and symbolic actions run throughout the book, but the overriding emphasis is the glory of God.

DANIEL

2:35b—- *"...And the stone that struck the image became a great mountain and filled the whole earth."* Filled with figurative prophecies concerning the rise and fall of subsequent empires, the emphasis is on the sovereignty of God and Him bringing the culmination of history to a climatic ending.

HAGGAI

1:4— *"Is it time for you yourselves to dwell in your paneled houses, and this temple to lie in ruins?"* Utilizing a combination of history and prophetic announcements, Haggai recounts the rebuilding of the temple.

ZECHARIAH

4:6B— *"'Not by might nor by power, but by My Spirit,' says the Lord of hosts."* With visionary and apocalyptic imagery, the prophet speaks about the rebuilding of the temple and gives a glimpse into the New Covenant future.

MALACHI

3:7B— *"'Return to Me, and I will return to you,' says the Lord of hosts."* Addressing the apathy among God's people, Malachi reminds them that God wants the best we have to offer, not mediocrity in our worship.

AMERICA & DEUTERONOMY 28

While America's prophetic destiny cannot be found anywhere in the 66 books, 1,189 chapters, and 783,137 words of the Bible, our country's pattern certainly parallels that of ancient Israel. Perhaps there is no better picture describing America than in Deuteronomy 28, a chapter with two divisions: blessings and curses. Throughout Deuteronomy God, through His prophet

Moses, warns the nation of the consequences of forgetting God.... His works, His ways, His Word. One such example is found in chapter 8: *"Beware that you do not forget the Lord your God by not keeping His commandments, His judgments, and His statutes which I command you today, lest—when you have eaten and are full, and have built beautiful houses and dwell in them....when your heart is lifted up, and you forget the Lord your God who brought you out of the land of Egypt, from the house of bondage.....then you say in your heart, 'My power and the might of my hand have gained me this wealth.'....Then, it shall be, if you by any means forget the Lord your God, and follow other gods, and serve them and worship them....you shall surely perish. As the nations which the Lord destroys before you, so you shall perish, because you would not be obedient to the voice of the Lord your God."* (Deut. 8:11-14, 17-19-20)

The crescendo chapter where God so clearly spells out the blessings for obeying and the curses for disobeying is Deuteronomy 28. It could not have been more clearly stated. It would be like saying to your child, "Now son, I love you and as your father I truly want to bestow upon you gifts that you'll enjoy. I take pleasure in blessing you this way. However, such blessings only come as you honor me through your obedience. If you rebel and refuse to obey, then I will withdraw those blessings and replace them with things you'll not like. In fact, you'll wish you had never defied me. So, don't ever forget this conversation we've just had because the choices you make will determine whether you choose to be blessed or choose to face the consequences of your disobedience. Now here are the blessings that await you and here are the curses that await you. The choice is yours."

The blessings described by God were certainly experienced by Israel, but sadly, so were the curses. The same can be said of America. See if you do not agree.

THE BLESSINGS

28:1—*".....If you diligently obey the voice of the Lord your God....the Lord your God will set you high above all nations of the earth."* From the days of her founding, our nation was begun by God-fearing men who esteemed the Word of God and incorporated His holy principles into our founding documents. As a result, God gave America preeminence above all the nations of the world.

28:8, 11-12—*"The Lord will command the blessing on you in your storehouses and in all to which you set your hand, and He will bless you in the land....And the Lord will grant you plenty of goods, in the fruit of your body, in the increase of your livestock, and in the produce of your ground.....You shall lend to many nations, but you shall not borrow."* America's economy was once blessed by God as evidenced by our generosity in lending money and aid to other nations. Our surplus of grain and other agricultural crops allowed us to be a blessing to the rest of the world.

28:7—*"The Lord will cause your enemies who rise against you to be defeated before your face..."* America's military success has been recognized throughout the world as the most dominant power in history.

28: 10,13—*"....all peoples of the earth shall see that you are called by the name of the Lord, and they shall be afraid of you..... The Lord will make you the head and not the tail; you shall be above only, and not be beneath..."* Global respect was America's legacy. At one time, we were the most religiously committed and moral nation on earth. Our currency still says, "In God We Trust." We did not lead from behind. We were the head and not the tail. Nations knew better than to resist the United States of America.

28:4—*"Blessed shall be the fruit of your body, the produce of your ground and the increase of your herds, the increase of your*

cattle and the offspring of your flocks." "The fruit of your body" refers to children who come into the world without defects. "The fruit of your ground" describes gardens, pastures, orchards, and fields. Healthy animals will reproduce helping to create a robust economy.

28:5—*"Blessed shall be your basket…"* This speaks to an abundance of food.

28:6—*"Blessed shall you be when you come in, and blessed shall you be when you go out."* This refers to the normal everyday activities of life.

28:12—*"The Lord will open to you His good treasure, the heavens, to give the rain to your land in its season, and to bless all the world of your hand."* This is a reminder that God controls the weather, and He promises to make the rain favor the nation that honors Him.

THE CURSES

28:16—*"Cursed shall you be in the city, and cursed shall you be in the country."* This is God's way of saying, "It makes no difference where you are in the nation. Nothing will work for you.

28:17—*"Cursed shall be your basket…"* Food supply will diminish.

28:18—*"Cursed shall be the fruit of your body and the produce of your land, the increase of your cattle and the offspring of your flocks."* Again, this is a reversal of the blessing stated earlier. Childless wombs and a depletion of livestock for their economic well-being would be seen as expressions of God's displeasure.

28:19—*"Cursed shall you be when you come in, and cursed shall you be when you go out."* In the normal activities of life, there will be no success or peace.

28: 21, 22, 27-28, 35—*"The Lord will make the plague cling to you until He has consumed you....The Lord will strike you with consumption, with fever, with inflammation, with severe burning fever, with the sword, with scorching, and with mildew...The Lord will strike you with the boils of Egypt, with tumors, with the scab, and with the itch, from which you cannot be healed. The Lord will strike you with madness and blindness and confusion of heart....The Lord will strike you in the knees and on the legs with severe boils which cannot be healed, and from the sole of your foot to the top of your head."* An epidemic of incurable diseases will plague the land. Mental diseases that cause confusion, along with other medical conditions for which there is no remedy, will create extraordinary discomfort.

28:23-24—*"And your heavens which are over your head shall be bronze, and the earth which is under you shall be iron. The Lord will change the rain of your land to powder and dust..."*

Rather than blessing the nation will favorable weather patterns, God's curse involves a lack of rain that produces drought conditions which, in turn, impacts the economy.

28:25—*"The Lord will cause you to be defeated before your enemies; you shall go out one way against them and flee seven ways before them...."* A weakened military causes the nation to be humiliated before the rest of the world. Once the world leader that never knew defeat in military campaigns, now America must admit her inability to succeed in such endeavors.

28:43—*"The alien who is among you shall rise higher and higher above you, and you shall come down lower and lower. He shall lend to you, but you shall not lend to him; he shall be the head, and you shall be the tail."* As the world's largest debtor nation, we now borrow from other countries just to pay our obligations. We now lead from behind, in the words of President Obama.

These curses continue through the remaining 68 verses of the chapter, but suffice it to say that they are relentless. As the nation is utterly destroyed under God's judgment, verse 37 says, *"And you shall become an astonishment, a proverb, and a byword among all nations where the Lord will drive you."* As we observe all that is taking place within our nation, a legitimate question to ask is, "Why would God not judge America if He judged Moab, Edom, Babylon, the Amorites, the Perizzites, the Hittites, and most importantly, Israel? In fact, He is. The curses listed in Deuteronomy 28 have now fully settled over 75 percent of America. [2] In referring to the Old Testament judgments that occurred due to sexual immorality, idolatry and Israel's departure from God, 1 Corinthians 10:11 reminds us that *"....all these things happened to them as examples, and they were written for our admonition, upon whom the ends of the ages have come."* So, to casually dismiss these warnings as non-applicable to America is to make a serious mistake.

LEVITICUS 26

Following the same warnings of Deuteronomy 28, God once again vividly describes the judgments that await the nation unless there is repentance and remorse for their sinful departure and blatant defiance of His Law. Let's call this the Five D's.

DISTRESS

26:16-17—*"I also will do this to you: I will even appoint terror over you....and cause sorrow of heart...I will set My face against you, and you shall be defeated by your enemies. Those who hate you shall reign over you...."* Terrorism could be an application for us, but seeing the nation's decline and inability to win as it once did, creates emotional and mental distress as expressions of God's judgment.

DROUGHT

26:19-20—*"I will break the pride of your power; I will make your heavens like iron and your earth like bronze."* By controlling the weather, God brings the nation's economy to a standstill and thus, humbles the nation. Man can do a lot of things, but one thing he cannot do is control the weather. Few things are more humbling than the sense of helplessness in knowing that we are completely incapable of pulling ourselves out of economic morass, especially when natural disasters are beyond our control.

DREAD

26:21-22—*"....If you walk contrary to Me, and are not willing to obey Me, I will bring on you seven times more plagues, according to your sins. I will also send wild beasts among you, which shall rob you of your children, destroy your livestock, and make you few in number; and your highways shall be desolate."* This speaks of violence, the future population will decline, disasters will increase, and the killing of children becomes more prevalent.

DISEASE

26:16, 25—*"I will even appoint....wasting disease and fever which shall consume the eyes...I will send pestilence among you."* Pestilences would include everything from wild animals to pests, diseases, and environmental hazards. As in Deuteronomy 28, incurable diseases become more prevalent, something that we are seeing today despite our advances in medical technology.

DESTRUCTION

26:17, 31-33, 37-38—*"....You shall be defeated by your enemies. Those who hate you shall reign over you....I will lay your cities waste....I will bring the land to desolation and your enemies who dwell in it shall be astonished at it. Your land shall be desolate and your cities waste....you shall have no power to stand before your enemies. You shall perish among the nations, and the land of*

your enemies shall eat you up." The nation will be utterly destroyed, even to the extent that the enemies who dwell within the nation will be stunned by the massive collapse. The military muscle, once to be feared, will be unable to stand against the enemy.

All of the preceding verses are extractions from the lengthier texts and only summarily describe the extent of God's judgment. The language used by the Lord is some of the most graphic imaginable, but goes to show the seriousness of the nation's transgressions and its inability to escape the justice of God.

HABAKKUK & THE JUDGMENT OF TERRORISM

Habakkuk is burdened about the injustice permeating the nation. He looks around and cries out unto God, *"Why do You show me iniquity, and cause me to see trouble? For plundering and violence are before me; There is strife, and contention arises. Therefore the law is powerless, and justice never goes forth. For the wicked surround the righteous; Therefore perverse judgment proceeds."* Bottom line, he's impatient and wants God to do something about the injustice that prevails throughout the nation.

We touched on this in an earlier chapter, but America's injustice is equally disturbing. Criminals getting light sentences, murderers portrayed as victims, immorality being defended, valedictorians forbidden to speak of their faith at graduation ceremonies, cop killers getting leniency, children refused the right to pray, read their Bibles, or quote the Ten Commandments in school. In the name of free speech, all kinds of indecency and immorality are permitted, but someone sharing the Gospel is prohibited by the courts. Yes, whoever has the best lawyer or political clout seems to be the one who goes free. Increasingly, it seems the guilty go free and the innocent are prosecuted. Out of every 1,000 violent crimes committed in America, only 2.4 criminals are brought to justice. [3]

So, we feel right at home with Habakkuk's concerns regarding the injustice of his day. As he sought the face of God regarding this matter, he most likely was expecting God to send revival, but to his dismay God delivered a message that left him stunned and speechless. *"Be utterly astounded," God said. "For I will work a work in your days which you would not believe, though it were told you (1:5)."* What could God possibly do that would be so unbelievable? *"For indeed I am raising up the Chaldeans, a bitter and hasty nation which marches through the breadth of the earth to possess dwelling places that are not theirs. They are terrible and dreadful; Their judgment and their dignity proceed from themselves. Their horses also are swifter than leopards, and more fierce than evening wolves. Their chargers charge ahead; Their cavalry comes from afar; They fly as the eagle that hastens to eat. They all come for violence; Their faces are set like the east wind. They gather captives like sand. They scoff at kings, and princes are scorned by them. They deride every stronghold… (1:6-10)."* You get the picture.

The Chaldeans were more wicked than Israel. They were terrorists. That's what was so unbelievable. The Chaldeans, of all people, were going to become instruments in God's Hand to inflict pain upon Israel, God's chosen nation. As a wicked and cold-hearted people, God was permitting the Chaldeans to succeed in their terroristic pursuits of Israel, only because they were God's rod of reproof upon the nation, reminding Israel once again that "You will not defy Me endlessly without paying the consequences." America needs the same reminder.

HOSEA & THE JUDGMENT OF TERRORISM

Reading Hosea is like looking at a reflection of America, as is the case with so many of the prophetic books. Once again, Israel had sunk to the lowest ebb of immorality and idolatry. Social injustice, foreign alliances, religious hypocrisy, violent crime, you name it and Israel was guilty. For two hundred years Israel had abandoned the God of their fathers. Their religious heritage came to mean nothing. So, God intervened through His prophet, Hosea, a man whose style was abrupt and his message, as you may have guessed, was unpopular. Throughout the entire book, Hosea spends his time telling the nation where they had gone wrong. As in Habakkuk, the Lord does the unthinkable. He raises up Assyria, the biggest sponsor of terrorism in that day, and afflicts Israel.

Let's just call a timeout and assess where we stand as a nation, because I believe that we are just as defiled as Israel. America has become the epitome of everything God hates. We are the primary global exporter of all kinds of evil. Immorality is pervasive, marriages are dissolving, our political leaders lie to us, the mainstream media is biased in its reporting, drug addiction is rampant, babies are murdered, children are routinely molested, teenagers are shooting classmates, homosexuality is celebrated with Gay Pride parades, Gay Pride Day at Disney World, gay clubs in high schools, Gay Day at sporting events, and now the redefining of marriage with the legalization of same-sex marriages. Our nation is increasingly refusing to worship the Lord. In the coming days, hostility toward Christianity in America will become more and more common. At this present time, we are seeing the collapse of everything, from our economy to our freedoms. Every institution is in decline. We live under a false prosperity with the only thing holding our economy together being the money that other nations loan us. As the bible teaches, we have become a slave to the lender so that we now are in bondage. Considering the Light America has been given and the abundance of Truth to which we've been exposed, can you think of a nation more deserving of God's judgment today? No amount of political rhetoric, no religious vocabulary, no form of godliness, no elected official is going to save our nation. God's desire is not to punish, but to protect. But as a prosecuting attorney, the Lord would bring a charge to us as He did in Hosea 4:1-2: *"For the Lord brings a charge against the inhabitants of the land: There is no truth or mercy or knowledge of God in the land. By swearing and lying, killing and stealing, and committing adultery, they break all restraint, with bloodshed upon bloodshed."*

Indeed, God is doing with America what Hosea declared to Israel. That is, he has changed our glory into shame (4:7). Nations abroad no longer respect us. Repentance is the only escape from God's judgment. Our hope is not to be found in an economic recovery, the rebuilding of our military, technological advancements, or education reform. We, no doubt, will strive toward doing all of these and more, but these things are only symptomatic of a nation that has departed from its spiritual landmarks. Only a return to God, accompanied by repentance for our sin, will restore America to wholeness. And this will not occur until the pulpits of our land begin to boldly and courageously sound the trumpet and rally the people of God to such a movement. As Peter declared in his epistle, judgment first begins at the house of God. In light of the gravity of our situation, one would think our churches would be packed with repentance and prayer meetings. But no, just the opposite is occurring with declining attendance, sparse prayer meetings, and no Sunday evening service.

DOES THIS REALLY APPLY TO AMERICA?

Certainly, there will be those who say that the dispensation in which we live is entirely different from that of thousands of years ago. And they are entitled to their opinion and welcome to defend it. However, when studying the Judeo-Christian heritage of America, there can be no question that the Pilgrims and the Puritans used God's prescription for Israel as the basis for establishing our nation. In fact, Deuteronomy 28 was a key concern to them. America's connection with Israel was strong in the minds of our Founders, so much that some considered making Hebrew the official language of the United States. Hebrew is found on the seals of some of our

Ivy League schools including Columbia, Dartmouth, and Harvard. Hebrew was even taught by the presidents of these schools. Why this emphasis on Hebrew? Quite simply, the Hebrew Scriptures of the Old Testament were at the heart of the Puritan society, even desiring to make the Law of Moses the basis of law in the colony of Massachusetts. Some of the Founders actually suggested that America should provide a section of land for the Jews to form a nation of Israel inside of America. Many of the rural towns in early America were given Biblical names as evidence that early settlers were conscious of God's hand in their plans. I'll not go on, but it's a fascinating study, one that is overwhelmingly convincing that our Founders had a strong connection to how Israel began its journey as a nation. The resemblance is not coincidental. Again, there is no nation on earth whose early history parallels Israel, only the United States.

So, while God did not write the Constitution, it was written with God in mind. From the three branches of government to tax-exempt status for churches, all came directly from the Old Testament. While not a perfect nation by far, nor have we ever been; we continue to enjoy the residual blessings from previous generations. And despite the decline of Christianity in America, it is those vestiges of Christian influences that provide the nation with whatever moral restraint is left. As Christianity continues to decline, such restraint will also decrease, thus giving rise to persecution. As in Deuteronomy, God has placed before us blessings and curses. The choice is ours. So are the consequences.

Thomas Jefferson's Warning and Prayer for America

"Can the liberties of a nation be thought secure if we have removed their only firm basis; a conviction in the minds of men that these liberties are the gift of God? That they are not to be violated but with His wrath? Indeed, I tremble for my country when I reflect that God is just; that His justice cannot sleep forever.

Almighty God, Who has given us this good land for our heritage, we humbly beseech Thee that we may always prove ourselves a people mindful of Thy favor and glad to do Thy will. Save us from violence, discord, and confusion, from pride and arrogance, and from every evil way. Defend our liberties, and fashion into one united people the multitude brought hither out of many kindreds and tongues. Endow with thy spirit of wisdom those to whom in Thy Name we entrust the authority of government, that there may be justice and peace at home, and that through obedience to Thy law, we may show forth Thy praise among the nations of the earth. In time of prosperity fill our hearts with thankfulness, and in the day of trouble, suffer not our trust to fail; all of which we ask through Jesus Christ our Lord, Amen." [1]

— Thomas Jefferson (1743-1826)
3rd U.S. President, author of the Declaration of Independence, Governor of Virginia, and Secretary of State under Washington along with many other titles to his credit.

CHAPTER 19

Voices for Hope & Change (Part 1)

If you have read the previous eighteen chapters, congratulations. It has been a long, laborious journey of wading through the literary sludge of political sewage, the stench of moral refuse, the sensation of freefalling into economic oblivion, accompanied by the emotions of outright anger from the ineptitude and utter irresponsible behavior from those whom we've elected to lead us. I also hear frustration and disgruntled comments from Christians who are perplexed by the silence in the pulpits of churches they attend. "Everyone" seems to understand the dire straits America is in. Perceptive Christians understand that the nation is at a tipping point....morally, spiritually, economically, domestically, and in so many other areas. However, many are wondering "If this is, indeed, the case, then why isn't my pastor sounding the alarm, calling for prayer and fasting, or doing something to inform the congregation? I thought desperate situations called for desperate measures. So, where's the urgency?" Feelings of despair and hopelessness are completely understandable, if the focus is exclusively on the horizontal plane. However, instead of looking around we must look up. And yes, there are pastors who understand the times we are living in. And yes, they are sounding the alarm. Sadly, their number is too small, but I believe that is about to change.

"STAY OUT OF POLITICS, JUST PREACH THE GOSPEL"

This is the mantra of many well-meaning laymen and preachers alike. It sounds so "right on" and no doubt would elicit loud "amens" in conference gatherings, but preaching the whole counsel of God does not exclude what the Bible teaches about the Christian's involvement in civil government or political activism. While the road to redemption does not travel through Washington, D.C., and while Jesus did not come to restore old creatures through government reform, but to make new creatures through the transforming power of the Gospel, this does not negate the responsibility for the believer's political involvement nor does it nullify evangelical preachers from addressing the relevant moral issues of our day that may contain political overtones.

A failure to hold the government or the legislative bench accountable for their unbiblical actions by refusing to preach such from the pulpit due to the pressures of political correctness leaves the impression that we are adhering to separation of church and state when, in fact, our Founding Fathers (many of whom were preachers) did just the opposite. It leaves the false impression that the government has nothing to do with advancing God's kingdom. Yet, anti-God governments do, indeed, hinder the spread of the Gospel through persecution and coercion. Where there is freedom, the Gospel thrives. So yes, governments can allow people to evangelize or they can prevent evangelization through the force of law. North Korea and South Korea are two examples of governmental polar opposites and we clearly see the church flourishing in South Korea while being oppressed in North Korea. Thus, to say the Church should keep silent is to cower to the forces of political correctness where the salt never penetrates this spectrum of society.

From changed lives, to changed families, to changed neighborhoods, to changed schools, to changed businesses and ultimately to changed governments should be the goal and strategy of every evangelical church in America. Transformed lives that result in a transformed world is a worthy aspiration; one that cannot be attained without preaching the whole counsel of God. As God-called preachers, what right do we have not to preach on Romans 13:1-7 or 1 Peter 2:13-14, or Daniel's influence on the government of Babylon. And what about the kings of the Old Testament and what about the prophetic books that speak of national judgment? Are we to simply skip the plethora of Old Testament passages that deal with God's judgment on nations that "forget His law" under the pretense that such subjects are not appropriate for our day or that the principles no longer apply to the twenty-first century and thus, America is exempt from such harsh language? Is this our idea of "just preach the Gospel" while ignoring the fact that the nation is on fire, teetering on collapse, wallowing in the mire of unprecedented wickedness that is destroying the very foundations for which our forefathers paid the ultimate price to preserve? We dare not ignore the fact that God uses the government to restrain evil. Certainly, a change of heart through the proclamation of the Gospel is the ultimate and best way, for restraining the evil that is loose in society. But since there are many who do not trust Christ, God uses the government to punish those who do evil (1 Peter 2:14).

It was through the involvement of Christians, many of whom were clergymen, that our Declaration of Independence and Constitution were formulated. It was through the involvement of Christians and the preaching of clergymen that influenced government to abolish slavery. History is replete with examples of governmental changes that occurred through the efforts of thousands of Christians who worked tirelessly and courageously to bring about the much-needed improvement in their respective cultures. These defining moments in history would never have occurred if they had adopted the philosophy of "stay out of politics, just preach the Gospel." It is not either-or, but both-and.

Granted, it is risky. Unbelievers who attend church may decide not to return. Even some Christians may conclude that a line has been crossed and they choose to join another church. Just to be clear, I am not advocating anything that violates the laws of our land. What I am suggesting is that we have been silent far too long on far too many moral issues on which the Bible is loud and clear. Yes, hearts must change. That's what the Gospel does. But minds must also change in conforming to the moral standards of the Bible. That comes through bold, compassionate preaching and teaching (i.e. discipleship). How do people know that divorce is wrong? How do pagan converts know that living together unmarried is wrong? How are new Christians expected to know that pornography is wrong? Why should we expect converted gang members to know that profanity is wrong? How are Christians to know that alcohol consumption is unwise and in violation of biblical counsel? How are teenagers supposed to know that homosexuality is wrong? How are young pregnant women supposed to know that abortion is wrong? The list could go on, but the point is this. Our pulpits, for the most part, have been silent on so many of today's moral issues that we now have churches filled with members who see nothing wrong with these things. Let's face it. Most do not seriously read the Bible. And when you add the silence from our pulpits, the end result is a Christian community that has capitulated to the cultural norms surrounding it. Thus, the accusation from the unbelieving world is that the church is filled with hypocrites. So, while the Church has been waiting for the world to get right with God, the world is still waiting for the Church to get right with God.

Judgment must first begin at the house of God. There is no implication in the aforementioned comments that a political savior is the answer to our nation's ills. It is not just the White House, but it is God's House that must get its "act" together. As 2 Chronicles 7:14 clearly specifies, it is "If My people," not "If the politicians." So, the eyes of the nation may be on the White House, but the sins inside the Beltway are only a magnified reflection of what is going on inside God's House. So, let the healing of the nation begin, but let it first begin with the Church. That being said, listen to these voices of hope from some of America's most influential Christian leaders, some of whom are no longer with us, but their voices continue to reverberate beyond their grave.

D. James Kennedy

(Late Pastor of Coral Ridge Presbyterian Church in Ft. Lauderdale, Florida and founder of Evangelism Explosion)

"We face imminent and irreversible catastrophe. Today there are people in this nation who want to rewrite our history and revise the facts of our cultural and moral heritage according to a more modern politically correct view. They want to shake off the restraints and the responsibilities of Christian virtues and to guide the nation toward a new world order of cultural and moral diversity. The democrats have promised to "reinvent" the American form of government and to "redefine" what it means to be Americans in this century. We are a nation at risk as never before in our history. If we empower people to rule this nation whose views are absolutely contrary to the beliefs of the founders and deliberately opposed to the principles that made this nation great, then the changes they bring about will not be for the better.

Christians have avoided the dirty business of politics for too long. While Christians have withdrawn into their holy huddles, the nation has been taken from us and transformed by secular liberals and humanists into a nation we no longer recognize. The place to start is at the local level, in the schools, on the zoning boards, town and county councils, in the local courtrooms, and serving on state advisory committees. There is just one thing those people want from Christians: our silence.

Unless we regain the moral authority upon which the nation

was founded, and unless we return to the godly principles that allow society to function in harmony, there is very little hope that this nation can avert imminent disaster. The only thing that prevents us from claiming the victory is the level of our personal commitment and dedication to the task, whatever the cost. First of all, tell others about the Gospel of Jesus Christ, and then about the values of the cultural mandate. We must also speak out about the principles upon which this nation was built. We have no desire to force our beliefs down anyone's throat. But the crime raging through the land is a sign of judgment; broken homes and ruined lives are evidence of judgment. Storms, floods, tornadoes: All these things are a wake-up call to this nation to get right with God.

Second, write letters, register to vote, speak out in public forums, run for office, and stand up in whatever way you can for those principles on which America was built. If we remain silent, we have no right to complain when things get worse.

If every Christian were to lead someone to Christ next week, the whole nation would be transformed....in one week. Most won't even bother to invite someone to church. The sacred cows—such as abortion and homosexuality—are among the most defiling sins according to a biblical worldview. What one system calls good the other calls evil. The prospects for revival in this nation have never been greater. The problem is that eighty-six percent of Americans claim to be Christians already. A part of our task is to lead those who are merely "nominal" Christians—Christians in name only—to a true encounter with the Messiah.

Our nation has been seduced into the far country. Now, with God's help, we shall reclaim this land and awaken this world to an eternity of wonderful blessings. Are you engaged in the struggle for the soul of America? Or are you just one of those poor, listless Christians sitting on the sideline, watching the destruction of your hopes and dreams? If I could say only one thing to touch your heart and make a difference in your life, it would be to urge you to join the army of the Lord, to accept His challenge to become a part of the greatest movement of the Spirit of God in the history of the world."[2]

James Dobson

(Founder of the nationally syndicated radio program and ministry Focus on the Family.)

"Faith and freedom are inseparable. They are two sides of the same coin. On one side is freedom, and on the other is responsibility, which is itself derived from an individual's internal moral standards. As for the concept of revival, I believe that it is essential—not only in terms of changing the hearts and lives of individuals, but in terms of improving our society on a broad scale. If we are to effectively halt the advance of immoral ideals, a sweeping spiritual revival must take place. I pray that it might happen in our lifetime."[3]

Ravi Zacharias

(Christian apologist and host of the nationally syndicated radio program "Let My People Think.")

"America is living in what I consider one of the hinges of history that will determine the country's future. How can we return to our essential faith tradition with such a pluralistic mix in American society? Is a full-blown revival necessary? I'm a firm believer in the fact that unless theological institutions and our seminaries start training leaders to think again and think well, and to be able to articulate their positions well, we'll be running for a long time against the wind. We'll be swimming against the tide. Secondly, we need to go back in our homes and teach our young people how to think properly, how to think critically. Our institutions and our homes are places of great importance. Our musicians have a very key role here because this is culture of music and the arts. We need to return to solid thinking in the lyrics of our songs, not just the floaty feeling that punctuates our worship. The best way to lose a battle is to stop moving and to sort of get behind your own fort and think you'll be safe out there. We have to be in the public arena. We need to pray that our leadership will continue to be of the caliber and the quality that is willing to stand against the tide. We, I think, have statesmanlike material in the country, and that's what the nation will need to be strong, courageous, and humble at the same time."[4]

David Limbaugh

(Lawyer, political commentator, and nationally syndicated columnist.)

"The task of preserving our liberties will be exceedingly more difficult to the extent that our culture and our courts suppress Christian religious expression and ostracize those who advocate Christian principles. Christians committed to their faith and to American freedom, I believe, have an unmistakable right, if not a duty, to engage in the political arena and to influence the course of this country. They must not be intimidated from participating in the political process by distorted notions of the proper role of religion in politics."

"There appears to be a consensus that America, to remain a free nation, must rededicate itself to its foundational Judeo-Christian moral underpinnings. And for that to happen, Christians must champion unfettered religious freedom, oppose those forces that threaten it, and strengthen their own churches, without which any hope to influence the political system and our culture will be futile."[5]

Todd Starnes

(Host of Fox News & Commentary, author, political commentator)

"Hostility against religious liberty has reached an all-time high. The freedom of religion is being pushed out of public life, schools, and even churches. The time has come for people of faith to rise up. We need patriots who will take back this land. We need patriots who will say we are still one nation under God. The storm clouds are gathering. The winds of revolution are blowing. Religious liberty is under attack. Will you, church member, be a sunshine citizen or an all-weather patriot? Will you, pastor, be willing to take unpopular position in the pulpit? I believe God is raising up a new generation of believers—young people who are fervent in their faith, a new generation of Billy Grahams and Billy Sundays.

The most pressing problem facing America can't be solved in Washington, D.C. True hope and change can't be found at 1600 Pennsylvania Avenue. It can only be found at the foot of the cross on Calvary. When militant homosexual activists launched attacks on Chick-fil-A and the Duck Dynasty family, millions of Christians rose up and took a stand. Remember what happened when Cracker Barrel announced they would no longer sell Duck Dynasty merchandise? Within 24 hours of their announcement, the restaurant chain reversed their decision—and apologized for offending Christians. We saw firsthand what could happen when people of faith mobilize. Hollywood and the mainstream media would have you believe we are the minority in this country. Together we are a mighty force.

We are in the midst of a culture war. American values are under attack. They may spy on our phone lines. They may throw us in jail. They may take away our shops and bakeries. They may demand to know the content of our prayers. But we will not be bullied. We will not be intimidated. We will not be silenced. Onward, Christian soldiers. Onward." [6]

Jim DeMint

(Former United States Senator and author)

"The real problem is not simply bad people in politics, but "good" people who are willing to ignore facts and common sense in order to do "good" things with other people's money. As I continue to watch my country's journey toward destruction, I fear I've reached the breaking point. I am fed up with being fed up. By always being outraged, I am now outraged out. We are mindlessly destroying the world's last bastion of freedom and hope. We are carelessly frittering away humanity's greatest achievement—a nation where even the lowest among us has the opportunity to use their God-given talents to achieve dreams unimaginable anywhere else in the world. We are needlessly turning our backs on a precious gift handed down to us by men and women who sacrificed their lives, their treasures, and their sacred honor. Ronald Reagan's shining city on a hill grows ever dimmer. America's future becomes dangerously dark.

On a radio interview in the summer of 2011, I said bluntly that Barack Obama was the most antibusiness and anti-American president of my lifetime. I believe my statement was true and needed to be said. It still needs to be said, and often. President Obama's policies are also anti-American. Everything this President has proposed or passed through Congress continues to routinely transfer power and money away from individuals and the states and place more of both in the hands of Washington politicians. He has effectively socialized American health care and nationalized our banking system. He has expanded federal control of America's energy resources. He has attempted to expand the power of national labor unions at the expense of small businesses. This is not the American way.

We may not get another opportunity. This could be our last chance. It is now or never that we decide if we are going to continue the American Dream. Getting involved with politics can be messy and unpleasant. But if the citizens who make America work continue to just mind their own business, protect first their dignity, profess enlightened nonpartisanship, or look down their noses at those of us who appear to be mud wrestling in public, we will lose everything that generations of Americans have fought to give us. Those who understand what's truly at stake must join this fight.

Has America reached a low point from which we cannot escape? Absolutely not! A bankrupt and declining nation is not our inevitable fate. It will happen only if we choose to ignore the threats and refuse to solve our problems. We must choose to fight for the principles that have always made America unique and exceptional. And we must choose to elect representatives who will take this fight to Washington. These problems will not be solved by the same people who created them. The majority of Americans still understands and believes in the principles of freedom. The only pertinent question is this: Will they get active in the political process? We can win this fight, but only if those who love and understand America are willing to fight."[7]

Robert Jeffress

(Pastor of First Baptist Church in Dallas, Texas and Fox News Contributor)

"Those outside the church—and many within the church—become agitated whenever the pastor begins to confront the culture with the truth of God's Word. It's one thing for pastors to talk about building self-esteem, experiencing strong marriages, and even understanding the end times. But when a pastor criticizes a city council for approving a topless bar in his community, calls for the board of education to adopt textbooks that present a balanced view of evolution, or organizes a protest in front of a local abortion clinic, he is accused of neglecting his primary calling for "politics."

The Old Testament prophets refused to compartmentalize their message. They confronted their cultures as a whole for their departure from the commands of God. They did not recognize the modern divorce between religion, and especially the ministerial office, on the one hand, and social and national duties on the other. In the Old Testament, a prophet was simply a man who confronted his culture with God's Word. What leads us to believe that God's interests have changed?

Some pastors and many laymen believe that the so-called separation of church and state prohibits pastors from addressing controversial issues like abortion and same-sex marriages, because such topics are political rather than spiritual. There is a concerted effort today by groups such as Americans United for the Separation of Church and State and the American Civil Liberties Union to intimidate pastors and their churches from attempting to influence legislation and elections by threatening their tax-exempt status. They are almost always directed at conservative pastors.

Historically, churches in our country have spoken passionately for and against candidates for public office. From the birth of our nation, pastors preached against Thomas Jefferson for being a deist and against William Howard Taft for embracing Unitarianism. Churches have also been at the forefront of significant social changes including ending segregation and abusive child labor practices, along with advancing civil rights.

No local church has ever lost its tax-exempt status or been fined by the IRS for sermons a pastor has preached. Even when a group of thirty-seven pastors chose to challenge the constitutionality of the IRS prohibition against endorsing candidates in the 2008 presidential campaign by supporting Republican candidate John McCain from their pulpits, their actions were ignored by the Internal Revenue Service. Although I would not encourage pastors to officially endorse or oppose specific candidates for elected office from the pulpit, I would strongly urge pastors to preach their convictions about moral issues without being intimidated by those who would seek to muzzle God's prophets. God has charged you with the responsibility to confront your culture with His Word. Preaching biblically-based messages on controversial topics, encouraging and equipping your members to vote, and challenging laws that violate God's standard of righteousness are just some of the ways pastors can fulfill their role as a prophet. Such actions may cost you your reputation, your security, and even your livelihood. Prophets and their messages have never been popular.

No one feels threatened as long as pastors stick to their major job assignment of being nice people who encourage other people to do nice things. But a pastor who dares to point his finger in the face of unrighteousness and declare, "Thus saith the Lord" is going to become a target of criticism and persecution from without and from within the church.

More believers find themselves faced with the dilemma of choosing between obeying government and obeying God. When ordered to keep silent about our faith in Christ, we have no choice but to disobey human authorities. In these last days, Christians will increasingly be challenged to courageously stand firm against those who deliberately—or sometimes innocently—attempt to abrogate our constitutional rights and our biblical mandate to spread the message of Jesus Christ. The certainty that we are living in America's last days should not paralyze us with fear but energize us to pour our time and resources into expanding God's kingdom.

The fortress Satan has erected is formidable, but it is no match for the spiritual firepower of Jesus and His followers. Instead of hunkering down and holding on until the Lord rescues us from this chaotic world, God is calling us to go on the offensive by aggressively pushing back against evil and proactively expanding God's kingdom. God has left you here at this critical time in history for a greater purpose than simply eking out a living and trying to survive the unexpected challenges life throws at you every day. You and I represent the first wave of attack God has sent to infiltrate this enemy-controlled world and soften it up before our Commander returns for the ultimate reclamation of what is rightfully His. [8]

As for pastors, "Jesus confronted his culture with truth—and He ended up being crucified because of it. I believe it's time for pastors to say, 'You know, I don't care about controversy, I don't care whether I'm going to lose church members, I don't care about building a big church. I'm going to stand for truth regardless of what happens.'" [9]

Frank Page

(President and CEO of the Southern Baptist Convention Executive Committee)

"We have a God-given and constitutionally-granted opportunity to help shape the destiny of our nation by selecting its top official, as well as numerous other elected leaders who will also be on the ballot. No one is more keenly aware than I of the dire straits in which we find ourselves in the twenty-first century. Gone are the days when our leaders governed by Judeo-Christian principles shaped by a biblical worldview. Gone is the time when we had a cultural consensus on matters of good and evil, of right and wrong, of moral and immoral. Gone are the days when elected officials at every level of government truly believed that one day we will all stand before the Great Lawgiver and be judged by the Book…or by the books (Revelation 20:12-15).

Why not ask the Lord to guide you to cast your ballot for the greater good for the nation? For the greater good for our Christian liberties? For the greater good for our children and their children and their children's children? But, most importantly, for the greater good for God's will and purposes for our nation and for us as His people? Regardless of who sits in the seat of power now—God is still in control. His will and purposes will not be thwarted by mere mortals. God has blessed us to live in this golden age of democratic governance. The franchise is more than a mere right. It is a responsibility. It is a stewardship of trust, a stewardship that billions of earth's inhabitants would love to have.

At the end of the day, we confess with those gone before that we are merely strangers and pilgrims on the earth, for our citizenship is in heaven. Our hope rests not in political parties, powerful personalities, or prestigious positions. Our hope is in God. As we approach the ballot box in our individual precincts, let each of us render unto God the loyal obedience He is due. But let us also render unto Caesar the elective influence God has graciously granted to us at this strategic juncture in history." [10]

Steve Gaines

(Pastor of Bellevue Baptist Church in Cordova, Tennessee; author)

"Unless the Spirit of God falls upon our churches, we really don't have chance. The (decline in) baptisms are just evidence of the fact that we're not as much in love with Jesus and in love with people as we need to be. So spiritual awakening is a big thing. It starts with the pastor. It starts with me, it starts with you. The church was birthed in a prayer meeting, not a business meeting. And missions was birthed when they were ministering to the Lord and praying to the Lord.

I'm praying for a real, bona fide spiritual awakening like we've had six times in this country. And I'd like to be a catalyst for spiritual awakening, not just in Memphis but in the United States. I pray for the United States every day across the nation. I pray for the leaders in our Southern Baptist Convention every day by name, with the institutions.

I'm just telling you, we've got to cry out to God and plead with the God of heaven because we're in trouble. And we're beyond a political solution; we're beyond just having another method. We need an outpouring from Almighty God. We need for God to come down in our churches. And so that's what my life's about. I'm giving the rest of my life—if it's five minutes or thirty more years—I'm giving my life to God pouring out His Spirit on His churches and upon the Southern Baptist Convention. I would like to see the Southern Baptist Convention be the leader in revival instead of somebody else doing it. I think that we need to be the catalyst for spiritual awakening in America, and that's what I hope for, where I want to lead our Convention." [11]

Michael Catt

(Pastor of Sherwood Baptist Church in Albany, Georgia; author; executive producer for Sherwood Pictures)

"I believe the greatest deterrent to revival is the church. The church in America is playing games at the foot of the cross. Carnality abounds. The devil is no longer fighting churches, he's joining them. Many churches are nothing more than religious social clubs. Many churches say they are 'Christian' but they are more Corinthian than we dare admit. The church is in trouble. Prophets are an endangered species. Truth is sacrificed for numbers. Righteousness is sacrificed on the altar of a 'good time was had by all.' We need Pentecostal power, not a party at Hooters. Lacking holiness, we have nothing to offer the world. If we aren't distinctive, we are nothing. There is no hope if the church looks like the world. What's happening is nothing more than a 21st century version of Corinthians. A revived church calls sin, sin. She demands repentance. God's looking for a bride, not a prostitute dressed in a wedding gown. Most believers don't know their Bibles well enough to discern where the subtle sidetracks are taking them. It's easier to go with the flow than swim against the tide. What the church and pastors need today is a good dose of Martin Luther, Finney, Spurgeon, A.W. Tozer, John Wesley, and others. These men were willing to stand up to the crisis of the hour. We need to get back to our roots. The pygmies of today's pulpit couldn't hold a match to these men.

Until the church in America sees the need for a purifying, Holy Ghost movement, we are never going to see a national movement of God. There will be pockets, but our greatest resistance, I believe, will come from carnal churches and apostate pastors. After all, when the money is rolling in, the parking lot is full and the seats are jammed for multiple services, WHO NEEDS GOD?" [12]

The church is in need of a prophetic voice. I believe it is important for EVERY pastor, regardless of his spiritual gift, to speak with a "thus saith the Lord" voice. The church will not repent if we ignore sin in the church and the consequences of unconfessed sin. This may be our last and best hope. The cloud of blessing is moving off our land. God is moving in power in other parts of the world. Here, we seem to be content to be worldly Christians. I can't accept that. Nor do I want to resign myself to defeat. I believe the Spirit of God still desires to see the American church return to first love. Erwin Lutzer said, 'Mired in a moral and spiritual crisis, America's only hope is a national revival.' Although I believe we should be engaged in the elections, I do not believe elections are the cure for what is wrong with America. The cure is confession, repentance, and crying out to God in desperation.

I do not believe one message will be sufficient to arouse an apathetic, carnal church. We need to drive this message home. I choose to keep pressing this message down the court until I see a glimpse of what God has done in past awakenings. If not today, maybe tomorrow. Until then, I'm praying, planning, preaching, and preparing for God to do a mighty work." [13]

"It's as if I am reading the front page of every newspaper and seeing the trends of our times unfolding in the book of Judges. NO BOOK in Scripture has more to say to this carnal, backslidden, godless nation than the book of Judges. I can't tell you how serious I think the times are. Not just because we have elections this year (One commentator has said this election is the most important in our lifetime), but because we are pushing the patience and grace of God to the limit. God is not going to sit back and let us mock Him, mock marriage, mock laws, mock morality, and get away with it. We were founded and blessed to be a blessing. Now we are a mockery of all that our nation once was.

I'm telling you, we need Sunday morning crowds on Sunday night. I know God has more for me and for us than we are experiencing. I believe we are wallowing in undeserved blessings. I know I am. God has been better than I deserve, and I've settled for less than He demands of me. I need to be all in. I need you to be all in. Time is short. Hell is hot. Eternity is long. We only get this life to do what we are going to do for the Lord."[14]

The heart-cry of these men is nothing short of a massive spiritual awakening throughout our land. Anything less will not suffice and places us in greater peril. Go forward to the next chapter and let's hear the perspective of other great men throughout the nation.

The "Father of Public Schools" Perspective on the Bible & Education

"Surely future generations wouldn't try to take the bible out of schools. In contemplating the political institutions of the United States, if we were to remove the Bible from schools, I lament that we could be wasting so much time and money in punishing crimes and would be taking so little pains to prevent them. The only foundation for a republic is to be laid in religion. Without this there can be no virtue, and without virtue there can be no liberty, and liberty is the object and life of all republican governments."[1]

— Benjamin Rush (1745-1813)
twas a physician, signer of the Declaration of Independence, and known as the "father of public schools." He served as the Surgeon General of the Continental Army, helped write Pennsylvania's Constitution, and was the treasurer of the U.S. Mint. He founded five universities.

CHAPTER 20

Voices for Hope & Change (Part 2)

One of the benefits in reading these accounts from other Christian leaders throughout the nation is that God is giving us a glimpse into what His Spirit is doing in the hearts of some of His choice servants. That is, we clearly see God rallying His Church with the unified message of revival that includes the ingredients of confession, prayer, fasting, and repentance. The explosive growth of the New Testament Church was preceded by prayer (Acts 4:31), birthed in prayer, and occurred when they were in one accord (Acts 2:1) and of one heart and one soul (Acts 4:32). This oneness seems to have been an essential ingredient before the manifest Presence of God could be experienced. Thus, it is encouraging to see the Holy Spirit doing a similar work in the hearts of believers throughout our land. With increasing awareness, the body of Christ is awakening to the fact that an invasion of the Spirit of God is our only hope. One of the great hindrances in accelerating the awakening for which many prayerfully await is the reluctance of pastors to prophetically preach with the boldness necessary to arrest the attention of the congregants and grip hearts in conviction of sin. But, that too, is changing. The cumulative impact from the following accounts encourage us to conclude that the wind of God's Spirit is gently blowing. It will be the prayers of God's people that fan this gentle breeze into a mighty, rushing wind.

Russell Moore

(President of the Ethics and Religious Liberty Commission of the Southern Baptist Convention; author)

"Carl F. H. Henry, then nearing the end of his life, was on the campus of the seminary where I was working on my doctoral degree. It turned out to be the last time I ever saw him. And that one conversation changed my life. I had asked rhetorically, whether there was any hope for the future of Christian witness in the public square. The old theologian said, 'of course, there is hope for the next generation of the church. But the leaders of the next generation might not be coming from the current Christian subculture. They are probably still pagans. Who knew that Saul of Tarsus was to be a great apostle to the Gentiles? Who knew that God would raise up a C.S. Lewis, once an agnostic professor, or a Charles Colson, once Richard Nixon's hatchet man, to lead the twentieth-century church? They were unbelievers who, once saved by the grace of God, were mighty warriors of the faith.'[2]

The hope for the future is not that Christianity will be seen as more respectable or more influential in the sectors of American power. The hope for the future is churches filled with people who never thought they fit the image of "Christian." If the church is powered by the gospel, then the Body of Christ has tattoos. The next Jonathan Edwards might be the man driving in front of you with the Darwin fish bumper decal. The next Charles Wesley might be a misogynistic, profanity-spewing hip-hop artist right now. The next Charles Spurgeon might be managing an abortion clinic right now. The next Mother Teresa might be a heroin-addicted porn star right now. The next Augustine of Hippo might be a sexually promiscuous cult member right now, just like, come to think of it, the first Augustine of Hippo was. But the Spirit of God can turn all that around, and seems to delight to do so. The new birth doesn't just transform lives, creating repentance and faith; it also provides new leadership to the church. After all, while Phillip was leading the Ethiopian eunuch to Christ, Saul of Tarsus was still a murderer. And that happens over and over again, as God raises up leaders who seem to come out of nowhere, with shady pasts and uncertain futures. And none of us would be here apart from them.

Jesus never promised the triumph of the American church. He promised the triumph of the church. Most of the church, in heaven and on earth, isn't American. Maybe the hope of the American church is right now in Nigeria or Laos or Indonesia or Argentina. We ought to always recognize that those we are arguing with, including sometimes the most vitriolic of our opponents, just may be our future brother and sister in Christ. Yes, we face difficult times, every generation of the church does. But we also face unprecedented opportunities, as cultural Christianity falls all around us. So we need to be ready for those who—like the woman at the well in Samaria—need to hear of living water that can alone satisfy. We must labor to preserve something ancient, something ever new, not just for us, and not just for our children, but for our future brothers and sisters in Christ, many of whom hate us right now."[3]

Joel Rosenberg

(Best-selling author, cofounder of the Joshua Fund, communications strategist, former senior advisor on two U.S. presidential campaigns)

"It is the church through whom Christ chooses to reveal that he alone has the ultimate answer for the ills that plague any nation. A weak church—one whose members give lip service to Jesus but are really spiritually asleep or intoxicated by the things of the world rather than walking in the light of God's Word and the power of the Holy Spirit—can provide little help to a weak nation in danger of imploding. You see, while the economic, political, and security failings of our country are deeply troubling, there is a much more insidious danger facing our country. It is a danger that threatens to make restoration and revival impossible. I am speaking of the spiritual blindness in America. The blindness is the cause of deep moral brokenness. And unfortunately, the church too often acts as though she either is blind herself or is unwilling to be the source of the only true light available to mankind." [4]

After the 9/11 attacks, the wake-up call came, and startled people jumped out of bed—but before long, they went back to sleep, back to business as usual. God is shaking us because he loves us and he wants us to repent. Americans desperately need to wake up from the moral and spiritual slumber we are in. Most importantly, the church in America needs to wake up, purify herself, abide in Christ more faithfully and passionately than ever before, and once again offer families, communities, our nation, and the world the wonder-working power of Christ Jesus and His Holy Spirit. The church is truly America's last best hope. If we don't show the way back to the Lord, who will?

It is critical that we as a nation seriously consider, understand, accept, and then discuss with our fellow Americans just how precarious our situation really is. We must not put our heads in the sand. We must not allow ourselves to become paralyzed by fear or consumed by the thought that our fate is sealed. Will God in his mercy unleash a dramatic period of sweeping spiritual revival and moral renewal and reform that will fundamentally transform our nation and help us get back on the right track before it's too late? I believe such a dramatic revival is possible.

The CENTRAL QUESTION of our time for Americans is this: Will God in his grace and mercy decide to allow the American people to experience a Third Great Awakening? We are desperate for his help. If not, then I believe our days are numbered and a terrible implosion is coming. There is no middle ground. It is one or the other.

The second most important question of our time for Americans is this: How will we invest our time, talent, and treasure now, before either revival or implosion comes? What we urgently need is a national U-turn. We require a wholesale national turning from our current path of pride, materialism, narcissism, selfishness, unkindness, and vulgarity. These are not normal times. We are not facing normal problems. We dare not continue with business as usual. We cannot keep tinkering around the edges and procrastinating and living in denial. We are in mortal danger as a nation. We are on the verge of seeing God's hand of favor removed from us forever. We are on the brink of facing God's fair but terrifying judgment.

How, then are the spiritual leaders, ministers, and elders of the church supposed to respond. The second chapter of Joel makes it crystal clear: (1) **Blow a trumpet in Zion, and sound the alarm (v. 1).** That is, wake up the people and call them to action. (2) **Consecrate a fast (v. 15)**. Make serving God more important than eating food or reading e-mails or being entertained or anything else. (3) **Proclaim a solemn assembly and gather the people (vv. 15-16)**. Encourage people to spend more time with the Lord in their homes as individuals and families. Bring the people together for a special event or a series of events for serious self-reflections, prayer, fasting, repentance, and time in the Word. (4) **Sanctify the congregation (v. 16)**. Encourage people to make a list of things they are doing that God doesn't want them to be doing. Find other ways to encourage your congregation to sanctify themselves from sin. (5) **Assemble the elder and urge the Lord's ministers to weep and ask the Lord to spare his people (vv. 16-17)**. Focus on leaders; spend time in prayer and fasting and repentance with and for them. (6) **Return to the Lord with all your heart, with fasting, with weeping, with mourning; rend your hearts and not your garments (vv. 12-13)**. This is a call to get on our faces and beg and plead with the Lord to have mercy on us as individuals, as families, and as a nation. Consider radically changing your schedule; give people time and space to get on their knees—or on their faces. Take this issue of mourning and weeping very seriously. Have lots of Kleenex ready. **(7) Return to the Lord, because he is gracious and compassionate, slow to anger, abounding in loving-kindness, and relenting of evil (v. 13)**. Don't let people simply dwell on their sinfulness; teach people the stories of the First and Second Great Awakenings to remind them of what God can do.

If you and I are too lazy or too proud or too busy or too self-absorbed to obey the Lord, why should God give America a Third Great Awakening? America is on the brink of collapse. We desperately need God's mercy. Without his grace, we will implode. It's not a matter of if but when. Thus, now is the time we must urgently ask the Lord to give us a sweeping series of spiritual revivals in every part of our nation that will culminate in a Third Great Awakening.

Are you just planning to watch from the sidelines and do nothing to help? America is not finished—not yet. America has not imploded—not yet. So I refuse to give up. I choose to believe there is hope. I choose to pray that God will save this country. So long as there is still time, I choose to press on and do everything I can possibly do. Mobilize people to work together and pray together to turn this ship around before it really is too late. I'm not blind to the enormity and gravity of the challenges we face. But neither am I blind to the power and might of our God. The Bible says, "Nothing will be impossible with God" (Luke 1:37). I believe that, and that is what gives me hope.

The evidence suggests we may very well be aboard the Titanic, heading for icebergs and inexplicably increasing our speed toward disaster. So many on board are unaware of the dangers fast approaching and not concerned in the slightest. We haven't hit the icebergs yet, but if we don't make a sharp turn fast, we soon will, and we will sink. Who will serve as our captain and crew going forward? Will they understand the gravity of the threat and have the wisdom, courage, and speed to take appropriate action before it is too late? I believe with all my heart if we are to avoid implosion as a nation, we must repent of our sins and turn to Christ—personally and nationally."

Marlin Maddoux

(The late Host of Point of View Radio Talk Show, Founder & President of USA Radio Network and The National Center for Freedom & Renewal; Co-Founder of the Alliance Defense Fund; noted journalist and author)

"America must be reshaped! The good news is that there are still enough people in this country who hold to the values of our Founding Fathers and are willing and able to join us in launching an effective counterattack against the liberal, humanist forces that are carrying out a philosophical reign of terror in this country. This is a war for the heart and soul of America. The task is daunting and not for the weak at heart.

Christianity in America is at a crossroads. Unless there is an immediate moral and spiritual awakening in this country, Christianity could continue its drift into cultural irrelevance. For a picture of what America could look like in another decade or two, we have only to look at Europe. We have learned the bitter lesson that, regardless of who occupies the Oval Office, the same political elitists—from administration to administration—continue to control the policies that are driving America toward socialism and moral decadence. It has also become apparent that simply appointing one or two "good" people to the Supreme Court is no guarantee of the Court's protection of our constitutionally decreed rights and privileges. The survival of our entire civilization is at risk; pray we do not fail."[5]

Wayne Grudem

(Prolific author and Research Professor of Theology and Biblical Studies at Phoenix Seminary, Phoenix, AZ.)

"If pastors and church members say, "I'm going to be silent about the moral and ethical issues that we face as a nation," that will leave a moral vacuum, and it will not be long until the ultimate adversaries of the Gospel—Satan and his demons—will rush in and influence every decision in a way contrary to biblical standards. And if that happens, then governments around the world will increasingly use their tremendous power to silence the church. Governments will in effect say to Christians and to churches, "Keep your homophobic, misogynist, oppressive, fear-inducing, intolerant, militarist, hate-mongering Christianity out of our lives, and out of our schools, and off our college campuses, and off our radio and TV stations, and out of any part of government and out of our quiet suburbs where you are never going to get permission to build any more churches; and keep your hate-mongering Christian religion locked up in the privacy of your own home.

I still believe that pastors have a special responsibility to preach and teach from God's Word on at least some issues affecting laws and government and politics. After all, these topics are part of the teaching of God's Word. The mere fact that something is "controversial" does not excuse pastors from the responsibility to preach about it and the responsibility of a church to take a stand on it. Good judgment is required for each issue along with an ability to distinguish between the clear teachings of Scripture and disputed areas of relevant, present-day facts. In all cases, however, the decisive question should not be, "Will people disagree with me?" but rather, "What does Scripture teach, and how can I faithfully teach that to my congregation?" The question is faithfulness to God and his Word, not simply avoiding divisions in the church at all costs. So, it seems apparent that pastors have some responsibility to preach and teach about the significant moral issues that are at stake in each election. They should use wisdom (and seek the wisdom of their elders or church board) in deciding which issues are addressed by the moral teachings of Scripture and by the teachings of Scripture on civil government, and then they should faithfully instruct their congregations in these issues.

After all, who else is going to teach these Christians about exactly how the bible applies to specific political issues? Would pastors think it right to leave their congregations with such vague guidance in other areas of life? Would we say, "You have a responsibility to bring up your children according to Christian principles," and then never explain to them what those Christian principles are? Would we think it right to say to people in the business world, "You have a responsibility to work in the business world according to Christian principles," and then never give them any details about what these Christian principles are? No, the responsibility of pastors is to give wise biblical teaching, explaining exactly how the teachings of the Bible apply to various specific situations in life, and that should certainly include instruction about some policy matters in government and politics.

The United States at the present time has a tremendous need for moral guidance. I am convinced that there is a great need for Christians to study and discuss and then speak publicly about these issues. But if pastors and church members say, "I'll let somebody else speak about that," where will a nation's moral standards come from?" To put it another way, if Christians do not speak publicly about moral and ethical issues facing a nation, who will? Where will people learn about ethics? Where will a nation learn how to tell right from wrong? The simple fact is that if Christians do not speak publicly about what the Bible teaches regarding issues of right and wrong, there aren't many other good sources for finding any transcendent source of ethics, any source outside of ourselves and our own subjective feelings and consciences. If Christians are silent about such moral and ethical issues, then where will moral standards come from?

I am concerned that God in heaven might bring judgment on the nation—judgment in terms of economic collapse, an incurable disease epidemic, a military attack from powerful enemies, the imposition of totalitarian government or some other means. If God does bring revival, one of the first indications will be much evidence of deeper love for God and commitment to prayer on the part of God's people. Another step will be a deeper sense of repentance for sin and commitment to personal holiness among God's people. Churches will begin to see many thousands of new Christians flocking to them for fellowship and teaching and ministry to various kinds of needs. Personal evangelism will suddenly begin to bear much fruit, perhaps at the highest levels of government—in the Supreme Court, in Congress, and among the Executive Branch—many will find themselves turning to Jesus Christ in faith for the first time. University presidents and senior professors will begin to publicly profess faith in Christ and repentance from sin. Hollywood movie directors and network news anchors, one after another, will begin to profess genuine personal faith in Christ and repentance from sin. And so it will be through all levels of society.

Until such a revival comes, the work of Christians today at all levels of society—and especially at all levels of political influence—is essential in order to protect the freedoms necessary to bring about such changes. Still, no matter what happens, at the end of our days—whether we find ourselves like Paul, in prison in a place like Rome, or find ourselves in the midst of great revival and societal transformation—it is important for us to continue to pray and act in faith, trusting in God's power for any success that might come."[6]

George Barna & David Barton

(George Barna is the executive director of the American Culture & Faith Institute, called "the most quoted person in the Christian church today." He is founder of The Barna Group. David Barton is founder/president of WallBuilders and named one of America's twenty-five most influential evangelicals by Time Magazine.*)*

"Our choices over the past fifty years have been steadily redefining who we are. These choices of societal disengagement have put us on a path of self-destruction. Our success over the last couple of centuries is fully attributed to God's blessings, and the current state of decline is fully attributable to our own arrogance and ignorance apart from Him. The accumulation of decades and decades of atrocious choices has annihilated the possibility of an easy restoration process. We are at a stage of the disease where all of the necessary medicines are harsh.

In early America Congress issued such regular public calls to recognize God, forsake sin, and pursue personal holiness that by 1815, some 1,020 call to public days of humiliation, fasting, and repentance had been issued—792 by governmental bodies and leaders, with an additional 238 by church leaders. First Timothy 2:1-2 directs us to pray "first of all" for all people especially for leaders and those in authority. Thus, the command is to make praying for governmental leaders a top priority, right along with praying for our families, churches, jobs, or ourselves. There is nothing else in the Bible that God directs us to pray for "first of all," thus indicating the importance that he Himself places on the governmental arena.

Proverbs 14:34 declares that "righteousness exalts a nation, but sin is a reproach to any people" (NKJV). Numerous Bible passages make clear that on the one hand, a nation will be blessed only when its public policies are such that God can approve, and on the other, that if God opposes a nation's public policies for their lack of righteousness and conformity to His general principles, then that nation will begin to decline and lose its stability, prosperity, freedoms, and other national blessings. Whenever the wrong types of leaders make it into office, then a nation's law and form of government, no matter how good they have been previously, are in dire jeopardy of becoming absolutely worthless. Consider Israel as an example. Did any nation in the history of the world have better civil laws? Certainly not, for God Himself had written their laws. Yet how good were those laws under rulers such as Ahab and Jezebel, or Manasseh, Jeroboam, Rehoboam, and other wicked leaders? Even though their laws had come directly from God, they were disregarded when placed in the hands of corrupt and deficient leaders.

Americans have a responsibility to vote, but when turnout is highest among registered voters, one out of four don't bother to cast a ballot. More specifically, in the 2012 presidential election, nearly ninety million adults who were qualified to vote made a conscious decision not to participate. Pew Research Center demonstrated that only one-third of adults might be deemed "high knowledge" voters, with another one-third possessing moderate knowledge and the final one-third being largely clueless about public affairs. President James A. Garfield (a gospel minister in the Second Great Awakening) bluntly affirmed: 'Now, more than ever before, the people are responsible for the character of their Congress. If that body be ignorant, reckless, and corrupt, it is because the people tolerate ignorance, recklessness, and corruption.'

Noah Webster, Founding Father and one of America's leading educators, addressed this biblical responsibility in one of his most famous public school texts, telling students: 'When voting for public officers, God commands you to choose for rulers, just men who will rule in the fear of God (Exodus 18:21). If the citizens neglect their duty, and place unprincipled men in office, the government will soon be corrupted: laws will be made, not for the public good, so much as for selfish or local purposes; corrupt or incompetent men will be appointed to execute the laws; the public revenues will be squandered on unworthy men; and the rights of the citizens will be violated or disregarded.'

The message was clear: if citizens became negligent in electing competent, godly leaders to office, government would become corrupt. Voting was therefore stressed as one of the most important of Christian responsibilities, never to be taken lightly. Each of us will one day individually stand alone before the great judgment seat to be held accountable for everything we did—and did not do. And when the Almighty asks us, "And what did you do with that government I entrusted to you? What did you do with that vote I placed in your hands?" what will be our reply? Answers such as, "I chose to keep myself unsoiled by the rough-and-tumble nature of politics" or "I let the professionals deal with it" will be unacceptable.

The failure of the Christian body to do as both the bible and the US Constitution encourage—that is, to stand up for righteousness and freedom—will result in a nation where Christianity itself could one day be outlawed as an intolerant, exclusive faith system that is detrimental to the health and well-being of the country, where preaching the Word of God is construed as "hate speech," and where the Bible is banned because of its politically incorrect teaching. Instead, the expectation is that churched people will know the Scriptures better and eagerly wait for God do something miraculous—without recognizing that the Scriptures they are studying consistently demonstrated that God always uses His genuine followers to change the world, regardless of how many are available. With our backs against the wall, it is time for the believers in America to clarify their beliefs and put them into action in order to save what is left of the freedoms that so many Americans have fought and even died for.

When a majority of senior pastors of Protestant churches proclaim that there must be a separation of religion and politics and that it is unacceptable for pastors to use the pulpit to incite people to "political" action (that is, to exert any biblical influence on public policy and thus shape the culture), we are a nation in grave danger. American culture is dying because too many Christians and pastors in church pulpits refuse to boldly speak truth about the issues occurring around them. For example, Romans 1:32 unequivocally states that God does not approve of homosexuality and that He also does not approve of those who do approve of homosexuality. And the same with those who now believe that sex outside of marriage, or divorce, or any of the other things we've discussed earlier are "moral." Standing up and speaking out may be difficult and may not be well received by others; especially if what you say contradicts something they might be doing or believing at the time. It is our duty to do what is right even when it is uncomfortable to do so. Ezekiel 3:16-21 makes clear that if we do not clearly warn others of what God has said is right and wrong and that if those others wander off the path, then we ourselves will be held personally accountable. Leviticus 5:1 similarly talks about the sin of silence. Silence is not an option for a biblical Christian.

Early Americans believed that God's Word applied to every aspect of daily life—a fact documented by any perusal of early sermons. If something important was in the news, then it was also covered from the pulpit with a biblical perspective. Consequently, it is easy to find countless early sermons on numerous topics never covered today, such as earthquakes, fires, droughts, hurricanes, national defense and foreign affairs, the duties of civil rulers and of citizens toward government, immigration, education, economics and taxation and other practical topics. As John Adams affirmed, "It is the duty of the clergy to accommodate their discourse to the times...how much soever it may move the gall (the critics).

The data makes clear that the Church in America is being influenced by society more than it is influencing that society. As our nation decays from the inside out, the sole solution for that deterioration is for the Church to be the Church that Jesus intended, called, and prepared us to be.

Exodus 18:21 instructs: "Select from all the people able men, God-fearing, trustworthy, and hating bribes. Place them over the people as commanders of thousands, hundreds, fifties, and tens." Notice the four characteristics that are to be common to every elected official, whether a local dogcatcher or the president of the United States: (1) able and competent (2) God-fearing, (3) trustworthy, and (4) hating bribes. Only one demands skill and experience; the other three address qualifications of character and morality. Proverbs 8:13 explains that "to fear the Lord is to hate evil" (NIV), and evil is defined as "any deviation…from the rules of conduct prescribed by God." Therefore, God-fearing actually means someone who hates variances from God's standards of morality, or, in the words of Psalm 139:21, it is hating what God hates and loving what He loves. Thus, a God-fearing leader is one who recognizes and supports biblical morality—one who stands for what God approves and opposes what God opposes.

If a candidate does not embrace God's views of right and wrong, then he/she is not, biblically speaking, God-fearing. True love for God is measured by the standard that Jesus Himself erected in John 14:15: "If you love me, keep my commands" (NIV). To determine if a candidate meets the qualification of being God-fearing, a biblical citizen should ask, "What is your position on abortion? Homosexuality? Debt? Military? Welfare?" and other issues about which God has established clear moral standards. Sadly these are questions that most Christian voters don't consider at election time, largely because they themselves don't personally know God's stand on these issues.

Founding Father John Witherspoon (a signer of the Declaration of Independence and the president of Princeton University) reminded Americans: *"That he is the best friend to American liberty, who is most sincere and active in promoting true and undefiled religion, and who sets himself with the greatest firmness to bear down profanity and immorality of every kind. Whoever is an avowed enemy of God, I scruple not to call him an enemy to his country."*

Founding Father and chief justice John Jay restated the same principle when he answered a question posed him by the Rev. Dr. Jedidiah Morse, one of America's leading theologians and educators. Morse inquired whether it was permissible for a godly person to vote for someone who did not support biblical positions, to which the chief justice replied: *"This is a question which merits more consideration than it seems yet to have generally received, either from the clergy or the laity. Second Chronicles 19:2 says, 'Should you help the wicked and love those who hate the Lord? Because of this, the wrath of the Lord is on you.' Jay therefore held that God would not bless those who voted for and placed unbiblical leaders (and thereby unbiblical policies) into office. He concluded: "Providence has given to our people the choice of their rulers, and it is the duty, as well as the privilege and interest, of our Christian nation to select and prefer Christians for their rulers."* It is our duty to elect individuals to office who embrace and reflect biblical values, regardless of whether or not they call themselves Christians.

Benjamin Franklin noted: *It is observable that God has often called men to places of dignity and honor, when they have been busy in the honest employment of their vocation. Saul was seeking his father's asses, and David keeping his father's sheep, when called to the kingdom. The shepherds were feeding their flocks when they had their glorious revelation. God called the four Apostles from their fishery, and Matthew from the receipt of custom; Amos from among the herdsmen of Tekoah, Moses from keeping Jethro's sheep, Gideon from the threshing floor…*

God never encourages idleness, and despises not persons in the meanest employments (i.e., simplest vocations).

Simple, busy, hard-working, common individuals were chosen by God for public service rather than glamorous, credentialed, and pedigreed ones. The government of this nation can be blessed only to the extent that citizens become God-fearing and moral and then place God-fearing and moral individuals into office.

America is at a crossroads. We must choose—very, very soon—who we will be for the coming decades: a nation of grateful and humbled people who grasp the miracle that God has been performing on our shores and who choose to honor and obey Him; or a nation that continues its emergence as a self-indulgent, arrogant, self-reliant people who increasingly reject God's existence, His love, and His principles. No nation that has resisted doing it God's way has ever prevailed.

Do not get caught up in the focus on what "the nation" must do. The heart of the matter is what you must do. Every one of us must slow down, take time to examine ourselves, and figure out what commitments we personally must make to pull our weight in the national turnaround. It is so much easier to point the finger at society and wait for it to change. But that's not how cultural transformation works. It takes place one life at a time, and the first life that must change is yours.

No, you're not the president or chief justice of the Supreme Court or the CEO of a major global corporation. But you are a child of God who has the responsibility and the capacity to impact the thinking and behavior of other people. Think about the family members, friends, work associates, neighbors, fellow volunteers in community organizations, and church members who interact with you, not to mention your social media contacts. What you say and do matters. These relationships represent a chance for you to impact and expand the restoration process. This isn't rocket science. It's the art of making good choices, the art of thinking and living biblically, the art of spending your life on the purposes of God. Make a U-turn. Now!"[7]

There is much to absorb, digest, and process in this chapter. The wisdom articulated from these men and that quoted from our founders so needs to be heard in the public square and today's pulpits. In private conversations with friends and colleagues, I have often said that I feel like a voice crying in the wilderness. Any time strong stands for righteousness are taken, public opinion is not in our corner. That's a given. But more concerning is the prevailing indifference, apathy, and lethargy within the body of Christ. Every pastor knows what I am talking about and it is the change that must come in order for there to be a conducive environment that ignites the spiritual awakening for which we are diligently working and prayerfully awaiting.

The Necessity of Christian Morals in Government

"Without morals a republic cannot subsist any length of time; they therefore who are decrying the Christian religion....are undermining the solid foundation of morals, the best security for the duration of free governments." [1]

— Charles Carroll
was a signer of the Declaration of Independence and member of the Continental Congress.

CHAPTER 21

Voices for Hope & Change (Part 3)

For years my wife has endured excruciating pain, but because she seldom complains about it, even her closest friends have been unaware to the extent of her discomfort. From one specialist to another, Debbie would describe her symptoms only to have the physicians stare at her as if to say, "Lady, your blood work, your MRI, and all of your other tests appear to be normal. Perhaps you need your head examined!" So, the pain persisted as did our prayers.

In recent months, however, it became increasingly apparent that her mobility was becoming more limited due to the level of pain tolerance. Struggling to walk laps around the track, forced to have a slower gait, or being required to sit and rest after only a few minutes of walking or standing due to shooting pain in the hips, knees, and feet were just one more reminder that it wasn't her head that needed examining. Through the years she has diligently watched her diet, followed the instructions of her nutritionist, and produced "healthy" drinks from the blender that required me to hold my nose before swallowing. She subscribes to various nutrition newsletters and takes customized supplements. Despite her best efforts, there have been several occasions when her muscles lock up and she is writhing in pain for up to three hours.

Long story short, last night we returned from seeing one of the nation's top physicians in Nashville, Tennessee who administers prolotherapy, an unconventional approach to identifying and treating the cause for pain rather than merely temporarily relieving the symptoms. This physician himself had endured similar pain for twenty-five years and experienced the same frustration in trying to find a cure. He was a leading urologist in America who did robotic surgery, but has now transitioned into this new field of medical treatment and is helping hundreds of people with "incurable" diseases such as arthritis, fibromyalgia, and many other health-related issues that normally require surgery. Debbie received 15 injections. Yes, each was painful. I stood beside her and cringed. The assistant said, "For your first treatment you did the best of anyone I've ever seen." The doctor said, "You did great! You're tough as nails. No one knows the pain that you've been enduring on a daily basis." This was the first of several more monthly treatments and trips to Nashville. There's a 90% success rate, so we're hopeful.

So, what's the point? America is sick and in pain. We've tried everything from government bailouts to healthcare reform, immigration reform, airport security reform, welfare reform, and after spending hundreds of billions of dollars we're in more pain than ever. We've gone from one specialist to another seeking answers and hoping for solutions only to have our disappointment compounded with further political rhetoric and empty promises. Roundtable discussions with Ivy League economists and Rhodes Scholar politicians have proven to no avail because we have been treating the symptoms instead of addressing the source of our problem. Furthermore, we have factored the wisdom of God out of the equation by looking to man instead of consulting the Great Physician who alone can heal our land. His success rate is 100%, but there is a price to be paid if such healing is to occur. There is no such thing as a painless revival. Yet, anything less will not suffice.

The citizens of our country know that we're sick. They understand that something is wrong. Each election cycle creates another false hope. Like prolotherapy, the cure may sound strange to some and the treatment seem unconventional to the "professional" politicians, but the results cannot be disputed. My wife's physician has endured the ridicule of his colleagues for leaving a lucrative realm of medicine and the stellar reputation as a top urologist in the nation in order to bring relief and complete healing to ailing people. No, insurance does not cover the cost and no, the American Medical Association does not recognize the validity of what he is doing. But yes, healing occurs! Just as Debbie stretched out on the physician's table and submitted to his expertise by allowing him to inject her body with the healing properties, so it is with the Christian. Each of us must humble ourselves in yielded submission to our Great Physician, seek His face, and cry out for His mercy to find expression in reviving His Church and healing our land. One of the Hebrew names for God is Jehovah Rapha, the God who heals. That's who He is. So, what is He waiting for? It would seem the mobilization of God's people to cry out in humble repentance.

Once again, let's hear from some of our nation's spiritual leaders.

Erwin Lutzer

(Senior Pastor of The Moody Church in Chicago, renowned author, and a featured speaker on Moody Broadcasting Network).

"America is rapidly degenerating into a godless society. The church in America appears powerless to redirect the rushing secular currents. America's only hope is a national revival. The powers in America today have chosen a path rejecting God and His ways. Federal courts have interpreted our Constitution as requiring that the bible, prayer, and religious discussion be removed from classrooms, community buildings, and places of public gatherings. Government officials and educators across the country are systematically eliminating any vestiges of God from society. Militant secularists will not be satisfied until God is expunged from every facet of American life. American laws are being reinterpreted and rewritten to sanction what is abominable to a holy God. Our society is fast becoming openly hostile to Christian values. America is reaping the consequences of rejecting God. The church in America has no measurable effect in reversing this downward spiral. Our culture has begun to permeate our churches. The church has condoned sinful compromise. There is moral decay within the church, with highly publicized scandals involving ministries and divorce statistics which are not much better than those outside the church.

The present powerlessness of the church may be a sign that God has withdrawn His blessing that we might seek Him. A national revival is needed. I am convinced that every human resource is now inadequate and only the direct intervention of God can reverse our country's spiritual decay. We need a renewal that can only be affected by widespread repentance. The forces of evil are so deeply entrenched that any cultural shifts will only be cosmetic unless they are accompanied by a spiritual awakening that affects large segments of our population.

There is hope. Revival is possible as long as God is God. [2]

If we continue along the path we have chosen as a nation, I have little doubt that preaching the gospel in any context in America will be deemed hate speech. All that will be necessary is for one person to claim they are "offended' by our message and we will have a lawsuit on our hands. If the present trend continues, we just might have the opportunity to stand with the apostles who were imprisoned and beaten for preaching Jesus—indeed they were warned that they should not speak to anyone about "this name." But they would not be silenced and reported, "Judge for yourselves whether it is right in God's sight to obey you rather than God. For we cannot help speaking about what we have seen and heard" (Acts 4:17-20 NIV).

Hate speech laws will not silence us from preaching the Gospel. It is just that in the future some pastors might have to preach it in a different place—in a jail, for instance.

I believe that the spiritual climate of America will never be changed unless we have a revival of what we call "the layman." That is, we need ordinary people living authentically for Christ in their vocations, among their neighbors, and positions of influence. We cannot look to a man or even a movement as much as to the common person who is committed to Christ and living for Him. It is not how loud we can shout but how well we can suffer that will convince the world of the integrity of our message.

With no political base in the Roman government, without any majority in the culture, the Gospel changed the spiritual and moral climate of the Roman Empire. Christianity competed with paganism and, for the most part, won the hearts and minds of the populace. Christians were radicals in the best sense of the word—radically committed to community in worship, radically committed to serving their pagan neighbors, and radically committed to living out the implications of their redemption.

Without freedom of religion, without a media presence, and without the ability to redress the wrongs against them, the Christians discovered that the Gospel had the power to change individuals, families, and the culture. Their faith was not in their beleaguered numbers but in a simple message that they unashamedly proclaimed. They were not intimidated by the odds against them but were invigorated by the power of the Spirit.

We must ask ourselves: At what point do we have to become lawbreakers rather than betray our faith? At what price are we willing to take the cross into the world and identify with our Savior? As Christians we can welcome an assault on our freedoms as long as we see this conflict as an opportunity to bear an authentic witness for Christ."[3]

Al Mohler

(President of the Southern Baptist Theological Seminary in Louisville, KY. Described by Time Magazine as the "reigning intellectual of the evangelical movement in the U.S.")

"As identifying with Christ comes with greater cost, cultural Christianity, which so many millions of Americans claimed when it was to their advantage, is disappearing. The church is now tempted to declare that same-sex behaviors are not sin and that the moral precepts of the gay liberation movement should be welcomed and celebrated as advances in an arc of progressive human morality. To accommodate to the moral revolution and affirm its morality is to look at what the Bible calls sin and call it something else. Such a shift would mean turning from the authority of Scripture to a new authority. It would mean declaring to our friends and neighbors that their sin is not actually sin. It would mean disregarding their need for a Savior. When it is demanded that Christians respond with compassion at the expense of truth, we must understand that any compassion severed from truth is false compassion and a lie against the truth. Scripture teaches that the truth is itself compassionate.

Pastors who fail to teach the whole counsel of God will give an answer for their failure to teach Christians what must be known for faithful discipleship in the Lord Jesus. The church finds itself now in alien territory in a post-Christian culture. The choice before the church is clear: we will either ground this generation in the grandeur and glory of all that biblical Christianity represents, or we will see the roster of the "missing in action" grow to even more tragic proportions. The confessing church is always a moral minority. Those who seemed to share our morality in times past, without sharing our theology, were quick to exchange their own moral understanding when the morality of the culture changed around them. The collapse of cultural Christianity was not the collapse of the Christian church—merely the collapse of those who were living off of the social capital of Christianity.

The hardening of the culture toward Christian morality must not dissuade us from boldness in communicating Christian truth. We must stand our ground. Carl F.H. Henry encouraged his generation of evangelicals to avoid any surrender of cultural and moral responsibility by volunteering to be "a wilderness cult in a secular society with no more public significance than the ancient Essenes in their Dead Sea caves." Christians must look each other in the eye and remind one another of what is now required of us—to speak the truth, to live the truth, and to bear witness to the truth whether we are invited to the White House or treated as exiles. The rest is in God's hands."[4]

David Wilkerson

(The late senior pastor of Times Square Church in New York City and Founder of Teen Challenge)

"God is dealing with America in the same way he's dealt with all nations who have forsaken him. Whenever nations turned away from God, he sent them warnings through prophets. If the people didn't respond, God often sent violent storms and drastic weather changes and plagues to wake them up. America is racing toward ruin! Our country is morally crippled. Any thinking citizen can see we're sinking into a mire of degradation beyond all comprehension. We elect people to our highest offices knowing they're liars, adulterers, immoral and two-faced. We Americans seem to be saying, 'Just give us a good economy. We want to be left alone. It doesn't matter if he's a scoundrel—as long as we can prosper!' The Bible warns that when God pours out his judgments on nations, he begins by crippling the economy.

Beloved, the evidence is overwhelming: God has a detailed plan to help us face the worst of times. We may suffer in the coming days, but our Lord will make sure we won't have to beg for food and that we'll always have a roof over our heads. Our Lord pledges to be totally involved in the daily care and keeping of all who trust him in times of panic and collapse. God wants us to know that no matter how difficult things may get for us, he will sustain all who trust in him.

In the coming crisis in America, God is going to set apart a people who'll be an example to the rest of society. These set-apart ones won't be caught up in the panic. Instead, they'll walk in total peace, because they trust the Lord with their whole being. And they'll hear God speaking to their hearts. Yes, God is going to purge America, because his holiness demands its. But I don't believe this signals the end of our society. I don't know how long his judgment will last—but I do know he'll keep his people throughout the crisis, even if we have to face a great measure of suffering. And even in the most difficult times, we'll enjoy a time of great rejoicing—because he will reveal himself to us as never before."[5]

Charles Stanley

(Senior Pastor of First Baptist Church in Atlanta, GA., author, and president of the global outreach of the radio and television " In Touch" Ministries)

"There may be people who question whether Christians should be involved in issues of government at all. However, I do not find one verse in Scripture that calls us to disengage from the responsibilities of citizenship. We need to be actively involved in overcoming the issues that confront us as a nation—whether we are fighting the battle on our knees or writing to our lawmakers to influence their votes. Our hope in God compels us to proactively influence those who are in power.

I readily admit I do not know how or if our nation will recover from all that is coming against us. But I do believe this: We must fast, pray, and trust the Lord for the answers. More than ever in our history, it is time to speak up for what we know is right, good, and beneficial. There is nothing to be gained by our silence—- but there is much to be lost. The more we keep silent about the wrongs in our nation, the further we will lose our ability to speak out about them in the future. For some, this signifies running for public office. For others, it means writing letters to representatives, speaking out publically about certain issues, and taking a more active role in civil matters.

I think we can all agree that a terrible tide is rising and our country is under serious threat. With the continuing onslaught of economic difficulties, socialism, increasing immorality, eroding personal freedoms, and lawmakers who often offer empty optimism rather than real solutions, we are facing a wave of trouble that promises to devastate our nation. If we don't act decisively and quickly, we will suffer loss and persecution unlike anything you and I have experienced before. Now more than ever, we need the spirit of determination and the will for absolute victory over the forces that are assailing us—just as our fellow countrymen showed after the attack on Pearl Harbor.

I have been in ministry for more than fifty years, and I readily admit that I could become discouraged when I see the direction our country is taking. But I'm not giving in to pessimistic feelings, because I wholeheartedly believe that our good and all-powerful God understands our situation. I also have faith that His purposes continue to advance in our nation. Therefore, we must never give in to despair. He promises to respond to those who seek Him in humility and to look with favor on those who honor Him. So let us do so; let us humble ourselves before the Father and serve Him faithfully, knowing for certain He will forgive us and shower His favor upon us once again.

The reality is our time is short. You and I do not know how much longer we have to influence those around us and affect the course of the country. So take part in being the real change this nation desperately needs. Allow the Father to work through you to turn this tide. Do not back down. Never surrender. What is at stake is far too important for us to ever give up."[6]

Franklin Graham

(Evangelist, President & CEO of the Billy Graham Evangelistic Association and Samaritan's Purse)

"Our nation is changing so quickly. We have turned our back on God, and we are beginning to celebrate and flaunt sin. The only hope for this country is God. While we were relaxing, secularism, which is exactly the same as communism—they're both godless, slowly over the last 40 years has taken this country. It's gone into Washington. It's gone into our state capitals. It's gone into our local offices. It's in our schools. What godless communism could not do, godless secularism has done. We're going to lose the opportunity, not only to spread the gospel, but we're going to lose our religious freedoms to even live out our faith.

If we can get Christians to run for mayors, to run for city council, to run for school boards, to run for the state house, we can win this thing. It doesn't matter who the presidents are. We can win at home, and we can win big. As Christians, our voice needs to be heard. We're not to be silent. God has not called us to be quiet and to sit on a pew like a church mouse. No, we're to speak out. We're to be salt and light. Churches have been derelict by not engaging in important public debates. So many churches now are more concerned about political correctness than they are about God's Word and His righteousness. I would encourage Christians and churches to take a bold stand and not be afraid.

The world says if you get involved in politics then you're being intolerant. Oh really? Well then, let's be intolerant. We should be intolerant. We should not tolerate sin, and we should not tolerate sinful behavior. Absolutely we should be intolerant, not of the individual but of the sin they represent. [7]

An estimated 20-30 million evangelical Christians stayed home from the polls in the last election. Christians must be willing to vote, supporting candidates that stand for biblical truth and biblical principles, who are also willing to live them. America will only be saved by turning back to God. Unless America turns back to God, and repents of its sin, and experiences spiritual revival, we will fail as a nation. I believe God honors leaders in high places who honor him. I have no hope in the Democratic Party. I have zero hope in the Republican Party. I have no hope in the Tea Party or any other party. My only hope is in almighty God and His Son Jesus Christ. Our country is in big-time trouble. The moral and political walls of our nation are crumbling. It's not that the enemy is at the gate, they've come through the gate. We've left the gates wide open and allowed our moral walls to fall down. Men and women of faith, living their faith, in all aspects of life, is the only way things will get turned around in the United States. [8]

I believe we are at a historic moment in our nation. I have talked with a number of leaders in Washington in recent months, and the recurring theme is that if we don't do something now to return our nation to the strong moral convictions that guided us through the centuries, it could be too late. Nothing less than the future of our nation is at stake. [9]

America is in critical condition. We've got maybe one election left to preserve America's liberties or "the game will be over." [10]

Tim LaHaye

(The late Tim LaHaye was president of Family Life Ministries and associate minister at Montrose Baptist Church. He was a prolific author, including the popular "Left Behind" *series.*

"I am convinced that if the church in our country will begin to take seriously her responsibility of being that restraining influence, we can still turn this nation back to God. Even as morally dark as America is today, we could yet experience a moral, spiritual revival—not because we deserve it, but because God is a merciful God. Just as he spared the wicked city of Nineveh in the days of the prophet Jonah, so he may yet spare America. America may even now be experiencing the judgment of God. Our nation has experienced the worst two years of natural phenomena in history, with devastating hurricanes in Florida, floods in the Midwest, deadly blizzards in the northeast, and earthquakes in southern California. Add to those events riots, our unprecedented crime wave, and the ever present threat of nuclear proliferation and terrorism.

While we may be living in a post-Christian culture at the present time, we should not allow ourselves to limit God. Instead, we should expect him, one way or another, to bring glory to Himself, perhaps through giving us one more chance for a revival that will return this nation to moral sanity by reestablishing the moral traditions we once held.

The Christian who doesn't vote has lost his right to complain about how the secularists run his community or country. If the ministers of America would fearlessly expose the unfruitful secularizers who control our culture and are leading it to Sodom and Gormorrah, we could turn this country around in one decade. People in this country are looking for men of God who have enough guts to stand up and warn the church that moral barbarians are storming the gates. Unfortunately, far too many Christians remain silent in the face of moral chaos and impending doom. They may be concerned enough to express themselves privately, but their policy is never to mix politics and religion. Many of them are actually proud of their silence, either because they don't understand what the Bible says about being salt and light or because they were trained in seminary to believe that religion and politics don't mix. What they don't understand is that the secularizers themselves have politicized morality. In the good old days you could talk about abortion, prayer, and homosexuality without offending anyone's politics because these issues had not been politicized. But today you can't speak out on abortion, homosexual rights, gambling, pornography, or prayer in school without the liberals screaming that you're trying to legislate morality.

Frankly, I am ashamed of some of my minister colleagues who rarely use their God-given influence to take a stand for morality in the public square. Instead, they feel more comfortable remaining politically aloof in this morally depraved period of American history. That way they avoid being called controversial. In this day, my friend, the minister who isn't controversial is too quiet. It is not possible today for a minister to preach the "whole counsel of God" as it appears in the Word without offending someone's politics. We need watchmen who aren't afraid to speak out. Secularists don't hesitate to impose their speech or promote their godless candidates on their networks or through their various communication vehicles, but many in the Christian media are intimidated into silence. [11]

David Jeremiah

(Senior Pastor of Shadow Mountain Community Church in El Cajon, California and a New York Times bestselling author.) He hosts the international broadcast of "Turning Point.")

"Though the world may seem to be crashing down around us, it really changes neither our basic duty nor our ultimate security. We know the truth. We know who we are and to whom we belong. We are God's people, living under His grace and assured by His promises that whatever happens, we are in His strong and dependable hands. Lions' dens, fiery furnaces, storms that crash our world down around our heads don't matter. Our task is still the same: greet the approaching sunrise with joy. The sun will come up. It always does for those who love the Lord.

God is still in control. He has a plan, and His Bible is a book of hope. When we walk in fellowship with God, we find ourselves lifted by the irresistible updraft of biblical hope. If we maintain this hope, nothing can destroy our real security. As Christians, we should never place our hope in the systems of this world. The real hope that Christ gave us does not depend on the shifting sand of politics and economics. We can only lose hope if we take our eyes off the God of Hope."[12]

Greg Laurie

(Senior Pastor of Harvest Christian Fellowship in Riverside, California. He is Honorary Chairman of the task force for the National Day of Prayer.)

"The answer to America's problems is a spiritual one. We need a spiritual awakening. America has two options: judgment or revival. The heart of the problem is the problem of the heart. The fate of the country hangs in the balance. We know this much: America's days are numbered. Rome, once the reigning superpower, collapsed internally before it collapsed externally. The freedom we enjoy was built on the foundation of absolute truth. And when you remove that foundation, freedom can turn into anarchy.[13]

If God can bring a mighty revival in Nineveh with no better representative than Jonah, and no more Gospel than he preached, certainly God can do the same for the United States. Do we think that we can continue to thumb our nose at God and not face any consequences? God warned Israel over and over that her judgment would come if she did not repent from her sins and turn from her idolatry. Israel just ignored God's wishes....and then one day the nation of Babylon overtook her. There's going to come a day when the United States of America, the greatest superpower on the face of the earth, will no longer exist in the present form. [14]

We need to humble ourselves and pray. The word used in 2 Chronicles 7:14 for "pray" is interesting. Of the 12 Hebrew words employed in Scripture to express the verb "to pray," the one used here means to judge self habitually. We must examine ourselves. We must seek His face. We cannot organize a revival, but we can agonize for one in prayer. We can prepare the ground—or perhaps I should say "pre-prayer" the ground—for revival to take root in. There has never been a prayerless revival in history, so it does start with prayer. There must be repentance. [15]

The United States of America is standing at a crossroads. We have never been in worse shape morally. The fabric of society continues to unravel. Revival can be described as waking up from a state of sleep. A revival is when God's people come back to life again, while an awakening is when a nation comes alive spiritually and sees its need for God and turns to God. The church needs a revival. And America needs an awakening. Nothing can happen through us until it first happens to us. It has to start with us.

Everywhere the apostle Paul went; there either was a riot or a revival. It never got boring. I feel the time has come for the church to start making a disturbance again. Revival is when God gets so sick and tired of being misrepresented that he shows up himself. That is what we need to pray for now." [16]

Larry Bates & Chuck Bates

(Larry is an economist and publisher and editor of "Monetary and Economic Review." He is a former member of the Tennessee House of Representatives and chairman of its Committee on Banking and Commerce. He is also CEO off the Information Radio Network and IRN USA Radio News. Chuck is an economist and the executive vice president and news director for IRN USA Radio News. He has served in the Office of Political Affairs in the White House.)

"We are at the precipice of losing an entire generation to lackluster, namby-pamby "preaching." Sitting in a pew, waiting for someone to feed you the same milk week after week will render you practically useless for the kingdom. We have to grow up as a church. The Western church has become lazy, and this, my friend, is manifest disobedience. Pastors, you need to wake up to the world around you; lead your flock to become relevant to the society around them. Stop seeking answers from the world; instead, become the answer center for the world. You may not realize just how many in the congregation are ready to cry out and demand that you tell the truth and challenge the church to get up and get with it. Because of the tentative and uncertain message coming from many of our nation's pulpits, spiritual men are increasingly skeptical about the institution that masquerades as God's church. You would be amazed at the many spiritual warriors waiting for the leaders of churches to take a stand on the truths of God. Much of the church has more fear of man than fear of God. We have decided that our concerns over what man may think of us outweigh our responsibility to God and to our congregations as preachers of the truth.

It is time for the world to take notice of the people of God. Lives are not changed, pastor, when you hold back on the truth of God from the pulpit.

You can't just put a fish and a cross on the world system and call it of God. You can't just wear your favorite Christian jewelry and expect total protection from the evils in the world system, and you can't just show up at your favorite house of worship and get equipped for what is facing us. We have a responsibility to be involved. We are to be proactive as salt and light. [17]

Jim Cymbala

(Pastor of Brooklyn Tabernacle for more than forty years and author of many bestselling books)

I believe followers of Jesus in America are on the cusp of something horrible. I, and many others, see the early warning signs all around. The freedom to preach and practice the truth of the Bible is ever so slowly eroding before our eyes.

In the last twenty years there have been more conferences and more books published on church growth than in all the prior history of our country. As new models of how to grow your church have increased in popularity, we have actually witnessed a precipitous decline of Christianity in America. The numbers are irrefutable. So, if all these ideas are so great, why are we here? How is it we are going backward while still clinging to every new thing coming down the pike? Maybe they are the very thing pulling us down.

One of the beautiful results of the Holy Spirit's blessing is a changed pulpit with more powerful preaching. Today we suffer from a distinct lack of the prophetic when it comes to preaching. I am not referring to foretelling future events (a type of prophecy), but rather the Spirit-given insight to apply God's Word and heart into a given situation—-a "forth telling." We need more than just a clinical dissection of what the words of Scripture mean. We need both Word and Spirit.

Many will argue that cultural differences make it harder for us to make true converts than it was with Paul. Centuries ago, they say, Paul didn't face the same opposition that we do. In these days of secular humanism, failing political leadership, and declining morality, Christian leaders claim we have more opposition to the spread of the gospel. The truth is just the opposite.

The early church lived in a totally pagan culture. Degenerate emperors like Caligula and Nero were worshiped as gods and reigned over the world the apostles lived in as part of the Roman Empire. On top of that, the emperors required taxes be paid to them. There was no prevailing sense of morality, as we call it. The emperors themselves were often immoral monsters who murdered their own family members. Belief in one God was ridiculed, and both Jews and Christians became easy targets for persecution.

We complain about the culture today, but despite their greater obstacles, we don't hear any complaints coming from the early Christians. How are we going to build the church with Nero as the emperor? Come on. Let's be real. There's a totally pagan mentality over there in Rome. Instead, they trusted the Holy Spirit to overcome the challenges in front of them. Our complaints don't match up with the reality of their more challenging circumstances.

Does anyone really believe that the Republicans, Democrats, White House, Supreme Court, or Congress will transform one human heart? Are these civil servants supposed to be light and salt, or is that the task of the church of Jesus Christ? Unless there is a new heart, there won't be a new person. Unless people are changed, we can't have a transformed society, no matter who's in charge.

For the first time in church history, spiritual leaders are being sold new methods instead of an opportunity to meet God in a fresh way. Pastors tell me repeatedly that it's a "new day," and we must be careful not to offend or else folks might not visit again next Sunday. But when the message is catered to the people's tastes, soon it is no longer a message with God's power behind it. This is sad and has tragic consequences. We had better face the fact that Christ never asked us to be clever, entertaining communicators, but rather to declare his love and salvation to everyone we can.

Paul didn't end up in prison getting whipped and beaten, early Christians didn't face persecution, and Stephen didn't become martyred because they were broadcasting a "user-friendly" message. No, we are called by God to share the truth as it is in Jesus. We have to declare the pure, unadulterated gospel. The Lord warned us that when we do it that way, in some situations, we will face the same hatred, the same rejection, and the same persecution that he faced. Muslims are persecuting Christians in Egypt, and there have been dozens of church burnings. When Christians are discovered in Iran or in North Korea, terrible persecution occurs, including imprisonment and death. But the message won't change. It can't change. We must preach Christ and him crucified. Otherwise, we fail as followers of Jesus.

Thirty minutes of Spirit-aided intercessory prayer is more effective than all the new programs and stylistic changes we are constantly tinkering with. [18]

OBSERVATIONS

Some of what you have just read is comforting and yes, some is convicting and disturbing. It is especially noteworthy that a few of the men quoted passed away over 20 years ago, but their insights and projections are relevant as if they were living today. They spoke of the signs of God's judgment and the cultural signs of decay that were activating God's displeasure. My attention is arrested and my heart is compelled to cry out all the more to God, knowing that His mercy has striven with us for decades.

Today, however, we see further evidence of the very signs that concerned these men decades ago, now intensifying and serving as additional proof that God is disciplining us in greater measure. Without question, the weight of His corrective hand is resting heavily upon us. It is time for the Church to rise from its slumber, for we have already overslept.

George Mason's View of God's Judgment on Nations

"As nations cannot be rewarded or punished in the next world, so they must be in this, by an inevitable chain of causes and effects. Providence punishes national sins by national calamities." [1]

— George Mason (1725-1792)
was called the "Father of the Bill of Rights."

CHAPTER 22

Voices for Hope & Change (Part 4)

I have been blessed with a fairly strong family tree. My mother far exceeded her expected longevity, living until 82 and my Dad remains healthy and vibrant at age 91. No one in our family has died due to cancer. However, I can imagine reading the diagnoses of this array of leaders, whether they are religious, political, military, sociologists, or economists, all are in agreement that our beloved nation is terminally sick. Like a family member reading for the first time the medical report of an ill parent who has known nothing except health and happiness, but now is faced with the undeniable reality that an untreatable malignant tumor has been discovered. Apart from divine healing, there is nothing the best doctors in the medical world can do. Death looms on the horizon. It is a shocking reality check for the family. Memories of the way things used to be flooding their minds. The laughter, energy, and fun times make the doctor's pessimistic diagnosis seem so surreal. Denial seems to be the initial reaction, but deep in their hearts they know the report is accurate. Now, more than ever, they agree to desperately cry out for God to glorify Himself through a supernatural healing. They have known of such reports occurring with others, so now they're committed to seeking God as never before.

Pertaining to our nation, as you have read the assessment of various leaders, your initial reaction may have been similar to the above illustration. The nation of our past contains pleasant memories of military might, a robust economy, pride in her manufacturing industry, and an educational system that was the envy of the world.

It is difficult coming to grips with where we stand today. A tumor has metastasized and continues to spread. The diagnosis is in. The report is in. We've received more than a second opinion. With few exceptions, and those all from the liberal side of the aisle, America's days are numbered. Revival in the church that leads to spiritual awakening throughout the nation is our only remedy. And that comes only from God's people seeking His face in prayer and repenting of our sin.

Dinesh D'Souza, a former White House analyst, writes that in talking to people outside our nation, "they sound as if the West is already finished; one of their stock phrases is, "After America…" The debate abroad is not over whether America will be done, but what will replace America. The main candidates are Russia, Brazil, India, and China but the smart money is on China." [2] As America's economy continues to decline and our decisions become less impactful in the world, our irrelevance will become increasingly apparent and accepted. Of course, this will place our national security at a higher risk. Granted, it is difficult to envision how we will be perceived globally but D'Souza gives this analogy: "Think of the way Americans view Mexico, with a mixture of condescension and contempt. That's the way that we are going to be viewed. Among many educated people outside the West, that's the way we are viewed now." [3]

Paul Nyquist, president of Moody Bible Institute, joins the chorus of men who have expressed the same concerns and agree with the same remedy. He says, "Our culture is in the midst of a radical makeover. The current trends show no sign of abating—only accelerating as the generational shift continues. Unless the hearts of Americans are gripped and changed through another Great Awakening, believers can expect antagonism—with its attendant physical, emotional, and financial effects—to steadily increase. To salvage our nation.….we need an unrelenting, nation-changing, awe-inspiring, church-filling movement of God." [4]

As we conclude our section of Voices for Hope & Change, it crescendos with the following insightful comments from another selection of spiritual giants whose finger has been, and remains, on the pulse of this radical shift in American culture.

Billy Graham

(Evangelist, spiritual advisor to American presidents, Founder of the Billy Graham Evangelistic Association, and has appeared 55 times in Gallop's Most Admired Men and Women.)

"Our great need is not for more economic prosperity. Our great need is for a real spiritual awakening. In my opinion we've had four major crisis periods in American history. The first was the Revolutionary War. We did not even know whether we could be born as a nation or not. The next great crisis in American history came when a Constitutional Convention was called in Philadelphia to ratify a Constitution for the new country that was being born. The delegates got angry with each other; they couldn't agree on a thing. Benjamin Franklin eloquently called on the Convention to pray for God's assistance. Out of that Convention came the Constitution of the United States.

The next great crisis came during the Civil War. Men on both sides were killing each other, brothers against brothers, and it seemed that our little country would be torn apart. It seemed that we would become two separate nations or that some European power would come and take us over because we had weakened each other. President Lincoln called the nation to a day of prayer, and in his call of prayer he recommended individual repentance. The day that General Lee surrendered, President Lincoln called the Cabinet to prayer, and at the suggestion of the president the whole Cabinet dropped to its knees and offered thanks to Almighty God for the victory that preserved the Union.

The fourth great crisis in American history was not World War I. We were never threatened in World War I. Nor was it World War II. We were really never threatened as a nation in World War II. The fourth great crisis in American history is the crisis of the present moment. Our nation at this moment is being threatened as it has not been threatened since the Civil War. We are being threatened by moral deterioration. The same symptoms that were in Rome during its last days are now seen and felt in America. Walk down the streets of our cities and see the current names of today's films. Many are either psychopathic or centered on sex. We need a spiritual revival that will put a new moral fiber into our society, or we will have collapsed internally before any enemies even get here. We are being softened up right now by the devil for the kill.

I am convinced that our nation is in peril. The handwriting is on the wall. The signs of the times are everywhere. A cancer is eating at the heart and core of the American way of life. The great need in America is not for more guns or more smart bombs—it is for more men and women who have been transformed by the power of Christ and are living dedicated lives for Christ in the office, on the production line, and in the school. The great need is for men and women who will take their stand for the Lord Jesus Christ, no matter what the cost. The place where we belong is at the foot of the cross."[5]

David Kupelian

(Award-winning journalist, vice president and managing editor of online news giant WND, *editor of* "Whistleblower" *magazine, and a featured guest on Fox News, CBN, and other radio venues)*

"There is still hope for America. Even if something like half the country has become either indoctrinated, or corrupted, or hopelessly dependent on a nanny state, what about the other half? What about the tens of millions of right-thinking Americans who haven't abandoned the nation's founding value—the soldiers and veterans; the hardworking farmers, ranchers, business-owners, and entrepreneurs; the grateful immigrants who came with nothing and achieved the American dream; the inventors and visionaries; and most important, the patriotic citizens who love their country, its history, and its values, as well as the God who blessed them with it? A lot of them are still here!

Columnist Don Feder concludes that grassroots fervor has never been stronger: *Those with a passionate commitment to life, marriage, border security, Second Amendment rights, the free market, and fighting jihad are energized and mobilized. The National Rifle Association has 4.5 million members. The National Right to Life Committee has more than 3,000 chapters. Rush Limbaugh has a weekly audience of 13.25 million. Sean Hannity has 12.5 million. There is 7 million each for The Glenn Beck Program and The Mark Levin Show, and 5.25 million for The Savage Nation. The only liberal talk-show in Talkers magazine's list of most-listened-to-radio programs is Thom Hartman, with a weekly audience of 2 million.*

Consider taking your precious children out of the government indoctrination centers called "public schools" and either homeschooling them or enrolling them in a private school compatible with your values. Remember Lincoln's warning, "The philosophy of the schoolroom in one generation is the philosophy of government in the next"—which is exactly how we got the government we have today!" [6]

Mark Hitchcock

(Senior Pastor of Faith Bible Church in Edmond, Oklahoma; prolific author and lecturer on Bible prophecy)

"Three main keys to national blessing are set forth in Scripture. The first biblical key to national blessing is the Jewish people. All the way back in Genesis 12:3, God made an amazing promise to

Abraham and his descendants that has never been revoked. "And I will bless those who bless you, and the one who curses you I will curse." Literally, we could translate this, "Those who bless you I will bless, and the one who curses you I must curse." This is God's only "direct" foreign policy statement in the entire Bible. Those who support the Jewish people will be blessed and those who curse them must be cursed. This ancient promise from God has never been repealed or abrogated. It still stands today.

American support for Israel today is more important than ever. Israel's problems, threats, and challenges are much more complicated and deadly than in the past, and at the same time, standing with Israel is becoming much more unpopular. An anti-Israel, and anti-U.S. attitude pervades the United Nations. Add to that the jihadist hatred for Israel; America is under growing pressure to "throw Israel under the bus." It's a key line of defense for our nation. Charles Dyer states the issue forcefully: "The minute the United States turns its back on the State of Israel, we have made ourselves the enemy of God."

The second biblical key to national blessing is faithfully sharing the good news (the gospel) of salvation with a needy world. A key ingredient in God's blessing on America is its active promotion and support of the gospel around the globe. God has been merciful to the United States simply because so many people have financed missions and have personally taken the good news of the gospel to others in this world. No other nation's faithfulness in this respect even comes close to America's. This is beautiful to God, and He blesses it.

In a nutshell, that's God's foreign policy for nations today: bless Israel and spread the good news to the nations. The third and final way we can invoke the blessing of God upon our nation is by practicing justice and righteousness in our own lives and promoting righteousness in the society at large. The fate of a nation is not ultimately dependent upon politics, military might, or economics, but on righteousness, goodness, and mercy.

Psalm 33:12 says, "Blessed is the nation whose God is the Lord." Proverbs 14:34 is crystal clear: "Righteousness exalts a nation, but sin is a disgrace to any people." Psalm 9:17 states the promise negatively: "The wicked will return to Sheol, even all the nations who forget God."

One important way we can ensure the continued outpouring of God's blessing is to elect godly leaders, to pray for them (1 Timothy 2:2), to support and vote for government policies that are righteous and good, to speak out and vote against government policies and actions that are unrighteous and harmful, and to practice personal holiness in our own lives."[7]

Tony Evans

(Founder and Senior Pastor of Oak Cliff Bible Fellowship in Dallas, Texas; founder and president of The Urban Alternative. His radio broadcast is heard on over 1,000 US radio outlets; He is former chaplain of the Dallas Cowboys)

"America is not the first nation to be in a situation of seeming hopelessness on a number of levels. Far too often in America today we fail to make the connection between our sin and society's circumstances. We fail to recognize that it was greed—plain and simple—that led to the housing collapse of 2008 and the subsequent $700 billion bailout. When we fail to make the connection between the spiritual and social, we fail to seek the solution that can bring real and lasting impact. We fail to address the spiritual root of the physical mayhem. Our spiritual situation in America has led to our social disintegration.

Our nation is poised for revival. We have reached the end of ourselves—that place where we realize that we cannot solve nor resurrect the death around us on our own. Much of what we witness today in American culture has been misdiagnosed by members of our news media. News analysts often give a political diagnosis for what has gone wrong, or an economic one, or even a social diagnosis. Yet what is happening in our land today and what is happening in our lives is spiritual at its root and must be diagnosed spiritually. The right diagnosis is personal and corporate rebellion against our maker.

The church is to be the key to the transformation of the culture, not the other way around. In the past, the church effectively influenced the society in many ways. In fact, it was because of the emphasis of the freedom of religion, as promoted by the body of Christ, that America was born. It was also because of the promotion of freedom and equality for all, in large part through the church, that civil rights for African-Americans was achieved. In both cases, the church went against the grain of what was commonly accepted in the culture.

The absence of righteousness in our culture has everything to do with the absence of God's people living as His disciples and thus influencing the culture. He has a lot of fans. Every Sunday around the country, our churches are packed with fans of Jesus who are content to remain in the stands rather than advance His kingdom down the field of play. Jesus doesn't need more fans. He needs more followers.

Almost everyone recognizes the fact that the task of national renewal in the areas of faith and freedom is too big for any one group or church to accomplish effectively. It will require the collective cooperation of the masses to leave a lasting impact for good. People have met in cities, churches, and their homes to call on God and access heaven's intervention in our nation. Many of these gatherings lasted one night, one Sunday, or perhaps two Sundays back-to-back. Yet in the busyness of the American lifestyle, it is easy for these experiences to be lumped into another long list of good things to do and—as a result—lose the collective impact they were intended to have. Because many of these gatherings occurred segmented by denomination, church, or location, we did not experience renewal on the greater level that it is so desperately needed. But have we ever done this collectively and comprehensively with unity from our nation's spiritual leaders?

We will need to set aside personal agendas, organizations, denominations, structures, and the like, and come together once and for all as the body of disciples whom Christ died to procure, and call on the name of our great God and King. Have you ever noticed how "special interest groups" in our country carry far more weight in influencing our land (policies, opinions, etc.) even though their numbers are but a small fraction of the number of evangelicals and believers in America? The reason they carry so much weight and influence is because they unite. We may have the numbers in our favor as an overall body of believers, but we have rarely, if ever, truly united over anything.

It is time to set our preferences and egos aside and go before the Lord as one body. It is also time for more than an evening event or Sunday morning assembly. It is time for a comprehensive season of seeking our Lord's hand and face in our great land. One of the ways to do this is to focus an entire segment of time—whether that is a week or several days—on each of the four covenantal areas of God's involvement with humanity: individual, family, church, and society.

If every serious Bible-believing church would do their own solemn assembly simultaneously with the others—whether that be for a solid week, or spread out over four weeks allowing time for personal reflection during the weekdays—we would see God as a nation together. If church and organizational leadership would come together in humility and unite, we could actually see the hand of God move in our midst in a way we may have never imagined.

We are too far down the road in our country of turning away from God for us to just ignore it, or simply bemoan it, and do nothing about it from a biblically strategic vantage point. We must set aside our personal, church, denominational, and organizational biases and egos, and come together underneath the overarching rule and call of Jesus Christ. [8]

Ronnie Floyd

(Senior Pastor of Cross Church in Springdale, Arkansas; author)

You may have given up on America, but God hasn't. As the foundation of our nation is cracking and our culture is crumbling before our eyes, never and I mean never in our generation, have we needed to call out to God in prayer more than Sunday, September 11. On September 11, 2016, on the 15th anniversary of 9/11, with great conviction, I want to ask each pastor and church in America to allocate the day to praying for our nation. Not just mention it, not just pray, but pray extraordinarily. Make no mistake about it: America's greatest need is the next Great Spiritual Awakening. Only revival in the church, a gospel explosion through the church, and awakening in the nation will turn around the church and nation. We need a Jesus revolution in America!

Surely, as the churches in America, we can agree on one major thing: America needs prayer now! We have no right to prognosticate doom about America, upon evangelicals, upon the church, or anyone else unless we are willing to humble ourselves before God and pray. Prayer brings the walls down! Prayer crosses over the perceived barriers of ethnicity, race, and generations, bringing down the walls that divide us.

I believe the polarization and division in America, the multiple crises in America and across the entire world, and the extreme division occurring in the church of America is a strong call from God to us: Come back to Me! Let me be clearer: The church cannot call America to repent until the church repents. We need to repent of our prayerlessness. We need to repent of our unbelief. We need to pray for ourselves to get right with God and right with one another.

The stakes couldn't be higher in America. Our hope cannot be in politics, positions, possessions, or people. Our eyes need to be fixed on Jesus alone. Our hope is not in Washington, DC or your state capitol, but in the cross and resurrection of Jesus Christ. God can do more in a moment than you could ever do in a lifetime. [9]

As spiritual leaders, there is not one of us who can sit out in this critical hour. Now is not the time for the churches in America to call time out and retreat to their land of comfort and sit around dissecting their theology and the theology of others. To every Southern Baptist layperson who operates daily in the arena of business, healthcare, education, entertainment, sports, law, politics, government, or serves in our military, please understand that the stakes have never been higher in this generation. Our pastors and churches need you to be more engaged on Sundays than ever before, but we also need you intentionally integrating your faith on the front lines of our culture in everything you do daily regardless of where you are.

One of the major reasons this is important is that our religious liberty in America is at stake. We are on the precipice of either experiencing spiritual awakening or falling into an abyss. We cannot be adrift in denial any longer; we must face our future honestly. We are at a turning point. This is our moment of decision. All other crises surface due to the spiritual crisis we are facing as a nation. We need to stop treating just the symptoms. It is time to go to the root of our problems. America is in a major spiritual crisis, perhaps the worst in our generation.

We all want to bring prayer back into our public schools, but I wish we would bring prayer back into our churches. [10]

Rick Warren

(Founding pastor of Saddleback Church in Lake Forest, California. He is a New York Times Bestseller, author of The Purpose Drive Church and Purpose Driven Life, named one of the 100 Christian books that changed the 20th century)

I believe God is preparing the church for another reformation. The first reformation focuses on what the church believed; this one will focus on what it does. Every time a new reformation has come, five renewals preceded it: (1) Personal renewal. You might call it rededicating your life, being filled with the Spirit or the "deeper life." I don't care what you call it. Just get it! (2) Relational Renewal. You've got to get right with others. When you have relational renewal in your church, the gossip goes down and the joy goes up. How do you know when a church has been through relational renewal? People hang around longer after the service. If people don't want to hang around after your services, you have a performance, not a church. (3) Missional Renewal. This is when a church discovers what God wants it to do. We have a kingdom assignment. We're not here just to bless one another. God wants to bless the world through us. (4) Cultural Renewal. Once the first three renewals have happened in the church, God will change the culture. (5) Structural Renewal. As your church gets healthier and healthier, the structure has to change. A great spiritual awakening is on the horizon. [11]

America is in its worst condition in our generation. Politically, our government has been paralyzed by partisanship. Culturally, we're becoming more and more secular. And internationally, our reputation has never been lower. America needs healing. We need healing in our economy. We need healing in our businesses. We need healing in our schools. We need healing in our marriages and our families. And, most of all, we need healing in our hearts. But our wounds are not fatal. I'm very hopeful.

So what is it that will heal America? We have to do the four things that God told Solomon and the nation of Israel to do. (1) **We must confess with humility.** The source of all our problems is pride. We think we know better than God what will make us happy. Hiding our sins is the opposite of humility. We need to lead our churches in a time of confession. (2) **We must pray with tenacity.** We simply give up too soon. That's why we don't see answers. That's why America doesn't see the widespread healing the Bible talks about in this verse. The tenacity of your prayer life will say a lot about how serious you really are. (3) **We must seek God with intensity.** You don't just seek God in your spare moments. It has to be our primary focus. God doesn't want to be our profession. He wants to be our passion. Most people want just enough of God to bless them but not bug them. (4) **We must repent with sincerity.** When we repent, we change the way we think about ourselves and God. We change the way we think about our values, other people, our past, our present, and our future. National repentance must begin with personal repentance.

America is in deep trouble right now. If God is going to judge America, he'll start with us. America will not be healed because we passed a certain law. Healing won't happen because we elect the right people to government positions. God will heal our land when his people—the church—confess, pray, seek him, and repent. National healing will start with our churches, or it won't happen. Will it start with you? [12]

James Robison

(Founder and President of LIFE Outreach and host of the daily television program LIFE Today.

"We are clearly witnessing the judgment and wrath of God revealed against all ungodliness as we see people given over to ravenous and demonic appetites and practices. The only hope for America lies in the effective witness and influence of the local church for the transformation of the individual, not in the power of government or social movements.

Voting is not just an inherent right or a mere privilege, but it is our responsibility. Edward Everett Hale, former chaplain of the US Senate, said, "I am only one. I cannot do everything, but I still can do something." The most basic "something" we can do is to vote. All citizens should get and out and cast their votes on the issues that live beyond today and will affect our children and grandchildren. Someone will determine our future; why not Christians? We have the power not only to change people's lives today but also to help shape the future for generations to come.

Christian influence on government was primarily responsible for the Declaration of Independence, the Constitution, and the Bill of Rights. These are three of the most significant documents in the history of governments on the earth, and all three show the marks of significant Christian influence in the foundational ideas of how governments should function. These foundations of our country did not come about as a result of the "do church, not politics" view. If our founders had adopted the "do church, not politics" views, we might not have a country today. But we do, because Christians realized that if they could influence laws and governments for good they would be obeying the command of their Lord.

We can kiss freedom in America good-bye unless those who say they know and love God stand together against the forces of evil.

If we don't act now, it will be too late to halt evil's intent. Satan's goal has always been the destruction of life and freedom, and in our day he often appears to be winning. We need a spiritual revival of our hearts and minds, which starts in our churches, changes our communities, and reforms the culture.

Whenever issues of national and moral importance are addressed by a religious leader, we hear the outcry, "Stay out of politics!" In other words, they say ministers must avoid real-life issues, problems, and challenges on the national stage by never standing up with hopeful, helpful solutions. The truth is, Christians, all people of faith, and certainly preachers of the Word of God are obligated to speak out boldly and to stand for their convictions. Ministers must not be timid and fearful or they will have a church filled with spineless, fear-filled people who will never become a "city set on a hill." Pastors must join together to sound a clear alarm on the trumpet of truth so the people will prepare for the right battle in the right way and win by choosing righteousness. Christians, pastors, and church leaders must totally reject the lie that "separation of church and state" means that people of faith must remain silent, uninformed, and uninvolved.

It is my firm opinion we are in the process of actually losing our national freedom—a freedom built on moral absolutes and a strong, but limited, government. Right now, I don't see how we are not headed toward the imprisonment of pastors and other Christian leaders. I don't see how Christian media can survive. I don't see how religious schools and universities can operate without fully embracing homosexuality. I don't see how companies that don't advocate gay marriage can be allowed to engage in business. Given all of this, I don't see how we are not headed toward civil unrest or complete collapse. That's why we need to pray—and pray hard.

Our nation will not be spared from catastrophic economic and moral collapse unless we turn to God and experience the necessary spiritual awakening. The collapse is imminent but by no means necessary. We can correct our course. Our nation is heading in the wrong direction, and much of the responsibility lies in the church. Still, there is hope—and it lies in the church as well. Repentance, beginning on the part of the church, is where we start. We must recognize that we have failed to be rightly inspired, adequately informed, and totally involved. I fully believe that if the church becomes prayerfully involved in the political process, then we can see this nation turn back to the light and glory of liberating truth. Freedom's future rests on the shoulders of bold people who will not be silent about truth and the absolute principles upon which it stands."[13]

OBSERVATIONS

This book could be filled with hundreds of other entries from leaders throughout our land, all of whom will agree with what has been written. The common thread that weaves its way throughout these Voices of Hope & Change contains at least four elements: (1) America is on the verge of collapse. We stand at a defining moment in our history, unlike anything we've seen in our lifetime. As Billy Graham observed, this is the worst crisis since the Civil War. Our destiny hangs in the balance. Of this assessment, all the leaders aforementioned are in agreement. (2) The basis of our crisis is spiritual in nature. Thus, before there can be national awakening, there must be revival in the church. The church is out of step with God in its priorities. I know of no spiritual leader who does not agree that the church is lukewarm and in desperate need of God's reviving power to be manifested. (3) All agree that prayer is the essential component to such an awakening. It must begin with God's people. More specifically, it must begin with God's pastors calling their congregations to such a time of protracted prayer. This calls for an interruption of our regularly scheduled programming.

The hour is late. The stakes are high. Desperate times call for desperate measures. (4) Finally, most of these men are in agreement that pastors must be more vocal, bold, and proactive in addressing the issues of the day and raising the awareness of our plight among their congregations. Christians must get involved in the political process, most fundamentally by showing up at the polls to vote.

Of the above four elements there is consensus. Certainly, there are other elements mentioned by leaders and much wisdom must be exercised in proceeding forward to "flesh out" the details necessary to mobilize the body of Christ throughout America so that we come together in unity with "one heart and one soul" as Acts 4:32 describes. The fact is, it is doable. This is not out of the question. With the technology today, such a massive movement could occur in a relatively short time. Once they hear a clarion call from the pulpits of America, I believe God's people will understand the seriousness of the moment and will agree to engage in this mighty movement. Even concerned unbelieving citizens, I think, will nod their heads in agreement when the church rises to this occasion. I believe politicians will welcome the churches of our land crying out to God in their behalf. It is simply time for the church to be the church. As in days of old during similar national crises, when the church raises the standard and marches forth in unity, the gates of hell will not prevail. It starts in the pulpits, then in the pews, and onto the streets. What are we waiting for?

The America That Once Existed

"The American population is entirely Christian, and with us Christianity and religion are identified. It would be strange indeed, as such a people, if our institutions did not presuppose Christianity, and did not often refer to it, and exhibit relations with it." [1]

— John Marshall (1755-1835)
was Chief Justice of the United States for 34 years

CHAPTER 23

Severe Weather Alert

In this age of sound bytes and twitter feeds, one of the purposes for writing this expansive volume is to issue a severe weather alert as it pertains to our nation's survival. My sense is that the overwhelming majority of Americans are oblivious to the precarious future facing us. When severe storms approach the area, sirens scream throughout the neighborhoods, television stations interrupt regularly scheduled programming, and the radio stations fill the airwaves with their shrill alarms warning the public to take shelter. Yet, what confronts us as a nation is far more ominous than severe weather. Our very future hangs in the balance. Our religious liberties are on the verge of being lost. Our total economy teeters on collapse. The very identity of America is at risk of totally disappearing. Everything we hold dear and near to our hearts as God-fearing Americans is vanishing.

Alarm bells are ringing. The lights on the dashboard are flashing. The sirens are blasting. Yet, it appears that we are deaf and blind to it all. The church is sleep-walking its way through this dark hour completely unaware of what lies ahead if we refuse to wake up. As James Robison stated, "I don't see how we are not headed toward the imprisonment of pastors and other Christian leaders. I don't see how we are not headed toward complete collapse." [2] Many view such comments as fear-mongering and rightwing extremism, but unless we change course, there is coming a day (sooner than later) when we will regret our refusal to heed the warnings God has so graciously been giving us.

WHERE ARE THE WATCHMEN?

Watchman is not a word we often use, but if I counted correctly, it is used 31 times in the Old Testament. A watchman was the first line of defense for those on the inside of the fortress. For you see, the watchman's job was to stand in the tower and search the horizon for any sign of a threat that may place the safety of the citizens at risk. Actually, it was a dangerous assignment because his position in the tower made him vulnerable. Upon sighting danger, the watchman would blow the trumpet alerting all citizens to prepare for approaching danger.

Since the watchman was the first line of defense, it can readily be seen that any apathy or laziness in his duty would jeopardize the safety of those within the fortress. Thus, he was required to be alert and vigilant in dispensing his duties. Now, whenever the watchman sounded his trumpet, the threat had better be legitimate. If he was guilty of sounding false alarms, then the people themselves would become complacent and the watchman would lose his credibility. So, there were two charges given to the watchman: Not to sound false alarms and not to sound the alarm too late.

If the watchman waited too long for confirmation of a coming crisis, then it could prove to be fatal. Understandably, sufficient data needed to be gathered and proper assessment needed to be made before blowing the trumpet. However, taking too much time to acquire the necessary information meant sacrificing time, time that could prove to be fatal. Thus, the timing of the watchman was extremely vital. Of course, the goal of the enemy is to go undetected so that it will be too late to reverse the consequences of a surprise attack.

It stands to reason, therefore, that the enemy will do his best to eliminate the watchman. In fact, targeting the watchman is often the enemy's top priority because once the watchman is removed, then success is practically guaranteed. One of the strategies of the enemy for going undetected is to disguise himself by appearing to be a friend. Thus, the attack comes from both outside and inside.

God has designated preachers and other spiritual leaders to serve as His watchmen. This is part of our role and yet a great percentage have capitulated to the political correctness of our day and cowered to the whims of influential opinions that say "politics and religion" don't mix. Indeed, there is a delicate line to be respected, but I must agree with George Barna and David Barton in their excellent book, *U Turn*: "When a majority of the senior pastors of Protestant churches proclaim that there must be a separation of religion and politics and that it is unacceptable for pastors to use the pulpit to incite people to "political" action, we are a nation in grave danger."[3]

Our congregations are uninformed and asleep through this revolution that has transformed our nation and much of the blame lay at the feet of pastors who have a greater fear of man than the fear of the Lord. God is telling us to wake up, but we have repeatedly hit the snooze button.

WAS THE ELECTION OF 2016 OUR LAST?

On January 20, 2017, the presidential inauguration of Donald J. Trump was made official and concluded a campaign unlike any in American history. Both candidates had the highest disapproval numbers of any in history. With each passing week there were new "revelations" regarding Hillary's ineptitude and scandalous actions during her stint as Secretary of State. Lie after lie, deceit upon deceit, contradictions galore haunted her every step of the way. A new batch of emails was uncovered marked as "Classified." She actually stated not to know what the "C" at the top of the page meant. Using her personal email address to transact government business was unprecedented. And then it was revealed that she had 13 mobile devices that were smashed and destroyed with a hammer. Avoiding the media by refusing to hold a press conference for 300-plus days was unheard of for such a candidate, but only compounded the suspicions of her guilt. The aura surrounding this lady reeks with corruption. But the very fact that many of the analysts were forecasting a landslide victory in her favor only exposed the character flaws of Trump. More importantly, it reflected the culture itself. Throughout the campaign Trump threw one verbal grenade after another only to have them boomerang in his own face. Had he displayed the temperament of an adult rather than the thin-skinned name-calling of a sixth grade bully whenever he was insulted, he would have done himself well. Even so, the populace forgivingly turned the other cheek (or the other ear) and rallied behind his mantra, "Make America Great Again!" He obviously had hit a nerve with his rhetoric and had his finger on the pulse of millions that was unforeseen by practically all prognosticators.

Despite such antics and despite criticizing Hillary for reading off a teleprompter, Trump acquiesced to the counsel of his advisors and he himself became more scripted by utilizing the teleprompter. His speeches were more substantive and his ranting more subdued. He looked more presidential, his temperament more controlled, and his poll numbers began to narrow the gap.

Also to his credit he formed an evangelical advisory board with such names as: Ronnie Floyd, Cross Church in Springdale, Arkansas; Jentezen Franklin, Free Chapel in Gainesville, Georgia; Jack Graham, Prestonwood Baptist in Plano, Texas; David Jeremiah, Shadow Mountain Community Church in El Cajon, California; Robert Morris, Gateway Church in Southlake, Texas; James MacDonald, Harvest Bible Chapel in Rolling Meadows, Illinois; James Robison, Life OUTREACH International in Euless, Texas; Jay Strack, Student Leadership University in Orlando, Florida and several others. Trump told the board that "Our laws prevent you from speaking your minds from your own pulpits. I am going to work very hard to repeal that language and to protect free speech for all Americans."[4]

Former Congresswoman Michele Bachmann, who also serves on Trump's advisory board, says, "I believe without a shadow of a doubt this is the last election. If Hillary Clinton is elected, she'll let people into the country who will change the demographics of states like Florida and Texas and make it impossible for Republicans to win there. If we can't win Florida and Texas, it's game over." This is the last election when we even have a chance to vote for somebody who will stand up for godly moral principles. [5]

To clarify her position, Bachmann went on to say, "It's a math problem of demographics and a changing United States. If you look at the numbers of people who vote and who lives in the country and who Barack Obama and Hillary Clinton want to bring into the country, this is the last election when we even have a chance to vote for somebody who will stand up for Godly moral principles. This is it." She went on to rebuke the "Never-Trumpers" by saying, "Get over it. All the establishment Republicans that are out there saying, 'We'll just take our chances and four years from now we'll have a better candidate, then we can take the White House.' It's not going to happen." [6]

Bachmann, a strong Christian herself, says "the choice facing Americans this fall is one of 'life and death.' God says to every nation for all of time, 'I set before you life and death, what are you going to choose?' If you look at the book of Genesis, you don't even have to get beyond chapter 3 to see that the first thing he gives mankind is life. What does man choose? Death. We choose rebellion and death. You go from Genesis all through the Bible to the book of Revelation; man stupidly makes the same decision over and over again by rejecting life and choosing death. What I'm telling you is that's what we're looking at now in this country." [7]

Concluding her remarks, Bachmann passionately declared, "I don't think God sits things out (as if to send a message to those who refused to vote in 2016). He's a sovereign God. Donald Trump became our nominee. I think it's very likely that in the day that we live in, Donald Trump is the only individual who could win in a general election of the 17 who ran. Maybe I'm wrong. I actually supported Ted Cruz. I thought he was fabulous, but I do know that the Bible is true and that Daniel teaches the Most High God, which is one of God's names, is the one who lifts up who he will and takes down who he will."[8]

WHERE DO WE GO FROM HERE?

I have no doubt that both sides of the aisle love America. The problem is we each love a different America. One side loves the America that was built upon Judeo-Christian principles, an educational system that was fortified with biblical principles, and a political system that reinforced those values from the White House to the school house to the houses of everyday citizens. This is the side that believes in hard work and flag-saluting veterans and the spirit of capitalism and small government. This is the side that believes in traditional values and the right to life for the developing babies inside millions of mother's wombs. The other side loves a different America. It's the America that believes in the redistribution of wealth, social entitlements, women's rights, gay rights, gay marriage, abortion, and big government. Clearly, we are divided. Only as the true Church of Jesus Christ allows its voice to be heard and only as God's people seriously seek the face of our Almighty Savior through prayer and fasting, will the nation avert total collapse. That's right; the future of the most important nation on earth hangs in the balance.

When Ted Cruz announced his presidential candidacy at Liberty University, he made a revealing statement: "Today roughly half of born-again Christians aren't voting. They're staying home. Imagine, instead, millions of people of faith all across America coming out to the polls and voting our values."[9] Let's explore this further.

PolitiFact concluded that 42 percent of evangelical Christians stay home on Election Day. Since over 70 percent of Americans self-identify as Christian with more than 25 percent being evangelicals, we're talking tens of millions of potential voters who refuse to exercise their right to vote by participating in the electoral process. [10] To think about the sacrifice made by our Founders who fought, bled, and died to preserve our freedoms, and then to think about the millions of Christians who cannot get motivated to set aside their personal agendas to go cast a ballot on Election Day and vote their values, is sickening.

THE DECK IS STACKED

How can we possibly think that exposing millions upon millions of our children to an educational system that denies the existence of God has no impact on their mental health and well-being? How can we possibly think that teaching millions upon millions of young impressionable minds that they are the product of a random, accidental process called evolution does not affect their self-esteem? Do we not think that aborting 60 million children since 1973 will impact the mother's mental health in the aftermath of realizing what she has just done? How in the name of moral sanity could we ever justify the legalization of marijuana in multiple states when for years it has been proven to be a gateway drug for hardcore addicts? Do we not think that easy access to graphic nudity by young adolescents does not put them on a path of future relational, marital, and emotional problems? Why should we be surprised by the low morale of our soldiers when they see the reduction of our military, forcing our best commanding officers into retirement, and allowing our aircraft to embarrassingly deteriorate beyond repair? With millions unemployed or under-employed and watching the economy teeter on total collapse while observing the irresponsible spending habits by our political agencies, why are surprised by the epidemic of prescription drug addictions? When young children are taught the value of same-sex marriage and they see two men kissing one another and told it is normal behavior, why should we be surprised by their depression and decline of mental health? When homosexual school teachers manipulate their classrooms by making students ashamed if they don't embrace same-sex marriage, why are we shocked by transgender bathrooms and then high incidents of rape? When the liberal professors in our universities denounce God's existence and berate political conservatives, why are we surprised that those with a strong Christian upbringing renounce their Christian heritage?

We are a nation spinning out of control and the deck is stacked against those who embrace conservatism or traditional Christian values. Every major institution in America has been radically transformed. Obama promised to transform the nation, but no one bothered to ask what he meant by such change. We were too caught up with charisma, charm, eloquence, and swagger. Certainly, he doesn't bear all of the blame. This stuff was well underway decades earlier, he just accelerated the process.

IS IT TOO LATE TO TURN BACK?

Only God really knows the answer to that question, but I have to believe that because He is full of grace and mercy, desiring that none should perish, if the Church in America awakens from its slumber and becomes proactive in pursuing the biblically prescribed solutions, then yes, there is hope. "Just what does that entail?" you may ask. One thing is for sure, it will not be in the form of a Democrat or Republican savior.

I borrow the suggestion of a prolonged solemn assembly from Tony Evans which involves a weeklong solemn assembly starting on Sunday morning and culminating with a "Break-the-Fast" breakfast on Saturday morning. As the name implies, there is a sacrifice in giving up personal needs (such as food) in order to call on God for His manifest presence upon our nation. But it also involves meeting together as a church body six times in the week and as individual families one night. The schedule looks something like this:

Sunday Churches across the nation teach the practice of the solemn assembly while individuals continue to pray for personal revival.

Monday Churches convene with families for family revival.

Tuesday Churches convene with their leadership teams for a time of solemn assembly while congregants are equipped with the tools to pray for God's hand in their leadership and church revival.

Wednesday Churches are united via a televised simulcast to participate in the culmination of the week through a national focus of prayer and seeking God for national revival. [11]

Another option is for the church to focus on a four-week national solemn assembly with the following possible format:

Week One. A Sunday gathering focuses on matters of **personal revival**, followed up with study notes, questions, and prayer guide for personal time Monday through Saturday related to individual confession, renewal, vision, and praise.

Week Two. A Sunday gathering focusing on **matters of family revival**, followed up with study notes, questions, and prayer guide for personal time Monday through Saturday related to familial confession, renewal, vision, and praise.

Week Three. A Sunday gathering focusing on **matters of church revival**, followed with study notes, questions, and prayer guide for personal time Monday through Saturday related to church confession, renewal, vision, and praise.

Week Four. A Sunday gathering focusing on **matters of societal revival**, followed up with study notes, questions, and prayer guide for personal time Monday through Saturday related to societal confession, renewal, vision, an d praise, and culminating in a national collective solemn assembly held in one location, and/or groups of community gatherings of churches. [12]

As an evangelist/revivalist, I am praying for God to reveal the course of action our ministry is to pursue and how He would have us to proceed in making a difference within the body of Christ throughout our Land. I am pleased to report that He is, indeed, doing just that. It is extensive, but premature to print the detail. However, one component of the strategy is that of conducting *Heal Our Land* rallies and *Heal Our Land* crusades as the catalysts for revival in the church and the prayerful expectation of spiritual awakening throughout the Land.

The great awakening that occurred in 1857-1858 began with a lone 48 year-old businessman who was burdened for the country. Doing the only thing he knew to do, he began handing out flyers in downtown New York and invited businessmen to take a portion of their lunch hour to pray for the city and nation. As you might suspect, only a handful showed up. But Jeremiah Lanphier persisted. Then, the unexpected occurred. The stock market crashed, people fell to their knees. Within six months, 10,000 people were gathering for prayer in New York City. Broadway venues were being rented during lunchtime for the exclusive purpose of calling upon God to intervene.

Amazingly, 50,000 New Yorkers reportedly gave their lives to Christ from March to May. Throughout the nation, the figures were estimated to be 50,000 new converts each week for about two years. All total, one million people received Jesus Christ as personal Lord and Savior. It all began with one businessman, burdened by God, and doing what little he knew to do. God honored it. The nation was saved. This kind of awakening does not stand in isolation. Such divine intervention is in America's heritage and DNA. We now stand at another critical crossroads unlike anything the nation has known. You are reading this book because you too are concerned. Could you be the one to ignite the spark in your community, your church, or your school?

The Prayer That Caused Uproar

The date was January 23, 1996. Pastor Joe Wright, senior pastor of Central Christian Church in Wichita, Kansas, had been invited to serve as the House's guest chaplain by Rep. Anthony Powell, A Wichita Republican who was also a member of Wright's church. After reading his prayer at the opening of the legislature, Pastor Wright left the assembly unaware of the ruckus he had caused. While returning home in his car, his secretary called to ask what he had done. You see, the church phone had been ringing "off the wall," with a total of over 6,500 calls coming in from every state, including many foreign countries. His prayer even continued to create controversy the next month when Nebraska's chaplain coordinator read it before the legislature.

House Minority Leader Tom Sawyer (a Democrat) claimed the prayer "reflects the extreme radical views that continue to dominate the House Republican agenda since right-wing extremists seized control of the House Republican caucus last year." Some walked out during the prayer and others prepared speeches that blasted his "message of intolerance." So, what exactly did the prayer say that was so offensive to Democrats? Here it is:

Heavenly Father, we come before You today to ask Your forgiveness and seek Your direction and guidance. Lord, we know Your Word says, "Woe to those who call evil good," but that's exactly what we've done. We have lost our spiritual equilibrium and inverted our values.

We have worshipped others gods and called it multi-culturalism.

We have endorsed perversion and called it an alternative lifestyle.

We have exploited the poor and called it the lottery.

We have neglected the needy and called it self-preservation.

We have rewarded laziness and called it welfare.

We have killed our unborn and called it choice.

We have shot abortionists and called it justifiable.

We have neglected to discipline our children and called it building esteem.

We have abused power and called it political savvy.

We have polluted the air with profanity and pornography and called it freedom of expression.

We have ridiculed the time-honored values of our forefathers and called it enlightenment.

Search us, oh God, and know our hearts today; try us and see if there be some wicked way in us; cleanse us from every sin and set us free.

Guide and bless these men and women who have been sent here by the people of Kansas, and who have been ordained by You, to govern this great state. Grant them Your wisdom to rule and may their decisions direct us to the center of Your will. I ask it in the name of Your Son, the Living Savior, Jesus Christ. Amen. [13]

The political and media firestorm that resulted from this simple prayer serves as one more reminder that standing for truth comes with a price. Over twenty years have passed since that prayer was articulated in the chambers of Kansas' legislature. I fear that if such a prayer was to be offered today, even from the pulpits of many of our churches, it would create controversy and perhaps result in the resignation of many pastors. That's how far down the politically-correct road we've travelled.

BRACE FOR THE DESCENT

The verdict is still out. I am encouraged by the increased talk about spiritual awakening. We see it at our national denominational gatherings. We even hear it from some of our politicians. As the spiritual rhetoric gains momentum I am hopeful that the unity we find in Jesus Christ will bring together the Church in America of all denominational persuasions. I am hopeful that the leadership of these denominations will assemble, ask God for His direction, and come out with a strategy designed to compel the Church to cry out in repentance. This must be the starting point.

However, if this fails to occur and if the political atmosphere remains more of the same, then we will see persecution as we never imagined. And America's decline will continue as we fade off the scene as the global leader we once were.

For those who travel by air, the flight attendants have a rehearsed speech that frequent fliers practically have memorized. There is one for takeoff, one for turbulence, one for landing, and one for deplaning. However, there is also one for descent that seems appropriate for the subject before us: *"Ladies and gentlemen, as we start our descent, please make sure your seat backs and tray tables are in their full upright position. Make sure your seat belt is securely fastened and all carry-on luggage is stowed underneath the seat in front of you or in the overhead bins. Thank you."*

In the earlier part of the flight the attendant reminds the passengers that "In the event of an emergency, please assume the bracing position. Lean forward with your hands on top of your head and your elbows against your thighs. Ensure your feet are flat on the floor. Your seat cushion can be used as a flotation device. Pull the cushion from the seat, slip your arms into the straps, and hug the cushion to your chest."

Passengers are also told that "If you are seated next to an emergency exit, please read carefully the special instructions card located by your seat. If you do not wish to perform the functions described in the event of an emergency, please ask a flight attendant to reseat you."

Sound familiar? *Storm Warnings* has made the case that our nation has begun its descent but our "bracing position" is not with hands on top of our heads, but hands lifted toward the heavens. Our arms are not hugging a seat cushion, but embracing the truth of God's Word. No doubt, turbulent times lie ahead. The atmosphere will be bumpy, perhaps even a little unsettling. We are in "emergency mode," but politicians and media seemingly do not want the nation "at large" to know the extent of our crises. They spin it as positively as possible with a game face and demeanor that appears calm and confident, but putting lipstick on a pig does not change the reality. The instruction card is as nearby as your Bible. Contained within are the admonitions necessary to avert a crash landing. Ignoring the oncoming danger and pretending that it's embellished rhetoric or extremist fearmongering does not change the reality of what lies ahead.

It was the legendary Vance Havner who said, "Snowflakes are frail, but if enough of them stick together, they can stop traffic." You are one person, one voice, and one vote. But if enough of us stick together we can make a difference. We've heard the English statesman Edmund Burke oft quoted, "The only thing necessary for evil to triumph is for good people to do nothing." [14] Please review what you have highlighted in this book. Read it. Take it to heart. Act upon it. You, and others like you, are America's only hope as together we bond together through the power of our risen Lord to make a difference. Doing nothing is not an option.

Words of Wisdom from America's First President

"You do well to learn our arts and our ways of life, and above all the religion of Jesus Christ. It is impossible to rightly govern the world without God and the Bible."[1]

— George Washington (1732-1799)
the first President of the United States and Commander-in-Chief of the Continental Army during the Revolutionary War

CHAPTER 24

The Mother of All Storms

Although *Storm Warnings* is not a book that addresses Bible prophecy, there can be little doubt that underlying all of the aforementioned crises is a sovereign God whose plan for the ages will not be diverted or defeated. Regardless who sits in the Oval Office, we know who sits on the Throne. At this present time, things in the world look ugly. Spiritual darkness is increasingly prevalent. Lawlessness abounds. Truth is embraced only when convenient. Integrity is a rare trait. Prophetic voices that thunder "Thus says the Lord" are quickly becoming a fading memory. Compromising churches are the norm rather than the exception. Political corruption is rampant. Cynicism toward politicians and skepticism toward preachers are commonplace. The culture is inundated with immorality. Profanity and obscenity dominate the airwaves. For those who say it can't get much worse, think again.

Since this is not a book on Bible prophecy, I must refrain from getting too technical in identifying signs of the times or offering a theological treatise on end-time events. This has been a lengthy read and it's time to put down the landing gear, but before doing so it is important to be reminded that history is His Story. The unseen sovereign hand of God is orchestrating the events of history, even those discussed in this book. Rather than get distressed and depressed, let's keep an eye on the Eastern sky because it's time to stop looking at the signs and start listening for a shout. Jesus is returning. All signs are pointing in that direction. With a newspaper in one hand and the Bible in the other, it is clear that prophecy is unfolding at an unprecedented rate. The Rapture of the Church could occur at any time. However, staying consistent with the theme of storm warnings, it only seems fitting to conclude with the mother of all storms, Armageddon. This is the storm that ends all storms. Armageddon makes all other wars look like "kids play," minor skirmishes. There will no final curtain call. Contrarily, this is God drawing the curtain on modern civilization.

Former President Ronald Reagan said, "You know, I turn back to your prophets in the Old Testament and the signs foretelling Armageddon and I find myself wondering if we're the generation that's going to see that come about. I don't know if you've noted any of these prophecies lately, but believe me, they certainly describe the times we're going through." [2] One has to wonder what Reagan would say today. With the global threat of terrorism, the Israelis and Palestinians in a life-and-death struggle, Afghanistan a hotbed for radical jihad, Iraq being overrun by ISIS, Iran as the world leader in training terrorists, and hundreds of thousands of Syrian refugees fleeing their countries murderous regime, the entire world is becoming one big power keg. All of this, and more, seems to be a foreshadowing for Armageddon to take center stage.

Billy Graham says, "There is no doubt that global events are preparing the way for the final war of history—the great Armageddon!" [3]

I am fully aware that some who read this chapter may not believe the Bible or may be skeptical at best. Thus, reluctance to embrace prophetic predictions is understandable. It may seem mystical, anti-intellectual, and simply hocus-pocus. Certainly, each is entitled to his or her opinion, but it is important for the reader to know that of the hundreds of prophecies contained in Scripture, not one has ever failed. The Bible is the only book that dares to predict the future in great detail. Museums across the planet contain mountains of evidence regarding the historical reliability of the Bible. Whenever archeologists have dug up the evidence, the Bible has been proven to be one hundred percent accurate and skeptics proven to be wrong. I only mention this to validate the fact that unlike other religious books, the Bible has an unblemished track record. Indeed, it is the inerrant, infallible Word of God.

That being said, promises of the second coming of Christ dominate both the Old and New Testaments. There are 1,845 references to Christ's return in the Old Testament with 17 books giving it prominence. Of the 260 chapters in the New Testament, there are 318 references to His return. In fact, 23 of the 27 New Testament books refer to this climatic event. Of the four books that do not refer directly to the Second Coming, three are single chapter letters which were written to persons on a specific subject. Since this is the only Book that God ever wrote, there is a reason He devoted so much ink to this subject. It is His desire that no one perish, but that all come to repentance and saving faith in Jesus Christ.

Much of what we've read in the preceding chapters is the result of God withdrawing His protective hedge from our nation and the crises surrounding America come as an expression of such divine judgment. However, this pales in comparison to what awaits the world during the seven-year Tribulation Period and culminating with the Battle of Armageddon, the cosmic battle of the ages. Leading toward this climatic battle are seven judgments in which God pours out His wrath upon the planet. Commonly referred to as "The Seven Bowls" of judgments, each corresponds with the Egyptian plagues in the Old Testament. You may recall that in his hardness of heart, Pharaoh refused to set God's people free from their captivity until these judgments persuasively arrested his attention. Briefly, here are the seven bowls of judgments that await those who rejected Jesus and received the mark of the beast by worshiping the Antichrist.

(1) Revelation 16:1-2 speaks of painful boils and sores which corresponds with the Egyptian plague in Exodus 9:8-9. Some

scholars suggest that the sores are the result of radiation poisoning from the fallout of an atomic bomb.

(2) The second bowl that follows is in the next verse (16:3) in which the sea is turned into blood and all sea creatures die. Again, this is similar to the Egyptian plague in Exodus 7:17 where the Nile River was turned into blood. With a little imagination you can picture what this does to the fishing industry, the unbearable stench, and potential disease.

(3) Next, the rivers and springs of water are turned into blood as well. This can once again be compared to the first Egyptian plague in which the water became undrinkable.

(4) Then, Revelation 16:8-9 describes the fourth angel administering the judgment of scorching heat in which the skin is burning like fire. Keep in mind that the wars during the Tribulation Period have impacted the earth's atmosphere, most likely destroying the ozone layer. Now, without sufficient blockage from the ultraviolet rays of the sun, men are scorched with a fiery heat.

(5) In Revelation 16:10-11 the fifth angel pours out a bowl of darkness similar to the ninth Egyptian plague in Exodus 10:22. Mark 13:24 corresponds to this by saying, "*But in those days, after that tribulation, the sun will be darkened, and the moon will not give its light.*" This could be the aftermath of nuclear war. Regardless, the planet will be covered with a pitch-black darkness, unlike the typical dark nights we experience. This will be a judgment of darkness.

(6) The sixth bowl of judgment may seem strange at first glance. Revelation 16: 12-16 describes the sixth angel drying up the Euphrates River which is in present day Iraq. Then it speaks of three evil spirits that looked like frogs coming out of the mouth of the dragon, the beast, and the false prophet. These

spirits (demons) are performing miraculous signs and they go out to all the leaders of the earth and gather them for the Battle of Armageddon. More on this later. Suffice it to say that evil spirits are behind this global mobilization in which the armies of the earth are rallied to fight.

(7) The final bowl occurs when the seventh angel (Rev. 16:17-21) activates thunderings, lightnings, and a great earthquake along with large hail stones falling from Heaven. Verse 18 says that *"such a mighty and great earthquake as had not occurred since men were on the earth."* We've read about some massive earthquakes in our lifetime, not the least of which occurred in 2004 which set off a tsunami, killing 500,000 near Indonesia. But this earthquake will dwarf 2004's catastrophe. The hailstones mentioned in verse 21 weigh about 135 pounds each. Try to imagine the earth being pounded by these massive stones coming down from Heaven. Again, this judgment parallels that found in Exodus 9:13.

The Stage is Set

Keep in mind that this is all a backdrop of events leading to the Armageddon. Zechariah 14:2 says *"For I will gather (The Lord is speaking) all the nations against Jerusalem to battle..."* Again, none of this catches God by surprise. He's orchestrating the events even though it appears otherwise. Humanly speaking, Antichrist is in power. He's in control of the government, the economy, religion, commerce. No one can buy or sell anything without the mark of the beast. By an impressive display of miraculous signs, he rallies the leaders of the world and all of their armies to surround Jerusalem and annihilate the Jews. Revelation 16:14 says....*he assembled them at the place that in Hebrew is called Armageddon."* Ar means "mount" and Mageddon means "slaughter." So, it's the Mountain of Slaughter. But there is no Mountain of Armageddon, but there is a valley of Armageddon at the base of Mount Carmel known as the Valley of Jezreel. This is the staging area from where the troops will march toward Jerusalem. Megiddo located about 18 miles southeast of Haifa, 45 miles north of Jerusalem and 10 miles from Nazareth.

No doubt, the armies are feeling invincible. They've seen miracles in nature that defy science. The demonic spirits have produced unexplainable phenomena in the skies, in warfare, and every conceivable venue to convince these leaders they have nothing to worry about. Again, it is all for the purpose of persuading them to go to war against Israel. You may wonder, "Why destroy Jerusalem? What's the big deal about this city?" First, the hatred Satan has for Jesus is beyond fathoming. Jerusalem is God's city. It's the place where the Lord made promises to the Jewish people. In fact, He made promises regarding that very city, so by destroying Jerusalem God would be a promise-breaker.

Therefore, today's hatred of all the surrounding Moslem nations toward the Jews and Israel is instigated and inspired by none other than Satan himself. Ironically, radical Moslems call Israel the little Satan and America the Great Satan. The Valley of Jezreel where the armies of the world are gathered is the same place where Gideon's 300 soldiers routed the Midianites in Judges 7. It's where Elijah destroyed the servants of Baal in First Kings 18. It is where King Saul was slain during a war with the Philistines. Josiah was slain here by the Egyptians (2 Kings 23). Napoleon once stated that it was the world's natural battlefield, no place in the whole world more suited for war. Indeed, more than 200 battles have been fought here.

Once again, we find Joel 3:12 looking down the corridors of time and prophesying, *"Let the nations be wakened, and come up to the Valley of Jehoshaphat; for there I will sit to judge all the surrounding nations."*

Revelation 9:16 tells us that an army of two hundred million march across the Euphrates. It is one of four rivers that flowed out of the Garden of Eden. It begins in the Turkey and flows for 1,800 miles and serves as a boundary between the east and the west. While it was once the cradle of civilization, it now becomes the grave of civilization.

On the surface it may seem ludicrous for two hundred million foot soldiers to be gathered in one place when they could be traveling in sophisticated armory and using missiles and warheads. However, with further contemplation it makes perfect sense. The Antichrist not only wants to exterminate the Jews, but his goal is to take the entire Middle East with all of its rich resources. Using atomic weapons would only destroy the land and its resources.

THE MISMATCH OF THE AGES

Warnings are now over. Timelines are completed. It's now "game-on." God has already given a brilliant display of power as described in Ezekiel 38:19-23: *"For in My jealousy and in the fire of My wrath I have spoken: 'Surely in that day there shall be a great earthquake in the land of Israel, so that the fish of the sea, the birds of the heavens, the beasts of the field, all creeping things that creep on the earth, and all men who are on the face of the earth shall shake at My presence. The mountains shall be thrown down, the steep places shall fall, and every wall shall fall to the ground. I will call for a sword against God throughout all My mountains," says the Lord God. "Every man's sword will be against his brother. And I will bring him to judgment with pestilence and bloodshed; I will rain down on him, on his troops, and on the many peoples who are with him, flooding rain, great hailstones, fire, and brimstone. Thus I will magnify Myself and sanctify Myself, and I will be known in the eyes of many nations. Then they shall know that I am the Lord."*

Get the picture. The nations have surrounded Jerusalem. They are on the cusp of victory, or so they think. But then something happens. Revelation 19:11 says, *"Now I saw heaven opened, and behold, a white horse. And He who sat on him was called Faithful and True, and in righteousness He judges and makes war. His eyes were like a flame of fire, and on His head were many crowns. He had a name written that no one knew except Himself. He was clothed with a robe dipped in blood, and His name is called The Word of God. And the armies in heaven, clothed in fine linen, white and clean, followed Him on white horses. Now out of His mouth goes a sharp sword, that with it He should strike the nations. And He Himself will rule them with a rod of iron. He Himself treads the winepress of the fierceness and wrath of Almighty God. And He has on His robe and on His thigh a name written: KING OF KINGS AND LORD OF LORDS."*

Did you notice that Jesus is riding a white stallion but the armies in heaven followed him on white horses? Who might that be? That's you and me, assuming of course that you know Jesus as your personal Savior. You may never have ridden a horse and you may never have taken horseback riding lessons, but this will be the ride of your life. The sword that proceeds from His mouth is the Word of God. God spoke the world into existence through His Word and He will destroy the armies of the world with a simple Word. It will not even be a contest. Just a word.......and they're defeated. It's no wonder that Psalm 2 says, *"The kings of the earth set themselves and the rulers take counsel together; against the Lord and against His anointed saying, 'Let us break their bonds in pieces and cast away their cords from us.' He who sits in the heavens shall laugh...."* God laughs at the feeble, puny attempts by man to unseat Him from His throne.

THE PURPOSE OF ARMAGEDDON

Armageddon is the completion of God's judgment upon Israel for their rejection of Jesus, their Messiah. Time and again the Jewish people were given an opportunity to return to God, but in their hardness of heart, they defiantly denied the Savior whom God sent in behalf of their sins. But Armageddon is also the finalization of God's judgment upon the nations that have persecuted Israel. Joel 3:2 describes it by saying, *"I will also gather all nations, and bring them down to the Valley of Jehoshaphat; and I will enter into judgment with them there on account of My people, My heritage Israel, whom they have scattered among the nations; they have also divided up My land..."*

As previously stated, Satan is on a mission to destroy the Jewish people and has been since God's promise to Abraham that the Messiah would come through his lineage. One of his greatest attempts was through the extermination of millions of Jews under Hitler's Third Reich. But Armageddon, commandeered by his puppet, the Antichrist, will seem to be the perfect strategy to finally exterminate the Jews once and for all, not to mention ruling the entire planet.

It needs to be said that Armageddon is not a single battle, but actually three-and-one-half-year military campaign. The Greek word translated "battle" is the word *polemos,* which means war or campaign. Thus, it is a series of conflicts that span throughout the last half of the Tribulation Period, no doubt intensifying with this final push that we've been describing. Revelation 14:20 describes the gruesomeness of this cosmic war by saying that the blood will flow up to the horses' bridles, about 4 and one-half feet deep for 200 miles. It will take seven months to bury the dead and seven years to clean up the rubble.

WE WIN!

I can only say that I'm glad to be on the winning team. There are many, however, who cannot make that claim. They hope to win in the final analysis....they hope God will let them into Heaven.... they hope to be riding on one of those white horses....But deep in their soul resides a lingering question mark. They're just not sure. If this describes you, please read the following carefully.

FIRST, going to Heaven when we die is the desire of most people but much confusion surrounds it and opinions abound. Everybody seems to think they have it figured out so that when death knocks at their door, with fingers crossed, they breathe their last and hope for the best. The most prevalent misconception goes something like this: "If I just try to live by the Ten Commandments and obey the Golden Rule, you know, do unto others as I would have others do unto me, then I believe that covers most of the bases. I mean, I don't claim to be perfect, but I gotta believe that if I just do the best that I can, then when I die God in His mercy, love, and grace will let me into Heaven." Sadly, no He won't. Say what? That's right; the Bible declares that the very best of our good works are like filthy rags when compared to God's holiness. The Bible tells us that God's standard for Heaven is perfection. Obviously no one attains perfection and that's why the Bible says, "All have sinned and come short of the glory of God." So, when comparing ourselves with others, we may measure up just fine. But "others" are not God's standard for Heaven, Jesus is. Thus, when compared with Him, we've all blown it.

Therefore, we are "forced" to agree with God's assessment that we've all sinned and come short of His standard for Heaven.

But SECONDLY, God has more to say about this sin issue. He tells us that the wages or payment of sin is death. That is, separation from God for all eternity. After all, God is the very essence and source of life. Our sin has created a void in our souls and a chasm between us and God. Since we're all sinners, this means that we all have the death penalty hanging over our heads.

THIRDLY, there is good news when the Bible says, "But God has demonstrated His own love toward us in that while we were yet sinners, Christ died FOR US." This is incredible! The righteous One died for the unrighteous. The innocent for the guilty and the sinless One for the sinner. This is the supreme expression of God's love for humanity. John 3:16 says, "For God so loved the world (your name) that He gave His only begotten Son (Jesus) that whoever (your name) believes on Him should not perish, but have everlasting life." At the Cross Jesus shed His own spotless, stainless, sinless blood to make a way for you to enter into a personal relationship with God and ultimately go to Heaven upon your death.

FOURTHLY, the greatest news is that Jesus did not simply die for us, although that's a big deal, but He arose from the dead as testified by 500 eyewitnesses at the time and millions today will testify that we serve a living, risen Savior. He stands ready to come into your life. The Bible says, "Whoever will call upon the name of the Lord will be saved." We call upon Him in faith and in repentance. Repentance is a word that means to have a change of mind. It depicts a person who is calling his own shots, making his own decision, and setting his own agenda with disregard for God's plan and character. In other words, he's doing his own thing with little thought about God. Repentance is when a person comes before God in prayer and says, "God, I desire Your plan for my life. I invite you to take over the steering wheel of my life. I want you in the control tower of my life."

I chose not to elaborate on these four points because this is the simple, but amazing, plan of God's salvation. It is His desire that no one perishes. Many will stumble and refuse to yield their lives to God because it seems too simple. While it is, indeed, simple to understand it is not easy to do. Human pride resists God at every turn. The nature of man wants to be in control and chart his own destiny. Thus, it is all too easy to point a finger at other Christians who may not provide the best role model of what a Christian should be or to assault the Church for its shortcomings, or to reduce Christianity to a set of rules, restrictions, or rituals. Thus, God is cast in a distorted light as some Celestial Killjoy or Cosmic Policeman who's come to rain on their parade and cramp their style. Nothing could be further from the truth. Nevertheless, if you're looking for excuses, you'll have no problem finding them.

Without trying to be morbid and using scare tactics, the reality is this. We are all going to die. Last time I checked, the stats say that 10 out of 10 people die. You'll be no exception. Ecclesiastes 3:11 says that God has set eternity our hearts. Simply stated, you'll never cease to live. Created in the image of God, we're all going to live forever, either in hell or in heaven. The sobering truth is that you and I are a heartbeat from eternity. No wonder the Bible warns of the urgency behind this decision. In fact, the Bible says that "Now is the time and today is the day of salvation." Receiving Jesus Christ into your life is truly a game changer. Not only does this decision redirect your eternity, but Jesus said, "I have come to give you life and give it more abundantly." I make no pretentions that the Christian life is easy, nor does the Bible promise that you will experience only health and wealth upon receiving Christ. What I can tell you is that I have never spoken to anyone who had regrets and I can testify that it's the best life this side of eternity. Knowing Jesus is to discover life and the reason we've been placed on the planet. There is no magic formula in the following prayer. The words do not save you, but if these words express the sincere desire of your heart, then pray them to the Lord.

A PRAYER OF SALVATION

Dear Lord Jesus,

I need you and want you in my life. But I have sinned against you. I'm sorry. Please forgive me. By your power and grace, I now turn from my sin, believing that you died on that cross and took the punishment I deserved. But because you're alive right now, by faith, I open to you the door to my life. Come on in, Lord Jesus, and please save me. As best as I know how, I choose to follow you from this day forth. So, I surrender all that I am to all that you are. Thank you for hearing my prayer, and thank you for saving my soul. I humbly ask this in your strong name. Amen.

If, indeed, you made this decision to follow Jesus as your Savior, please email our office and I would like to send you a booklet that will greatly assist you getting started on this new journey. The address is: shea@fbcw.net.

Declaration of John Hancock

"We think it is incumbent upon this people to humble themselves before God on account of their sins, for He hath been pleased in His righteous judgement to suffer a great calamity to befall us, as the present controversy between Great Britain and the Colonies. (And) also to implore the Divine Blessing upon us, that by the assistance of His grace, we may be enabled to reform whatever is amiss among us, that so God may be pleased to continue to us the blessings we enjoy, and remove the tokens of His displeasure, by causing harmony and union to be restored…" [1]

— John Hancock (1737-1793)
was a Revolutionary leader and the first member of the Continental Congress to sign the Declaration of Independence.

CHAPTER 25

The Historic 2016 Election: What We Learned

The election of 2016 was the most historic in our lifetime and will go down in the history books as one for the ages. Many have called it the most epic election since George Washington's. Hillary Clinton seemingly had every demographic in her corner with the exception of evangelicals, white males, and veterans. Virtually all the research had her winning handily. Almost unanimously, talking pundits and experienced pollsters were predicting an easy win, if not a landslide. After all, Trump was a businessman who had never held an elected political office and now facing the much-acclaimed Clinton machine. To think that he could become the leader of the Free World sounded more like a fictitious novel than reality. His profane language, bombastic personality, narcissistic comments, and moral indiscretions from the past made him seem an even more unlikely victor. Furthermore, mainstream media and the existing Republican Establishment were opposed to his candidacy. He was a rookie, a novice, and a reckless buffoon whose unfiltered antics bordered on the absurd in the eyes of millions. He was the butt of jokes from those on the other side of the aisle.

Furthermore, with a biased liberal media to free celebrity concerts to a massive ground game and a two billion dollar campaign budget in her corner, Secretary Clinton was a shoo-in. Add to this the fact that prominent Republican leaders such as Paul Ryan, Jason Chaffetz, Ted Cruz, John Kasich and many others refused to endorse Trump, the deck was clearly stacked against him. The residual bitterness from a hard-fought Primary cut so deeply that Kasich, the Republican

Governor of the key swing state of Ohio, even refused to attend the Republican Convention that was hosted in his own state and made it clear that he was casting his vote for John McCain whose name was not even on the ballot. Point is, there was a lot of collateral damage strewn across the political landscape all caused by Trump's bombastic name-calling and checkered history of sexual indiscretions. Trump attempted to reconcile the differences by extending an olive branch to Cruz, inviting him to be a keynote speaker at the Republican Convention, a move that surprised everyone given the animosity that existed between the two of them. Trump had labeled Cruz as Lyin' Ted and made derogatory remarks about his wife and father. Despite Trump's congenial gesture, to the chagrin of the Republican Hall, Cruz refused to reciprocate with an endorsement of Trump. Such animosity was seen as unthinkable, childish, and divisive as evidenced by the chorus of boos throughout the Republican Hall. Political analysts were saying that Cruz shot himself in the foot and destroyed whatever future hopes he had of running for President. Fox News Contributor, Charles Krauthammer, called Cruz' decision a miscalculation and political suicide.

Trump's campaign spent a fraction of the money compared to Clinton, something unheard of for modern-day elections. He had a small ground game, another unconventional approach to elections. Twitter became a primary source of communication for Trump which seemed to make the nightly news. Given all of these realities, one can easily understand why the talking pundits and political analysts would write him off. Yet, in this David versus Goliath contest, it seems they failed to take into account that he had already defied the odds by defeating 16 experienced, competent opponents in the Republican Primary. Yes, he was a novice. Yes, was a political outsider. Yes, he was a popular reality star (The Apprentice). And yes, he was a real estate mogul who knew how to make business deals. In short, he was an anomaly. America had never seen anything like it. News commentators did not know how to explain his sudden burst of popularity as a politician. All the while, the Republican establishment was wringing its hands preparing for a humiliating defeat and knowing that the future of the Party was at stake.

Yet, there were four unexpected and uncontrollable events that no one could have predicted. First, upon discovering 650,000 Clinton emails on the laptop of Anthony Weiner, the FBI announced the reopening of its investigation just days before the election. It also continued the inquiry into the Clinton Foundation which allegedly was guilty of soliciting hundreds of millions of dollars in exchange for political favors. This caused Americans to further question her ability to lead and further validated the charges of corruption which Republicans reminded voters would continue to plague her well into the Presidency. Second, a dramatic increase on premiums for Obamacare were announced just as the election was coming into the final stretch. Trump used this timely development to capitalize on his repeal and replace policy which resonated deeply with middle class voters. Third, Clinton brought in celebrity pop stars such as Jay Z, Beyonce', Stevie Wonder, Bruce Springsteen, Jennifer Lopez, and others to perform free concerts. By all appearances, it was counterproductive. It sent a message that she was unable to draw a crowd on her own merits and policies. By contrast, Trump was packing out arenas, even at 1:00 in the morning with thousands standing outside unable to get in. This further highlighted her inability to connect with voters. Fourth, when CNN staffers were found to be guilty of slipping questions to Clinton prior to the debates and also asking the DNC what questions they wanted to ask Trump, this provided further verification of the corruption charges which they had been denying.

Add to this the Benghazi scandal and her repeated lies before the congressional committee and FBI interrogation, the cumulative impact from all of this led to her demise.

Many Christians interpret these unforeseen developments as

divine intervention. Indeed, there is no polling, map, or graphs to quantify the impact made by the power of prayer. This was not, and is not, a time to gloat or to have any false sense of security. The fact is, America was, and is, just as sinful and defiant toward God the day after the election as it was prior to the election. Furthermore, the answer to the ills that plague our nation remains the Gospel of Jesus Christ because the solution is not, nor has it ever been, political in nature. Yes, it will be good to repeal and replace Obamacare. Yes, it will be good to lift government regulations off the backs of small businesses. Yes, it will be good for the Iran nuclear deal to be repealed. However, if the unseen sovereign hand of God was instrumental in this monumental victory, it was not for the purpose of prospering us but rather for the propagation of the Gospel. Through conservative Supreme Court appointees and through the appointment of conservative federal judges throughout the Land, perhaps God is giving us a measure of revival (Ezra 9:8) in the our bondage so that an environment is now created for increased religious freedom in the public square without fear of legal consequences such as imprisonment or fines or the biased scrutiny of a politicized Internal Revenue Service. In short, the Lord may be preparing the way and creating an atmosphere conducive to fanning the flame of spiritual awakening throughout the Land.

Clinton had made it clear that her position on religious liberty was to not only confine it within the four walls of the church but also silence it from the public square. Although she had articulated this repeatedly, during the Women in the World Summit in 2015 she boldly stated that she would bring the power of the government against people of faith. There is nothing dearer to the heart of God than the Gospel for which Christ died and arose from the dead. Since it is the will of God that no one perish and since America has been the launching point for the greatest missionary enterprise in world history, such oppressive policies would be a frontal assault against the very heart of God. Therefore, while it remains to be seen what a President Trump will do, it is significant that for the first time since 1928 we have a Republican President and a majority Republican House and Senate. The ground is fertile, the environment is conducive, and there will now be evangelical Christians in high places for spiritual awakening to occur throughout the nation. The only open-ended question is this: Will the Church rise to the occasion? Will pastors find it within themselves to be bold and not wimp out? Will the laity be courageous in sharing the Good News? Will teenagers serve to be the catalyst for such a movement as in past Awakenings. These are questions that remain to be answered. But for now, there is every reason to be encouraged. The church must pray as never before and be more assertive to seize the moment. God has had mercy on us by giving us a space of grace. Now, what we do with it remains to be seen but God has placed the ball in our hands. This may be our last chance to save this nation from imminent collapse.

WHAT DID WE LEARN FROM THE 2016 ELECTION?

This is not intended to be a comprehensive analysis of the most historic election in our lifetime, but there are some observations that must not go unmentioned. I saw a yard sign that was placed in the center of highway median. It said, "Trump-Pence Win! ....There is a God!" Indeed, this was a political miracle, a modern day David & Goliath contest, one that will leave political pundits and pollsters scratching their heads for years to come. Larry Sabato, the esteemed political pollster from the University of Virginia who often appears on Fox News, had this to say on the morning following the election: "Before I say anything else, I have a sincere apology to offer the American people. I missed it. I completely blew it. I don't just have egg on my face, I have an omelet. Somehow, none of the polls saw this coming. We must get this corrected, and corrected soon." So, now that the dust has settled and smoke has cleared, here are a few takeaways from this election.

(1) As mentioned above, we learned that the polls are not always accurate. They missed this one by a longshot. The seismic inaccuracies of the pollsters were a devastating blow to their credibility. Of the 67 national polls, only four gave Trump the lead, according to RealClearPolitics. The pollsters overestimated Clinton's support among minorities and underestimated Trump's support among white voters.

(2) Evangelicals still make a difference. The exit polls indicate that the evangelical turnout for this election was the greatest in history. Experts are pointing to this reality as a tipping point in the election. In 2012 twenty-five million evangelicals failed to vote, but such was not the case in this election cycle. The result was a historic victory that may have spared the nation from imploding and created a more conducive environment for the spiritual awakening for which millions are praying.

As many as 61 percent of evangelicals voted in this election and 79 percent voted for Trump while only 18 percent voted for Clinton. [2] Interestingly, 71 percent of non-Christians voted for Clinton as compared to 21 percent for Trump. [3] Evangelicals made up 1 in 4 of all voters and with 4 out of 5 casting ballots for Trump, this demographic was undoubtedly a game-changer. [4]

(3) The Bible says, "Be sure your sin will find you out." Hillary Clinton's repeated lies, massive cover-up, and corruption charges were simply too numerous to be ignored. When the light was shined on her indiscretions, she found the Proverbs 28:13 to be true: "He who covers his shall not prosper." Of course, Trump was no angel as his moral indiscretions were also uncovered, a warning to all of the truth from this Scripture.

(4) Two realities that must not be overlooked are the fact that Clinton narrowly won the popular vote and Bernie Sanders, a self-proclaimed socialist and liberal Jew, garnered almost half of the Democrat votes winning multiple states over Clinton. Despite Trump's victory, the liberal views of both Clinton and Sanders' popularity further exposes how the culture has rapidly and radically shifted to the left.

(5) Trump's assertion that the "system is rigged" seemed to resonate with voters. Ordinary people see political crooks getting off scot free and this election allowed them to voice their displeasure at their voting precincts. It was within the Democratic Party that the corruption surfaced like a neon flashing sign and Clinton's email scandal only confirmed what many had suspected. Attorney General Loretta Lynch's 40 minute meeting with Bill Clinton on the tarmac of Phoenix's Sky Harbor airport toward the end of Hillary's email investigation was highly suspicious. Then, FBI Director James Comey's admission that Clinton had repeatedly lied about her use of classified information on a personal computer, but his refusal to prosecute her raised more suspicions that the FBI had been politicized. The American people were beginning to conclude that Trump was correct. The system is rigged and corruption runs deep from top to bottom, from the institutions of the IRS to that of the FBI and to that of the United States Justice Department. That was the perception and perception is reality to the one who perceives it.

(6) Media bias was never more evident than in this election. What's more, some of the news commentators unashamedly admitted it. CNN discovered that some of its staffers were actually slipping questions to Hillary Clinton prior to the presidential debates. Wolf Blitzer inquired of Democratic elites as to what questions he should ask Trump. This was a

dagger into the heart of a news organization that was already suffering poor ratings. Therefore, the claims that mainstream news outlets are biased in their reporting are not overblown. Objective journalism seems to be a thing of the past and the viewer must get his information from multiple sources and be extremely discerning in deciphering truth from falsehood.

(7) Political polarization is greater than ever. The two political platforms could not have been more different ideologically. Everything from Clinton's determination to open our borders to massive numbers of foreign refugees, increased funding for Planned Parenthood, the endorsement of partial birth abortion, the continuation of Obama's healthcare plan, her threat on religious liberty, her appointment of liberal judicial activists, to her views on gay rights, are just a few of the positions that created a Great Divide with no indication of it being bridged. Add to the mix Trump's "in your face" style and antithetical views, the result is a nation divided and a polarization America has not seen in decades. The election was a choice between socialism versus capitalism. Sadly, as already stated, various metrics indicate the nation has drifted rapidly to the left, despite Trump's election.

(8) Trumps criticism of political correctness and America's failure to win at anything seemed to resonate deeply with the American people. Voters were frustrated with Obama's foreign policy of leading from behind and watching China and Russia surpass our military. Again, whenever Trump mentioned the term "political correctness" in his speeches, there was an obvious approval from his audiences and the sense of relief that someone was finally verbalizing what they were thinking. It was readily apparent that a large segment of the country was fed up with a government controlled by, paralyzed by, and enamored with political correctness. Trump's brash

pronouncement of "Merry Christmas" and then saying, "Doesn't it feel good to say Merry Christmas again," was a slap in the face to liberals and their agenda.

(9) Trump's theme of "Make America Great Again" implied that America had lost its respect and global standing as a superpower in the world. While this was not shocking news, the fact that a candidate was so bold as to acknowledge it and the fact that the American people bought into it was a significant admission. For we cannot move from where we are until we acknowledge where we are. As Dr. Phil says, "You cannot change what you do not acknowledge."

(10) When Trump won the Republican Primary, it was another case in point for the perceived irrelevance of Christianity. Of the seventeen candidates, at least half of them identified with strong Christian values. Donald Trump was rude, bombastic, profane, and narcissistic. Yet, he won the Primary in record-setting fashion. Despite his character flaws, use of profanity, and the denigration of women, Hispanics, Latinos, and Muslims, Christian leaders such as Robert Jeffress and Jerry Falwell, Jr. publicly endorsed him. Securing a record-setting number of votes against the strongest Republican field ever assembled was no small feat. But again, this only unveiled the coarseness of American culture and the reality that character no longer carries the weight as in days past.

(11) Stating the obvious, Americans are incensed with the Washington Establishment and they voiced their disapproval at the voting booth. As a political outsider, Trump tapped into the anger of the American people, a reality the political and media establishment failed to understand.

(12) The Wikileaks hacking of John Podesta's email account was a reminder that social media accounts are not as safe as many would have us think. Without a doubt, the revelation

> of Clinton's classified information on a personal computer placed our national security in jeopardy and is generally agreed that hostile nations accessed it. The constant dumping of her private conversations dealt a fatal blow to her character, her untrustworthiness, and ultimately her political future.

While these lessons revolve primarily around social and political policies, we dare not lose sight of the fact that God was superintending all of this. I repeat what was said earlier. There is no graph, no poll, and no map to quantify the power of the prayers from God's people that were brought to bear upon this election. So, any statement that I make is only speculative. However, when God's people pray spiritual forces are set into motion that otherwise would have remained stagnant. Given this political miracle that defied all odds and given the uncanny and unpredicted events of the closing days of the election, I choose to believe that God intervened and spared America from imminent collapse. Certainly, the future remains undetermined, but there will be no one to blame but ourselves if we as God's people fail to seize this historic moment.

IS THIS THE GREATEST EVANGELICAL PRESENCE FOR A PRESIDENTIAL CABINET?

The answer to the above question is "Yes, it may very well be, at least in modern times." While it is difficult to deliver an emphatic "yes," it is safe to say that the eleven men and women who occupy the label as being "Christian" in Trump's administration are not the silent, in name-only type. Each person in the following list has publicly and unashamedly spoken of his/her faith without flinching, without apology, and with firm conviction. In other words, these are not nominally committed, blow-in-the-wind, wishy-washy Christians. From all reports and letting their track records speak for themselves, these individuals have pledged their unwavering allegiance to Jesus Christ. Here is a small sampling of whom Trump has chosen to surround himself with on his cabinet:

(1) **Mike Pence (Vice-President):** Pence has said, *"My Christian faith is at the heart of who I am. I'm a Christian, a conservative and a Republican, in that order. I try and spend a little time on my knees every day."*[5]

(2) **Dr. Ben Carson (Department of Housing and Urban Development):** Unusual for his profession as a world-renowned surgeon, Dr. Carson is a creationist who talked about his Christian conversion as part of his narrative on the campaign trail. He said, *"I fell on my knees and said Lord, you have to help me because I can't fix this."* Unashamedly, Carson says, *"I would describe myself first of all as a Christian—evangelical in the sense that I believe we have a responsibility to proclaim the Gospel and show other people why we live the way that we do and hopefully that will affect their lives. I think that's a very important component in what we do."*[6]

(3) **Scott Pruitt (Environmental Protection Agency Chief):** Pruitt serves as a deacon at First Baptist Church in Broken Arrow, Oklahoma and is a trustee for Southern Baptist Theological Seminary. Pruitt says, *"A Christian worldview means that God has answers to our problems. And part of our responsibility is to convey to those in society that the answers that he has, as represented in Scripture, are important and should be followed."*[7]

(4) **Betsy DeVos (Education Secretary):** Mrs. DeVos was raised in the Reformed Christian Church and attended Christian schools, including a Christian Calvinist college. In addition, she sent her children to Christian schools so it is no surprise that she is an advocate for school vouchers that would allow the government to fund religious education. This is a radical departure from anything ever seen within the Beltway and is

sure to be met with staunch resistance. She says, *"I want to impact our culture in ways that are not the traditional funding-the-Christian-organization route, but that really may have greater Kingdom gain in the long run by changing the way we approach things—in this case, the system of education in the country."* If you have seen her speak, then you know that she is up to the task. She is focused, internally strong, and ready to take the heat for what she is advocating.

(5) **Rex Tillerson (Secretary of State):** A devout Christian, Tillerson attends church weekly and teaches a Bible study.

(6) **Reince Preibus (Chief of Staff):** A life-long member of the Greek Orthodox Church, the man is a devoted follower of Christ. While he was serving as Chairman of the GOP, during Easter Priebus delivered this message: *We celebrate the resurrection of Christ and the love of God in providing a savior. Just as the first Christians praised God at the sight of the empty tomb, we too praise our good and merciful God today for his victory over the grave. Christ's sacrificial work provides an example for us all, and we join the Psalmist in saying, 'You make known to me the path of life.' Easter is a time for the celebration of new life, and I pray we will all draw on that new hope throughout the year."* [8]

(7) **Rick Perry (Energy Secretary):** Well-known for his conservative Christian stance, Perry has been outspoken for Christian values. For example, during a prayer service in 2009 he stated his belief that non-Christians will be condemned to hell, he called evolution "a theory that's out there," and as governor of Texas he promoted the teaching of creationism in public schools. In 2011, he held at a 30,000-strong Christian national prayer rally for "a nation in crisis." No stranger to controversy, Perry said, *"There's something wrong in a country where gays can serve in the military but our kids can't open*

celebrate Christmas." In 2014, he was re-baptized in a Texas river. [5]

(8) **Ken Blackwell (Domestic Policy Advisor):** Blackwell is a senior fellow at the conservative religious Family Research Council organization and is responsible for the domestic side of the transition. He calls homosexuality "a transgression of God's law" and supports conversion therapy for gay claiming that their sexual tendencies can be changed the same as an arsonist or kleptomaniac. It was Blackwell who was instrumental in consolidating evangelical support by forming a religious advisory board. [9]

(9) **Mike Pompeo (Head of the Central Intelligence Agency):** Pompeo serves as a deacon at Eastminster Presbyterian Church and teaches Sunday School to fifth-graders.

(10) **Nikki Haley (Ambassador to the United Nations):** Nikki is a powerhouse for Christ. Steely and determined, she says, *"I believe in the power and grace of Almighty God. I know, and have truly experienced, that with Him all things are possible. I have looked to Him for leadership throughout my career and will continue to do so. My faith in Christ has a profound impact on my daily life and I look to Him for guidance with every decision I make. God has blessed my family in so many ways and my faith in the Lord gives me great strength on a daily basis. Being a Christian is not about words, but about living for Christ every day."* Nikki dedicated her life to Christ at age 24. [9]

(11) **Jeff Sessions (Attorney General for the United States):** Sessions has been a lay leader and Sunday School teacher at his church, Ashland Place United Methodist Church in Mobile, Alabama. He served as chairman of the church's Administrative Board and was a delegate to the annual Alabama Methodist Conference. Sessions opposed the Supreme Court's 2015 ruling on same-sex marriage by saying, *"Today's ruling is part*

of a continuing effort to secularize, by force and intimidation, a society that would not exist but for the faith which inspired people to sail across unknown waters and trek across unknown frontiers. The ruling divorced morality from law and has far-reaching ramifications."[10] During his confirmation hearings, Session repeatedly referred to "secularists" which was offensive to many sitting on the panel. During the interrogation Sessions said, *"I have a little concern that we, as a nation, are reaching a level in which truth is not sufficiently respected, that the very idea of truth is not believed to be real and that all of life is just a matter of your perspective and my perspective, which I think is contrary to the American heritage."*Then came the "gotcha" question from Rhode Island Democratic Senator Sheldon Whitehouse. "And a secular person has just as good a claim to understanding the truth as a person who is religious, correct?" Sessions replied, "Well, I'm not sure." What followed was a period of uncomfortable silence, as if the panel was stunned to hear such a response from an astute lawmaker. [11]

(12) **Sonny Perdue (Agriculture Secretary):** Although a former Governor of Georgia and holding a doctorate, he is affectionately known as "Sonny." He's a former member of my home church, First Baptist Woodstock where he and his wife taught a couple's Sunday School class while serving as Governor. Before accepting Trump's invitation to serve on his cabinet, Sonny asked Pastor Johnny Hunt to pray with him about the matter. His son is a Southern Baptist pastor. Having spoken in our church's pulpit, I can testify to his Christian commitment and godly spirit. While giving the commencement address at Truett-McConnell College, Perdue boldly said, *"I'm going to use a word that would be very, very rare in commencement speeches across the United States. It's a powerful word; It's Jesus. The name of Jesus marks history's calendar. It's the name above all names and is a name at which*

'every knee shall bow' one day. You can't utter that word in polite society because you will be labeled a peculiar person, weird and strange if you talk about the name." Regarding his run for Governor, Perdue said, *"I never intended to run for Governor. But the Holy Spirit started scribing on me with a Brillo pad... and the message was, get out of your comfort zone."*The address concluded by reminding the students, *"Your faith will be challenged in the marketplace if you are resolved to stand for Jesus."*[12]

(13) **Tom Price (Secretary of Health & Human Services):** While there is scant information on Dr. Price's Christian commitment, his voting record certainly aligns with conservative Christianity such as opposing same-sex marriage, abortion, and other issues important to Christians. He is a Presbyterian.

(14) **Elaine Chao (Secretary of Transportation):** Mrs. Chao is the wife of Senate Majority Leader, Mitch McConnell, a Southern Baptist. For 15 years the two of them faithfully attended the conservative megachurch, Southeast Christian in Louisville. Chao grew up in a devout Christian family in China. It was in 2008 that she describes witnessing "God's glory" in the Beijing Jiaotong University. She says, *"For the help of faith and church, we can always get comfort in Jesus' love."* Referring to her upbringing, Chao recalls that after meals they went to church nearby and prayed there. She says, *"Christian values strengthened us and my sisters and praise God and my parents for what we have achieved."*[13]

(15) **Dan Coats (Director of National Intelligence):** Google Dan Coats' name and you will have no trouble finding an exhaustive list of this man's admirable career and his stellar reputation as a dedicated Christian. Without going into great detail, suffice it to say that he is a member of "The Fellowship,"

> a highly secretive association of Christian lawmakers. That speaks volumes. Regarding the Court's decision on same-sex marriage, Coats retorted, *"Decisions of faith are the most personal and precious we make in this lifetime. Guided by my Christian faith, I believe that marriage is a solemn covenant made between a man and a woman before God."*[14]

Granted, the fact that these individuals are known for their commitment to Christ does not guarantee their level of competence for the task to which they are assigned. However, their record of past success speaks for itself and this was the primary litmus test that attracted President Trump. Whether their evangelical Christianity was a "coincidence" or a deliberate part of Trump's vetting process, the reality is that God has placed these men and women in high offices of influence for such a time as this. We have every reason to be heartened by this President's unabashed identification with the Christian community. Robert Jeffress, pastor of the historic First Baptist Church in Dallas, Texas, says that Trump may very well prove to be the most faith-friendly President in America's history. From all appearances at this point in time, who's to argue with such an assertion.

THE TRUMP EFFECT CONTINUES

Since the time of his election to the first week of being sworn into office, the stock market on January 25 reached a historic high of exceeding the 20,000 point plateau, up 2,000 points from the day he was elected. Even before assuming office he began cutting deals with companies like Carrier and Ford, persuading them to keep manufacturing jobs in America rather than moving to Mexico as previously planned. This was unprecedented and further proof of following through on campaign promises. On his first day in office Trump met with CEO's from Ford, Lockheed Martin, Dow Chemical, Under Armour, Dell, U.S. Steel, Whirlpool, Johnson &

Johnson, Arconic, Corning, International Paper, and others. The next day he met with the three automobile manufacturers. Later in the week he planned to announce his nominee for a Supreme Court justice to replace the vacated seat of conservative champion Antonin Scalia. As you may recall, well in advance of the election Trump announced a list of twenty potential nominees who met the litmus test for conservatives. Point being, during the campaign he talked the talk and now he is walking the walk. Next, the infamous wall for the southern border is now on his agenda along with a trillion dollar proposal for infrastructure. Aggressive, focused, bold, and courageous could all be used to describe this man's first week in office. Sean Hannity called it transformative and revolutionary. Reporters who have covered the White House for decades say they have never seen so much get done in so little time as with this President. Reince Priebus said, "I thought I had a good work ethic with 16-hour days, but this President never stops, he doesn't sleep. I've never seen anything like it."

Millions watched the press conference where Trump legally and officially divested himself from the management of the Trump Organization and turned control over to his two sons. Keep in mind that he is not mandated by law to do so, but to make America great again and put America first, his exclusive focus is on that task. Beside the podium was a stack of legal papers looking to be at least a foot in height and serving as a visual aid confirming in the viewer's mind of his sincerity. He terminated pending business deals with foreign entities and pledged to donate all profits from foreign government payments to his luxury hotels into the U.S. Treasury. Add to this the fact that he is refusing to take a salary as President of the United States, one cannot help but be impressed by such selfless choices. He is sending a message from his own life of putting America first.

He also placed a ban on the construction of a Boeing Air Force

One stating that the price was too high. He instructed Boeing to return with a fairer price tag. Again, this is staying true to his slogan "America First." Certainly, it is much too early to draw any conclusions. As President, he continues the habit of early morning tweets to which voters became accustomed. But this is calculated as a strategy for bypassing the mainstream media's biased reporting.

THE CONTROVERSIAL INAUGURATION

Trump's inauguration festivities were unable to attract the performance of headliner celebrities as one artist after another declined to be associated with the GOP. In typical Trump fashion, he brushed it off by stating, "It's not about the celebrities and never has been. It's about the American people."

His inaugural speech was the shortest since Jimmy Carter's, only 1,400 words in length. Yet, it carried a punch with rhetoric that many found inflammatory and insulting to those of the Democratic Party and Republican Establishment who were seated directly behind him. For instance, he said, *"For too long, a small group in our nation's capital has reaped the rewards of government while the people have borne the cost. Washington flourished, but the people did not share in its wealth. Politicians prospered, but the jobs left and the factories closed. Their victories have not been your victories. And while they celebrated in our nation's capital, there was little to celebrate for struggling families all across our land. That all changes starting right here and right now, because this moment is your moment, it belongs to you."*[15]

Critics described his tone as dark and negative, but Republicans described it as realistic. One can only imagine the cheering in front of television screens when he launched an attack on the very politicians who were sitting around him, chastising them for being all talk and no action. *"We will no longer accept politicians who are all talk and no action, constantly complaining but never doing anything about it. The time for empty talk is over. Now arrives the hour of action."*[16]

Suffice it to say that the goal of most inaugural speeches is to unite the country, but this one seems to have been counterproductive. He entered office with a historically low approval rating of 53 percent and a reported 10,000 people attended the concert at Lincoln Memorial compared to the 400,000 who came out for President Obama's concert eight years earlier. The Great Divide was made even more conspicuous by the 60 Democratic House members who stayed home from the inauguration event. On the day following the inauguration one million women throughout the nation took to the streets in a march protesting Trump's election and his denigration of women.

There were several pungent quotes, but two of the more powerful, memorable lines from the speech were as follows: *"We will follow two rules—Buy American and Hire American." "Whether we are black or brown or white, we all bleed the same red blood of patriots."*[17]

DRAINING THE SWAMP

I am cautiously optimistic by what this man has done thus far. Whenever speaking to school assemblies, I often say "There are no born losers, only born choosers. But the choices we make create the foundation upon which the rest of our lives are built. Those choices determine our mark in history and the destiny that we obtain." Though he has just come out of the gate, and though the starter's gun has just sounded, and although this is a marathon and not a sprint, the choices President Trump has made early-on are to be commended and have created a trajectory that should encourage any conservative, especially those in the evangelical camp.

President Trump has repeatedly promised to drain the swamp. Well now he finds himself in the swamp and much of it has already been drained. However, he is sure to find a few rats and snakes in the grass. He, along with all of his cabinet and those serving in Congress, deserve our prayers at the very least. May this not be a cliché or empty religious rhetoric. Please join me in committing to pray for this Administration. The resistance coming against him and all who reflect his agenda is a daily grind and even life-threatening. May God place His hedge of protection and impart wisdom from on High as we navigate the turbulent political waters that lie ahead.

A Word from The Father of Public Schools

"The only foundation for....a republic is to be laid in Religion. Without this there can be no virtue, and without virtue there can be no liberty, and liberty is the object and life of all republican governments."

"If moral precepts alone could have reformed mankind, the mission of the Son of God into all the world would have been unnecessary. The perfect morality of the Gospel rests upon the doctrine which, though often controverted has never been refuted: I mean the vicarious life and death of the Son of God." [1]

— Benjamin Rush (1745-1813)
was a physician, signer of the Declaration of Independence, "father of public schools," and a principal promoter of the American Sunday School Union. He served as the Surgeon General of the Continental Army and also helped write the Pennsylvania Constitution. He was the treasurer of the U.S. Mint.

CHAPTER 26

Heal Our Land

Let's take a step back and assess what we now know. The statistical information and research invested in the preceding chapters have accentuated the brokenness of America. We have seen that our courts are broken. Our government is broken. Our schools are broken. Our families are broken. Our inner cities are broken. There is very little in our beloved nation that is not in decline. A self-centered, victim-minded, government-dependent, entitlement mentality prevails throughout the Land. The Election of 2016 exposed just how divided we are as a nation: red states versus blue states, whites versus blacks, police versus citizens, the establishment versus the common man, the rich versus the poor, conservatives versus liberals.

THE TRUMP TRAIN HAS ARRIVED!

Yes, the Trump Train has pulled into 1600 Pennsylvania Avenue, Washington, D.C. and with it comes car loads of optimism. At least that's what we are hearing from the conservative side of the aisle. Reducing taxes, removing regulations on small businesses, building the wall, appointing conservative justices to the Supreme Court, renegotiating trade deals, rebuilding our military, reducing crime, repairing our infrastructure, incentivizing corporations to manufacture once again in America, and on it goes. And make no mistake, this goes beyond political rhetoric. Remember? Trump is no politician. He's a businessman with high energy, an incredible work ethic, a strong vision, a proven negotiator, and based on his cabinet he has surrounded himself with what many are calling the most competent cabinet in history. He has accomplished more in the first three days than many Presidents would accomplish in their first 100 days. Seriously, his performance has been impressive to say the least. And the stock market thinks so as well as it hit historic highs during his first week in the Oval Office.

At this moment in history it appears that we are witnessing a political revolution unlike anything seen in our lifetime. Admittedly, it is dangerous to use such hyperbole in describing a movement that remains in its infancy, but historians are already penning chapters of what they describe as unprecedented. Experienced pollsters remain stunned and questioning, "How could we have missed it so badly?" Reporters are testifying to the most productive first week in office by a President that they have seen in decades. Much of the optimism lies in the fact that Trump the President is actually lining up with Trump the Campaigner. His actions are matching his promises. Americans have grown so accustomed to hearing empty rhetoric and broken promises from the campaign trails of our politicians that to see one who wastes no time in fulfilling his pledge to the American people is refreshing and energizing.

A WORD OF CAUTION

In President Trump's inaugural address he said, "We're going to make America strong again. We're going to make America wealthy again. We're going to make America proud again. We're going to make America safe again. And yes, we're going to make America great again." Strong, wealthy, proud, safe, and great. Who doesn't want that, right? People are fickle. If the economy is good and money is in the bank account, then all is well and the populace is happy. However, there is such a thing as a pseudo-wealth and pseudo-greatness. It depends on who is defining the terms. The Bible says, "Blessed (great) is the nation whose God is the Lord" (Psalm 33:12). It is noteworthy to observe that the President did not say, "Make America moral again." Perhaps it was implied, but let's go back to the quote of General Douglas McArthur: "History fails to record a single precedent in which nations subject to moral decay have not passed into political and economic decline. There has either been a spiritual awakening to overcome the moral lapse, or a progressive deterioration leading to ultimate national disaster."

In this quote McArthur makes the astute observation that economic and political decline are traced back to moral decay. *Storm Warnings* has thoroughly documented that America is a world leader in immorality. We are accelerating down the slippery slope of moral relativism which denies absolute rights and absolute wrongs. Such a false value system is the recipe for anarchy and the sets up each person as a god unto himself. It is a subtle form of idolatry that blatantly opposes everything the true and living God stands for. So, while the political landscape is now in a transitional and transformational state with a new incoming Presidential Administration, the answer to America's problems goes beyond political solutions. Politics never has been and never will be the ultimate answer to what ails the nation. That's because the heart of the problem is the problem of the heart.

As stated in an earlier chapter, moral decay is the problem and a declining economy and political system are only symptoms of this reality. If, indeed that is true, then where do morals come from? They come from theology. Where does theology come from? It comes from the Bible. To whom has the Bible been entrusted? The Church. So, once again the bread crumbs lead back to the doorstep of our local churches throughout the Land. In Matthew 15:19 Jesus says, "For out of the heart proceeds evil thoughts, murders, adulteries, fornications, thefts, false witness, blasphemies." We see the record number of murders in Chicago, the decaying buildings around Detroit, the riots in Baltimore, the anger spewing from the mouths of protesters, the epidemic of heroin and opiates. All that ails the nation is traceable to the heart. Hearts are broken needing to be healed. Captives enslaved to sin need to be liberated. There is only one solution. That is, Jesus Christ and the Gospel that He has entrusted to His people, the Church. As well-intentioned this Administration is and for all that has been accomplished thus far, they deserve our applause of approval. But just as the Big Government of liberals is not the answer, neither is a finely tuned, smaller competent Government of conservatives the answer.

Let us not forget Alexis de Tocqueville's quote upon traveling to America for the purpose of determining the secret of our greatness: "I sought for the greatness and strength of America in her fertile fields and boundless prairies but I didn't find it there; in her rich mines and worldwide commerce, but I didn't find it there. In her commodious harbors and ample rivers, but I didn't find it there.....not until I stepped inside her churches and found her pulpits aflame with righteousness, then I discovered the source of America's greatness." He concluded that "America is good. And as long as America is good, America will be great. But when America ceases to be good, then she will cease to be great." Therefore, if we truly want to make America great again, our pulpits must be re-ignited and aflame for righteousness. The greatness of America cannot be separated from the foundation upon which that greatness was built, and that is the Word of God. This is why each page preceding the chapters of Storm Warnings contains a quote from one of our Founding Fathers documenting America's strong Christian heritage.

TRUMP AND THE JOHNSON AMENDMENT

Trump's perspective on the Johnson Amendment is hugely significant. I'm assuming it's been years since you took a political science class, so here is what the Johnson Amendment is about. At the risk of over-simplification, the Johnson Amendment forbids preachers from political speech in their pulpits and threatens to remove a church's tax exempt status if such does occur. However, it is worth noting that the IRS has never taken such action. In his own words, here is Trump's journey into the tall weeds of this Amendment:

"I had 50 pastors in a big conference room. And we were all talking and we were there for two hours. And at the end, it was a love-fest. We all agreed. It was like a love-fest....And I said to them, I'd love your support....And they didn't really know what I was talking about. And I said, "What's going on here?" They said, "Well, sir, we can't do that because we would be violating laws."

And I said, "What's the punishment?" "Well, we could lose our tax exempt status," which of course is a massive penalty. I said, "Tell me about this." And we sat down. They talked about it....So we were looking down onto the sidewalk and there were people walking on the sidewalk. I said, "So, folks, what you're telling me is those people walking way, way down there on the sidewalk have really more power than you do because they're allowed to express their feelings and thoughts openly and without penalty?"....They looked at me and they said, "That's actually right. They have more power than we do. We're now allowed to express."

Upon learning and reading more on the subject, Trump later gave these words on the campaign trail: *"The Johnson Amendment has blocked our pastors from speaking their minds from their own pulpit. If they do speak out, they are punished with the loss of their tax-exempt status. All religious leaders should be able to freely express their thoughts and feelings on religious matters, and I will repeal the Johnson Amendment if I am elected President."*[2]

Time will tell, but if Trump chooses to wade into the tall weeds of political correctness, this is a jungle awaiting him with spears, drawn swords, and knives. However, he has a Republican Congress and if preachers are no longer restrained by the fear of preaching on abortion, same-sex marriage, homosexuality, and other moral issues that have political overtones, an environment of religious liberty will have been created that could fan the flames of revival. Oh, do not misunderstand. It is not preaching on these moral issues that ignites revival, but the freedom from fear that paralyzes so many preachers may bring a greater boldness and prophetic approach to the pulpits of America. Once again, the point taken to heart is that Trump is a faith-friendly President who is bold as a lion and not intimidated by the opinions of others. Yes, he is unconventional and unorthodox, but also refreshing in many ways.

THE ESSENCE OF WHAT DIVIDES US

America is experiencing the clash between two polar-opposite worldviews. A worldview is how we see problems and the approach we take to solving those problems. It is the lens through which we view life. If the lens is distorted, then how we view the world will be distorted. Thus, the moral compass will be off-center and with the passage of time, this could be disastrous.

There is indisputable historical evidence that America's Founding Fathers held unwaveringly to a Christian Theistic worldview that interpreted circumstances through the lens of Scripture. They believed in the existence of a loving, good, just, and merciful God who is actively involved in the affairs of mankind, just as the Bible describes. The Christian worldview embraces an attitude of optimism knowing that God is in control and we are citizens of another world with Heaven awaiting us.

The secularist worldview, on the other hand, sees religion as oppressive and irrelevant. This is the view of atheism in which there is no absolute moral truth nor is there an objective standard for determining moral behavior. Right and wrong are defined by situation ethics or what seems/feels right at the moment. This worldview was the basis of Charles Darwin's *The Origin of Species* and is the premise for the theory of evolution, the atheistic doctrine taught in our public schools. The end-game of this worldview leads to a futile and empty existence. While Christians are tolerated by secularists, their attitude is, "Just don't take your faith into the public square."

With few exceptions, the Democratic Platform has increasingly drifted to a secularist worldview which helps explain the radical leftist views of same-sex marriage, transgender bathrooms, and host of other legislation diametrically opposed to Scripture.

AMERICA IS HUMPTY-DUMPTY

The nursery rhyme we learned as children says, "Humpty-Dumpty sat on a wall. Humpty-Dumpty had a great fall. All the king's army and all the king's men couldn't put Humpty-Dumpty back together again." Sadly, America is Humpty-Dumpty. At one time America sat on a wall atop of the world in everything we accomplished whether it was economically, politically, militarily, or domestically. America had no rivals. But then the unthinkable occurred. America had a great fall. Actually, it has been a gradual decline. To make America great again requires acknowledging the Source of our greatness in the first place, God Himself. Many of the men and women whom Trump has selected to serve on his Cabinet understand this reality, so for that I am encouraged.

However, inside the Beltway there is a strong demonic, delusionary spirit that seems to engulf good men and women who travel there with pure motives and godly intentions, but are sucked in by lobbyists and special interest groups. Let it be said again, only the supernatural transformational power of the Lord Jesus Christ can bring healing to our nation. In short, we have forgotten God, but He is giving us a window of opportunity to return.

RE-LIVING THE 2016 ELECTION

He did not stand a chance in the Republican Primary, running against 16 outstanding, accomplished candidates. Yet, he won. He did not stand a chance in the General Election with Hillary Clinton amassing two billion dollars, a well-oiled political machine with a superb ground game. Yet, he won. He did not stand a chance with practically every demographic in Clinton's corner including a biased media that served as wind to her back. Yet, he won. With one or two exceptions, all the polls pointed to a landslide victory for Clinton. Yet, he won. It did not appear that he would carry the unlikely swing states of Florida, Ohio, and North Carolina. Yet, he won. The Democratic states of Pennsylvania, Wisconsin, Michigan, and Iowa were considered shoo-ins for Clinton, so much so that she hardly campaigned in those regions. Yet, he won.

With voting precincts closed and the votes still being counted into the wee hours of the morning, around 1 a.m. it was announced that Florida had gone to Trump. Then, it was Ohio. Next, it was North Carolina. In fact, of the 3,141 counties in the United States, Trump won 3,084 of them. Of the 62 counties in New York, Trump won 46 of them. While it is true that Clinton won the popular vote, five counties that encompass New York City (Bronx, Brooklyn, Manhattan, Richmond, and Queens) gave Clinton two million more votes than Trump. This fact alone accounts for Clinton winning the popular vote. Those five counties comprise 319 square miles with the rest of the United States comprising 3,797,000 square miles. In other words, the large, densely populated liberal cities do not speak for the rest of the nation.

While Trump was not the first choice of most evangelicals, 81 percent of them marched to the voting booths in record numbers to let their voices be heard. Defying all odds, when the dust had settled the next morning, celebrities and liberal pundits were at a loss for words. It was nothing short of miraculous. Whether it was divine intervention or not, you be the judge. In his Inauguration Day message to President Trump, Dr. Robert Jeffress, pastor of First Baptist Church in Dallas, Texas said, "President-Elect Trump, you, Vice-President-elect Pence, and your team have been called by God and elected by the people to do a great work."

FROM POLITICAL REVOLUTION TO SPIRITUAL REVOLUTION

Along with the rest of the nation, I have sat back and marveled at how quickly things have changed on the political landscape. Literally overnight Republicans gained controlled of the Presidency, the House, the Senate and 36 governorships. These are leaders who, if not at least sharing the heart of evangelical Christians for a massive spiritual awakening, they are sympathetic to it. The transformational revolution that has occurred on the political scene needs to be mirrored throughout the ecclesiastical landscape as well. The climate is conducive. The stronghold of political correctness is being weakened. Pulpits have less reason to fear speaking out for righteousness. Religious liberty will increasingly find greater reception.

Socialism, liberalism, secularism, hedonism, and atheism need not be our national identity. Godly principles, moral legislation that reflects biblical values, and family-friendly policies can all be reinstated. The heavy hand of politically-correct government policies is being lifted off the throats of Christians who simply want to exercise religious liberty in the public square, the same rights given to other citizens. However, the Church must awaken from its slumber. Judgment begins first in the house of God. It seems that God is tossing the ball into the Church's court. He's in our corner, but prophetic voices calling for repentance and renewal must sound forth a clarion call.

I read of a school that was under a tornado warning and all the students were ushered into a shelter waiting for the storm to pass. Huddled in the lower halls of the school, one student began softly singing, "Mary Did You Know," a popular Christian song during the Christmas season. Others joined in. Soon, scores of students were harmonizing and exalting Christ with joyful voices while the turbulent winds from the outside raged overhead. This is a composite picture of a similar contagious movement that God desires to ignite throughout our Land. It begins with one person, one school, one church, one community, one state and the winds of revival will once again blow throughout the Land as in days past.

National Blessing Tied to a Biblical Worldview

In my book *Truth Decay* there is a chapter on America's Christian heritage with quote after quote documenting the biblical worldview that established our nation. However, another potent example is South Korea. In 1960, Ghana had the same per capita income as South Korea. Ghana chose to follow a socialistic model of government while South Korea followed a biblical worldview and pursued a free-market model. As a result, over ninety percent of South Koreans express a belief in Jesus Christ and embrace a biblical worldview and South Korea today sits as the twelfth wealthiest nation in the world while Ghana has fallen to the one-hundredth. The correlation cannot be denied. Clearly, America must get off the path of socialism/big government and return to the path that made us the most prosperous nation in history, a biblical worldview.

RESTORING A BIBLICAL WORLDVIEW TO OUR EDUCATION SYSTEM

There is nowhere that a biblical worldview needs to be restored more than in America's educational system. Since a previous chapter was devoted to this subject, I'll refrain from being redundant. However, the following quotes from two of our Founding Fathers seem appropriate. Thomas Paine was the least religious of our Founders, but he could not comprehend teaching science that excluded God. He said, *"It has been the error of the schools to teach astronomy, and all the other sciences and subjects of natural philosophy, as accomplishments only; whereas they should be taught theologically, or with references to the Being who is the author of them: for all the principles of science are of Divine origin. Man cannot make, or invent, or contrive principles. He can only discover them; and he ought to look through the discovery to the Author.*

When we examine an extraordinary piece of machinery, an astonishing pile of architecture, a well-executed statue or a highly finished painting where life and action are imitated, and habit only prevents our mistaking a surface of light and shade for cubical solidity, our ideas are naturally led to think of the extensive genius and talents of the artist. When we study the elements of geometry, we think of Euclid. When we speak of gravitation, we think of Newton. How then is it, that when we study the works of God in the creation, we stop short, and do not think of God? It is from the error of the schools in having taught those subjects as accomplishments only and thereby separated the study of them from the Being who is the author of them.

The evil that has resulted from the error of the schools in teaching natural philosophy as an accomplishment only has been that of generating in the pupils a species of atheism. Instead of looking through the works of the creation to the Creator himself, they stop short, and employ the knowledge they acquire to create doubts of His existence. They labor with studied ingenuity and ascribe everything they behold to innate properties of matter, and mump over all the rest, by saying that matter is eternal."[3]

Noah Webster was called the "Father of American Scholarship and Education." Authoring the original textbooks used in our early classrooms, Webster spent 27 years studying 26 different languages and compiling 70,000 words into the first-ever dictionary, *The*

American Dictionary of the English Language. Being a devout Christian, Webster incorporated biblical truths in all of his textbooks for children. To do otherwise would have been unthinkable as seen by the following statement: *"The Christian religion is the most important and one of the first things in which all children under a free government ought to be instructed. No truth is more evident than that the Christian religion must be the basis of any government intended to secure the rights and privileges of a free people."*[4]

Sadly, students today have little understanding of America's true history, our Christian heritage, or the biblical convictions of our Founding Fathers. Instead, the authors of our textbooks intentionally avoid the truth and write about a different nation, one that adheres to their political agenda and secular worldview. No one argues that the NEA is one of the most powerful and liberal lobbyist groups in the nation. Thus, the future of America is being shaped by an educational system that, as pertaining to our history, is deceptive, liberally biased, immersed in political correctness, and written by authors who are either delusional or victims of their own misguided system. Our universities are even more blatant in their opposition to a biblical worldview, so today it is no small miracle for a graduate to emerge from the system spiritually unscathed.

Judges 2:10 says, *"And there arose another generation who did not know the Lord, nor what He had done for Israel."* This describes America. We have forgotten the principles upon which we were founded. It saddens me to know that teenagers and their parents have no clue (for the most part) of the biblical underpinnings of our nation.

Thomas Jefferson has oft been criticized for being a Deist and less than a biblical follower of Jesus Christ as were his colleagues. Yet, Jefferson, the primary author of the Declaration of Independence, said, *"I am a real Christian, that is to say, a disciple of the doctrines of*

Jesus. I have little doubt that our whole country will soon be rallied to the unity of our Creator."[5]

Ironically, after the Declaration was signed into effect, one of the first congressional acts was to purchase 20,000 copies of Scripture for the American people. This certainly reflects the high esteem our leaders had for God's Word, the Bible. In fact, the first component of the educational system was that of learning to read. And why was that? They considered literacy to be essential in order for the children to read the Bible and understand the strategies of Satan so they would not be deceived. Today, the same Bible, the Ten Commandments, prayer, and the teaching of creationism have all been judicially kicked out of our schools. Joshua 1:8-9 says, *"This Book of the Law shall not depart from your mouth, but you shall meditate in it day and night, that you may observe to do according to all that is written in it. For then you will make your way prosperous, and then you will have good success."* Our lack of educational success, prosperity, and all that ails America is directly tied to the rejection of God's Truth.

Betsy DeVos, Trump's selection for Education Secretary, understands the nation's Christian heritage, for she was trained in Christian schools, both elementary, high school, and college. She is an advocate for school choice and the use of vouchers that would allow the government to fund religious education. This could be a game-changer. Once again, another piece of the puzzle is in place for the Church to let its voice be heard without fearing a backlash from political elitists in Washington. Oh, to be sure, there will be staunch resistance on the local level and from others inside the Beltway, but knowing that we have a faith-friendly Education Secretary is comforting.

Our education standing globally is of such concern that in 2001 it was considered to be the second greatest threat to America's security—after a terrorist attack with a weapon of mass destruction.

How can we ever hope to compete with other nations like China whose students walk or ride bikes an average of five miles arriving at school by 7:30 a.m. and sitting at desks until 7:30 p.m. with no music, no athletics, no art, and no drama—just an immersion into the academics that has earned China global respect. It is no small problem, but one that must be corrected. Instilling a biblical worldview into the curriculum is a good place to begin.

A BIBLICALLY ILLITERATE NATION

When Jay Leno hosted the *Tonight Show* his "Jay Walking" interviews were an entertaining segment of the show. It was not unusual for him to ask biblical questions that elicited hilarious responses. One responder thought the Red Sea was parted so that Noah's Ark could pass through. Another thought Cain and Abel were friends of Jesus. Another guessed that Jesus was born 400 years ago while still another took a stab in the dark by saying he was born 300 million years ago. But the one that really makes the head spin was the lady who said that Jesus could not have been a carpenter because they didn't have carpet back then. Welcome to the New America! When Jesse Watters of Fox News randomly interviews people on the street and asks the most basic questions regarding America's history, the responses are equally as absurd, even among our Ivy League students. It truly makes you scratch your head and ask, "What are these students being taught?"

HEALING IS POSSIBLE

This is no time for cynicism, skepticism, or defeatism. Our constitutional system was based upon a biblical worldview. We the people, particularly God's people, must demand it. We cannot be fainthearted. We are living in a period of American history where it is not a time to sleep at the wheel. Nor is it a time to cheerlead from the grandstands. Ezra 10:9 says, "*.....all the people sat in the open* *square before the house of God, trembling because of this matter and the heavy rain."* The rain may have contributed to their trembling, but the primary source of their shakiness was the realization that they had forgotten God. And this eye-opening moment occurred in front of the house of God.

Why should we not do the same? Gather God's people in our houses of worship and with a prophetic voice call them to repentance. Yes, even our regular attenders have forgotten the God of their salvation and left their first love. Our casual Christianity has declined into a casual commitment requiring little sacrifice so that today's level of commitment to Christ is as low as it has ever been. Remembering and reconnecting with God is where the healing begins. This necessitates a prophetic voice. Someone must stand up and address the issues, guide the people, and point them back to God. This is what the prophets of old did. The day for such a prophetic voice to return to our pulpits is now.

Pastors know that such proclamation will not be met with applause. Yet, we cannot depend on our political leaders to do what God has admonished His church to do. Certainly, our politicians know that our economy is broken, our families are broken, and our inner cities are broken, but they cannot fix America at the most fundamental level because the problem starts in the heart. Only the Gospel can change the heart and only the Church, God's people, have been commissioned to share it. Yet, I fear that the Church has been waiting for the world to get right with God and all while the world has been waiting for the Church to get right with God.

The Church cannot be divided into red states or blue states. While the Church can be, and should be, a voice for righteousness, her role is not political activism. For too long her prophetic voice has been drowned out by the cultural trends and popular fads. "Thus says the Lord" sounds too archaic, old school, and antiquated. Scandals, hypocrisy, and liberal theology have all combined to assault the Church's credibility. It will take an invasion of God's Spirit whether initiated by one man, one student, one church, or one denomination. It is the only real hope for America. The time is now. We cannot await another election cycle because be assured those on the other side are strategizing and mobilizing their troops in an effort to avoid another humiliating loss. This is our time for the Church to seize the moment.

The One Who Discovered The Law of Gravity

"We account the Scriptures of God to be the most sublime philosophy. I find more sure marks of authenticity in the Bible than in any profane history whatsoever.....There is one God, the Father, ever-living, omnipresent, omniscient, almighty, the Maker of heaven and earth, and one Mediator between God and man, the man Christ Jesus....To us there is but one God, the Father, of whom are all things, and one Lord Jesus Christ, by whom are all things, and we by Him. That is, we are to worship the Father alone as God Almighty, and Jesus alone as the Lord, the Messiah, the Great King, the Lamb of God who was slain, and hath redeemed us with His blood, and made us kings and priests."

— Sir Isaac Newton (1647-1727)
the famous discoverer of the laws of universal gravitation and helped develop calculus into a comprehensive branch of mathematics. Newton was a mathematician, scientist, and philosopher. He constructed the first reflecting telescope, laid the foundation for the great law of energy conservation and developed the particle theory of light propagation.

CHAPTER 27

Ask For The Old Paths

We have been on quite a journey. Thanks for taking the ride with me. If you read the entire book without skipping chapters, you're to be commended. While I pray that each chapter fulfilled its intended purpose, the one you are about to read is among the most significant. Cultural statistics, political trends, and quotes from esteemed leaders all have their place, but there is no substitute for the Word of God. Certainly, Storm Warnings is saturated with Scripture and clarion warnings echoed from biblical prophets have sounded the alarm throughout these pages, but it is now time to call it a wrap with one final prophetic voice, none other than Jeremiah. Perhaps there is no prophet who speaks with such relevance to the current state of America's culture as does this weeping prophet of Scripture. For Judah once stood where America now stands. And though our nation appears nowhere in the holy writ, the principles and warnings issued to Judah apply to America. Judah's failure to heed the prophet's message resulted in God's ultimate judgment, captivity by a foreign nation. In Jeremiah 30:23, he exclaims, ***"Look! It is a storm from the Lord!...Punishment will come like a storm..."*** *(NCV)* The storm warnings God issued to Judah are reflective of what we are witnessing in America. Clearly, we stand on the precipice of an intensified storm from the Lord Himself that threatens our very survival as a nation. Storm clouds are gathering, thunder is rumbling, and the distant lightning is striking. We can only nod our heads in agreement, bow our hearts in contrition, and confess, "Guilty as charged!" But God, through His prophet, offers hope and a solution. For Judah, it was too late. For us, there is still time.

A LITTLE BACKGROUND ON JERRY

No irreverence intended, but his best buddies in ministry may have affectionately called him "Jerry." Come to think about it, he probably had very few friends. His message was certainly discomforting and his style elicited shouts of anger rather than applause. He was scorned, reviled, and exiled. He began his ministry about 60 or 70 years after Isaiah's death and was a contemporary of Zephaniah, Habakkuk, and Daniel. God told Jeremiah in 7:28, *"You shall say to them, 'This is a nation that does not obey the voice of the Lord their God nor receive correction. Truth has perished and has been cut off from their mouth.'"* It is especially noteworthy that Jeremiah's ministry began during the reign of King Josiah, the boy ruler who became Judah's king at only eight years of age. His father (Amon) and grandfather (Manasseh) were both evil men who led Judah into the most hideous forms of idolatry. Yet, Josiah did what was right in the sight of God (2 Kings 22:3) and issued executive orders to purge Judah and Jerusalem of all pagan gods. Josiah reintroduced the nation to the Word of God when the sole manuscript copy of Scripture was discovered in the House of God while it was being rebuilt. Think about it, the nation's only copy of Scripture had been lost in the House of God while it sat abandoned for years. Consequently, the people had not heard a word from the Lord in their lifetime. Their minds were darkened and susceptible to the lies of false prophets.

Sadly, God's Word has likewise been lost in a great percentage of our churches with the name of Jesus never being mentioned and sin never being identified and rebuked. Many of today's popular preachers are little more than motivational, positive-thinking, health & wealth, self-esteem boosters peddling the latest heretical trend. Similarly, Judah's false prophets were telling them that they were good people deserving of prosperity and wealth. You can practically hear their false prophetic voices declaring, "How dare Jeremiah should preach such a harsh message! God is good and loving." If they had television in those days, ratings would have soared and their best-selling books would have been featured throughout the nation. Not so with Jeremiah. And so it is today. There is an eerie silence in America's pulpits when it comes to a bold prophetic, "Thus says the Lord."

King Josiah's efforts were well-intentioned and we dare not minimize his courage in destroying the idols and temples of false worship, but the spiritual reformation ushered in was shallow, short-lived, and more cosmetic than heart-felt. Outwardly, it had the appearance of genuine revival, but Josiah's executive orders could not legislate a change of heart. Yes, they changed the name of their god and the place of their worship, but they were the same sinners they had always been, still pursuing their immorality and self-centered agendas. The "spiritual reformation" was superficial and this was the setting that Jeremiah was instructed to expose their hypocrisy.

I fear the same to be true within America's evangelical world. As I now write, there is much excitement over President Trump and his new administration. As stated earlier, given the evangelicals he has appointed to his cabinet, he may prove to be the most faith-friendly executive the White House has seen in our lifetime. He has already repealed federal funding for abortions. Thus far, the checklist for his agenda has been consistent with evangelical thinking and his aggressive economic policies have created optimism among conservatives, not to mention his pledge to restore religious liberty and remove much of the political correctness from the nation. Christians must be careful, however, not to fall prey to a superficial optimism that excludes a change of heart produced only by repentance and a return to Jesus Christ. Once again, anything short of a massive, authentic movement of God's Spirit that is initiated and perpetuated by the local churches of our Land will fall short of the remedy for what ails America. By in large, the Church (Christians) in America has left its first love (Jesus) and revival is the need for the hour. Let Josiah be a reminder that the wind of God's Spirit cannot be legislated and revival cannot be dictated by executive orders. What I see God doing is answering the prayers of multitudes of Christians who prayed for the 2016 election and God seems to be creating a more conducive atmosphere for such an awakening to occur. But the ball is now in the church's corner. If the Christian community fails to seize the moment, take the ball and run with it, then our days are numbered regardless of how successful Trump's economic policies are. There is no act of Congress that can substitute for what only the Church can do, so come on Church and come on men and women of God, let's rise to the occasion! For years, the Lord has repeatedly warned America through the judgments mentioned in previous chapters. This may be our last chance, one that we don't deserve, but one that we desperately needed.

Without trying to beat a dead horse with redundancy, America's greatest need is spiritual, not political. Yes, we need jobs. Yes, we need an economic resurgence. Yes, we need to get immigration under control. Yes, we need to strengthen our military. Yes, we need education reform. Yes, we need to be unified. Yes, yes, yes, and a thousand more. We are a nation in great need. Can you name one institution that is not in decline? But a return to biblical principles will do more to heal the wounds of our nation, cure our problems, and solve our polarization than any law Congress can pass. Why? Because fundamentally America does not simply have a crime problem, illegitimacy problem, divorce problem, drug problem, or greed problem. We have a heart problem and the Gospel of Jesus Christ is the only remedy for changing the heart. Furthermore, the Gospel has been entrusted to the Church and the Church has been commissioned by our Commander-in-Chief to share it with those around us. The Church's refusal to do so is a great starting point for our repentance because our silence is deafening and high treason in the courts of Heaven.

Josiah was a religious celebrity and the people were following instructions out of love for him rather than their love for God. He was their spiritual hero whom they adored. They thought they were in the midst of real revival, but within three months of Josiah's death, they fell back into their idolatrous, immoral ways. That's when the truth surfaced and their true colors were revealed. Today, churches bring in celebrities to draw the crowds and even mega-church pastors often are placed on pedestals as thousands throng to their auditoriums with hands raised in what appears to be genuine worship. But, if another person fills the pulpit or if the pastor resigns for another ministry assignment, attendance often plummets and it begs the question, "Who were the people really worshipping? Does such tendency reflect a depth of love for Christ or merely a loyalty to the pastor and his personality?" It was in the middle of this pseudo-revival that God raised up Jeremiah as His spokesman to expose their hearts. Not a popular assignment, but he did so for 42 years without any measurable results.

ASK FOR THE OLD PATHS....

In one of his sermons, Jeremiah offered hope for his nation by declaring, *"Stand in the ways and see..." Another translation says, "Stand at the crossroads and look. Ask for the old paths, where the good way is, and walk in it; then you will find rest for your souls."* (6:16) For America, the old paths were from inception of our nation to 1960. Frankly, we have been aggressively intentional in driving God out of the public square, so the problems we're facing should come as no surprise. Contrarily, it would be surprising if such were not the case. Now, like Judah, we are standing at the crossroads but do we hear anyone asking for the old paths? That is, the Christ-centered, biblically-based principles that captured the hearts of our Founders, compelled them to action, inspired their writings, and gave birth to America and its founding documents. Clearly, the Word of God permeates the foundational documents of our nation and incessant prayer was at the heart of it all. All of this encompasses the "old paths." Lest anyone thinks such statements are historically inaccurate, the research is available for all to see. Patrick Henry is one of hundreds we could quote, but hear him again: *"It cannot be emphasized too much or repeated too strongly that America was founded not by religionists, but by Christians, not upon religions, but upon the gospel of Jesus Christ."* This is the old path to which we must return. Not coincidentally, the old path reflected the glory days of our nation because, "Blessed is the nation whose God is the Lord." (Ps. 33:12)

America has chosen a new path as seen in the following examples:

- The Affordable Care Act mandated tax-payer funded abortions and contraceptives to children.
- Matthew Reynolds, the valedictorian for his high school in Victor, Iowa, was told by authorities that his graduation speech must be secular after he expressed a desire to attribute his success to Jesus Christ. [1]
- A federal judge threatened "incarceration" to a high school valedictorian unless she removed references to Jesus from her graduation speech.
- A cross was removed from a veteran's memorial in San Diego after the U.S. Court of Appeals for the 9th Circuit held that the memorial was unconstitutional.
- A Cisco employee was fired for expressing his views on traditional marriage in his book, even though he never voiced his religious opinions at work.
- Samantha Schulz, 8, was barred from singing "Kum Ba Yah" at a Boys and Girls Club in Port Charlotte, Florida because the song included the word, "Oh, Lord."

- City officials prohibited senior citizens from praying over their meals, listening to religious messages, or singing gospel songs at a senior activities center.
- A public school official physically lifted an elementary school student from his seat and reprimanded him in front of his classmates for praying over his lunch.
- Public school officials prevented a student from handing out flyers inviting her classmates to an event at her church.
- A public university's law school banned a Christian organization because it required its officers to adhere to a statement of faith that the university disagreed with.
- The U.S. Department of Justice argued before the Supreme Court that the federal government can tell churches which pastors it can hire and fire.
- The state of Texas sought to approve and regulate what religious seminaries can teach.
- The U.S. Department of Veterans Affairs banned the mention of God from veterans' funerals, overriding the wishes of the deceased's families.
- A federal judge held that prayers before a state House of Representatives could be to Allah but not to Jesus. [2]

The individuals cited above were seeking the old paths, but were refused by those in authority over them. It is a clear picture of two worldviews clashing, atheistic secularism and biblical Christianity. I often encounter it when speaking in school assemblies. For example, this week I received a call from an Oklahoma pastor where I will be serving in a few weeks. The principal of the local high school is a member of his church and wants me to conduct a school assembly, but is disallowing me from mentioning the youth rally where I will be speaking later that evening. The fear is that by naming a church someone might be offended and a lawsuit may be filed. The operative word is "fear." The ACLU and other anti-Christian organizations have school administrators paranoid and largely uninformed of our First Amendment constitutional rights. The separation of church/state card has been played so many times and our distorted understanding of its mythological interpretation literally has paralyzed Christians from exercising their God-given rights and liberties.

Nevertheless, these are only a few of the hundreds of examples that reflect the new path America has chosen. The collateral damage can be seen in the fragmentation of families with divorce rates skyrocketing since the 1960's, crime and teenage suicides are off the charts, and in some cities the illegitimacy rates are as high as eighty percent! Our government spends millions of tax-payer dollars per year teaching our kids how to use condoms and then uses that same money to attack abstinence-based sex education. The result? We lead the industrialized world in sexually transmitted diseases. Our kids are more familiar with the lyrics of the latest pop star than with the words of Jesus Christ. No surprise there since the Bible, prayer, and Ten Commandments have been legislated from America's classrooms. Granted, it never has been the school's responsibility to spiritually train our children, but the message is clear and millions have concluded, "If our government declares exposure to the Bible, prayer, and God's Commandments to be illegal in school and potentially harmful to our kids, then perhaps we should not give it priority in our homes either."

We are a divided nation, old path vs. new path, biblical worldview vs. secular worldview. We see it reflected in pro-life vs. pro-choice, traditional marriage vs. gay marriage, capitalists vs. socialists, small government vs. big government, conservatives vs. liberals, and the list seems endless. But whatever cultural or political issue is being debated, almost always it is battle between a biblical worldview and secular worldview. Just by the sheer numbers, if the church of Jesus Christ in America experiences genuine life-changing revival that rocks our complacency, restores our marriages, removes our prejudices, and restructures our priorities, then a secular culture will take notice that we've been with Jesus and these peripheral issues become moot because something else, no Someone else, has invaded our world. Life change is what's missing in most our religious activity. Deep in the hearts of unbelievers resides the question, "What is there about your life that distinguishes you from me?" The prevailing answer is, "Very little." Thus, the false assumption and inaccurate conclusion is, "The Church is irrelevant and this Jesus stuff is inconsequential." Of course, the problem with many of our religious institutions and religious activity lies in a cold, dry, inauthentic, watered-down message that excludes the necessity of embracing the cross, denying ourselves, or repenting of sin. Rather, millions merely conform to a religious code of ethics, attend the required classes, adopt a system of morality, get sprinkled, and join the church. That may be an over-simplification, but the point to be made is that America may be a religious nation, but no longer are we a Christian nation in the sense that we abide by the Founding principles established by our forefathers. Our churches are filled with good, moral, religious folks who do not have a personal walk or relationship with Jesus Christ. And the world at large is perceptive enough to pick up on that reality. Again, there are very few problems in America that could not be solved if the American Church encountered an earth-shaking, life-changing revival.

Statistically, it is undeniable that the new path we embarked on is not working. In 1950, 78% of all households contained a married couple, but today the marriage rate is at an all-time low (48%) with more than half of all couples cohabiting before marriage. It comes as no surprise, therefore, that America is the world leader in divorce resulting in one out of every three children without a father in the house. For women under 30, more than half of all babies born in our country are out of wedlock. [3] There was a day when homosexuality was the litmus test for religious apostasy and culturally, it was actually against the law. Our new path has seen the highest court in the Land abolish America's long-standing definition of marriage as described in the Bible and redefine it by legalizing same-sex marriage. As with Judah, America has made a mockery of God's standards and Jeremiah asks, *"Were they ashamed when they had committed abomination? No! They were not at all ashamed, nor did they know how to blush."* (8:12) Nor do we. In arrogant defiance of God's Holy Word, President Obama had the audacity to celebrate the same-sex ruling (which the Bible calls an abomination) by lighting up the White House in rainbow colors, just the opposite of blushing!

THE THREE SINS THAT INVOKED GOD'S JUDGMENT ON JUDAH

(1) The guilt of shedding the innocent blood of their children

Jeremiah 19:4-8 is graphic: *"Because they have forsaken Me and made this an alien place, because they have burned incense in it to other gods whom neither they, their fathers, nor the kings of Judah have known, and have filled this place with the blood of the innocents (they have also built the high places of Baal, to burn their sons with fire for burnt offerings to Baal, which I did not command or speak, nor did it come into My mind), therefore behold, the days are coming," says the Lord, "that this place shall no more called Tophet or the Valley of the Son of Hinnom, but the Valley of Slaughter. And I will make void the counsel of Judah and Jerusalem in this place, and I will cause them to fall by the sword before their enemies and by the hands of those who seek their lives; their corpses I will give as meat for the birds of the heaven and for the beasts of the earth."*

On 9/11 of 2001, 3,000 Americans were slaughtered in the name of Allah. That same day 4,000 unborn Americans were also slaughtered in the name of convenience. In fact, 4,000 were slaughtered on September 10 and September 12 and every day since 1973. Our landscape is polluted with the innocent blood of 58 million innocent, defenseless babies. Adolph Hitler was responsible for the death of 12 million Jews in concentration camps and we call him deplorable. Joseph Stalin was responsible for the deaths of 20 million citizens and we call it inhumane brutality. Yet, here in America we have our own Valley of Slaughter like that of Judah in which millions of fully developed babies can be seen moving and sucking their thumbs in the womb of their mothers during the third trimester of pregnancy but that innocent human being is killed in a procedure called partial birth abortion. Forgive the imagery, but the woman's cervix is dilated, the baby's legs are grabbed with forceps and pulled through the birth canal and then the baby's entire body is exposed, with the exception of the head. The abortionist inserts a sharp object into the back of the baby's head, removes it, and then a vacuum tube sucks out the baby's brain. The head collapses and the child is discarded like a piece of trash. Granted, not all abortions fall into the partial birth category and it is illegal in 19 states, but that leaves 31 states performing this barbaric procedure. So, while only a minority of abortions fall into the partial birth category, just one is too many. What we do know is this: Modern science tells us that by Day 4 the sex of the baby can be determined and by Day 20 the heart begins to beat. Life begins at conception, but our culture of death has exterminated over a million babies each year since 1973.

A phrase that leaps off the page in the Jeremiah passage is when God says, "It did not come to my mind." That's how hideous, hard-hearted, and calloused the people had become. At the root of killing their innocent children was a misguided theology with deception, greed, lust, and idolatry at its core. Judah had exchanged gods, departing from the True and Living God for a false god made of stone and created by the hands of man. Their false god appealed to their comfort, was less demanding, accommodated their immorality and conformed to their convenient lifestyle. However Americans may try to justify it, we are just as guilty and just as deserving of judgment. Thankfully, God is giving us this window of opportunity.

(2) Sexual Sin

God, through His prophet, says in Jeremiah 5:7-9: *"How shall I pardon you for this? Your children have forsaken Me and sworn by those that are not gods. When I had fed them to the full, then they committed adultery and assembled themselves by troops in the harlots' houses. They were like well-fed lusty stallions; everyone one neighed after his neighbor's wife. Shall I not punish them for these things?" says the Lord. And shall I not avenge Myself on such a nation as this?"*

Judah was a sex-crazed nation guilty of all kinds of perversions. Marriage had lost its sanctity. Immorality was common. Troops of citizens were lined at the door to commit sin with prostitutes. We know from other passages that a part of Judah's violation of God's covenant involved homosexual activity. You name it, Judah did it. God describes them as being like horses in heat. A horse has no shame having sex with the whole world watching. That was a picture of Judah. But is it not also a clear portrayal of our nation? With the click of a mouse or the push of a button on cell phones, a person can watch the most perverted acts of sex by those who have no shame whatsoever. They even boast, laugh, and gloat in their perversion. Multiple research claims that men in America spend more money on pornography than all the combined revenue generated from CBS, NBC, and ABC. More is spent on porn than major league baseball, the National Football League, or the National Basketball Association combined. America indulges its pornographic appetite more than the combined revenue of rock music concerts, jazz concerts, classical music performances, ballet, or country music concerts. Our nation is responsible for 89% of all porn produced and exported throughout the world. Research shows that 79% of men age 18-30 view porn at least once a month. [4] Other reports tell us that Americans spend more on pornography each year than groceries. [5] So, even our appetite for food is exceeded by a lust for unfaithful sexual activity. Jeremiah mentions adultery with their neighbor's wife. Again, the stats for America are off the charts with more than half of all couples living together outside the bonds of the marriage covenant. We dare not miss the point. If God's judgment fell upon His chosen people for these violations of His moral law, why should we falsely assume that America's fate will be any different?

(3) Abandoning God's Word

Let's hear the Lord's indictment of Judah once more: Jeremiah 16:10-13 says, *"And it shall be, when you show this people all these words, and they say to you, 'Why has the Lord pronounced all this great disaster against us? Or what is our iniquity? Or what is our sin that we have committed against the Lord our God?' then you shall say to them, 'Because your fathers have forsaken Me,' says the Lord; 'they have walked after other gods and have served them and worshiped them, and have forsaken Me and not kept My law. And you have done worse than your fathers, for behold, each one follows the dictates of his own evil heart, so that no one listens to Me."*

A few observations are compelling. First, they were defending their immoral actions as though God was wrong and they were right. They had convinced themselves that they were the innocent party. They were in denial. Listen to the arrogance of their claim: *"Why has the Lord pronounced all this great disaster on us? What is our iniquity? What is our sin that we have committed against the Lord our God?"* Their moral compass was so skewed, their minds so deceived, that they saw no harm in their porn, their adultery, or their activity with prostitutes. In their minds, this was normal. All the while, they continued with their religious rituals. They still claimed that “the Lord is our God.”

A second observation is that disobeying God’s law is associated with forsaking Him. But, this was beyond the pale. It was blatant defiance of God’s Word and actively worshiping false gods. As in Romans one, Judah had exchanged the truth of God for the lie. Also as in Romans one, this exchange of truth found expression in their vile passions of sexual activity. It is difficult to conclude that Judah’s apostasy was any different than America’s.

A third observation is when God says, *“Each one follows the dictates of his own evil heart.”* This is another way of saying that each one had become a little god unto himself. The ideology was, “What’s right for you may not be what’s right for me. What’s wrong for you may not be what’s wrong for me. You have your truth and I have my truth. And besides, there is no objective standard by which to judge right from wrong. So, who are you to judge?” This is the philosophy of moral relativism, one that is held by over 90% of youth and over 75% of adults in America. Everybody follows what seems right in his or her own heart. God’s Word never enters the equation of their decision-making process. They just followed their own consciences. “If it feels right in my heart, then what could be wrong with it?” Well, as Jeremiah says in 17:9, *“The heart is deceitful above all things, and desperately wicked.”* Again, Judah’s faulty reasoning and misguided value system was no different than America’s today.

As a result, Judah faced financial problems, family problems, health problems, and social problems. The social infrastructure of the nation was turned upside down. And while America has always had its share of problems, today America is inundated by an educational crisis, an economic crisis, a military crisis, an immigration crisis, a crime crisis, a racial crisis, a healthcare crisis, a terrorism crisis and a host of incurable diseases along with the social unrest that pervades the nation. Never in our history have we encountered so many problems simultaneously and never have they been so complex. In short, America is where Judah was at the end of her days. That fact alone should drop us to our knees.

There is a Balm in Gilead

It's another way of saying, "There is still hope." I remember singing out of an old hymnal in my grandmother's church, "There is a balm in Gilead." As a child I had no idea what I was singing. Jeremiah 8:21-22 says, *"For the hurt of the daughter of my people I am hurt. I am mourning; Astonishment has taken hold of me. Is there no balm in Gilead, is there no physician there? Why then is there no recovery for the health of the daughter of my people?"*

The balm of Gilead was a rare ointment made from the gum of a tree. The balm had the power to soothe and to heal. On the mountains of Gilead was a special kind of tree and when removing its bark, resin would flow. The resin would be collected and ground into a powder and then physicians would know how to apply the balm so that healing would occur. Today, we look into the Scriptures and see another special tree found on another mountain…Mt. Calvary. Hung on that tree was the Great Physician and flowing from His side was the healing blood of Jesus. Therein lies the secret to our healing. The balm is the blood of Jesus Christ. Judas called it "innocent blood" (Mtt.27:4). Peter called it "precious blood" (1 Peter 1:9). John called it, "cleansing blood" (1 John 1:7 and "washing blood" (Rev. 1:5). Paul called it "purchasing blood" (Acts 20:28), "redeeming blood" (Eph. 1:7), "justifying blood" (Eph. 1:7), "peacemaking blood" (Col. 1:20). Hebrews calls it "sanctifying blood" (Heb. 13:12) and "powerful blood" (Heb. 13:20). We see in Scripture that "without the shedding of blood there is no remission for our sins" (Heb. 9:22).

Wouldn't it be a shame to be diagnosed with a terminal disease with no miracle drug to eradicate it? Cancer fits into this category. But wouldn't it also be incredible if someone discovered a pill or a vaccination that could prevent anyone from ever getting cancer? If so, would you be willing to take the shot or swallow the pill? Who in their right mind would say, "No thanks, I'll take my chances. Friend, you and I have a disease that is terminal. It goes by the name of sin. It comes with a death penalty. "All have sinned and the penalty of sin is death," so says the Bible. But this disease not only comes with a terminal diagnosis but also eternal consequences. Yet, God in His great mercy and love has provided us with a balm, a remedy. It does not cost you a dime and this cure will not only increase the quality of your life in the here and now, but it will increase the longevity of your life into all eternity. I am speaking about salvation made possible through the precious blood of Jesus Christ.

WILL YOU RECEIVE CHRIST AS YOUR PERSONAL SAVIOR?

Look, I realize that the opportunity was extended for trusting Jesus as your personal Savior back in chapter twenty-four. Nothing wrong with asking again, right? After all, eternity is no small thing nor is experiencing the best life this side of Heaven something to shrug off, so let's re-visit the balm, the remedy, the CURE that God offers to all of us through Christ Jesus, His Son.

Yes, we have all sinned. We're all damaged goods standing in need of a Savior. Regardless of how good you may be or how high your standard of morality may reach, we still fall short of God's standard of holiness. No doubt, the human tendency is to compare ourselves with those around us and in doing so, you'll probably measure up just fine. However, the problem with this approach is that God's standard for Heaven is not "others" but Jesus Himself. That's why we all fall short. Despite this reality, God still loves us and desires to forgive us, come into our lives, and provide an eternal home for us in Heaven. "How can I receive Christ into my life?" you may be asking. There is no magic formula in the words we pray because God is looking mostly at the attitude of our hearts. Romans 10:9-10 says, *"If you confess with your mouth the Lord Jesus and believe in your heart that God has raised Him from the dead, you will be saved. For with the heart one believes unto righteousness, and with the mouth confession is made unto salvation.....For whoever calls on the name of the Lord shall be saved."*

God is saying, "You do the calling and I'll do the saving." Will you allow this prayer to express the sincere desire of heart? You may pray it silently or audibly but Jesus says, *"I stand at the door and knock. If anyone will hear my voice and open the door, I will come in to him."* Standing outside the door of your life, Jesus stands ready, willing and able to come into your life, cleanse your sin, and connect the bridge that separates you from God. While He is knocking, keep in mind that the doorknob is on the inside. Only you can open it. I can help you with this prayer of invitation to the Lord:

Dear Lord Jesus,

I need you and I want you in my life. I have sinned against you and I'm unable to save myself. Please forgive me. I now turn from my sin, believing that you died on that cross and that You took the punishment I deserved. So, come into my life, Lord Jesus, and save me now and forever. As best I know how, I now choose to follow You. I surrender all that I am to all that You are. Thank you for cleansing my sin and for saving my soul. I humbly ask this in the strong name of the Lord Jesus Christ.

If you just now offered this prayer to the Lord, I would like to send you some literature that will great help you to grow and mature in your new-found walk with Christ. Please contact me at shea@fbcw.net.

A Final Look at Judah's Destiny

The reason for all the calamities that surrounded Judah was simply her wickedness, her sinful defiance, and her idolatry. Jeremiah 30:15 says, *"Because of the multitude of your iniquities, because your sins have increased, I have done these things to you."* And let's not forget verse 23: *"Look! It is a storm from the Lord! Punishment will come like a storm…."* This has been the basis, the thesis for *Storm Warnings! America's Race to a Day of Reckoning.* One of the saddest verses in the Jeremiah is found in 8:20: "The harvest is past, the summer is ended, and we are not saved!" As a nation, Judah's opportunity had passed. It was too late. She had ignored the storm warnings that God had sent. For America, it is not too late. But time is running out. The window is narrow. But there is clear indication that God has opened it. America's only hope is for the preachers of our Land to call their congregations to prayer, humbling ourselves, seeking His face, and turning from our wicked ways (2 Chronicles 7:14). May God grant it to be so!

A WORD OF CAUTION TO EVANGELICALS

Donald Trump was an iconic businessman, a multibillionaire, and a reality star with the number one show on NBC. He was a political novice who had never held an elected public office in his life. I'll refrain from reiterating the "miraculous" phenomena that left political analysts dumbfounded, pollsters with egg on their face, and talking pundits speechless. Celebrities cried, women protested, and the Democrats declared him illegitimate with over 60 refusing to attend the Presidential Inauguration, an action that was unprecedented. The boycotting continued well into the nomination process of Trump's Cabinet as Democrats on the Senate Floor rallied an all-night effort to sway one more Republican from voting for Betsy DeVos as Education Secretary. For the first time ever a sitting Vice-President was required to cast the tie-breaking vote in her favor. Some Democrats refused to even attend the interrogation sessions for Cabinet appointees. So yes, there is deep-seated anger and division between the two parties.

Within weeks of his election Trump was renegotiating trade deals, appointed 14 conservative evangelical Christians to his Cabinet whom experts are saying may be the most competent cabinet in the history of politics, he nominated a conservative constitutional originalist to fill the Supreme Court vacancy, signed executive orders for the pipeline deal, to build the wall, to repeal the Affordable HealthCare Act, to repeal federal funding for abortions, and in the midst of it all the stock market hit 20,000, a historic high. Reporters who have covered Washington politics for decades say that he accomplished more in the first week than of any President they've seen in recent history. Those closest to him say that he practically never sleeps. He's high energy, rising at 3 a.m., and committed to putting America first in all of his decision-making. Robert Jeffress, pastor of First Baptist in Dallas, Texas, says that Donald Trump may be the most faith-friendly President in modern history.

As a result of all this, there is a renewed energy, optimism, and growing enthusiasm within the evangelical community, especially in hearing him pledge to repeal the Johnson Amendment which would allow preachers to address political and moral issues in the pulpit without fear of having their church's tax-exempt status revoked or censored by the IRS. As Trump has said, "We are witnessing something of historic proportions and what we have seen was not a campaign, but a movement, the likes of which has never been seen in all of American politics."

What you have just read is in no way intended to be a political endorsement, but to his credit, Trump wasted no time in fulfilling many of his pledges to the American people. However, in his inauguration speech he said, "We are going to make America strong again, wealthy again, proud again, safe again, and great again." But he did not say that he was going to make America moral again because morals come from theology and theology comes from the Bible and the Bible has been entrusted to the Church. Jesus said, "It's out of the heart that proceeds blasphemies, adulteries, murders, profanity, and all other immorality. Only the Gospel of Jesus Christ can change the heart. In other words, we cannot depend on our political leaders to do what God has admonished the Church to do. Politicians know that our economy is broken, our families are broken, our inner cities are broken, our military is broken, our healthcare is broken, our educational system is broken, our government is broken, immigration is broken, and the list goes on. There is not one institution in our nation that is not in decline, the Church included. But at our most fundamental level America does not have a crime problem, an illegitimacy problem, a divorce problem, a drug problem, or a greed problem. What we have is a heart problem and that's something that only the power of God through the Gospel of Jesus Christ can change. Yet, that's not going to happen until the Church gets its act together.

America has always had its problems, but it's not an overstatement to say that never in our history have we seen so many problems with such magnitude coming against us simultaneously and with such impactful ramifications. We are on the precipice of collapsing.

WAKE-UP CHURCH, THE ALARM IS GOING OFF!

What happened politically in terms of a movement sweeping the country and electing the most unlikely candidate in a field of 17, a similar movement must occur in the Church if we hope to survive as a nation. There, I said it. We saw the nation express its outrage for a do-nothing Congress, a dysfunctional government, Congressional gridlock, empty political rhetoric, broken promises, and millions could see this nation spinning out of control and spiraling downward. They had a wake-up call and instead of hitting the snooze button, they got out of bed and expressed their displeasure by going to the voting booths all across the Land.

In the same way, the churches of our Land need to have a wake-up call because there is no act of Congress that can produce what only God can accomplish. Regardless of how much good is accomplished politically, judicially, or legislatively, it will all be short-lived apart from an invasion of God's Holy Spirit that impacts the local churches of our Land through an authentic revival that spreads from county to county and state to state, and school to school. And while historians are writing about an unprecedented political movement in American history which no one has been able to explain, they will be forced to turn their attention to a spiritual movement which no one is able to explain. And while the swamp is being drain in Washington, the lethargy, complacency, and apathy is being drained within the Church. It will be a glorious day when the Church stops hitting the snooze button and starts responding to the wake-up call that God has been sending us for years!

God, I believe, is giving us one more opportunity. The movement we are seeing politically needs to be reflected in the Church spiritually. God is creating an environment politically so that His Church can more easily rise to the occasion spiritually with a reduced fear of persecution, lawsuits, or the over-reaching arm of the IRS. Whether it be through one man, one woman, one student, one church, or one denomination, it is time for the Church to be the Church and preachers in America to re-engage and rediscover their prophetic voice and with one mighty chorus, call our congregations to repentance and call our churches to revival. That most likely will require an interruption to our regularly scheduled programs. It may require turning the lights back on Sunday nights for prayer and fasting. But whatever it takes, there is no price too high to bring America back to God and its founding principles. So, while many are applauding President Trump's aggressive agenda to make America great again, those within evangelical circles must not be disillusioned into believing that the hope for our future lies in politics, regardless of how conservative the policies may be. Similarly, we must beware of a misplaced value system that expresses greater enthusiasm over a political speech or an executive order from the President than what is expressed by a well-delivered sermon an executive order from our Commander-in-Chief when reading His Word. No, America will never be great again apart from the foundation upon which that greatness was built, that is none other than the Word of God and the Gospel of Jesus Christ. May we fervently pray for our leaders, both spiritual and political, that this worthy and urgent goal may be attained sooner rather than later. "God, bless America to this end, we humbly pray."

APPENDIX A

Books That Served as Sources for *Storm Warnings*

Saving Freedom by Jim DeMint

Already Gone by Ken Ham & Britt Beemer

The Snapping of the American Mind by David Kupelian

Stop the Coming Civil War by Michael Savage

Culture Warrior by Bill O'Reilly

Bankruptcy of Our Nation by Jerry Robinson

Persecution by David Limbaugh

Broke by Glenn Beck

Public Education Against America by Marlin Maddoux

Bowling Alone by Robert D. Putnam

Undemocratic by Jay Sekulow

America: Imagine a World Without Her by Dinesh D'Souza

Reclaiming a Nation at Risk by Brannon Howse

Faith of Our Founding Fathers by Tim LaHaye

From Family Collapse to America's Decline by Mitch Pearlstein

Adios, America! By Ann Coulter

A Nation in Crisis: The Meltdown of Money, Government, and Religion by Larry Bates & Chuck Bates

Plunder and Deceit by Mark Levin

U Turn by George Barna and David Barton

Legislating Morality by Norman Geisler and Frank Turek

The Great Destroyer by David Limbaugh

Coming Apart by Charles Murray

Godless: The Church of Liberalism by Ann Coulter

One Nation by Ben Carson

The Twilight of American Culture by Morris Berman

America's Real War by Rabbi Daniel Lapin

Islam and Terrorism by Mark A. Gabriel

Rise of ISIS by Jay Sekulow

America's God and Country by William J. Federer

America: Turning a Nation to God by Tony Evans

Onward by Russell Moore

We Cannot Be Silent by R. Albert Mohler, Jr.

Godless America by Todd Starnes

Culture Shock by Chip Ingram

The Real Crash by Peter Schiff

The Great Evangelical Recession by John S. Dickerson

Epicenter by Joel C. Rosenberg

Now or Never by Jim DeMint

Obama's America by Dinesh D'Souza

Implosion by Joel C. Rosenberg

Our Kids: The American Dream in Crisis by Robert D. Putnam

The State of the American Mind by Mark Bauerlein and Adam Bellow

Islam and Terrorism by Mark A. Gabriel

Islam, Israel and Armageddon by Bob Gass

Strategic Failure by Mark Moyar

Truth Overruled by Ryan T. Anderson

Faith in the Voting Booth by Leith Anderson & Galen Carey

My Final Word by Charles Colson

The Conservative's Handbook by Phil Valentine

Culture of Corruption by Michelle Malkin

One Nation, Under Attack by Grant R. Jeffrey

Can America Survive? By John Hagee

Dispatches From Bitter America by Todd Starnes

The Immigration Crisis by James K. Hoffmeier

One Nation Under God by Bruce Ashford and Chris Pappalardo

Truth Decay by Steve Hale

The Coming Economic Armageddon by David Jeremiah

Signs of The Coming of Christ by Gary Frazier

Prepare: Living Your Faith in an Increasingly Hostile Culture by J. Paul Nyquist

Same-Sex Marriage by Sean McDowell & John Stonestreet

Politics According to the Bible by Wayne Grudem

Character & Destiny by D. James Kennedy

Twilight's Last Gleaming by Robert Jeffress

Storm by Jim Cymbala

Stream by James Robison

Awakening by Ralph Reed

Tough Faith by Janet & Craig Parshall

Why You Can't Stay Silent by Tom Minnery

Armageddon, Oil and Terror by John Walvoord and Mark Hitchcock

Future Events That Will Shake the World by Ed Hindson

Ask the Question by Stephen Mansfield

War in the Middle East by Grant Jeffrey

The Church Awakening by Chuck Swindoll

It's All About Islam by Glenn Beck

Inside the Revolution by Joel Rosenberg

The ISIS Crisis by Charles Dyer and Mark Tobey

Our Last Great Hope by Ronnie Floyd

Countdown to Apocalypse by Robert Jeffress

Healing America's Wounds by John Dawson

Praying for America by Dutch Sheets

Is God on America's Side? by Erwin Lutzer

Vision America by Aubrey Malphurs

The Late Great United States by Mark Hitchcock

A Nation Without a Conscience by Tim & Beverly LaHaye

War on Terror by Grant Jeffrey

When a Nation Forgets God by Erwin Lutzer

America's Last Call by David Wilkerson

APPENDIX B

Storm Warnings' Signature Sermon

For Pastor's Only

WHEN GOD REMOVES THE HEDGE

Abraham Lincoln once said, "If destruction be our lot, we ourselves will be its author and its finisher." Adrian Rogers said, "While God is America's greatest hope, He can also be our greatest threat." Both of these men are saying that the greatest enemies we face as a nation are none other than ourselves and God himself. And that means the most important battle we face is not the war on terrorism but a spiritual battle that is being waged for the very soul of our nation. Never in history have we seen America assaulted by so many complex problems occurring at the same time. Everywhere we turn we're faced with multiple crises....an economic crisis, an immigration crisis, a healthcare crisis, an education crisis, a moral crisis, a drug crisis, a racial crisis, and then when we look at crime, our marriages, our military, and our political institutions. The foregone conclusion is that there is not an institution in our nation that is not in decline, including the church.

Therefore, it is not an overstatement to say that we are a nation in distress and on the precipice of collapse. For many years we have travelled down this destructive path and with each passing year we have been sinking deeper and deeper and lower and lower into the quick sands of moral corruption and degradation. But as believers in Jesus Christ and as members of the Christian community the question we should be asking the question, "Does God have a Word for us and what course of action should His Church be taking?" So, I'm speaking tonight on the subject, "When God removes the Hedge." We're going to look at **Recognizing the Reality of the**

Hedge, Reasons for Removing the Hedge, and the Results of Removing the Hedge.

The doctrine of hedges is something we don't often hear preached, but the Bible speaks of its reality throughout Scripture. For example, Job 1:10 describes God placing a hedge of protection around Job so that Satan was unable to penetrate it. Ecclesiastes 10:8 says, "Whoever breaks through a hedge or a wall will be bitten by a serpent. In other words, when the hedge is removed Satan moves in to kill, steal, and destroy. The Hebrew words for "hedge" actually mean "a wall." So, in biblical times a hedge was a defensive wall built around a city and comprised of stones. And inside these stone hedges were poisonous serpents. When the hedge was broken, the serpent would strike innocent victims.

In Isaiah 5:1-5 we see that God had placed a hedge of protection around the nation of Israel. It reads like this: **"Now let me sing to my Well-beloved. A song of my Beloved regarding His vineyard: My well-beloved has a vineyard on a very fruitful hill. (He's referring to Israel as a vine or vineyard). He dug it up and cleared out its stones, and planted it with the choices vine. He built a tower in its midst, and also made a winepress in it; so He expected it to bring forth good grapes, but it brought forth wild grapes. And now, O inhabitants of Jerusalem and men of Judah, Judge, please, between Me and My vineyard. What more could have been done to My vineyard than I have not done in it? Why then, when I expected it to bring forth good grapes, did it bring forth wild grapes? And now, please let Me tell you what I will do to My vineyard. I will take away its hedge, and it shall be burned."** God is saying, "I created the nation of Israel. I planted them, prospered them, and blessed them. I did all I could for them. I placed a hedge of protection around them. But when I came to get My fruit, instead of a sweet cluster of grapes, the fruit was rotten, wild, and worthless. And it was because of the nation's defiant attitude toward God and His Word that God declared to Israel,

"I am removing the hedge that I placed around you." That is to say, "The divine protection that I placed upon you and around you, I've decided to remove it and you're going to see the impact it has upon your economy, your weather patterns, your health, your military, and the blessings you've enjoyed will gradually be replaced with national distress, anxiety, and fear.

Were you aware that when our Founding Fathers came to this new Land to establish America as one nation under God, they used Israel's covenant relationship with God as a pattern for composing our Founding documents, structuring our government, and establishing our laws. Our Founders wanted the blessings described in Deuteronomy 28 to apply to America. Our Founders understood that "Blessed is the nation whose God is the Lord." They understood that "righteousness exalts a nation, but sin is a reproach to any people." Most of our Founding Fathers were highly educated and extremely godly. Our constitution was born out of a prayer meeting. The first 100 colleges were for the purpose of training ministers. The first public buildings constructed were churches and the first school teachers were ministers. No wonder that Patrick Henry set the record straight by saying, **"It cannot be emphasized too much or repeated too strongly that America was founded not by religionists, but by Christians, not upon religions, but upon the gospel of Jesus Christ."** Throughout the writings of our Founders we see time and again that the purpose of their journey to this Land was for the glory of God and the propagation of the Gospel of Jesus Christ. In fact, political science professors from the University of Houston wanted to know where our founders came up with the idea for our form of government, so they spent 10 years researching 15,000 documents and to their surprise, 94% of the content was either direct or indirect quotes from the Bible.

So, the point is simply this: With Israel being the exception, no other nation in all of history has had the kind of Christ-honoring, biblical foundation and Christian heritage as has America. And as a result, I am fully persuaded that God placed His hedge of protection and blessing upon our country as the Bible describes. I mean, have you ever stopped to wonder why our nation has been so blessed beyond all others? Why is it that for over 200 years pestilence, terror, and war reached the shores of other nations, but not ours? Why is it that other nations have looked to us to lend them food and send them aid in times of international crisis just as Deuteronomy 28 describes? Why do millions of immigrants flee their countries and come to America with the hope of seeing their dreams fulfilled? It's because God has been the Source of our blessing and freedoms. Our first line of defense as a nation has not been the military, but God Himself and the hedge of protection that He placed around us.

But let's not just recognize the reality of God's hedge of protection, but what are the reasons for Him removing it? Take your Bibles and turn to Romans chapter 1. In verses 24, 26, and 28 we find three identical phrases that state, "God gave them up, God gave them up, and God gave them over." This is an example of backing off, removing His protective hedge, and giving the nation over to its own desires. Now interestingly enough, we find this very same terminology throughout the Old Testament as well. So, this is obviously a way in which God deals with nations. Let's take a moment to look at a few examples. In Psalm 78:62 it says, **"God *gave* His people over to the sword."** In fact, in verse 46 of that chapter it says, **"God gave their crops to the caterpillar." Verse 48 says, "He *gave* up their cattle to the hail." Verse 50 says, "He *gave* their life over to the plague." Psalm 81:12 says, "I gave them over to their own stubborn heart, to walk in their own counsels. And the reason is given in the previous verse, "My people would not heed My voice, and Israel would have none of Me." In verse 13 God pleads with them by saying, "Oh, that My people would listen to Me, that Israel would walk in My ways! I would soon subdue their enemies, and turn My hand against their adversaries."** In other words, "If your enemy is terrorism. If your adversary is a bad economy. Whatever is coming against you as a nation, I will fight in your behalf." However, God backed off and removed His hedge by giving them over to their own counsels and their own stubborn heart.

In Psalm 106:41 we see that **"God *gave* them into thc hand of the Gentiles so those who hated them ruled over them. Their enemies also oppressed them, and they were brought into subjection under their hand."** In this passage the thing that provoked God to hand Israel over to an enemy nation was in verse 35 where it says, **"They mingled with the Gentiles and learned their works. They served their idols which became a snare to them. They even sacrificed their sons and their daughters to demons. And shed innocent blood, the blood of their sons and daughters whom they sacrificed to the idols of Canaan."** That's when verse 35 says, **"The wrath of the Lord was kindled against His people, so that He abhorred His own inheritance."** And God's wrath found expression by backing off and removing His Hedge of protection which resulted in giving them over to be oppressed by an enemy nation. And by the way, you cannot read these verses without making the obvious comparison to America. We've not bowed down to wooden idols, but we've served false gods and since 1973 we've killed 58 million innocent babies through abortion, 98% of which were done on the altar of self-centered convenience. Just as verse 38 describes the land being polluted with the blood of their own children, so it is with our nation. The hands of our nation are stained with the innocent blood of millions of our children who were never given the chance at life and when the next verse says, "Therefore the wrath of the Lord was kindled against His people," if that be true for His own chosen nation what makes us think that America is an exception?

A similar pronouncement is found in Nehemiah 9:30 where God says, **"Yet they would not listen; Therefore You *gave* them into the hand of the peoples of the lands."** 1 Kings 14:16 says the same thing. Ezekiel 20:25 says, **"I also *gave* them up to statutes that**

were not good and judgments by which they could not live." God is telling us that a part of His judgment is allowing politicians to enact laws and pass legislation that is not in the best interest of the nation. So, just to be clear, when God removes His hedge from a nation, it simply means that He backs off or takes away His hand of protection and blessing, and in these passages we've just read, we see that the manifestation of this is found in everything from poor laws, poor counsel, bad advisors, oppression from other countries, decline in military strength, hail, pestilence, and disease. In most of the passages we read, the reason for all of these calamities and distress was idolatry. That is, the heart of the nation had exchanged gods; they had transferred their loyalty from the true and living God to false gods in order to accommodate their immoral lifestyle.

And listen, our nation has done precisely the same thing. We have transferred our loyalty from the God who once blessed us to other false gods. As Romans 1:25 says, "We have exchanged the truth for the lie." And the lie that 75% of American adults now embrace and that over 90% of teenagers embrace and that 62% of active church members embrace is the assertion that there is no such thing as absolute truth. It's the ideology that says, "What may be right for you may not be right for me and what may be wrong for you may not be wrong for me. You have your truth and I have my truth. You have your god and I have my god. Besides, who are you to judge? There is no objective standard for determining right from wrong." Folks, this is the deceptive philosophy that permeates our nation, our schools, our laws, our government, and now our churches. It's called moral relativism. We're told to be tolerant of everybody and everything because there is no such thing as an absolute right and absolute wrong. This is nothing more than atheism dressed up. You can put lipstick on a pig, but it still smells like a pig.

But go back to Romans 1:26. It says, **"For this reason God gave them up."** So God identifies the reason that He removed His protective hedge and it's found in the previous verse that we just read. "They exchanged the truth of God for the lie." This is a clear warning that when a nation begins to tamper with God's truth, it is a personal assault on the very character of God Himself and that's something He takes so personally that He's not about to passively sit on the sidelines indifferent to such transgression.

Now, if indeed America has exchanged God's truth for the lie, when did such a thing occur?

(1) It has been a process and not merely a one-time action. The fact is, our nation has been at war with God's truth for several decades but it never really surfaced legislatively until 1962 when the United States Supreme Court ruled that leading our children in prayer in the public schools of our nation had not become illegal.

(2) In the following year, the same Court ruled that reading God's Word to our children in public schools was now illegal. Remember that Jesus said, "God's Word is Truth."

(3) In 1965, it became illegal for a student to verbally pray over his meal in a school cafeteria.

(4) In 1969 it was ruled illegal for a war memorial to be erected in the shape of a cross.

(5) In 1970 it was ruled illegal to arrive at school early to hear a student volunteer read prayers, the very same prayers that are offered by the chaplains in the chambers of both the Senate and the House.

(6) In 1973, the same Supreme Court ruled in favor of killing unborn, innocent, defenseless babies through abortion on demand.

(7) In 1976 the Court ruled that it was illegal for the board of education of any public school to use or refer to the word "God" in any of its official writings. Incidentally, is it not ironic that we've gone from the Bible being the first textbook in our schools to now not allowing the word "God" to be used.

(8) In 1980 it became illegal for the Ten Commandments to hang on the walls or our classrooms and the reason the Court gave was that "It might lead our students to read them and obey them."

(9) In 1984, the Court ruled that if a legislator writes a bill with a religious activity in mind, then that bill becomes unconstitutional even though the wording of the bill is constitutionally acceptable.

(10) In 1984 the Court ruled it was illegal for kindergarteners to pray, "We thank you for the flowers sweet. We thank you for the food we eat. We thank you for the birds that sing. We thank you for everything."

(11) In 1985 the Court ruled that it was illegal for a school graduation ceremony to open or close in prayer.

(12) In 1987 it became illegal to teach creationism as a viable explanation for how the world began. And in that same year, students in Alaska were forbidden to use the word "Christmas" because it contained the name "Christ" in it. They could not even exchange Christmas cards or write the word on their notebooks.

(13) In 1992 clergy-led prayer at high school graduation exercises became illegal.

(14) In 1996 student-led prayer was likewise banned.

(15) A federal judge ruled that prayers before a State House of Representatives could be made to Allah but not to Jesus.

(16) In fact, back in 1995 a U.S. District Judge named Samuel B. Kent ruled that any student even uttering the word "Jesus" at graduation exercises would be arrested and incarcerated for six months. He threatened further by saying, "This court is going to have a marshal present who'll be censoring your language. Anyone who thinks I'm kidding about this order better think again. Anyone who violates these orders is going to wish he or

she had died as a child when this court gets through with it."

This is judicial activism out of control but we could be here for hours citing one ruling after another that has placed our nation in direct opposition with God and the biblical principles we were founded upon. And the cumulative effect from all of this is that God has increasingly removed His hedge of protection. And just for the record, from 1927 to 1962 there were never more than two consecutive years in which SAT scores declined. Since those rulings, SAT declined for 18 consecutive years and even then the only reason they leveled off was because of the home school and Christian school movement in the country.

Did you know that compared with other industrialized nations, America is at the bottom of the academic ladder in literacy, math, and science? Seventeen of the nation's 50 largest cities have high school graduation rates lower than 50%. In Detroit, only 25% graduate from high school, it's 31% in Indianapolis and 34% in Cleveland.

Since those rulings in 1962 and thereafter, there are indisputable statistics that show teenage pregnancies increased by 187% for the next 15 years. For girls 10-14 years of age it was an unbelievable 553% increase. Sexually transmitted diseases skyrocketed to 226% for the next 12 years.

Before 1962 divorce had been on the decline but after those rulings divorces increased by 300% for the next 15 years and violent crime increased by 544%, so you can look at every conceivable metric and see that when our Courts removed prayer and God's Word from the eyes and ears of our children, it was an attempt to remove God from their thinking. And with each passing year we have legislatively and increasingly taken legal action to remove any semblance of Christianity from the public life of this nation. So, 1962 was a defining moment which was subsequently followed by a dramatic increase in crime, STD's, premarital sex, illiteracy, suicides, drug use, and other social ills. And I submit to you that it is difficult to deny the correlation between the ungodly rulings by our Courts and the statistical decline in our nation's morality. In fact, the prayer that was ruled illegal contained 27 words and here's what it said, "Almighty God, we acknowledge our dependence upon thee. We ask thy blessings upon us, our parents, our teachers, and our nation." This was the prayer that led to the 1962 landmark decision, but don't you find it interesting that the four areas covered in that short prayer of blessing are the very four areas where we have seen dramatic decline. That is, education, our youth, our homes, and our nation.

It's as though we have raised a clinched fit toward heaven and have said, "God, you can take your prayers, take your commandments, take your Word, take your hedge, and take the name of Jesus and just go back to Heaven and leave us alone. We can make it on our own." By our actions that is precisely the message we have sent to God. And God has reciprocated by doing just that. And if you think that's an exaggerated assessment of where we are, then let me remind you of a national political convention a few short years ago (and I'll refrain from identifying the party but you have a 50-50 chance of guessing it), but for the first time ever, God was omitted from the party platform and it created enough unrest that the decision was made to reinstate God into its political platform. Now, this was on national television and when the chairman brought the motion to the floor for a vote to reinstate God into the party platform, there was a resounding NO from the delegates on the floor. I was stunned because this was a vivid example and representation of the nation's attitude toward God.

So much more could be said, but we need to move on to not just recognizing the reality of God's hedge of protection and the reasons from removing it, but what are results that come from the removal of the hedge?

We'll look at several, but let's first go back to our Romans 1 text. Verse 26 once again says, **"For this reason, God gave them up**

to vile passions." So, what were the vile passions that God gave them over to? **"For even their women exchanged the natural use for what is against nature. Likewise, also the men leaving the natural use of the woman, burned in their lust one for another, men with men, committing what is shameful and receiving in themselves the penalty of their error which was due."**

So, the nation is impacted morally when God removes His hedge. But I want you to notice that homosexuality and sexual immorality were not the causes of God's judgment. The text does not say, "God gave them up *because* of sexual immorality or because of homosexuality." No, the words read that "God gave them up TO vile passions." You see, while homosexuality and sexual immorality were not the causes of God's judgment, they were the consequences of His judgment. This is an incredibly important distinction to make. Homosexuality and sexual immorality were instruments of God's judgment upon the nation. Homosexuality and sexual immorality were expressions of God's wrath upon the nation.

Therefore, when God backs off and removes His protective hedge from the nation, sexual immorality and homosexuality not only become more prevalent, but they become expressions of His judgment. So, what we saw in the Court's 2015 ruling on same-sex marriage is Romans 1 being played out before our very eyes. The Washington elite interprets it as evidence of a nation that's in step with the times and tolerant, but in reality it is evidence of a holy God turning His back, giving us up, and removing His protective hedge. For these 9 unelected, unaccountable justices to ignore what has stood for thousands of years of civilization and disregard hundreds of documented studies on the benefits of traditional marriage and without a vote from the citizens whom the Court represents, these 9 justices redefined marriage which they never defined in the first place and legalized same-sex marriage, which God calls an abomination, and made it the law of the land. And what's even more embarrassing is that we now have the distinction of being one of the few nations on the planet to legalize same-sex marriage and we actually celebrated it by lighting up the White House in rainbow colors which represents the colors of the Gay Pride flag and stands for diversity.

Ladies and gentlemen, marriage is a divine institution which God Himself created and therefore God alone has the right to define it. But again, this is what happens when a nation exchanges the truth of God for the lie. So, America has redefined what God had already defined and in so doing, it substituted biblical morality for man's immorality and elevated man's opinion above God's Word. That is blatant defiance and arrogance, but this is the cumulative effect from decades of judicial activism that has created this environment of political correctness in which Christianity is marginalized and our religious liberties are being lost.

Once again, Romans one speaks of sexual immorality being a result of God removing His hedge and today over one-half of all couples live together before getting married, over 40% of all childbirths are out of wedlock (in some cities it's as high as 80%) and one out of every four teenage girls is carrying a sexually transmitted disease. Eighty-nine percent of all porn is produced in America and exported from America.

The result of God removing His hedge not only impacts our nation's morality, but it impacts us monetarily as well. In Deuteronomy 28 God promised to bless Israel for her obedience by saying in verse 11: **"The Lord will grant you plenty of goods, in the fruit of your body, in the crease of your livestock, and in the produce of your ground (and the next verse says) You shall lend to many nations, but you shall not borrow. And the Lord will make you the head and not the tail."** However, if you scroll down to verse 33 the Lord promises to curse the nation if she refuses to obey His Word. He says, **"A nation whom you have known shall eat the fruit of your land and the produce of your labor, and you shall be only oppressed and crushed continually. Verse 42 says, "Locusts shall consume all your trees and the**

produce of your land. The alien who is among you shall rise higher and higher above you, and you shall come down lower and lower. He shall lend to you, but you shall not lend to him; he shall be the head and you shall be the tail." Does the phrase "leading from behind" come to mind? But let's not miss the point. Clearly, God says that if a nation will honor Me and the principles of My Word, then I will prosper that nation. Tonight, we have a $20 trillion debt and an entitlement debt of unfunded liabilities of around $140 trillion that comes from Medicare, Medicaid, Social Security, military pensions, and government employee pensions. Now, none of us can wrap our brains around those kinds of figures but here are a couple of illustrations to show just how massive this debt is.

If you could pay one dollar of every hour of every day of the month, it would take 32,000 years just to pay off $1 trillion. To pay off $20 it would take 640,000 years.

Or we could say it like this: If you spent $10 million a day it would take 273 years to get to one trillion dollars and 5,460 years to pay off $20 trillion. That means that if you spent a million dollars every day going back to the birth of Jesus, it would not come close to a trillion dollars. That's why respected economists are shouting at us saying, "We are facing an economic disaster on an epic scale."

So, when God removes His hedge it impacts the nation's morality, the nation monetarily, but also meteorologically.

Throughout the Old Testament whenever Israel invoked the judgment of God upon the nation, it often found expression in the form of droughts and famines. That is to say, God caused inclement weather to come against the nation as an expression of His judgment and a means of getting the attention of the nation with the goal of producing a repentant spirit. In Deuteronomy 28 there is a lengthy list of curses that God promised to place upon the nation for her disobedience and among them is verse 23 where

He says, **"And your heavens which are over your head shall be bronze, and the earth which is under you shall be iron. The Lord will change the rain of your land to powder and dust; from the heaven it shall come down on you until you are destroyed."** Again, in Psalm 78 47-48 it says, **"He gave their crops to the caterpillar. He destroyed their vines with hail, and their sycamore trees with frost. He also gave their cattle to hail and their flocks to fiery lightning."** In these two passages alone we see drought, frost, hail, and lightning which came upon the land and was directly associated with the expression of God's judgment. Now, if God attributed adverse weather to Himself as a part of His judgment, who are we to say that He does not still do the same. Now, this is not to say that every thunderstorm or flash of lightning is God's way of administering His displeasure. But when the weather patterns of a nation become so extraordinary and historic in magnitude, then I think it's fair to stand back and reassess what God might be saying. Here are just a few examples:

In 2011 we had a record-breaking 89 natural disasters, but then the first six months of 2012 exceeded all of the 2011 record with 104 natural disasters. In 2011 our nation experienced the largest outbreak of tornadoes ever recorded with 343 ripping through the South in one month alone. Then, less than a month later Joplin, Missouri saw the deadliest tornado in American history with 160 people killed. That same year we also had the largest wildfires ever recorded and Oklahoma experienced its strongest earthquake in history.

Next, there was record-breaking rainfall in the Ohio Valley. The next year Texas experienced its most severe drought and worst heat wave in history. In fact, the entire Southern United States recorded a record-breaking heat wave from 2010 to 2013 and California endured its worst drought in over 130 years. The Drought of 2012 impacted 60% of the nation and devastated the country with crop and livestock losses.

Then in 2014 Washington State experienced its worst wildfire and mudslide in history. In 2015 the western part of our nation experienced the worst wildfire activity in recorded history.

One newspaper article asked the question, "WHY DOES THIS KEEP HAPPENING TO AMERICA?" It said that America has been absolutely pummeled by a devastating series of disasters and the most recent one may be the worst of all when in 2015 Missouri encountered what the news media called a historic flood. It said, "Nobody that is living has ever seen anything like this." But then Missouri's historic flood was eclipsed by West Virginia's flood in 2016. News reports called it a "once-in-a-thousand year flood."

The point is this. With each passing year it seems that America is encountering record-breaking tornadoes, hurricanes, ice storms, snow falls, floods, wild fires, droughts, and earthquakes. Meteorologists will explain it in scientific terms, but when I look at the natural disasters of Deuteronomy 28 and other passages of Scripture, I believe it is further evidence of God removing His protective hedge from the nation because God clearly stated that when a nation chooses to honor Him and give His Word the preeminence and respect it deserves, the He promised to cause even the weather of the nation to be in our favor.

So, I believe a strong biblical case can be made that when God withdraws His hedge of protection, the nation is impacted morally, monetarily, and meteorologically, and if we had the time we could also discuss militarily. It's significant to note that about 75% of the curses listed in Deuteronomy 28 now reside upon our nation. It would be the height of spiritual naivety to conclude that all of this is cosmic coincidence, global warming, or a random set of unfortunate circumstances.

Once again, we go to the prophetic book of Habakkuk where the prophet raises several concerns by asking, **"O Lord, how long shall I cry, and You will not hear? Why do you show me iniquity, and cause me to see trouble? For plundering are before me; There is strife, and contention arises. Therefore the law is powerless,**

and justice never goes forth. For the wicked surround the righteous; therefore perverse judgment proceeds." Then listen to how God responds to Habakkuk's questions: In verse 5 He says, **"Look among the nations and watch—Be utterly astounded! For I will work a work in your days which you would not believe, though it were told you. For indeed I am raising up the Chaldeans, a bitter and hasty nation which marches through the breadth of the earth, to possess dwelling places that are not theirs. They are terrible and dreadful; their judgment and their dignity proceed from themselves. Their horses also are swifter than leopards, and more fierce than evening wolves. Their chargers charge ahead; their cavalry comes from afar; they fly as the eagle that hastens to eat."**

If Habakkuk was alive today, he would be asking, "Why is our judicial system lenient on criminals? Why are murderers portrayed as victims? Why do the courts defend immorality and ridicule the righteous? Why are valedictorians forbidden to speak of their faith at graduation ceremonies? Why are our children taught tolerance toward immoral lifestyles and instructed on how to use condoms, but are refused the right to pray, read the Bible or quote the Ten Commandments in school? Why do our courts defend every kind of indecency in the name of free speech, but to share the Gospel or wear a Christian T-shirt is prohibited as being intolerant and a violation of the law? Why do the courts redefine what God has already defined and why do they legalize what God declares to be immoral?

So, God stuns the prophet by saying, "I hear what you're asking and I, too, am concerned….so much so that you're going to be astounded at what you're about to hear. I am going to use the Chaldeans, the terrorists of your day, and even though they hate me and want nothing to do with me, but they are going to be My instrument of judgment against the very nation that I brought into existence and chose at one time to bless unlike any other." Folks, if God could raise up a terroristic, foreign ungodly nation to come against His chosen people,

He has no problem doing the same with our nation.

I repeat what was said earlier. The decades of anti-God, anti-Christian, and anti-Biblical rulings of our courts, the immorality of our nation, and the backslidden complacency of the American church have collectively combined to activate the judgment of God upon our nation. Daniel Webster, the great American statesman, said, **"If we abide by the principles taught in the Bible, our country will go on prospering; but if we neglect its instructions and authority, no man can tell how sudden a catastrophe may overwhelm us and bury all our glory in profound obscurity."**

Now, we come to the most important part of the message. If we truly believe that our nation is under the judgment of God; if we truly believe that God has largely withdrawn His hedge of protection from American, then the real question becomes, "How do we restore God's blessing? How do we recover from such judgment? How do we regain God's favor rather than His wrath?" From observing many evangelicals you might conclude that the answer lies in a new political administration. And to his credit, Donald Trump has appointed 14 conservative evangelicals to his cabinet, he has promised to repeal the Johnson Amendment, he has chosen an incredibly conservative constitutional originalist nominee to replace Scalia on the Supreme Court, he has repealed federal funding for abortions and he is seemingly pushing all the right buttons to fulfill his campaign pledges. Robert Jeffress, pastor of First Baptist in Dallas, Texas says that he may be the most faith-friendly president in modern history. Many make the claim that what occurred in the 2016 election would fall into the "miraculous" category and was divine intervention.

In his inauguration speech, Trump said, "We're going to make America strong again, wealthy again, proud again, safe again, and great again." But he did not say that he was going to make America moral again and therein lies the root of all our problems. General Douglas MacArthur gave this profound assessment and word of warning to our nation: **"History fails to record a single**

precedent in which nations subject to moral decay have not passed into political and economic decline. There has either been a spiritual awakening to overcome the moral lapse or a progressive degeneration leading to ultimate national disaster."

MacArthur is reminding us that what often seems to be the problem is not the problem. The economy is not the problem. It's the moral decay that has resulted in the economic decline. Political decline is not our problem. It's the moral decay that has caused the political decline. Now here's the deal and please don't miss this. If, indeed, MacArthur's contention is correct....and I believe it is. Then, the attention should be focused on the morality of the nation. So the question becomes, "Where do morals come from?" They come from theology. Where does theology come from? It comes from the Bible. To whom has the Bible been entrusted? The church. And what is the responsibility of the Church? To be salt and light to the world. Salt is a preservative and keeps things from decaying. So, in tracing the bread crumbs and connecting the dots, we are forced to conclude that the church is at the heart of both the solution and the problems facing us. The church has failed to be the moral preservative in our culture.

The fact that America tonight leads the world in abortions, teenage pregnancies, prison incarcerations, crime, divorce, child poverty, sexually transmitted disease, illegal drugs, and pornography while at the same time having more Bibles, more churches, more Christian TV stations, more Christian radio programming, and more Christian schools only places the spotlight on the anemic condition of the church in America.

Jedoniah Morris was one of our Founding Fathers and known as the "Father of Geography." He issued this warning, **"In proportion as the genuine effects of Christianity are diminished in the nation, in the same proportion will the people of our nation recede from the blessings of genuine freedom. Whenever the**

pillars of Christianity shall be overthrown, our present form of government and all the blessings that flow from it must also fall."

It's another way of pointing back to the church and our responsibility for making a difference in the culture. There is no act of Congress that can do what God has called the church to do. Jesus said, **"It's out of the heart that proceeds blasphemies, adulteries, murder, profanity, and all other immorality and only the Gospel of Jesus Christ can change the heart.** Again, we cannot depend on our political leaders to do what God has admonished the Church to do. Our economy is broken, our families are broken, our inner cities are broken, our military is broken, our healthcare is broken, our educational system is broken, our government is broken, immigration is broken, and there is not one institution in our nation that is not in decline, including the church. But at the most fundamental level, America does not have a crime problem, an illegitimacy problem, a divorce problem, or a drug problem. We have a heart problem and that's something that only the Gospel of Jesus Christ can change, but that's not going to happen until the Church gets its act together.

So, here is my perspective on where we stand right now. **What happened politically in terms of a movement sweeping the country and electing the most unlikely candidate in a field of 17 competent, experienced candidates and then defying the odds in defeating the Clinton political machine, a similar movement must occur in the church if we hope to survive as a nation.** You see, the reality is that our nation was just as sinful and wicked the day following the election as we were the day before the election. This election did not change the hearts of the American people. Only the Gospel can do that. But what we saw in this election was the nation expressing its outrage for a do-nothing Congress, a dysfunctional government, Congressional gridlock, empty political rhetoric, and broken promises to the American people. The nation had a wake-up call and instead of hitting the snooze button, they got out of bed and expressed their displeasure by going to the voting booths all across our Land.

And in the same way, the churches of our Land need a wake-up call because regardless of how much good is accomplished politically, judicially, or legislatively, it will all be short-lived apart from an invasion of God's Holy Spirit that impacts the local churches of our Land through an authentic revival that spreads from county to county and state to state and school to school. And while historians are writing about an unprecedented political movement in American history which no one has been able to explain, they will be forced to turn their attention to a spiritual movement which no one is able to explain. And while the swamp is being drained in Washington, the lethargy, complacency, and apathy is being drained within the church. And it will be a glorious day when the church stops hitting the snooze button and starts responding to the wake-up call that God has been sending us for years! Politically and culturally, God seems to be creating an environment conducive to such a movement. And whether it is through one man, one woman, one student, one church, or one denomination, the world is waiting for the church to rise to the occasion, for the preachers in this nation to re-engage and re-discover their prophetic voice and with one mighty chorus, call our congregations to repentance and call our churches to revival.

The reality is, America will never be great again apart from the foundation upon which that greatness was built and that is none other than the Word of God and the Gospel of Jesus Christ.

And so I ask, "Where in this congregation is a Moses who will determine to obey God regardless of the repercussions? Where in this congregation is a Joshua who displays courageous leadership and can pray down walls? Where is a Joseph who walks with God and implements policies that reflect the will of God? Where are the teenagers like Shadrach, Meshach, and Abednego who will refuse to bow their knees to the false gods of political correctness and will boldly say, "Our God is able to deliver us, but if not, we're still not going to compromise. We'll pay whatever price is required to stand for what's right." Where are the mothers like Hannah who will pray for their children and give them back to God for His service? Where are the children like Samuel who pray to God through the night and honor their parents through the day? Where are the physicians like Luke whose concern for their patients goes beyond the physical, but are likewise concerned about their spiritual well-being? When these kinds of men, women, children, and teenagers step forward and rise to the challenge, then there is hope for America.

There are enough Christians in our nation that if we'll become bold in our witness, disciplined in our prayer life, passionate in our worship, and cultivate a thirst for righteousness and daily bombard the portals of Heaven crying unto God to bring an awakening to this nation, then I got to believe that God will restore the years that were devoured by the enemy. But He's daring us to trust Him, to seek Him, and to fast & pray. Now, will you accept the challenge? Be radical. Be bold. Be light and salt in your school, in your neighborhood, and in your business.

APPENDIX C

A PRAYER FOR AMERICA

Dear God,

We humbly approach Your throne of grace in the Name of Jesus Christ our Lord. For that is the only Name by which we have access to Your Presence and the assurance of You hearing the cry of our heart. For You said in Your Word that "This is the confidence we have in Him that if we ask anything according to Your will You hear us. And if we know that You hear us in whatever we ask, then we may be assured that we have the request that we've asked of Him." Therefore, O God, it is through the blood that Jesus shed for our sins that we approach You in confidence and with boldness because Your Word has exhorted us to come boldly to the throne of grace that we may obtain mercy and find grace to help in our time of need. We confess that we are a needy people desperately needing Your mercy.

You are an awesome God worthy of our praise. We acknowledge Your sovereign Lordship over the nations of the world. You rule and reign from Your throne. Your unseen Hand orchestrates the destinies of nations. You are all-powerful, Wonderful Counselor, the mighty God, everlasting Father, and Prince of Peace. We acknowledge that You are King of Kings and Lord of lords, so we bow in humble adoration for all that You are. Without You we can do nothing, but with You all things are possible.

So, while we thank You for giving birth to this nation, and while we praise You for all the blessings You've bestowed upon America, far too numerous to count, we have as a nation taken these Divine gifts for granted. Throughout history You have delivered us in war and prospered us in peace. Indeed, Your hand of favor has rested upon our nation as we have enjoyed the pinnacle success and prosperity unlike any nation in history. And it's only because Your Word teaches that righteousness exalts a nation. So, we thank You for the godly heritage that our Founding Fathers entrusted to us. But for decades now, we have been poor stewards of our rich heritage. We have defied and denied the biblical principles for which they stood. We have kicked You out of our schools. We have mocked Your Word. We have implemented laws sanctioning the deaths of untold millions of innocent babies who never had the chance to become what you created them to be. We have redefined the institution of marriage which You alone created and declared to be holy. We have removed Your Ten Commandments from the eyes of our children. We have eliminated You as our Creator from the education of our children while substituting man's theory of evolution. Publicly acknowledging You in prayer is forbidden in our schools and Valedictorians who dare to mention the name of Jesus are intimidated and forbidden to do so. Because of our godless policies and spiritual defiance, we are a testament to the Truth of Your Word which says that sin is a shameful reproach to any people. For indeed, we find ourselves at the bottom looking up to other nations in our debt, our education, our morals, our divorces, our corruption, and our crime.

We stand before You without excuse. Our wickedness indicts us. Our evil ways can no longer be denied nor justified. And while it is tempting to point a finger to the political corruption in our government, we know that Your finger is pointing elsewhere. You've reminded us that judgment must first begin at the house of God. You promised to not heal our Land until first we, as Christians, humble ourselves, pray, seek Your face, and turn from our own wicked ways. And so, forgive us for doing what Adam did in the Garden of Eden, shifting the blame to others when it's the sinful rebellion and wickedness in our own hearts that has set in motion the avalanche of crises now facing our nation.

It has been our complacency, our pride, our silence, our indifference, and our self-centeredness. We stand guilty as charged. In our abundance, we've refused to share with those in need. In our greed, we have failed to give generously to Your Kingdom. Pride has often silenced our witness. Indifference has hindered our involvement. Complacency has perpetuated the comfort of our inactivity. But we, Your people, are chronically sick with anxiety disorders, fear, depression, and a host of emotional maladies that cripple our effectiveness for Your Kingdom. The world looks at Your Church and sees little difference between us and them. We confess our failure to be salt and light to the culture.

We have gone astray and embraced the lie of this world's value system. And yet, we're reminded that a friend of the world makes himself the enemy of God. O God, we don't want to be opposed to You nor do we want You to be against us. Your Word says, "If God be for us, who then can be against us?" But God, if You're against us it makes little difference who is for us. So, we repent of our worldly ways. We pray for the light of Your Truth to be restored in our homes. We pray for our marriages to be strengthened so that our children see a reflection of Your love and know the security that comes from the warmth of a Christ-centered marriage. We pray for revival in our homes.

But we also pray for revival in Your Church and let it begin with each of us. We pray for our pastors and church staff that You will do a work of renewal in each of their hearts so that they will effectively lead us and feed us as they ought. Empower the preachers of our nation to be bold in the proclamation of Your Truth and then give our congregations the grace to obey it.

From the wealthiest mansions to the homeless street peddlers; from the white Caucasians to all ethnicities; from the most famous celebrities to the no-name stock clerks; from the professional athletes to the physically handicapped; from the mega-church to the country church; from the concrete jungles of our cities to the backroads of rural America; let the Gospel of Jesus Christ prevail throughout our Land. We pray for nothing less than a Divine visitation igniting revival in Your Church that expands beyond county and state lines into a massive awakening unexplainable apart from the manifest Presence of a holy God in our midst. For, O God, it's not just about saving America from economic destruction but saving millions of souls from eternal destruction.

Open the eyes of our understanding to discern the urgency of the hour in which we live. We pray for those who lead us from school boards to city councils; from secondary educators to university professors; from local magistrates to federal judges, from all of our congressmen to all of our Supreme Court justices. And then we pray for our President, his cabinet, and all of his advisors. For each of these we ask that You turn their eyes Heavenward in acknowledging their inadequacies and seeking Your face and the grace that You extend in their behalf. In each of their lives, we pray for the conviction of sin where it's needed.

More than anything, we pray for the Gospel of Jesus Christ to find a lodging place in the hearts of the American populace, from the highest office in our Land to most common dwelling; from the most prominent citizens to the millions of welfare recipients; from the church house to the school house; from the court house to the White House; and yes, Lord, to my house.

Until then, may each of us be found as courageous soldiers of the Cross and faithful ambassadors of the Gospel. Despite headlines in the news and spiritual darkness that engulfs our Land; keep our eyes fixed on You. May the spirit of repentance prevail and may there be restoration and healing from the self-inflicted wounds caused by our stubborn, wicked, and foolish choices. As Jehoshaphat prayed in a state of desperation, "O Lord God of our fathers, are You not God in heaven, and do You not rule over all the kingdoms of the nations, and in Your hand is there not power and might, so that no one is able to withstand You? For we have no power against this great multitude that is coming against us; nor do we know what to do, but our eyes are upon You." Father, like Jehoshaphat, our problems are greater than our human abilities or resources. But our eyes are upon You. Bring glory to Your Name with a Divine visitation that ignites the spiritual awakening that America so desperately needs and for which Your Church so prayerfully awaits. We offer this prayer in the Name that is above every name, the mighty and matchless name of Jesus Christ our Lord. Amen.

FIVE SPECIFIC PRAYER TARGETS

(1) **Pray for spiritual awakening on our high school and college campuses.** The spiritual awakenings in America's history have been initiated and perpetuated by students. It is all too easy to observe this generation of young people and conclude that they are biblically illiterate, drenched in porn and alcohol, obsessed with sex, and spiritually indifferent. I can certainly understand that stereotype, but let's remember the 1960's when the hippie culture was into drugs and rock music, but God heard the cry of His people which ignited the Jesus Movement. Think about it. There are 720,000 international students on our college campuses. Revival on our college campuses has far-reaching ramifications.

(2) **Pray for revival in our inner cities.** The inner cities of America resemble a Third World country. Vacated store fronts, fatherless homes, high school dropouts, and high crimes rates only to name a few of the social metrics that characterize these neighborhoods. If the Gospel of Jesus Christ prevailed in these parts of our cities, who knows what would happen to the rest of the nation.

(3) **Pray for the men in our churches to step up and lead this movement of God.** For years there has been a glaring void of godly men who will lead their families and take initiative in their churches. Sexual sin, divorce, and fatherless homes have left our men ridden with guilt. But any genuine awakening will impact our families and as fathers are restored to wholeness, they will become spiritual mentors to a broken generation of young men desperately needing their presence.

(4) **Pray for Christian women to be courageous witnesses in these defining days.** Like Deborah and Esther in Scripture, God still raises up women of courage to meet the challenges of the nation. It has happened throughout our history and needs to occur once again. It is common consensus that

women have a greater appetite for God than most men, so let's pray for women to do more than gather around circles for ladies Bible studies, but to be proactive in impacting their secular communities with the Gospel.

(5) **Pray for revival in all denominations.** Without exception, all of our Bible-believing denominations are in significant decline. The statistics are horrendous. While we see a renewed and intensified church-planting emphasis, there is a need for our denominations to recapture the vision of personal soul-winning, local church revivals, and city-wide crusades. From the top of denominational leadership who sit in executive offices throughout the week to the laity who sit in their pews on Sunday mornings, we must pray to be more proactive in sharing the Gospel and resist blending in with the complacency mindset that embraces a business-as-usual approach to ministry.

What we witnessed in the election of 2016 was a political miracle, one that was missed by virtually every pollster. Many would say that God intervened in response to the prayers of His people. What occurred politically can also occur spiritually. Let us join our hearts before His throne and trust Him to do it. The environment has never been more conducive and the need has never been greater.

ENDNOTES

Introduction

1 https://en.wikipedia.org/wiki/1991/PerfectStorm

2 Ibid

3 Steve Hale, *Truth Decay*, pp 13-14, Riverstone Group, Canton, Georgia, 2006, 2011, 2015

Chapter 1

1 Tim LaHaye, *Faith of our Founding Fathers*; Brentwood, TN: Wolgemuth & Publishers, Inc., 1987, p. xi-xii

2 *America's God and Country*, William J. Federer, 2013, Amerisearch, Inc.; St. Louis, MO., p. 648

3 www.triumphpro.com/america-into-the-darkness.pdf p. 8 by William F. Dankenbring

4 ibid p. 9

5 http://www.treasury.gov/resource-center/data-chart-center/tic/Documents/mfh.txt

6 http://www.revelationunderstoodcommentary.com/revelation-commentary-blog.html-----article entitled Prophecy Being Fulfilled in Current Events

7 "The Decline of a Nation" by Kerby Anderson. p. 1 http://www.leaderu.com/orgs/probe/docs/decline.html

8 Ibid

9 Ibid. p. 1

10 http://fortune.com/2015/07/20/united-states-decline-statistics-economic

11 Richard McCormack, "The Plight of American Manufacturing," *The American Prospect*, December 21, 2009, http://prospect.org/cs/articles?article=the_plight_of_american_manufacturing.

12 Ibid

13 Les Christie, "Foreclosures Up a Record 81% in 2008," CNN Money, January 15, 2009, http://money.cn.com/2009/01/15/real_estate/millions_in_foreclosrue/index.htm

14 Lynn Adler, "U.S. 2009 Foreclosures Shatter Record despite Aid," Reuters, January 14, 2010, http://www.reuters.com/article/2010/01/14/us-usa-housing-foreclosures-idUSTRE60DoLZ20110113.

15 Corbett B. Daly, "Home Foreclosures in 2010 Top 1 Million for First Time," Reuters, January 13, 2011, http://www.reuters.com/article/2011/01/13/us-usa-housing-foreclosures-idUSTRE70CoYD20120112.

16 Leah Schnurr, "Foreclosure Filings Hit Four-Year Low in 2011," Reuters, January 12, 2012, http://www.reuters.com/articlue/2012/01/12/us-usa-housing-realtytrac-idUSTRE80Bo8H20120112

17 John Gittelsohn and Kathleen M. Howley, "U.S. Home Price Face 3-year Drop as Inventory Surge Looms," Bloomberg, September 15, 2010, http://www.bloomberg.com/news/2010-09-15/u-s-home-prices-face-three-year-drop-as-inventory-surge-looms.html.

18 American Bankruptcy Institute, http://www.abiworld.org/AM/AMTemplate.cfm?Section=Home&CONTENTID=63164&TEMPLATE=/cm/cONTENTdISPLAY. Cfm; also, Jahn Hartgen, "Consumer Bankruptcy Filings Increase 9 Percent in 2010," Amercan Bankruptcy Institute, January 3, 2011, http://www.abiworld.org/AM/Template.cfm?Section=Home&TEMPLATE=/CM/CtonentDisplay.cfm&CONTENTID=62756.

19 "Bowles: 'These Deficits Are Like a Cancer," CBS News, September 13, 2011,

20 http://www.cbsnews.com/8301-503544_162-20105714-503544.html; see also Dan Balz, "Obama's Debt Commission Warns of Fiscal Cancer,'" Washington Post, July 12, 2010, http://www.washingtonpost.com/wpdyn/content/article/2010/07/11/AR2010071101956.html

21 Michael Crowley, "Deficit Dilemma: Will Washington Finally Tackle the Sacred Cows?" *Time*, December 2, 2010, http://www.time.com/time/politics/article/0,8599,2034358,00html#ixzz1Xw37VXlh

22 Testimony of Professor Simon Johnson to the Senate Budget Committee, February 9, 2010, http://baselinescenario.com/2010/02/09/revised-baseline-scenario-february-9-2010/

23 Nouriel Roubini, "A Presidency Heading for a Fiscal Train Wreck," Financial Times, October 28, 2010, http://www.ft.com/intl/cms/s/o/dd140d16-e2c2-11df-8a58-00144feabdco.html#axzz1XJFgtU82; see also "U.S. On Track for 'Fiscal Train Wreck': Roubini," reuters, October 29, 2010, http://www.reuters.com/article/2010/10/29us-roubini-idUSTRE69SoZJ20101029

24 Testimony of Alice Rivlin to the Senate Budget Committee, March 15, 2011, http://www.brookings.edu/testimony/2011/0315_senate_budget_rivlin.aspx.

25 Stuart Butler, et al, "Saving the Am3erican Dream: The Heritage Plan to Fix the Debt, Cut Spending, and Restore Prosperity," The Heritage Foundation, Special Report #91, May 10, 2011, http://www.heritage.org/Research/Reports/2011/05/Saving-the-American-Dream-The Heritage-Plan-to-Fix-the Debt-Cut-Spending-and-Restore-Prosperity

26 Paul Ryan, interview by Evan Harris, "Rep. Paul Ryan on Budget Work: "I Sleep Well at Night," ABC News, April 30, 2011, http://www.abcnews.go.com/ThisWeek/rep-paul-ryan-budget-work-sleep-night/story?id=13499775

27 David Brody, "Speaker Boehner to NRB Tonight: National Debt Is a 'Moral Threat' to America," The Brody File (blog), CBN News, February 27, 2011, http://blogs. cbn. com/thebrodyfile/archive/2011/02/27/speaker-boehner-to-nrb-tonight-national-debt-is-a-moral.aspx

28 Debt Position and Activity Report," U.S. Department of the Treasury, November 30, 2011, http://www.treasurydirect.gov/govt/reports/pd/pd_debtposactrupt_1111.pdf

29 See Patrick Tyrrell, "U.S. Debt Now Surpasses 2010 GDP," *The Foundry* (blog), Heritage Foundation, August 5, 2011, http://blog.heritage.oprg/2011/08/05/us-debt-now-surpasses-2010-gdp/; see also "U.S. Debt Reaches 100 Percent of Country's GDP," FoxNews.com, August 4, 2011, http://www.foxnews.com/politics/2011/08/04/us-debt-reaches-100-percent-countrys-gdp/

30 Andrew Malcolm, "New National Debt Data: It's Growing about $3 Million a Minute, Even During His Vacation," *Top of the Ticket* (blog), Los Angeles Times, August 23, 2011, http://latimesblogs.latimes.com/washington/2011/08/obama-national-debt.html.

31 One trillion seconds is 31,688 years; see "Billions & Trillions," DefeatTheDebt.com, Employment Policies Institute, http://www.defeatthedebt.com/understand-the-national-debt-/millions-billions-trillions/

32 Ibid

33 Ibid. There are about 500 billion stars in the Milky Way; see April Holladay, "Seeing the Milky Way and Counting Its Stars," January 2, 2006, USA Today, http://www.usatoday.com/tech/columnist/aprilholladay/2006-01-02-milky-way_x.htm.

34 Ibid

35 Ibid

36 "The Buzz: Need-to-=know News/Dollar Signs," WORLD, 15 August 2009, http://www.worldmag.com/articles/15710

37 http://www.dailycognition.com/index.php/2009/03/25/what-1-trillion-dollars-looks-like-in-dollar-bills.html

38 Robinson, *Bankruptcy of Our Nation*, p. 150

39 Ibid, p. 162

40 John Hagee, *Can America Survive?* Howard Books, New York, NY, 2010, p. 91

41 Grant R. Jeffrey, *One Nation under Attack*, WaterBrook Press, 12265 Oracle Boulevard, Suite 200; Colorado Springs, CO. 80921, p. 36

42 William McGurn, "For Obama, Taxes Are about Fairness," *Wall Street Journal* (Aug. 19, 2008 http://online.wsj.com/articlre/SB121010117767951201,html?mod=todays_columinsts

43 Jeanne Sahadi, "47% Will Pay No Federal Income Tax," CNN.com (Sept. 30, 1999). http://money.cnn.com/2009/09/30/pf/taxes/who_pays_taxes/index.htm?postversion=2009093012

44 Wayne Grudem, *Politics According to the Bible*, Zondervan, Grand Rapids, MI. 2010, p. 295

45 Ibid, p. 296

46 Jerry Robinson, *Bankruptcy of Our Nation*, New Leaf Press, P.O. Box 726, Green Forest, AR. 72638; p. 140

47 Annual Survey of Public Employment and Payroll Summary Report: 2010, Released January 2012, http://www2.census.gov/govs/apes/g10aspep.pdf

48 Ibid

49 http://www.washingtontimes.com/news/2010/oct/29/1-billion-paid-dead-eople-senate-panel-find

Chapter 2

1 Ibid, p. 5

2 Ibid, p. 10-11

3 Mark R. Levin, Plunder and Deceit, Simon & Schuster, Inc., 1230 Avenue of the Americas; New York, NY 10020; 2015; p. 24.) By 2026, our debt will explode to $30 trillion. (The Growing Crisis in America Is What No One Wants to Address; http://www.1.cbn.com/cbnnews/finance/2016/February/This-Growing-Crisis-in-America-Is....

4 America's National Debt, September 13, 2012 by Michael Kelley; http://www.usa.org/the-good0news/americas-national-debt-growing-with-no-end-in-sight

5 America's Coming Retirement Crisis; http://www.bloombergview.com/articles/2015-05-13/providing-for-a-secure-retirement

6 The Retirement Crisis is Read by Teresa Ghilarducci; http://www.huffingtonpost.com/teresa-ghilarducci/the-retirement-crisis-is_b_5910144.html

7 The Reality of the Retirement Crisis; Center for American Progress; https://www.americanprogress.org/issues/economy/report/2015/01/26/105394/the-reality-o...

8 Ibid

9 http://solutions.heritage.org/entitlements/social-security

10 Ibid

11 Charles Goyette, *The Dollar Meltdown: Surviving the Impending Currency Crisis with Gold, Oil, and Other Unconventional Investments* (New York: Penguin Group, 2009, p. 20

12 Ibid

13 Ibid

14 Ibid

15 Peter D. Schiff, *The Real Crash*, 2012, St. Martin's Press, 175 Fifth Avenue, New York, NY 10010, p. 166

16 http://www.socialsecurity.gov/OACT/TRSUM/index.html

17 http://paul.house.gov/index.php?option=option=com_content&task=view&id=1118&Itemid=69

18 Stuart Butler et al., "Saving the American Dream: The Heritage Plan to Fix the Deb, Cut Spending, and Restore Prosperity," The Heritage Foundation, Special Report #91, May 10, 2011, chart 2, "Hiking Taxes to Pay for Entitlements Would Require Doubling Tax Rates," http://www.heritage.org/Research/Reports/2011/05/Saving-the-American-Dream-The-Heritage-Plan-to-Fix-the-Debt-Cut-Spending-and Restore-Prosperity

19 Ibid

20 Levin, p. 30-31

21 Laurence J. Kotlikoff, "America's Fiscal Insolvency and Its Generational Consequences," Testimony to the Senate Budget committee, February 25, 2015, http://www.budget.senate.gov/republican/public/index.cfm?a=Files.Serve&File_id=5e701473-386f-4149-8db0-00e50fdcdbf8; p.2

22 Blake Ellis, "40 million Americans now have student loan debt," CNN Money, September 10-2014, http://money.cn.com/2014/09/10/pf/college/student-loans/

23 Robinson, *Bankruptcy of Our Nation*, p. 174-175

24 Brad Plumer, "Who Receives Government Benefits, in Six Charts," *Washington Post*, September 18, 2012, http://www.washingtonpost.com/blogs/wonkblog/wp/2012/09/18/who-receivs-benefits-from-the-federal-goverrnmnet-in-six-charts/ (accessed August 4, 2014); and Tami Luhby, "Government Assistance Expands," CNN Money, February 7, 2012 http://money.cnn.com/2012/02/07news/economy/government_assistance/index.htm (accessed August 4, 2014)

25 Associated Press, "New Retirees Receiving Less in Social Security Than they Paid in, Marking Historic Shift," August 2, 2012, http://www.foxnews.com/politics/2012/08/07/new-retirees-receiving-less-in-social-security-than-paid-in marking-historic/

26 Levin, p. 51

27 Major Foreign Holders of Treasury Securities Holdings," December 2009, http://www.treas.gov/tic/mfh.txt

28 Doug Andrew, "The US Economy Is a Sinking Ship and David Walker, "Missed Fortune.com 7 May 2009, http://blog.missedfortune.com/2009/05/economy-sinking-ship-david-walker

29 http://www.cnbc.com/id/39177278

30 http://www.ebri.org/pdf/surveys/rcs/2011/FS2_RCS11_Prepare_FINAL1.pdf

31 http://www.aarp.org/about-aarp/press-center/info-12-2010/boomers_turning_65.html

32 2014 Federal Budget in Pictures, "Publicly Held Debt to Skyrocket," The Heritage Foundation, http://www.heritage.org/federalbudget/national-debt--skyrocket (accessed August 4, 2014)

33 Daniel Halper, "Over $60,000 in Welfare Spent Per Household in Poverty," *The Weekly Standard*, October 26, 2012, http://www.weeklystandard.com/blogs/over-60000-welfare-spentper-household-poverty_657889.html (accessed August 4, 2014)

34 http://www.heritage.org/research/reports/2014/09/the-war-on-poverty-after-50-years

35 Ibid

36 http://solutions.heritage.org/entitlements/health-care/

37 Paul Ryan, "A Roadmap for America's Future," House Budget Committee, introduction, http://www.roadmap.republicans.budget.house.gov/Plan/#Intro

38 "How Government Killed the Medical Profession" by Jeffrey A. Singer; initially appeared in the May 2013 issue of Reason; http://www.cato.org/publications/commentary/how-government-killed-medical-profession

39 Ibid

40 Why Doctors Really Quit by Dan Diamond; http://www.forbes.com/sites/dandiamond/2015/06/02/why-doctors-really-quit

41 Ibid

42 Why Doctors Quit by Charles Krauthammer, Washington Post, May 28, 2015; http://www.washingtonpost.com/opinions/why-doctor-quit/2015/05-28/1e9d8e6e-056f-1...

43 Ibid

44 Jim Demint, *Now or Never*, Hachette Book Group, 237 Park Avenue; New York, N.Y. 10017, 2012, page 29

45 Robert Rector, "Marriage: America's Greatest Weapon against Child Poverty," Heritage Foundation, September 16, 2010;09;marriage-america-s-greatest-weapon-against-child-poverty.

46 "Our View on Kids: When Unwed Births Hit 41%, It's Just Not Right," USA Today, January 25, 2011, http://www.usatoday.com/news/opinion/editorials/2011-01-25-editorial25_ST-N-htm

47 http://www.heritage.org/research/reports/2014/09/the-war-on-poverty-after-50-years

48 Ibid

49 Exclusive: America has 'reached point of no return,' Reagan budget director warns." Nathan Diebenow, January 10, 2011; http://www.rawstory.com/2011/01/america-has-reached-the-point-of-no-return-reagan-bud...

Chapter 3

1 Jeffrey, One Nation Under Attack, p. 68

2 What Is the Size of the US Military?" EHow, www.ehow.com/about_4595933_what-siz-us-miliatry.html#ixzz1l02MuEWr.

3 "Pentagon Successfully Tests Hypersonic Flying Bomb," AFP, November 17, 2011, www.space-travel.com/reports/Pentagon_successfully_tests_hypersonic_flying_bomb_999.html

4 "U.S. Air Force struggles with aging fleet" November 4, 2012) http://www.usatoday.com/story/news/nation/2012/11/04/air-force-military-defense/1680069

5 America's Weakening Military Strength is Terrifying; http://ww.investors.com/politics/editorials/us-military-strength-is-in-steep-decline

6 "After Decades of Lagging Modernization, The Air Force is Losing Its Edge; http://www.forbes.com/sites/lorenthompson/2014/10/27/after-decades-of-lagging modernization

7 Ibid

8 Ibid

9 "Wiped Out: Air Force losing pilots and planes to cuts, scrounging for spare parts," by Jennifer Griffin and Lucas Tomlinson, May 14, 2016; http://www.foxnews.com/politics/2016/05/14/wiped-out-air-force-losing-pilots-and-planes

10 Ibid

11 Ibid

12 Ibid

13 The Declining State of the U.S. Military; http://www/heritage.org/research/commentary/2015/10/the-declining-state-of-the-us-military

14 U.S. Military No Longer Able to Fight Two Wars at Same Time; http://freebeacon.com/national-security/u-s-military-no-longer-able-to-fight-two-wars-at-same

15 America's Shrinking Military: The End of U.S. Primacy?; http://nationalinterest.org/print/feature/Americas-shrinking-military-the-end-us-primacy-13

16 Ibid

17 Rumsfeld: US Going into Decline Due to Weakness in Military; http://www.newsmax.com/Newsfront/Donald-Rumsfeld-miliary-spending-Iran/2014/02

18 America's weakening Military Strength is Terrifying; http://www.investors.com/politics/editorials/us-miliatry-strength-is-in-steep-decline

19 The Navy's Hidden Crisis by Robert C. O'Brien, February 5, 2015; http://www.politico.com/magazine/story/2015/02/navy-hidden-crisis-114943

20 Defense Cuts to an already weakened military exposes us to aggression; http://winteryknight.wordpress.com/2012/08/09/defense-cuts-to-an-already-weakened-military-

21 Report finds that shrinking armed forces are less able to respond to global threats; http://freeebeacon.com/national-security/u-s-military-no-longer-able-to-fight-two-wars-at-sa

22 http://www.bbc.com/news/world-us-canada-33440287

23 National Security, Defense Spending, and the Debt Quotes from Government Officials; http://www.heritage.org/research/reports/2011/08/what-people-are-saying-about-national-spending

24 Carter: Return to Sequestration Biggest Threat to National Security; http://www.military.com/daily-news/2016/03/17/careter-return-sequestration-biggest-threat

25 National Security, Defense Spending, and the Debt Quotes from Government Officials; http://www.heritage.org/research/reports/2011/08/what-people-are-saying-about-national-spending

26 Ibid

27 Ibid

28 Ibid

29 Ibid

30 Ibid

31 Ibid

32 Ibid

33 Ibid

34 Ibid

35 Ibid

36 Ibid

37 Ibid

38 Ibid

39 Ibid

Chapter 4

1 Articles by Warren Mass on August 5, 2014, "Immigrants From Over 75 Countries Illegally Crossing U.S. Border; The New American Magazine

2 Jeff Sessions, "Immigration Handbook for the New Republican Majority," January 2015, http://www.sessions.senate.gov/public/_cache/files/67ae7163-6616-4023-a5C4-534c53e6fc26/immigration-primer-for-the-114th-congress.pdf; Steve Camarota and Karen Zeigler, "All Employment Growth Since 200 Went to Immigrant," Center for Immigration Studies, June 2014, http://cis.org/sites/cis.org/files camartoa-employment_0.pdf (data derive and analyzed from U.S. Census Bureau data collected from 2009 to 2011)

3 http://www.cairco.org/issues/how-many-illegal-aliens-reside-united-states

4 U.S. Border Patrol Overview; http://www.usborderpatrol.com/BorderPatrol90h.htm

5 Anna Brown and Eileen Patten, "Hispanics of Mexican Origin in the United States," Pew Research Center Hispanic Trends Project, 2011, http://www.pewhispanic.org/2013/06/19/hispancis-of-mexican-origin-in-the-united -states-2011/

6 "Facts for Features: Hispanic Heritage Month 2014: Sept. 15-Octo. 15," U.S. Census Bureau, September 8, 2014, http://www.census.gov/newsroom/fact-for0features/2014/cb14-ff22.html

7 "Hispanic Americans by the Numbers, 2012," U.S. Census Bureau, 2012, http://www.infoplease.com/spot/hhmcensus1.html#ixzz3AlloS52Z; John P. Puman, David F. Damore, and Maria Jose' Flor Agreda, "Immigration and the Contours of Nevada's Latino Population," Brookings Mountain West, June 2013, http://www.unlv.edu/sites/defautl/files/24/BrookingsReport-ImmigrationAndContours.pdf

8 Lopez, "In 2014, Latinos Will Surpass Whites."

9 "Fingertip Facts on Education in California–CalEdFacts," California Department of Education, 2013, http://www.cde.ca.gov/ds/sd/cb/ceffingertipfacts.asp

10 "Rise in Public Benefits to Children of Illegal Immigrants in L.A. County Has Supervisor Very Concerned," Los Angeles Times, September 3, 2010, http://latimesblogs.latimes.com/lanow/2010/09/rise-in-public-benefits-to-children-of-illegal-immigrants-in-los-angeles-county-concerns-supervisor-michael-antonovich.html

11 http://www.cairco.org/issues/how-many-illegal-aliens-reside-united-states

12 "Immigrants in the United States, 2010: A Profile of America's Foreign-Born Population" http://cis.org/2012-profile-of-amnericas-foreign-born-population, Steven A. Camarota, Center for Immigration Studies, http://cis.org August 2012

13 http://www.washingtontimes.com/news/2015/jul/20/number-of-illegals-levels-off-fewer

14 "Presentation of Data on the U.S. Foreign Born, Average Incomes of the Bottom 90% of Tax Filers, and the Estimated Share of Income Held by the Bottom 90% of the U.S. Income Distribution, 1945-2013." Congressional Research Service, April 22, 2015, http://www.scribd.com/doc/262874867/CRS-Income-and Foreign-Born-Population

15 http://www.usborderpatrol.com/Border_Patrol90h.htm

16 Ibid

17 Ibid

18 Ibid

19 FBI Data Backs up Tump Claims on Illegals and Crime; by Aaron Klein, July 9, 2015; http://www.wnd.com/2015/07/fbi-data-backs-up-trump-claims-on-illegals-and-crime

20 Ibid

21 https://en.wikipedia.org/wiki/Economic-impact-of-illegal-immigrant-in-the-United-States

22 Office of Inspector General Department of Homeland Security, Detention and Removal of Illegal Aliens (Washington, DC: Department of Homeland Security, April 2006), http://www.oig.dhs.gov/assets/Mgmt/OIG_06_-33_Apr06.pdf

23 Fay Menacker et al., "Births to 10-14 Year-Old Mothers, 1990-2002: Trends and Health Outcomes," Table A, Centers for Disease Control: National Vital Statistics Reports, Novembers 15, 2004, http://www.cdc.gov/nchs/data/nvsr/nvsr53/nvsr53_07.pdf

24 John Ritter, "Drug Agents Can't Keep Up with Pot Growers," *USA Today*, October 13, 2005, http://usatoday30.usatoday.com/news/nation/2005-10-12-pot-growers-cover_x.htm; and Burke, "The Public Lands' Big Cash Crop."

25 "INS Accused of Giving In to Politics; White House Pressure Tied to Citizen Push," *Washington Post*, March 4, 1997.

26 "Expanding Citizenship: Immigrants and the Vote" by Tova Andrea Wang, Spring 2013, No. 28; *http://decocracyjournal.org/magazine/28/expanding-citizenship-immigrants-and-the-vote/*

27 "Latino vote key to Obama's re-election" by Cindy Y. Rodriquez, CNN, November 9, 2012; *http://www.cnn.com/2012/11/09/politics/latino-vote-key-election*

28 "Poll: Illegal immigrants favor Democrats 54 percent to 19 percent" by Aaron Blake, The Washington Post, July 22, 2013; *https://www.washingtonpost.com/news/post-politics/wp/2013/07/22/poll-illegal-immigrant*

29 "Most Democrats Think Illegal Immigrants Should Vote"; May 29, 2015; http://www.rasmussenreports.com/public_content/politics/general_politics/may_2015

30 Ibid

31 Newsmax, "Groups Seek to Register 1 Million Legal Immigrants against Trump," by Todd Beamon, May 11, 2016; newsmax.com

32 The Impact of Unauthorized Immigrants on the Budgets of State and Local Governments," Congressional Budget Office, Dec. 2009, p. 8

33 William Booth, "One Nation, Indivisible: is It History?" *Washington Post*, February 22, 1998, http://www.washingtonpost.com/wp-srv/national/longterm/meltingpot/melt0222.htm

34 Business Week-Econ 101 for Illegal Immigraton-S&P-April 2006 http://www.businessweek.co/investor/content/apr2006/pi20060407_072803.htm

35 "Breaking News and Opinion on the Huffington Post"Aolnews.com 2013-01-30

36 Is Illegal Immigration an Economic Burden to America? http://immigration.procon.org/view.answers.php?questionID=000788

37 Is Illegal Immigration an Economic Burden to America? http://immigration.procon.org/view.answers.php?questionID=000788

38 Coulter, p. 85

39 Ibid

40 Congressional Budget Office, "Migrants' Remittances and Related Economic Flows," February 2011, p. 2 http://www.cbo.gov/sites/defautl/files/cbofiles/ftpdocs/120xx/doc12053/02-24-remittances_chartbook.pdf. According to the U.S. Department of Commerce's Bureau of Economic Analysis (BEA), it is $20 billion a year

41 Steven Camarota, "Welfare Use by Immigrant Households with Children," Center for Immigration Studies, April 2011, http://cis.org/immigrant-welfare-use-2011 (analyzing the census's 2009 and 2010 Current Population Survey questions about welfare use in immigrant-headed families, legal and illegal, with at least one child under the age of eighteen

42 Congressional Budget Office, "Migrants' Remittances," 10

43 Ann Coulter, *Adios, America!*; Regnery Publishing 300 New Jersey Ave. NW; Washington, DC; 2015, p. 26

44 "The Massive Tidal Wave of Illegal Immigration That Threatens to Destroy the United States Economy. http://theeconimcalcollaspeblog.com/archives/the-massive-tidal-wave-of-illegal-immigrants

45 Forget Illegal Immigrants; Legal Immigration Will Soon Destroy America" by John Hawkins. http://rightwinnews.com/immigration/forget-illegal-immigrants-legal-immigration-will-so

46 A new estimate of the U.S. Muslim population; http://www.pewresearch.org/fact-tank/2016/01/06/a-new-estimate-of-the-u-s-muslim-population; http://www.pewforum.org/2013/05/17/the-religoius-affiliation-of-us-immigrants/#muslim

47 http://www.conservativecrusaders.com/commentary/destroy-america-through-immigration

48 Ibid

49 How America is Turning into a 3rd World Nation in 4 Easy Steps; http://www.alternet.org/print/economy/how-america-turning-3rd-world-nation-4-easy-steps

50 US On Road to Third Word by Paul Craig Roberts; http://www.paulcraigroberts.org/2015/10/29/us-on-road-to-third-world-paul-criag-roberts

51 Ibid

52 Six Ways America is Like a Third-World Country; http://www.rollingstone.com/politics/news/six-ways-america-is-like-a -third-world-country

53 Ibid

54 Ibid

55 Here is Evidence the United States is Becoming a Third World Country; https://timprosserfuturing.wordpress.com/2015/09/03/here-is-evidence-the-united-states-is

56 NIDOTTE, 1, 836

57 *The Immigration Crisis* by James K. Hoffmeier; Crossway, 1300 Crescent Street; Wheaton, Il. 60187; 2009, p. 51-52

58 Barrett Duke and Richard Land, "just Immigration Reform: Foundational Principles," in *Regent Journal of Law & Public Policy* 3:1, 67-94

59 Ralph Reed and Russell Moore, "Immigration Reform Is a Moral Imperative, in The Wall Street Journal (March 30, 2014), http://www.wsj.com/articles/SB10001424055270230418510445794372034361097 32?mg=id-wsj

60 Ibid

Chapter 5

1 Ibid, p. 26

2 Ibid, p. 281

3 National Center for Education Statistics, "Fast Facts: Expenditures," http://nces.ed.gov/fastfacts/display.asp?id=66

4 Organization for Economic Cooperation and Development (OECD), Program for International Student Assessment (PISA), 2000, 2003, 2006, 2009, and 2012, http://nces.ed.gov/surveys/pisa/idepisa

5 Ibid

6 NationMaster.com, "Education: Literacy (total population)," http://www.nationmaster.com/graph-T/edu_lit_tot-pop&int=1

7 Huff Post Books, "The US Illiteracy Rate Hasn't Changed in Ten Years."

8 Statistic Brain, "Illiteracy Statistics," April 28, 2013, http://statisticbrain.com/number-of-american-adults-who-cant-read

9 Statistic Brain, "Private School Statistics," July 21, 2013, http://www.statisticbrain.com/private-school-statistic; Home School Statistics" April 28, 2013, http://www.statistic brain.com/home-school-statistics

10 Plunder and Deceit by Mark R. Levin; Simon & Schuster, Inc. 1230 Avenue of the Americas, New York, NY; 2015, p. 76

11 "2013 SAT Report on College and Career Readiness," September 26, 2013, The College Board, http://media.collegeboard.com/homeOrg/content/pdf/sat-report-college-career-readiness-2013.pdf

12 2013 Mathematics and Reading: Grade 12 Assessments, National Assessment of Educational Progress ("NAEP"), "Are the nation's twelfth-graders making progress in mathematics and reading?" http://www.natoinsreportcard.gov/reading_math_g12_2013

13 Council on Foreign Relations, Joel I. Klein and Condoleezza Rice, Task Force Chairs, U.S. Education Reform and National Security, Independent Task Force Report No. 68, 2012, p. 9, http://www.cfr.org/united-states/us-education-reform-national-security/p27618

14 "Where Do Public School Teachers Send Own Kids?" by Larry Elder, October 17, 2013; http://townhall.com/columnists/larryelder/2013/10/17/where-do-public-school-teachers-send

15 Ibid

16 Ibid

17 Survey: 1 in 5 public school teachers send kids to private schools; by Patrick R. Gibbons, August 19, 2014; https://www.redefinedonline.org/2014/08/survey-1-in-5-school-teachers-send-kids-to-private

18 Ibid

19 "Teachers More Likely to Use Private Schools for the Own Kids" by Paul E. Peterson and Samuel Barrows, 1/11/2016; http://educationnext.org/teachers-more-likely-to-use-private-schools-for-their-own-kids

20 "Why I'm a Public-School Teacher but a Private-School Parent" by Michael Godsey; The Atlantic, March 4, 2015; http://www.theatlantic.com/education/archive/2015/03/why-im-a-public-school-teacher

21 Big Labor Does Gay Marriage," *The Wall Street Journal*, October24, 2008.

22 Scott Jaschick, "Moving Further to the Left," Inside Higher Education, October 24, 2012, https://www.insidehighered.com/news/2012/10/24/survey-finds-professors-already-liberal-have-moved-further-left

23 Levin, p. 81

24 "Fast Facts," U.S. Department of Education, National Center for Education Statistics, 2013, Digest of Education Statistics, Chapter 3, http://nces.ed.gov/fastfacts/display.asp?id=76.

25 Josh Zumbrun, "It Only Takes $10,400 to Be Richer Than Most Millennials," Wall Street Journal, September 4, 2014, http://blogs.wsj.com/economics/2014/09/04/it-only-take-10400-to-be-richer-than-most-millennials/, Board of Governors of the Federal Reserve System, "2013 Survey of Consumer Finances," October 20, 2014, http://www.federalreserve.gov/econresdate/scf/scfindex.htm

26 Dalton Conley, You May Ask Yourself: An Introduction to Thinking Like a Sociologist (New York: W.W. Norton & Company, 2013)

27 http://www.foxnews.com/us/2015/05/13/liberal-speakers-dominate-college-commencements-says-conservative-group

28 Levin, p. 90

29 Engel, 370 U.S. 422, (1962)

30 Jim DeMint and J. David Woodward, Why We Whisper, 79

31 Doe v. Santa Fe Independent School District, 168 F. 3d 806, 810 (5th Cir. 1999).

32 Jim DeMint and J. David Woodard, Why We Whisper, 115

33 Don Rowland, "Jimmy and Raymond at School," The Christian Informer, July, 1998

34 Ibid

35 Josh McDowell and Bob Hostetler, The New Tolerance, How a cultural movement threatens to destroy you, your faith, and your children (Wheaton, Ill: Tyndale House Publishers, Inc., 1998), 7

36 Persecution, How Liberals Are Waging War Against Christianity; David Limbaugh, Regnery Publishing, Inc.; One Massachusetts Avenue, NW, Washington, DC, 2003, p. 6

37 Roberts v. Madigan, 921 F2d 1047 (10th Cir. 1990)

38 Wallace v. Jaffree, 472 U.S. 38 (1985).

39 Don Rowland, "Jimmy and Raymond at School," The Christian Informer, July, 1998

40 Chandler v. Siegelman, 230 F. 3d 1313 (11th Cir. 2000)

41 "The Prayer Corner," Institute for First Amendment Studies, January/February 1999

42 Carrie Smith, "Payout for Prayer Lawsuit Irks Board. Schools Must Pay Attorneys $23,000 for Student's Suit," The Charleston Daily Mail, August 16, 2002.

43 David Limbaugh, "Enemies, Not Guardians of Religious Freedom," Creators Syndicate, September 14, 2002

44 Tanya I. Green, J.D., "political Correctness Hinders Religious Expression," Concerned

Women for America, December 20, 2001

45 Joe Kovacs, "School Bans Saying 'Christmas'; Veteran teacher dumbfounded by order precluding mention of holiday," Worldnetdaily.com, December 13, 2002

46 Bryan J. Brown, "SCASD's Christless Holiday," Center for Law & Policy Analysis Press Release, November 20, 2000

47 News Brief, "Parents Fight School Christmas Ban," Charisma News Service, December 23, 2002

48 David Barton, "Separation of Church and State" VHS (Aledo, TX: Wallbuilders, Inc., 1992)

49 "The Bible's Influence on American Education" by Tim Hoy, Superintendent of Upland Christian Academy, 909 Magazine

50 Ibid

51 US Supreme Court, Vidal vs. Girard's Executor, 1844

52 Valley Family Forum, http://valleyfamilyforum.org/david-barton-on-400-years-of-american-education

53 http://www.jesusuncensored.com/benjamin_rush.html

54 Ibid

55 Ibid

56 Benjamin Pierce, "A History of Harvard University (Cambridge, MA. Brown, Shattuck, and Company, 1833), Appendix, p. 5

57 The Harvard Graduates Magazine (Manesh, WI: Geroge Barna Publishing Co.), September 1933, p. 8, from the article "Harvard Seals and Arms" by Samuel Eliot Morison.

58 Documentary History of Yale University. Franklin B. Dexter, editor (New Haven: Yale University Press, 1916), p. 32, November 11, 1701, Proceedings of the Trustees

59 Daniel Dorchester, Christianity in the United States (New York: Hunt and Eaton, 1890), p. 245

60 The Catalogue of the Library of Yale College in New Haven (New London: T. Green, 1743), see also The Catalogue of the Library of Yale College in New Haven (New Haven: James Parker, 1755

61 The Laws of the College of New Jersey (Trenton: Isaac Collins, 1794), pp. 28-29

62 Columbia Rules (New York: Samuel Loudon, 1785), pp. 5-8

63 The Charter of Dartmouth College (Dresden: Isaiah Thomas, 1779), pp. 1, 4

64 The Charter and statutes of the College of William and Mary in Virginia (Williamsburg, VA: William Parks, 1736), p. 3

65 William & Mary Rules (Richmond,: Augustine Davis, 1792), p. 6

Chapter 6

1 Ibid, p. 288-289

2 American Patriots Bible, ed. Dr. Richard Lee; Nashville, Thomas Nelson, 2009, pp. 1-12

3 Education against America: The Hidden Agenda by Marlin Maddoux; Whitaker House, 1030 Hunt Valley Circle; New Kensington, PA. 15068; 2006, p. 19-21

4 Reverend Austin Miles, "Public Schools Embrace Islam---A Shocker," ASSIST News Service, January 10, 2002. http://www.jeremiahproject.com/prophecy/teachingislam.html (February 23, 2002)

5 Diane Lynne, "Islam Studies Spark Hate Mail, Lawsuits," World Net Daily, January 16, 2002. http://www.worldnetdaily.com/news/article.asp?ARTICLE_id=26074

6 Abby Nye, "Have No Fear of Them," World Magazine, August 23, 2003. http://www.worldmag.com/displayarticle.cfm?id=7628 (September 10, 2003)

7 Ibid

8 Robert Stacy McCain, "Poll Confirms Ivy League Liberal Tilt," *The Washington Times*, January 15, 2002

9 Ken Hamm & Britt Beemer, *already gone*, Master Books, P.O. Box 726, Green Forest, AR. 72638, 2010; p. 32.

10 Ibid, p. 33

11 Ibid, p. 40

12 www.news.com.au/couriermail/story/0,23739,25375117-23272,00.html

13 Maddoux, p. 82-83

14 John Dewey, My Pedagogic Creed," *National Education Association Journal* (May 1927), 26

15 Maddoux, p. 99

16 John Dewey, "Soul-Searching," *Teacher Magazine*, September 1933, 33.

17 John Dewey, *My Pedagogic Creed* (Washington, D.C.: Progressive Education Association, 1897), 6, 15, 17

18 John Dewey, *Impressions of Soviet Russia and the Revolutionary World (New York: New Republic, Inc., 1929)* 4, 15, 57

19 Kevin Alfred Strom, "Anti-American Agenda Threatens Our Nation," radio broadcast American Dissident Voices, March 13, 1993. http://www.national vanguard.org/story.php?id=3339 (July 25, 2002)

20 Maddoux, p. 105-106

21 Maddoux, p. 107

22 Anita Hoge, various excerpts from interview by Marlin Maddoux, *Point of View* radio talk show, NCFR, March 28, 1995.

23 B.K. Eakman, *Educating for the New World Order* (Portland: Halcyon House, 1991), 71.

24 B.K. Eakman, "EDUCATION: Bushwacking Johnny," *Chronicles Magazine*, September 2002. http://www.Chronicles magazine.org/Chronicles/September2002/0902Eakman.html (October 11, 2002).

25 Maddoux, p. 152

26 Ibid, p. 155

27 Ibid, 156

28 Ibid, p. 166

29 Ibid, p. 179

30 John Whitehead, Parents' Rights (Wheaton, Ill: Good News Press), 113

31 World Net Daily, "Dobson to Californians: Quit public schools," March 30, 2002. http://www.worldnetdaily.com/news/article.asp?ARTICLE_id=27023 (July 15, 2002)

Chapter 7

1 Ibid, 311,312

2 Ibid, 206

3 Terrence McCoy, "ISIS Just Stole $425 million, Iraqi Governor Says, and Became the World's Richest Terrorist Group," Washington Post, June 10, 2014, http://www.washingtonpost.com/news/morning-mix/wp/2014/06/12/isis-just-stole-425-million-and-became-the-worlds-richest-terrorist-group/

4 Terrence McCoy, "Islamic State 'Now Controls Resources and Territory Unmatched in the History of Extremist Organizations," Washington Post, August 4, 2014, http://www.washingtonpost.com/nws/morning-mix/wp/2014/08/04/islamic-state-now-controls-resources-and-territory-unmatched-in-history-of-extremist-organizations

5 New ISIS Video: 'We Will Raise Black Flag Over White House," Fox News Insider, August 8, 2014, http://foxnewsinsider.com/2014/08/08/new-isis-video-%E2%80%98we-will-riase-black-flag-over-white-house%E2%80%99

6 Majid Khadduri, *War and Peace in the Law of Islam* (Clark, JN: Lawbook Exchange, 2010), 48.

7 Simon Tomlinson and Amy White, "This Is Our Football, It's Made of Skin #World Cup: After Posting Sickening Beheading Video of Iraqi Policeman, Isis Boast of

Slaughtering 1,700 Soldiers," Daily Mail, June 13, 2014, http://www.dailymail.co.uk/news/article-2656905/ISIS

8 Glenn Beck, *It **IS** About Islam*; Mercury Radio Arts, 1230 Avenue of the Americas; New York, NY, 2015.

9 Gary Frazier, *Signs of the Coming of Christ*, Discovery Ministries, P.O. Box 13770, Arlington, TX. 76094; 2004, p. 114

10 Ibid, p. 114

11 Ibid, p. 115

12 Charter, quoting the Quoting the Quran (3:110-112), arts, 5,8

13 Jerry Markon and Ben Hubbard, "Review Finds Slurs in '06 Saudi Texts," Washington Post, July 15, 2008

14 See transcript of report on Al Jazeera, June 17, 2008; se "Al-Jazeera, Report on the Controversy over the Islamic Saudi Academy in Virginia," MEMRI, clip 1799, June 17, 2008, http://www.memritv.org/clip_transcript/en/1799.htm; also, "Critics Dubs Saudi Islamic School "Terror High," Associated Press, November 24, 2007

15 See Markon and Hubbard, "Review Finds Slurs in '06 Sadi Texts."

16 See R. James Woolsey, testimony delivered before the U.S. House Committee on International Relations Subcommittee on the Middle East and South Asia, May 22, 2002

17 See Stephen Schwartz, Director of the Islam and Democracy Program of the Foundation for the Defense of Democracies, "Wahhabism and Islam in the U.S.," testimony before the U.S. Senate Subcommittee on Terrorism, Technology and Homeland Security, June 26, 2003.

18 See findings from the Hartfordd Institute for Religion Research, http://hirr.hartsem.edu/research/quick_queston20.html. The data are drawn from "Mosque in American: A National Portrait," a survey released in April 2001.

19 See "New Dearborn Mosque to Be the Nation's Largest," Associated Press, January 7, 2004

20 "Saudi Publications on Hate Ideology Invade American Mosques," Special Report released by the Center for Religious Freedom, Freedom House, 2006, p. 2, http://www.freedomhouse.org/uploads/specialreport/45.pdf.

21 Ibid, p. 57

22 See Andrew Kohur, "Muslims in America: Middle Class and Mostly Mainstream," Pew Research Center, May 22, 2007, http://pewresearch.org/assets/pdf/muslim-americans.pdf

23 Ibid

24 See John Esposito and Dlia Mogahed, *Who Speaks for Islam? What a Billion Muslims Really Think,* pp. x-xi, 69-70

25 Dexter Filkins, "What We Left Behind," *New Yorker*, April 28, 2014

26 Jay Sekulow, *Rise of ISIS*, Howard Books, Simon & Schuster, 1230 Avenue of the Americas; New York, NY; 2014, p.90-92

27 Graphic, "Foreign Fighters Flow into Syria," *Washington Post* (March 8, 2013) (Located at: http://www.washingtonpost.com/world/foreign-fighters-=flow-to-syria/2015/01/27/7fa56b70-a631-11e7c2-03d37af98440_graphic.html)

28 Charles Krauthammer, "The worst agreement in U.S. diplomatic history," July 2, 2015; https://washingtonpost.com/opinions/the-worst-agreement-in-us-diplomatic-history

29 James Phillips, "The Dangerous Regional Implications of the Iran Nuclear Agreement" May 9, 2016; http://www.heritage.org/research/reports/2015/05/the-dangerous-regoinal-implication-of-the

30 James Phillips, "The Dangerous Regional Implications of the Iran Nuclear Agreement

31 Ibid

32 Charles Krauthammer, "The Worst Agreement in U.S. diplomatic history"

33 Omar Alnatour, "Muslims Are Not Terrorists: A Factual Look at Terrorism and Islam," December 9, 2015; http://www.huffingtonpost.com/omar-alnatour/muslims-are-not-terrorist_b_8718000.html

34 Ibid

35 Ibid

36 Ibid

37 "Non-Muslims Carried Out More than 90% of All Terrorist Attacks in America"; May 13, 2016; http://www.globalresearch.ca/non-muslims-carried-out-more-than-90-of-all-terrorist-attack

38 Ibid

39 Ibid

Chapter 8

1 Ibid, p. 318

2 Megan McCloskey, "More soldier suicides than combat deaths in 2012," Stars and Stripes, December 20, 2012, http://www.stripes.com/news/more-soldier-suicides, than-combat-deaths-in-2012-1.201440

3 Rush Limbaugh, "A Newly Minted NRA Member" (transcript), the official website of *The Rush Limbaugh Show*, January 16, 2013, http://www.rushlimbaugh.com/daily/2013/01/16/a_newly_minted_nra_member.

4 David Limbaugh, "Let's Recognize Who the Real Haters Are," Townhall.com, April 3, 2015, http://townhall.com/columnists/davidlimbaugh/2015/04/03/lets-recognize-who-the-real-haters-are-n1980212

5 Radicalization and Recruitment, pp. 2-6. U.S. Department of Homeland Security, April 7, 2009, http://fas.org/irp/eprint/rightwing.pdf. See also, Huffington Post/AP, "Homeland Security Report Warns of Rising Right-Wing Extremism," HuffPost Politics, May 15, 2009, http://www.huffingtonpost.com/2009/04/14/homeland-security-report_n_186834.html.

6 Jon Meacham, "We Are All Socialists Now," *Newsweek*, February 6, 2009, http://www.newseek.com/we-are-all-socialists-now-82577.

7 The Wall Street Journal, "The Terrorists Freed by Obama," by Stephen F. Hayes and Thomas Joscelyn, January 15, 2016; http://www.wsj.com/articles/the-terrorists-freed-by-obama-1452901430.

8 "Obama releases Gitmo detainees determined to keep trying to kill Americans," http://www.washingtontimes.com/news/2016/jan/14/obama-releases-guantanamo-detainee

9 "Anita Dunn Favorite Philosopher Mao Tse-Tung," OrthodoxNet.com, October 16, 2009, http://www.orthodoxytoday.org/blog/2009/10/anita-dunn-favorite-philosopher-mao-tse-tung/.

10 Aaron Klein, "Czar's communist manifesto scrubbed from Net," WND, August 30, 2009, http://www.wnd.com/2009/08/108445

11 DiscoverTheNetworks.org; Key Obama Appointees: Reflecting the President's Radicalism; http://www.discoverthenetworks.org/viewSubCategory.asp?id=2379

12 Ibid

13 Ibid

14 Ibid

15 "Obama Surrounds Himself with the Most Extreme Appointees in American History,"; http://www.westernjournalism.com/exclusive-investigative-reports/obama-surrounds-himself

16 Ibid

17 "Obama Surrounds Himself with the Most Extreme Appointees in American History," http://www.westernjournalism.com/exclusive-investigative-reports/obama-surrounds-himself

18 Ibid

19 Freedom Outpost, "Sharia Advisors–Barack Obama's Muslim Appointees in High Security Positions," by Leon Puissegur, April 29, 2014; http://freedomoutpost.com/2014/04/sharia-advisers-barack-obamas-muslim-appointees

20 Ibid

21 Dave Hodges, The Common Sense Show, "The Muslim Brotherhood Has Taken Over the White House," http://www.thecommonsenseshow.com/2015/12/07/the-muslim-brotherhood-has-taken

22 Ibid

23 "Islamist Infiltration of the Obama Administration," http://www.discoverthenetworks.org/viewSubCategory.asp?id=844

24 "discoverthenetworks.org, http://www.discoverthenetworks.org/viewSubCategory.asp?id=2390

25 http://religionandpolitics.org/2016/10/10/the-christian-worldview-of-mike-pence

26 https://hellochristian.com/4053-mike-pence-we-need-jesus-more-than-ever-right-now

27 "Onward Christian cabinet: Trump's White House picks are a Christmas gift for the religious right"; http://www.haaretz.com/us-news-premium-1.758733

28 Ibid

29 Nine Christians in the Trump Cabinet?; http://headhearthand.org/blog/2016/12/12/nine-christians-in-the-trump-cabinet

30 "Trump's Cabinet: A Motley Collection of Believers"; CBN.com/http://www.1.cbn.com/cbnnews/us/2016/november/trumps-cabinet-a-motley-collection-of....

31 "Trump's advisers: The faith factor"; http://www.stltoday.com/lifestyles/faith-and-values/trumps-advisers-the-faith-factor

32 https://www.gop.com/mc-message-celebrating-orthodox-easter; quoted in http://www.christianpost.com/news/who-is-reince-priesbus

33 Ibid

34 "Onward Christian cabinet: Trump's White House picks are a Christmas gift for the religious right; of Amway founder, Rich http://www.haaretz.com/us-news/.premium-1

35 Ibid

36 Ibid

37 Ibid

38 "Kellyanne Conway Has Walked the Walk"; https://stream.org/kellyanne-conway-has-walked-the-walk

39 Ibid

40 Huffington Post as reported in "The Daily Sheeple" by Doug Ross, July 14, 2013; http://www.thedailysheeple.com/president-barack-obamas-complete-list-of-historic-firsts

41 Ibid

42 United States Court of Appeals as reported in "The Daily Sheeple" see above

43 Department of Homeland Security documents uncovered by Judicial Watch and reported in "The Daily Sheeple" see above

44 CNN, as reported by "The Daily Sheeple" see above

45 ABC News, as reported by "The Daily Sheeple" see above

46 NBC News, as reported by "The Daily Sheeple" see above

47 Fox News, as reported by "The Daily Sheeple," see above

48 The New York Times, as reported by "The Daily Sheeple," see above

49 Heritage Foundation, as reported in "The Daily Sheeple" see above

50 Washington Examiner, as reported in "The Daily Sheeple" see above

51 Wall Street Journal, as reported in "The Daily Sheeple" see above

52 The Hill Newspaper, as reported in "The Daily Sheeple" see above

53 Competitive Enterprise Institute, as reported in "The Daily Sheeple" see above

54 National Review, as reported in "The Daily Sheeple" see above

55 Center for Individual Freedom, as reported in "The Daily Sheeple" ....see above

56 Jeff Sessions, as reported in "The Daily Sheeple" ...see above

57 Meeting with his Jobs Council as reported in "The Daily Sheeple" see above

58 The Hill, as reported "The Daily Sheeple" ....see above

59 CNS, as reported in "The Daily Sheeple" ...see above

60 The Arizona Republic Newspaper, as reported in "The Daily Sheeple"....see above

61 Peterson Institute, as reported in "The Daily Sheeple" ....see above

62 Heritage Foundation as reported in "The Daily Sheeple" see above

63 Detroit News, as reported in "The Daily Sheeple"....see above

64 Wall Street Journal, as reported in "The Daily Sheeple"....see above

65 Politico, as reported in "The Daily Sheeple," ....see above

66 ABC News, as reported in "The Daily Sheeple".....see above

67 ABC News, Rep. Michael Turner, as reported in "The Daily Sheeple"....see above

68 Judicial Watch, as reported in "The Daily Sheeple"....see above

69 American Thinkers, The Independent (UK), as reported in "The Daily Sheeple"....see above

70 White House Dossier, as reported in "The Daily Sheeple"....see above

71 "President Barack Obama's Complete List of Historic Firsts," September 21, 2013,

https://www.facebook.com/notes/dan-asmussen/president-barack-obamas-complete-list

72 Ibid

73 David Gardner, London *Daily Mail*, June 1, 2009, http://www.dailymail.co.uk/news/article-1189893/How-Obamas-romantic-120-trip-Broadway-racked-45-000-bill.html

74 Annals of Law, "The Obama Brief" by Jeffry Toobin, October 27, 2014, "How Obama Transformed the Federal Judiciary" The New Yorker; http://www.newyorker.com/magazine/2014/10/27/obama-brief

75 Ibid

76 Barack Obama, *Dreams from My Father*, Three Rivers Press, 2004, p. 220

77 Dinesh D'Souza, *Obama's America*, Regnery Publishing, INC., 2012, One Massachusetts Avenue NW, Washington, DC 20001, p. 42

78 Ibid, p. 69-70

79 Ibid, p. 128-129

80 Ibid, p. 128

Chapter 9

1 Ibid, p. 669, 671

2 John W. Whitehead, "The Breakdown of the Traditional Family: why Conservative Christians Should Rethink Their Blame Game." May 26, 2011

3 "The Collapse of the Family Unit as the Building Block of Society; http://www.akdart.com/culture2.html

4 Ibid

5 "27 Facts That Prove That the Family in America Is In The Worst Shape Ever" by Michael Snyder, July 10, 2013; http://theeconomiccollapseblog.com/archives/27-facts-that-prove-that-the-family-in-america

6 Ibid

7 "Child Poverty in the U.S. is among the worst in the developed world" by Christopher Ingraham, Washington Post, October 29, 2014; https://www.washingtonpost.com/news/wonk/wp/2014/10/29/child-poverty-in-the-u-s-is-a

8 "The U.S. Is Leading The Way in Fatherlessness And It's Hurting Our Kids," by Nikita Coulombe; Elite Daily; June 18,2015; http://elitedaily.com/life/culture/how-society-is-failing-fathers-photos/1069521

9 "How Far Has the U.S. Fallen? America Leads The World in These 36 Shocking Categories... by Michael Snyder; July 4, 2013, The Truth; http://thetruthwins.com/archives/how-far-has-the-u-s-fallen-america-leads-the-world-in-the

10 Ibid

11 Ibid

12 Ibid

13 Ibid

14 Institute for American Values, "The Marriage Movement: A Statement of Principles," January 2000, http://americanvalues.org/catalog/pdfs/marriagemovement.pdf

15 Cynthia Harper and Sara S. McLanahan, "Father Absence and Youth Incarceration," Journal of Research on *Adolescene* 14, no. 3 (2004), 369-397, http://www.gwu.edu/-pad/202/father.pdf

16 Todd Michael Franke, "Adolescent Violent Behavior: An Analysis Across and Within Racial/Ethnic Groups," Journal of Multicultural Social Work 8 (2000): 47-70, as quoted in iMAPP policy Brief, "Can Married Parents Prevent Crime? Recent Research on Family Structure and Delinquency 2000-2005," September 21, 2005, http://www.marriagedebate.com/pdf/imapp.crimefamstructure.pdf

17 Les B. Whitbeck et al., "Predictors of Gang Involvement among American Indian Adolescents," *Journal of Gang Research 10* (2002): 11-26, as quoted in iMAPP, "Can Married Parents Prevent Crime?"

18 Wade C. Mackey and Nancy S. Coney, "The Enigma of Father Presence in Relationship to Sons' violence and Daughters' mating Strategies: Empiricism in Search of a Theory," *Journal of Men's Studies 8* (2000): 349-373

19 United States Census Bureau, 2012 Family Income, "Married-Couple Families, All Races," http://www.census.gov/hhes/www/cpstables/032013/faminc/finc03_000.htm

20 Patrick F. Fagan and Robert Rector, "The Effects of Divorce of America," The Heritage Foundation, June 5, 2000 http://www.heritage.org/research/reports/2000/06/the-effects-of-divorce-=on-america

21 Institute for American Values, "The Marriage Movement."

22 Elizabeth Marquardt. *Between Two Worlds: The Inner Lives of Children and Divorce* (New York: Crown Publishers, 2005), 189

23 W. Bradford Wilcox, "The Evolution of Divorce," *National Affairs 1* (Fall 2009) http://nationalaffairs.com/publications/detail/the-evolution-of-divorce

24 Ibid

25 Cathy Meyer, "No-Fault Divorce Laws: The impact of No-Fault Divorce on Our Children," Divorced Women *Online*, March 22, 2011 http://divoredwomenonline.com/2011/03/22/no-fault-divorce-laws-the-impact-of-no-fault-divorce-on-our-children

26 Wilcox, "The Evolution of Divorce."

27 "The Breakdown of the Traditional Family: Why conservative Christians Should Rethink Their Blame Game", by John W. Whitehead, August 10, 2010; http://www.washingtonpost.com/john-w.-whitehead/the-breakdown-of-the-traditional

28 "Child Poverty in the U.S. is among the worst in the developed world" by Christopher Ingraham October 29, 2014; https://www.washingtonpost.com/news/wonk/wp/2014/10/29/child-poverty-in-the-u.s-

29 Ibid

30 National Institute of Child Health and Human Development; accessed from "The *Breakdown of Family in Secular Culture by Alex Colvin*; http://www.tparent6s.org/library/unification/talks/colvin/secular.htm

31 Center for Disease Control, Atlanta, GA.; Ibid

32 "Children in Need: Investment Strategies for the Educationally Disadvantaged"---Committee for Economic Development; Ibid

33 Center for Disease Control, Atlanta, GA.; ibid

34 Bureau of Justice Statistics, 1988; ibid

35 Judith S. Wallerstein, "Children after Divorce: Wounds That Don't Heal" in *Perspectives on Marriage*

36 "30 Years of Research: A Child Deserves a Mother and a Father" by Focus on the Family; http://www.focusonthefamily.com/socialissues/marriage/teach-your-children-about-marriage

37 http://www.clasp.org/resources-and-publications/states/0086.pdf

38 www.childtrends.org/wp-content/uploads/2013/03/rbo32601.pdf

39 30 Years of Research: A Child Deserves a Mother and a Father" by Focus on the Family

40 http://www.princeton.edu/futureofchildren/publications/journals/article/index.xml?journalid=37&articleid=107

41 30 Years of Research: A Child Deserves a Mother and a Father; Focus on the Family

42 Wilcox, "The Evolution of Divorce."

43 Barna Group, "Frames Wave 2" and OmniPoll 1-14." See Riffkin, "New Record Highs in Moral Acceptability"

44 See Gallup, "Gay and Lesbian Rights," Gallup.com, http://www.gallup.com/poll/1651/gay-lebian-rights.aspx; Lydia Saad, "Americans Evenly Divided on Morality of Homosexuality," Gallup.com, June 18, 2008, http://www.gallup.com/poll/108115/americans-evenly-divided-morality-homosexuality.aspx

45 "The Breakdown of the Traditional Family: Why Conservative Christians Should Rethink Their Blame Game, John W. Whitehead

46 Ibid

47 George Barna and David Barton, *U Turn,* Charisma House Books, 600 Rinehart Road, Lake Mary, Florida; 2014, p. 150

48 Mikhail Heller, Cogs in the Wheel (New York: Knopf, 1988),pp. 168-79

49 CNS News; http://www.cnsnews.com; "Report: Only 16% of Baltimore Teens Raised with Married Parents."

50 http://rttnews.com/2559041/2300-shooting-parts-of-chicago-are-a war-zone.aspx

51 "War Zone: Chicago Has the Bloodiest Start in Almost Two Decades" by Matt Vespa; http://townhall.com/tipsheet/mattvespa/2016/04/01/warzone-chicago-has-the-bloodiest-start

52 Huffpost Chicago; "Chicago Homicides Outnumber U.S. Troop Killings in Afghanistan; http://www.huffingtonpost.com/2012/06/16/chicago-homicide-rate-wor_n_1602692

53 "Nearly half of Chicago's young black men are out of work, out of school," http://www.chicagonow.com/city-limits/2016/01/out-of-school-out-of-work-young-chicago

54 "The 5 Worst Cities for Urban Youth-ABC News" by R.C. Donovan, November 14, 2009; http://abcnews.go.com/Politics/Politics/worst-cities-urban-youth/story?id=9083935

55 "Detroit has half the median income, three the poverty rate of nation, new Census numbers show" by Khalil Al Hajal, September 21, 2012; http://www.mlive.com/news/detroit/index.ssf/2012/09/detroit-has-half-the-median-income

56 Ibid

57 Ibid

58 http://abcnews.go.com/Politics/Politics/worst-cities-urban-youth/story?id=9083935

59 "Cleveland has fifth-highest violent crime rate in the U.S., according to 2013 FBI Crime Report" by Nikki Ferrell, November 12, 2014; http://www.newsnet5.com/news/local-news/cleveland-metro/cleveland-has-fifth-highest

60 "More than half of Cleveland kids live in poverty, and it's making them sick." By Brie Zeltner, The Plain Dealer; September 30, 2014; http://www.cleveland.com/healthfit/index.ssf/2014/09/more-the-half-of-cleveland

61 David Kupelian, *The Snapping of the American Mind*, WND Books, Washington, D.C., 2015, p. 106

62 "27 Facts that Prove That the Family in America is in The Worst Shape Ever." By Michael Snyder, July 10, 2013; http://theeconomiccollapseblog.com/archives/27-facts-that-prove-that-the-family-in-america

63 Ibid

64 Ibid

65 Ibid

66 "The Collapse of the Family Unit as the Building Black of Society"; http://www.akdart.com/culture2.html

67 Ibid

68 Ibid

69 Ibid

70 "The Collapse of the Family Unit as the Building Block of Society" http://www.akdart.com/culture2.html

71 Ibid

72 Ibid

73 Ibid

74 Ibid

75 Ibid

76 Ibid

77 Infidelity Statistics; http://menstuff.org/issues/byissue/infidelitystats.html; "Monogamy Myth," by Therapist Peggy Vaughn

78 Ibid; Atwood & Schwartz, 2002, Journal of Couple & Relationship Therapy

79 Infidelity Statistics; http://www.infidelityfacts.com/infidelity-statistics.html

80 Sex: Statistics; http://www.leaderu.com/everystudent/sex/misc/stats.html

81 "STD Facts: Shocking Statistics You May Not Know About STD's" The Huffington Post; 2/16/2012, http://www.huffingtonpost.com/2012/02/16/std-facts_n_1282151.html

82 George Barna, as quoted in Christine Wicker, "Dumbfounded by Divorce: Survey Inspires Debate over Why Faith Isn't a Bigger Factor in Marriage," Dalls Morning News, 2000, http://www.adherents.com/largecom/baptist_divorce.html

83 "Supreme Court rules in favor of same-sex marriage nationwide," by Arlane de Vogue and Jeremy Diamond, CNN, June 27, 2015; http://www.cnn.com/2015/06/26/politics/supreme-court-same-sex-marriage-ruling

84 Ibid

85 "James Dobson: Gay Marriage Signals "The Fall of Western Civilization." Right Wing Watch by Brian Tashman, May 4, 2015; http://www.rightwingwatch.org/content/james-dobson-gay-marriage-signals-fall

86 Ibid

87 Ibid

88 Rev. Graham on Gay Marriage Ruling: 'I Pray God Will Spare America from His Judgment,'" by Michael W. Chapman, June 26, 2015; http://cnsnews.com/blog/michael-w-chapman/rev-graham-gay-marriage-ruling

89 *Truth Overruled: The Future of Marriage and Religious Freedom* by Ryan T. Anderson; Regnery Publishing, 300 New Jersey Ave. NW, Washington, DC 20001; 2015, pp. 44-45

90 Ibid, p. 68

91 Ibid, p. 75

92 Brief of Amici Curiaw 100 Schlars of Marriage in Support of Respondents, *Obergefell v. Hodges*, 2, available online at http://www.supremecourt.gov/ObergefellHodges/AmicusBriefs/14-556_100_Scholars_of_Marriage.pdf

93 Ibid

94 Ibid

95 http://www.boxton.com/news/local/articles/2006/03/11/catholiccharities_stuns_state_end_adoptions

96 J. Adams, "Message to the Officers of the First Brigade of the Third Division of the militia of Massachusetts" (October 11, 1798) http://www.beliefnet.com/resourcelib/docs/115/Message_from_John_Adams__to_the_Officers

Chapter 10

1 Ibid, p. 407

2 General Douglas MacArthur (1880-1964), WWII supreme Allied Commander of the Southwestern Pacific, Supreme United Nations Commander. (http://quotes.liberty-tree.ca/quote/douglas_macarthur-quote_4070)

3 See, for example, The Trial of Samuel Tulley and John Dalton, on an Indictment for Piracy and Murder, Committed January 21, 1812, *Before the Circuit Court of the United States at Boston, 28th October 1812, Containing the Evidence at Large, a Sketch of the Arguments of Counsel, and the Charge of the Hon. Judge Story on Pronouncing Sentence of Death* (Boston: Joshua Belcher, 1814) 22-26; and New York Times, "The Slave Trade: Sentence of Capt. Gordon of the Slaver Erie," December 2, 1861, http://query.nytimes.com/gst/abstract.html?res=9804EFDD113FEE34 BC4A53DFB467838A679FDE; See also Thomas C McCarthy, "Why Was the Tombs the Execution Site for the Only American Ever Hanged as a Slave Trader?," New York Correction History Society, February 2003, http://www.correctionhistory.org/html/chronicl/tombs/gordon/whytombs1.htm; William B. Reed, *Life and Correspondence of Joseph Reed, vol. 2 (Philadelphia: Lindsay and Blakiston, 1847), 36-37; Jacob Rush, Charges and Extracts of Charges on Moral and Religious Subjects* (Philadelphia: George Forman, 1804), 144-147; and The Globe, "Sentence of Horn, the Murderer," December 6, 1843)

4 Donald S. Jutz, "The Relative Influence of European Writers on Late Eighteenth Century American Political Thought," *American Political Science Review* 78, no. 1 (March 1894):

191-193. See also Donald S. Lutz, The Origins of American Constitutionalism Baton Rouge: Louisiana State University Press, 1988), 141-142

5 Barna Group, "OmniPoll 1013," national survey among 1,005 adults, January 2013

6 Barna Group, "Frames Wave 2" and "OmniPoll 1-14." See also Riffkin, "New Record Highs in Moral Acceptability."

7 Barna Group, "OmniPoll May-08," national survey of 1,003 adults eighteen or older, May 2008

8 Pew Research Center for the People and the Press, "Partisan Polarization Surges in Bush, Obama Years," section 6; see also Pew Research Center, "Worldwide Many See Belief in God as Essential to Morality," March 13, 2014, http://www.pewglobal.org/2014/03/13/worldwide-many-see-belief-in-god-as-essential-to-morality

9 Zachary Taylor, "The President and the Bible," *New York Semi-Weekly Tribune*, 4, no. 11, May 9, 1849

10 Theodore Roosevelt, *A Square Deal* (Allendale, NJ: The Allendale Press, 1906), 203-204

11 Zephaniah Sift, *The Correspondent* (Windham, CT: John Byrne, 1793), 119

12 Vidal v. Girard's Executors, 3 US 127, 200 (1844), as quoted at http://supreme.justia.com/cases/federal/us/43/127/case.html

13 American Medical Association, introduction to the *Code of Medical Ethics Adopted by the Medical Association at Philadelphia in May 1847 and by the New York Academy of Medicine in October 1847* (New York: H. Judwig and Co., 1848

14 Actions of the Founding Fathers are documented in numerous places. See the chapter by Robert L. Cord in Restoring the Constitution. See also David Barton, *The Myth of Separation* (Aledo, TX.: Wallbuilder Press, 1992)

15 George Barna, as quoted in Christine Wicker, "Dumbfounded by Divorce: Survey Inspires Debate over Why Faith Isn't a Bigger Factor in Marriage," Dallas Morning News, 2000, http://www.adherents.com/largecome/baptist_divorce.html

16 Barna Group, "Barna Survey Examines Changes in Worldview Among Christians over the past 13 Years," Barna.org, March 26, 2009, https://www.barna.org/barna-update/21-transformation/252-barna-survey-examines-changes-in-worldview-among-christians-over-the-past-13-years#.Uv5fWMko6cx

17 Perspectives on Sexual and Reproductive Health 46, no. 1 (March 2014), http://www.guttmacher.org/pubs/journals/psrh.46e0414.pdf. See also Guttmacher Institute, "Fact Sheet: Induced Abortion in the United States," July 2014 http://www.guttmacher.org/pubs/fb_induced_abortion.html

18 Rachel K. Jones, Lawrence B. Finer, and Susheela Singh, "Characteristics of US Abortion Patients, 2008," Guttmacher Institute, May 2010, http://www.guttmacher.org/pubs/US-Abortion-Patients.pdf

19 "The Oath by Hippocrates," translated by Francis Adams, available at http://classics.mit.edu/Hippocrates/hippooath.html

20 "76 percent say living together before marriage OK," http://www.onenewsnow.com/culture/2016/01/31/76-percent-say-living-together-before

21 Ibid

22 Joel Rosenburg, *Implosion*, Tyndale House Publishers, Carol Stream, Illinois, 2012, p. 5

23 "The decline of the family and our moral values" by Bruce Cook; http://www.avidchristian.com/family.html

24 Jason DeParle and Sabrina Tavernise, "For Women under 30, Most Births Occur outside Marriage," New York Times, February 17, 2012, www.nytimes.com/2012/02/18/us/for-women-under-30-most-births-occur-outside-marriage.html

25 Ibid

26 *The state of America's Children, 1998 Yearbook, Children's Defense Fund*

27 "The Fatherless Generation" http://thefatherlessgeneration.wordpress.com/statistics

28 "The Decline of fatherhood and the male identity crisis," by Ray B. Williams; *Psychology Today*; http://www.psychologytoday.com/blog/wired-success/201106/the-decline-fatherhood

29 Jerry Ropelato, "Internet Pornography Statistics," Internet Filter Software Reviews, http://internet-filter-review-toptenreviews.com/internet-pornography-statistics-pg2.html

30 Ibid

31 Ron Luce, *Battle Cry for a Generation*, Cook Communications Ministries, Colorado Springs, CO., 2005, p. 87

32 Judith Reisman, *Soft Porn Plays Hard Ball*: Its Tragic Effects on Women, Children and the Family (Lafayette, LA. Huntington House, 1991

33 www.familysafemedia.com/pornography_statistics.html

34 "Porn in the U.S.A." www.CBSnews.com; November 21, 2003

35 McAlpine, "American Porn", August 2001

36 "Porn More Popular than Search" (Found at www.InternetWeek.com; June 4, 2004

37 Pamela Paul, *Pornified*; New York, NY: Henry Holt and Company, 2005, 54

38 http://timchester.wordpress.com/2010/03/10/porn-statistics

39 http://familysafemedia.com/pornography_statistics.html

40 Ed Stetzer, "The Pornification of the American Culture," The Lifeway Research Blog, July 27, 2011, http://www.edstetzer.comj/2011/07/the-pornification-of-american.html

41 "Pornography Statistics: Annual Report 2014," Covenant Eyes, http://www.covenanteyes.com/pornstats

42 *Journal of Urban Health: Bulletin of New York Academy of Medicine* article, reported by Jeanette Torres, ABC News Radio, December 20, 2011, http://abcnewsradioonline.com/health-news/teens-as-young-as 14-engaging-in-group-sex-study-finds.html

43 Carolyn Kellogg, *"Fifty Shades of Grey' trilogy tops 100 million in worldwide sales,"* Los Angeles Times, February 26, 2014, http://articles.latimes.com/2014/feb/26/entertainment/la-et-jc-fifty-shades-of-grey-tops-100-million-in-worldwide-sales-20140226

44 "How Many Pastors Are Addicted to Porn? The stats are Surprising," http://www.expastors.com/how-many-pastors-are-addicted-to-porn-the-stats-are-surprising

45 Ibid

46 'Porn Epidemic' is Sweeping the Church,' says Evangelical Leader," by Bill Berkowitz, January 22, 2016; http://www.smirkingchimp.com/thread/bill-berkowitz/65643/porn-epidemic-is-sweeping

47 Proven Men.org, "Pornography Addiction Survey (conducted by the Barna Group), http://www.provenmen.org/2014pornsurvey/pornography-use-and-addiction

48 "The Pornification of the Church" by John Stonestreet, September 9, 2014, 44180 Riverside Pkwy., Lansdowne, VA

49 Phillip Yancey, *Finding God in Unexpected Places*; Nashville, TN: Morrings, 1995; p. 16

50 Margaret L. Usdonsky, "Gay Couples, by the Numbers," *USA Today*, April 12, 1993, 8A

51 Philip Elmer-DeWitt, "Now the Truth About Americans and Sex," Time, October 17, 1994, 68

52 H.H. Hartfield, "Sexually Transmitted Diseases in Homosexual Men," 1981.

53 National Center for Infectious Diseases, 1992

54 "Sex Survey Results," Genre, October 1996, quoted in *"Survey Finds 40 Percent of Gay Men Have Had More than 40 Sex Partners," Lambda Report*, January 1998:20

55 Michael Slackman, "Same-Sex Marriages: Is There a Republican-Democratic Split?" (Baptist Press News; April 8, 2004)

56 Goldman, "Psychological Factors Generate HIV Resurgence in Young Gay Men," n.d.

57 Paul Cameron, PhD; William L Playfair, MD, Stephen Wellum, "The Longevity of Homosexuals: Before and After the AIDS Epidemic," *Omega: The Journal of Death and Dying 29* 1994: 3. Quoted in Dr. D. James Kennedy, "Homosexuality" (Today's Crisis, 2001). www.frc.org/insights/is_3g2hs.html

58 David Island and Patricia Letellier, *Men Who Beat the Men Who Love Them* (New York, NY: Haworth Press, 1991, p. 14

59 Alan P. Bell and Martin S. Weinberg, *Homosexualities: A Study of Diversity Among Men and Women* (New York, NY: Simon and Schuster, 1979)

60 Paul Cameron and Kirk Cameron, "What is a Homosexual?" *Journal of the Family*

61 David McWhirter and Andrew Mattison, The Male Couple Englewood Cliffs, NJ: Prentice-Hall, Inc. 1984, p. 207) *Research Institute 15, June-July 2000*

62 Maria Xiridou, Ronald Geskus, John DeWit, roel Coutinho, and Mirjam Kretzschamar, "The Contribution of Stead and Casual Partnerships to the Incidence of HIV Infection Among Homosexual Men in Amsterdam," (*AIDS* 17, 2003, 1032)

63 Centers for Disease Control and Prevention, "Cases of HIV Infection and AIDS in the United States, 2002"; HIV/AIDS Surveillance Report 14, 2002; http://www.niaid.nih.gov/factsheets/aidsstat.html

64 Substance Abuse and Mental Health Services Administration, Results from the 2013 National Survey on Drug Use and Health: Summary of National Findings, NSDUH Series H-48, HHS Publication No. (SMA) 14-4863. Rockville, MD: Substance Abuse and Mental Health Services Administration, 2014, http://www.samhsa.gov/data/sites/default/files/NSDUHresultsPDFWHTML. 2013/Web/NSDUHresults2013.pdf

65 "In an average year 30 million Americans drive drunk-10 million drive impaired by illicit drugs," Substance Abuse and Mental Health Services Administration, December 9, 2010, http://www.samhsa.gov/newsroom/press-announcemets/201012091230

66 Centers for Disease Control and Prevention, "CDC Grand Rounds: Prescription Drug Overdoses–a U.S. Epidemic," *Morbidity and Mortality Weekly report*, January 13, 2012, http://www.cdc.gov/mmwr/previeww/mmwrhtml/mm6101a3.htm

67 Ibid

68 David Kupelian, *The Snapping of the American Mind*, WND Books, Washington, D.C., 2015, p. 138

Chapter 11

1 Ibid, p. 265

2 Statistics and Reasons for Church Decline by Richard J. Krejcir; http://www.churchleadership.org/apps/articles/default.asp?articleid=42346&columnid=45

3 Ibid

4 Ibid

5 Ibid

6 Ibid

7 Ibid

8 *The Washington Post*, "Christianity faces sharp decline as Americans are becoming even less affiliated with religion" by Sarah Pulliam Bailey, May 12, 2015; https://www.washingtonpost.com/news/acts-of-faith/wp/2015/05/12/chrisitanity-faces-sharp

9 Ibid

10 "How Will The Shocking Decline of Christianity in America Affect The Future of This Nation?" by Michael, January 18, 2012; http://endoftheamericandream.com/archives/how-will-the-shocking-decline-of-christianity

11 Ibid

12 Ibid

13 Ibid

14 Barna Group, "10 Facts About America's Churchless"' December 10, 2014; https://www.barna.org/barna-update/culture/698-10-facts-about-americas-churchless

15 Tom Sine, "A Wakeup Call for Evangelicals," Patheos.com, August 13, 2010, http://www.patheos.com/Resources/Additional-Resources/A-wakeup-Call-for-Evangelicals.html

16 Christian Index, "A Sobering Reality," by Joe Westbury, November 9, 2015; http://christianindex.org/20151112-1-sobering-reality

17 Ibid

18 Alarming Facts, Trends and Statistics; XXI, No. 2, February 2008; http://www.baptistbanner.org/Subarchive 2/208%20/Alarming%20Facts%20Trends%20and

19 Baptist Press, "To reach millennials is to know teens, say youth specialists"; http//www.bpnews.net/2744

20 Southern Baptists' Millennial Problem, June 2, 2014; https://blogs.thegospelcoalition.org/trevinwax/2014/06/02/southern-baptist-millennial

21 Alarming Facts, Trends and Statistics, XXI, No. 2, February 2008; http://www.baptistbanner.org/Subarchive 2/208%20Alarming%20 Facts%20Trends%20and

22 Ibid

23 Christian Index, "A Sobering Reality," by Joe Westbury, November 9, 2015; http://christianindex.org/20151112-1-sobering-reality

24 Ibid

25 John S. Dickerson, *The Great Evangelical Recession*, 2013, Baker Books, Grand Rapids, MI, p. 26

26 Ibid, p. 51

27 2005 Evangelical Alliance, http://www.eauk.org/resources/info/statistics/2005 englishchurchcensus.com

28 Ibid, p. 82

29 Ibid, p. 82

30 Ibid, p. 84-85

31 George Barna, "Tithing Down 62% in the Past Year," Barna Research Group, May 19, 2003, http://www.barna.org/barna-update/article/5-barna-update/121-tithing-down-62-in-the-past-year?q=giving

32 John L. Ronsvalle and Sylvia Ronsvalle, *The State of Church Giving through 2004: Will We will?* Champaign, IL: Empty Tomb, Inc., 2006; http://library.generous giving.org/page.asp?sec=50&page=609#RonsvalleJS3

33 John L. and Sylvia Ronsvalle, *The State of Church Giving Through 2009*, 21st ed. Champaign, IL: Empty Tomb, Inc., 2011, 104-105

34 Kluth, "Twenty Mega-Trends Impacting Christian Fund Raising." http://kluth.org/fundraising/20MegaTrends.htm

35 Dickerson, *The Great Evangelical Recession*, p. 98

36 Ibid

37 McConnellon, "LifeWay Research Finds Reasons 18 to 22 Year Olds Drop Out of Church."

38 Tom Sine, "A Wakeup Call for Evangelicals," Patheos.com. August 13, 2010, http://www.patheos.com/resources/Additoinal-Resources/A-Wakeup-Call-for-Evangelicals.html

39 Dickerson, *The Great Evangelical Recession*, p. 108

40 Ibid, p. 116

41 Ken Ham & Britt Beemer, *Already Gone, 2009*, Master Books, Green Forest, AR., p. 31

42 Ham & Beemer, Already Gone, p. 39

43 Ibid, p. 41

44 Ibid, p. 42

45 Ibid

46 Ibid, p. 43

47 Ibid

48 Ibid

49 www.news.com.au/couriermai/story/0,23739,25375117-=23373,00html

50 Ibid, p. 103-104

51 Data drawn from Gallup. "Confidence in Institutions," June 1-4, 2013, http://www.gallup.compoll/`597/confidence-institutions.aspx

52 Edelman, "2012 Edelman Trust Barometer: Global Results," http://www.edelman.com/insights/intellectural-property/2012-edelman-trust-barometer/the-state-of-trust/key-findings

53 Keven Robillard, "Poll:Distrust of Media Sets Record." Politico, September 21, 2012,

http://www.politico.com/news/stories/0912/81504.html#xzz33inG00GO

54 Barna Group,"OmniPoll 1-03," national survey of 1,010 adults eighteen or older, conducted January 2003

55 Barna Group, "OmniPoll F-10," national survey of 1,022 adults eighteen or older; December 2010

56 Barna Group, "OmniPoll S-08," national survey of 1,003 adults eighteen or older, May 2008

57 Barna Group, "PastorPoll W-03," national survey of 601 senior pastors of Protestant churches, December 2002

58 Barna Group, "OmniPoll 1-14"; Barna Group, "OmniPoll 1-12," national survey of 1,005 adults eighteen or older, January 2012 and Barna Group, "omniPoll F-12," national survey of 1,008 adults eighteen or older, November 2012

59 Barna Group, "Frames Wave 1," national survey among 1,005 adults, June 2013

Chapter 12

1 Ibid, p. 274

2 Ibid, p. 274

3 "The Life Cycle of a Nation" by Ignatius Piazza, November 3, 2008; http://www.ignatius-piazza-front-sight.com/2008/11/03/the-life-cycle-of-nation

4 "The Life Cycles of Empires" by Eric Snow, July 6, 2011; http://www.ucg.org/the-good-news/the-life-cycles-of-empires-lessons-for-america-today

5 Ibid

6 Ibid

7 Ibid

8 "Rome and America–Comparing to the Ancient Roman Empire," by Kerby Anderson, May 25, 2009;https://www.probe.org/rome-and-america

9 Ibid

10 Ibid

11 Ibid

12 Ibid

13 Ibid

14 Ibid

15 Ibid

16 http://www.sermoncentral.com/print friendly.asp?SermonID=194890

17 Carl Zimmerman, *Family and Civilization*, New York: Harper and Brothers, 1947, pp. 776-777

18 "The Decline and Fall of America," study No. 66; http://www.giveshare.org/BibleStudy/066.decline.html

19 "When Nations Fall" The Good News: March/April 2009; http://www.gnmagazine.org/issues/gn81/when-nations-fall.htm

20 "The Fall of Rom and U.S." by Don Gettys; http://mcdonaldroad.org/sermons/10/100227.htm

21 "The Fall of the Roman Empire," http://www.rome.info/history/empire/fall

22 http://www.sermoncentral.com/p;rint-friendly.asp?SermonID=149495

23 Ibid

24 Ibid

25 "The Death of a Nation," by Doug Hamilton

26 Ibid

27 Ibid

28 "12 Signs America is on the Decline" by Jill Hamburg Coplan" 7/20/2015; http://fortune.com/2015/07/20/united-states-decline-statistics-economic

29 "When Nations Die"; http://www.leaderu.com/common/nationsdie.html

Chapter 13

1 Ibid, p. 204-205

2 Emma Green, "The U.S. Puts 'Moderate' Restrictions on Religious Freedom," *The Atlantic*; January 28, 2014.

3 Jocelyn Kiley, "Most Young Republicans Favor Same-Sex Marriage," *Pew Research Center*, March 10, 2014, http://www.pewresearch.org/fact-tank/2014/03/10/61-of-young-republicans-favor-same-sex-marriage

4 Charles Francis Potter, *Humanism: A New Religion*, cited by David A. Noebel, Clergy in the Classroom, The Religion of Secular Humanism (Manitou Spring, Colorado: Summit Press, 1995.), p. 8.

5 *Torcaso v. Watkins*, 367 U.S. 488, 81 S. Ct. 1680 (1961).

6 *Wallace v. Jaffree*, 472 U.S. 38 (1985)

7 *Chandler v. Siegelman*, 230 F. 3d 1313 (11th Cir. 2000)

8 Carrie Smith, "Payout for Prayer Lawsuit Irks Board. Schools Must Pay Attorneys $23,000 for Student's Suit," *The Charleston Daily Mail*, August 16, 2002

9 Don Rowland, "Jimmy and Raymond at School," *The Christian Informer*, July , 1998

10 Ibid

11 Ibid

12 *Roberts v. Madigan*, 921 F.2d 1047 (10th Cir. 1990)

13 Tanya L. Green, J.D., "Political Correctness Hinders Religious Expression," Concerned Women for America, December 20, 2001

14 Joe Kavacs, "School Bans Saying 'Christmas'; Veteran teacher dumbfounded by order precluding mention of holiday," *worldnetdaily.com*, December 13, 2002

15 News Brief, "Parents Fight School Holiday," Center for Law & Policy Analysis Press Release, November 20, 2000

16 John Leo, "Seasonal Symbols make Some People See Red," Universal Press Syndicate, December 17, 2001

17 Tim Wildmon, "Have a Merry _______mas?" AFA Online, December 19, 2000

18 "Madison School Board Removes Pledge of Allegiance Ban in Schools," Fox News, October 16, 2001

19 D. James Kennedy, "Christian History Censored from Public Schools," Kentucky Gateway Christian Coalition, 2001

20 *Paul Vitz, Censorship: Evidence of Bias in Our Children's Textbooks* (Ann Arbor, MI: Servant Books, 1986

21 Brian Kennedy, "Teaching American History in the Schools: The Claremont Institute & The Teaching Teachers Project," *The Progressive Journal*, Volume IV, Issue # 67, June 17, 2002

22 Amy E. Nevala, "Judge Backs Evanston Church," *The Chicago Tribune*, April 3, 2003

23 Valerie Richardson, "Home Bible Study Makes Colorado Woman a Lawbreaker," *The Washington Times*, August 12, 1999).

24 "ACLJ Secures Victory for Denver Couple Ordered to Limit Prayer Meetings in Their Private Home by City of Denver," ACJL Press Release, December 22, 1999

25 Todd Starnes, *God Less America*, Charisma House Book Group, 600 Rinehart Road, Lake Mary, FL.; 2014, p. 14

26 Ibid, p. 17

27 Ibid, p. 38

28 Ibid, p. 69

29 Ibid, p. 129

30 Ibid, p. 162

31 Ibid, p. 3

32 Ibid, p. 164-165

33 Ibid, p. 168

34 Ibid, p. 175

35 *Goodridge v. Department of Health*, SJC-08860 (2003)

36 *Varnun v. Brien*, No. 07-1499 (2009)

37 Wayne Grudem, *Politics According to the Bible*, Zondervan; Grand Rapids, MI.; 2010, p. 145

38 The 11 Most Devastating Quotes from John Roberts' Gay Marriage Dissent by The Federalist Staff, June 26, 2015; http://thefederalist.com/2015/06/26/here-are-the-11-most-devastating-quotes-from-john

39 Grudem, Politics According to the Bible, p. 154

40 Ibid, p. 187

41 Ibid, p. 190

42 Ibid, p. 186

43 Ibid, p. 224

44 Ibid, p.4-5

Chapter 14

1 Ibid, p. 113-114

2 Martyn Lloyd-Jones, "What is Preaching?" in *Knowing the Times*, Bann of Truth Trust, 1989, p. 263

3 http://www.rlhymersjr.com/Online_Sermons/2005/112705PM_preaching.html

4 Sermon by Reggie A. Braziel, Christian Hope Church of Christ; Plymouth, North Carolina, August 26, 2012, "The Famine of the Word of God."

5 "The scandal of Biblical Illiteracy: It's our Problem" by Albert Mohler; http://www.christianheadlines.com/columnists/al-mohler/the-scandal-of-biblical-illiteracy

6 CultureWatch, by Bill Muehelenberg, "Rampant Biblical Illiteracy" May 14, 2011; https://billmuehlenberg.com/2011/05/14/rampant-biblical-illiteracy

7 Ed Stetzer, "Biblical Illiteracy by the Numbers Part 1"; http://www.christianity today.com/edstetzer/2014/October/biblical-illiteracy-by-the-numbers.html

8 Wendy Griffith," Know Your Bible? Many Christians Don't" CBN News 24-7; July 24, 2009, http://www.cbn.com/cbnnews/us/2009/june/do-you-know-your-bible-many-christians-dont

Chapter 15

1 Ibid, p. 676, 678

2 Ibid, p. 678-679

3 "The Obama Judgment: America's King Ahaz, Part Two" by Dean Olson, August 1, 2015; http://www.raptureforums.com/forums/threads/the-obama-judgment-americas-king-ahaz

4 Ibid

5 Ibid

6 "President Obama: God's 'Gift' to America," by Dean Olson; Rapture Forums, http://www.raptureforums.com/FeaturedCommentary/presidentobamagodsgifttoamerica.cfm

7 "Rep Trey Gowdy rips into FBI Director James Comey on Hillary Clinton's 'intent'" by Arriana McLymore, July 7, 2016; http://www.cnbc.com/2016/07/07/rep-trey-gowdy-rips-into-fbi-director-james-comey

8 Fox News Sunday with Chris Wallace, July 31, 2016

9 "Hillary Clinton's 'honest' and 'trustworthy' numbers are lower than ever. It might not matter," by Chris Cillizza, March 8, 2016, Washington Post; http://www.washingtonpost.com/news/the-fix/wp/2016/03/08/hillary-clintons-honest-and-trustworthy

10 President Obama: God's "Gift" to America, Rapture Forum

11 "The Obama Judgment: America's King Ahaz-Part One" by Dean Olson, July 30, 2015; http://www.raptureforums.com/forums/threads/the-obama-judgment-americas-king-ahaz

12 Ibid

Chapter 16

1 Ibid, p. 701

Chapter 17

1 Ibid, p.703-704

2 https://www.washingtonpost.com June 28, 2016

3 David Bailey, June 26, 2016/ www.reuters.com/article/us-west-virginia-floods

4 Dan Ebner, October 7, 2015/ krcgtv.com/news/local 1000-year-flood

5 Adam M. Zaretsky/ www.stlouisfed.org/Octobeer 1993

6 Mike Lear/ www.missouirinet.com/ December 27, 2015

7 David Manzo and David Chic, October 5, 2015/ abcnews.go.com/us/Charleston-south-carolina-soaked-worst-rains-1000

8 Zoe Schlanger, December 29, 2015/ www.newsweek.com/mississippi-river-about-have-record-flood

9 KMOV.COM STAFF, December 30, 2015/ www.kmov.com/story/30855767/record-flopods-sweep-through-st-louis

10 May 29, 2015, WWW.NBCDFW/RECORD-BREAKING-RAIN-FLOODS

11 January 6, 2016 by Jon Erdman/ https://weather.com/mississippi-river-flooding

12 Chris Doice, Nick Wiltgen, Jonathan Erdman/ https://weather.com/plains-rain-flood-threat

13 December 31, 2015 www.reuters.com/article/usa-weather-iduskbnovdo8h20151231

14 Lydia O'Connor, October 5, 2015 Huffington Post/ www.huffingtonpost.com/record-breaking-weather-events

15 Deanna Conners in Earth Science Wire, January 12, 2016/earthsky.org/earth/2015-worst-us-wildfire-year-on-reocrd

16 Lucy Nicholson/Reuters, September 15, 2015

17 The Weather Channel, March 23, 2015/ Jon Erdman/weather.com

18 BY Madison Park, CNN, July 26, 2016/http://www.cnn.com/2016/07/26/us/California-wildfires

19 March 2, 2016, http://phys.org/news/2016-03-extreme-tornado-outbreaks

20 By Scott Huddleston, San Antonia Express-News, May 15, 2014/www.chron.com/http://droughjt-among-worst-in-texas-in-past-500

21 January 7, 2012; http://www.cbsnews.com/news/2011-was-texas-driest-year-on-record

22 http://www.visualnews.com/2015/04/13/californias-worst-drought-in-history

23 BY Mark Fischetti, February 12, 2015; http://www.scientificamerican.com/article/u-s-droughts-will-be-the-worswt

24 by Joseph Romm, July 13, 2012/ www.theenergycollective.com/drought-covers-one-third

25 BY Kukil Bora, December 6, 2014; http://www.ibtimes.com/california-drought-2012-2014-worst-1200-years

26 BY Michael Pearson and Melissa Abbey, CNN, July 17, 2012/ http://www.cnn.com/2012/07/16/us/us-drought

27 Washington Post by Niraj Chokshi, January 23, 2016 https://www.washingtonpost.com

28 WWW.NWS.NOAA.GOV

29 April 27, 2011, American Weather

30 WWW.LIVESCIENCE.COM/ April 28, 2011 by Brett Israel

31 BY Natalie Angley, CNN, December 10, 2011 http://www.cnn.com/2011/12/09/world-americas-impact-year-in-review

32 BY Michael Snyder, January 4, 2016/ http://www.charismanews.com/opinion/54173-record-breaking-flooding-bombards

33 http://rismedia.com/2011/12/15/the-more-you -know-record-breaking-year

34 BY Lydia O'Connor, the Huffington Post, October 5, 2015

35 By Andrew Freedman, July 8, 2013; Climate Central; http://www.climatecentral.org/news/study-projects-more-frequent-and-stronger-hurricanes-world

36 https://benheb.github.io/tornado-days

37 uk.businessinsider.com/worst-storms-in-history

38 http://www.infoplease.com/ipa/A0778688.html

39 Ibid

40 America's Most Devastating Wildfires. The Big Burn; http://www.pbs.org/wgbh/americanexperie3nce/features/general-article/burn-worst-fires

41 infoplease.com

42 Ibid

43 America's Most Devastating Wildfires

44 Ibid

45 infoplease.com

46 Infoplease.com

47 America's Most Devastating Wildfires

48 Infoplease.com

49 Ibid

50 Ibid

51 Ibid

52 Ibid

53 "Historic Drought puts over half of U.S. counties in Disaster zones, USDA says" by David Ariosto and Melissa Abbey; http://articles.cnn.com/2012-08-01/us/us-usda

54 "Record year for billion-dollar disasters, CBS News; http://www.cbsnews.com/8301-201_162-57339130/record-year-for-billion

55 "2010 a deadly year for natural disasters" by Julie Reed Bell, Seth Borenstein, December19, 2010 http://www.msnbc.msn.com/id/40739667/ns/us_2010_year_in

56 "U.S. Natural Disasters: 2011 An Extreme and Exhausting Year; Seth Borenstein, September 3, 2011; http://www.huffingtonpost.com/2011/09/03/disasters-in-us-an-extreme

57 "Severe Drought Seen as Driving Cost of Food Up" by Annie Lowrey and Ron Nixon, July 25, 2012; http://www.nytimes.com/2012/07/26/business/food-prices-to-rise

58 "Why Are There So Many Natural Disasters in 2011?" http://endoftheamericandream.copm/archives/www.why-are-there-so-many

59 The Tornadoes of 2011: The Worst Natural Disaster in the United States Since Hurricane Katrina by Michael, May 1, 2011; http://theeconomiccollapseblog.com/archieves/the-tornadoes-of-2011-the-worst

60 "Drought: A Creeping Disaster" by Alex Prudhomme, July 16, 2011; The New York Times, Sunday Review; http://www.nytimes.com/2011/07/17/opinion/sunday/17drought.html?pagewante3d=all

61 http://www.christiannet.com/1215711636.html

62 Blackaby: Natural Disasters can point to God's judgment" by Ken Walker, January 24, 2005; Baptist Press; http://www.bpnews.net/bpnews.asp?ID=19983

63 (Will God Impeach America? By Adrian Rogers; Love Worth Finding Ministries, P.O. Box 38300, Memphis, TN.; http://www.lwf.org)

Chapter 18

1 Ibid, p. 251, 246

2 "God's Final Warning to America," http://defendproclaimthefaith.org/blog/?p=2070

3 "The Decline of the U.S.: Habakkuk's Dilemma" by Chuck Missler, President of Koinonia Institute; http://www.khouse.org/articles/2011/979

Chapter 19

1 Ibid, p. 323, 328

2 D. James Kennedy, *Character & Destiny: A Nation in Search of Its Soul*; Zondervan Publishing House; Grand Rapids, MI. 1994; pp. 11-13, 274-288

3 Excerpt from *Persecution* by David Limbaugh; Regnery Publishing, Inc., One Massachusetts Avenue, NW, Washington, D.C.; 2003, pp. 343-343

4 Ibid, pp. 349-351

5 Ibid, p. 352

6 Todd Starnes, God Less America; FrontLine, Christian House Book Group; Lake Mary, FL. 2014; pp. 230-233

7 Now or Never: Saving America From Economic Collapse by Jim DeMint; Hachette Book Group, New York, NY; 2012, pp. 250-258

8 *Twilight's Last Gleaming* by Robert Jeffress; Worthy Publishing, Brentwood, TN.; 2011, pp. 150-158; 203-206, 211-212, 219

9 Quote appears in Starnes, *God Less America*, p. 231

10 Frank Page in *SBC Life, Published by the SBC Executive Committee, Summer 2016*; p. 22

11 Ibid, pp. 6-7

12 "The Greatest Deterrent to Revival, The Church" by Michael Catt, 2003; http://www.2prophetu.com/templates/!print/details.asp?id=35585&PG-resources&CID=1

13 "Why One Cry Matters" by Michael Catt, June 13, 2012; http://michaelcatt.com/2012/06/why-onecry-matters

14 "Our Need for Revival," by Michael Catt, July 10, 2012; http://michaelcatt.com/2012/07/our-need-for-revival

Chapter 20

1 Ibid, 543

2 *Onward* by Russell Moore; B&H Publishing Group; Nashville, TN.; 2015, pp. 206-207, 214-216

3 *Implosion: Can America Recover From Its Economic & Spiritual Challenges in Time?* By Joel Rosenberg, Tyndale Publishing; Carol Stream, Illinois; 2012, pp. 209-212, 227-228, 230, 258-259, 287, 290, 293-295, 317, 323, 348

4 *Public Education Against America* by Marlin Maddoux, Whitaker House Publishers; New Kensington, PA.; 2006, pp. 264-270

5 *Politics According to the Bible* by Wayne Grudem, Zondervan Publishing; Grand Rapids, Michigan, 2010; pp. 62-63, 69, 70-74, 596-597, 599-601

6 *U-Turn* by George Barna and David Barton; Charisma House Book Group; Lake Mary, FL., 2014; pp. 4, 7, 43, 45, 49, 55-63, 153-155, 167-178, 203-204

Chapter 21

1 The Life and Correspondence of James McHenry by Bernard C. Steiner 1907, in a letter from Charles Carroll, November 4, 1800

2 https://verticallivingministries.com/dr-erwin-w-lutzer-on-the-great-need-for-revival

3 *When a Nation Forgets God*, Erwin W. Lutzer, Moody Publishers, Chicago, 2010; pp. 94-95, 120-121, 133, 139-140

4 *We Cannot Be Silent* by R. Albert Mohler, Jr., Nelson Books, Nashville, TN.; 2015, pp. 135, 138-139, 145, 147-151

5 *America's Last Call* by David Wilkerson, Wilkerson Trust Publications, Lindale, TX., 1998; pp.11-12, 21-22, 130-132, 139, 141

6 *Turning the Tide* by Charles F. Stanley, Howard Books; New York, NY; 2011, pp. 27, 187, 215, 223, 229, 273-277

7 "Franklin Graham Urges America: Vote For Christians This Election," by Greg Corombos; 4/23/2016; http://www.wnd.com/2016/04/franklin-graham-urges-america-vote-for-christians

8 *"America will fall without a moral revival: Franklin Graham launches 50-state tour ahead of 2016 election"; Life Site, January 6, 2016;* https://www.lifesitenews.com/news/america-will-fall-without-a-moral-revival-franklin-graham

9 *"Rev. Graham Warns: 'Unless America Turns Back to God' and 'Repents of its Sin…. We will Fail As a Nation"* by Michael W. Chapman; February 29, 2016; cns news; http://www.cnsnews.com/blog/michael-w-chapman/rev-graham-warns-unless-america

10 *CNB News,* Charisma News, January 14, 2016; endtimesheadlines.org/2016/01/franklin-graham-warns-americas-in-critical-condition

11 *A Nation without a Conscience* by Tim & Beverly LaHaye; Tyndale House Publishers; Wheaton, IL., 1994; pp. 246-247, 252-253, 256-260, 262, 264

12 *The Coming Economic Armageddon* by Dr. David Jeremiah; FaithWords, Hatchett Book Group, New York, NY; 2010; pp. 257-259, 261-262

13 "America needs a revival" by Greg Laurie; http://www.faithstreet.com/onfaith/2013/05/02/on-the-national-day-of-prayer-time-for-a-revival

14 "Greg Laurie Warns America May Be Destroyed Like Pompeii for Godless Culture" by Katherine Weber; Christian Post, June 16, 2016; http://www.christianpost.com/news/greg-laurie-warns-america-destroyed-pompeii

15 Greg's blog, "Why Blaming the Government Isn't the Answer," http://blog.greglaurie.com

16 Greg's blog, "The "3 Rs" of Personal Revival," http://blog.greglaurie.com

17 *A Nation in Crisis: The Meltdown of Money, Government, and Religion* by Larry Bates and Chuck Bates; FrontLine, Lake Mary, FL., 2010; pp. 154, 160, 162-163, 193, 131

18 Storm by Jim Cymbala, Zondervan, Grand Rapids, MI; 2014, pp. 10, 19, 27, 84-85, 106-107, 112-113, 137-138

Chapter 22

1 Debates of the Constitutional Convention, August 22, 1787, William Federer, p. 423

2 *America: Imagine a World Without Her* by Dinesh D'Souza; Regnery Publishing, Washington, D.C., 2014; p. 248

3 Ibid

4 *Prepare: Living Your Faith in an Increasingly Hostile Culture* by J. Paul Nyquist; Moody Publishers, Chicago, IL,; 2015, pp. 183, 168

5 *"Billy Graham on the Crisis of Moral Deterioration"* by Billy Graham, May 27, 2015; https://billgraham.org/decision-magazine/june-2015/billy-graham-on-the-crisis=of-moral

6 *The Snapping of the American Mind* by David Kupelian; WND Books, Washington, D.C.; 2015, pp. 198-200, 202

7 *The Late Great United States* by Mark Hitchcock; Multnomah Books, Colorado Springs, Colorado; 2009, pp. 125-127, 133, 135-136

8 *America: Turning a Nation to God* by Tony Evans; Moody Publishers, Chicago, IL., 2015, pp. 112, 114-115, 117, 124-125, 137, 150, 170-173

9 "11 Minutes to 1 Hour on Sunday, September 11: Focused Prayer for America During Church Worship Services" by Ronnie Floyd; http://www.ronniefloyd.com/blog/10809/pastors/11-minutes-to-1-hour-on-sunday

10 "Ronnie Floyd's 2016 Presidential Address to the SBC: The Stakes Are High" by Ronnie Floyd, June 16, 2015; http://www.christianpost.com/news/ronnie-floyd-2016-presidential-address-sbc

11 "Will Your Church Be a Part of the Great Spiritual Awakening on the Horizon?" by Rick Warren; April 3, 2015; http://www.charismanews.com/opinion/49030-will-your-church-be-a-part-of-the-great

12 "America Needs Healing! How We Can See It Happen" by Rick Warrren; http://pastors.com/america-needs-healing-how-we-can-begin-it

13 The Stream by James Robison; Worthy Books; Franklin, Tennessee; 2016; pp. 11, 37, 40, 48-49, 55, 58, 60, 63, 71, 92, 135, 175, 231, 247, 254-255

Chapter 23

1 Letter to Jasper Adams, May 9, 1833

2 *The Stream* by James Robison; Worthy Publishing, Franklin, TN.; 2016, p. 231

3 *U Turn* by George Barna & David Barton; FrontLine, Lake Mary, Florida; 2014, p. 154.

4 "Michele Bachmann says 'This is The Last Election'" by Lauren Stephenson, September 3, 2016; TheDenverChannel.com

5 Ibid

6 "Michele Bachmann: This Will Be The 'Last Election' if Hillary Clinton Wins the Presidency," by Tre' Goins-Phillips; http://www.theblaze.com/stories/2016/09/02/michele-bachmann-this-will-be-the-last-election

7 Ibid

8 "Michele Bachmann: 'God Raised Up' Trump to Become Nominee" by Jason Devaney, August 30, 2016; http://www.newsmax.com/Politics/trump-bachmann-God-campaign/2016/08/30/id/745941

9 Transcript: Ted Cruz's speech at Liberty University, Washington Post, M arch 23, 2015, http://www.washingtonpost.com/politics/transcript-ted-cruzs-speech-at-liberty-university/2015/03/23/41c4011a-d168-11e4-a62f-ee745911a4ff_story.html

10 Pew, "America's Changing Religious Landscape."

11 *America: Turning a Nation to God* by Tony Evans; Moody Publishers, Chicago, Il., 2015; p. 174

12 Ibid, p. 174-175

13 Billy Graham's "Prayer for Our Nation" recited by Reverend Joe Wright, www.snopes.com/politics/soapbox/prayernation.asp

14 https://en.wikiquote.org/wiki/EdmundBurke

Chapter 24

1 Ibid, p. 644

2 John F. Walvoord and Mark Hitchcock, *Armageddon, Oil, and Terror*; 2007, Tyndale House Publishers; Carol Stream, IL., p. 171

3 Ibid, p. 171

Chapter 25

1 "More Than 60 Percent of Evangelicals Voted in 2016, Says Barna Study," http://www.christianitydaily.com/articles/8710/20161206/faith-played-huge-role-election

2 Ibid

3 "Trump Elected President, Thanks to 4 in 5 White Evangelicals," http://www.christianitytoday.com/gleanings/2016/november/trump-elected-president

4 "Onward Christian Cabinet: Trump's White House Picks Are a Christmas Gift for the Religious Right," by Allison Kaplan Sommer, December 14, 2016; http://www.haaretz.com/us-news/.premium-1.758733

5 Ibid

6 Ibid

7 "Who is Reince Priebus? 5 Things You Should Know," http://www.christianpost.com/news/who-is-reince-priebus-171487

8 "Nikki Haley's confession of faith," by David Waters; http://www.onfaith.com/onfaith/2010/06/09/nikki-haleys-confession-of-faith

9 "Donald Trump Picked Jeff Sessions for AG: What He Believes,"; http://time.com/4576787/jeff-sessions-attorney-general-donald-trump

10 "Can Jeff Session, in good faith, hire attorneys with no faith?" http://www.salon.com/2017/01/15/can-jeff-sessions-in-good-faith-hire-attorneys-with-no-faith

11 Gov. Perdue Addresses 102 Graduates at Truett-McConnell Commencement," by Jenny Gregory, May 27, 2014; http://truett.edu/news/archive/gov-perdue-addresses-102-graduates-at-truett-mcconnell

12 *"US Former Secretary of Labor, Christian, Elaine Chao 'Seeks Her Roots' and Donates Two Primary Schools in Anhui,'* by Ruth Wang, October 20, 2015; http:P//chinachristiandaily.com/2015-10-20/society/us-former-secretary-of-labor

13 *"A Deeply Personal Decision"* by redtravelmaster, June 27, 2015; http://www.dailykos.com/story/2015/6/27/1397243/-A-Deeply-Personal-Decision

14 *"The Astonishing Rhetoric of President Trump's Inaugural Address,"* by Nick Morgan; http://www.forbers.com/sites/nickmorgan/2017/01/20/the-astonishing-rhetoric-of-president

15 *"Eight things we learnt from Donald Trump's inaugural speech,"* by Harriet Alexander, January 20, 2017; http://www.telegraph.co.uk/news/2017/01/20/did-learn-donaldd-trumps-inaugural-speech

16 *"Donald Trump: President Donald Trump's inaugural address: Top quotes,"* http://timesofindia.indiatimes.com/world/us/president-donald-trumps-inaugural-address

Chapter 26

1 Federer, p. 543-544

2 *"Trump Completely Mangles the Meaning of the Johnson Amendment at the Values Voter Summit,"* by Josh Voorhees, September 9, 2016; http://www.slate.com/blogs/the_slatest/2016/09/09/trump-mangels-johnson-amendment

3 Ed Young, *Healing Broken America,* Winning Walk Family Publishers, 2011, Houston, TX., p. 99-100

4 Ibid, p. 101

5 Ibid, p. 106

Chapter 27

1 "It's Time for America to Wake Up!" by Jim McCutchen; August 30, 2012; http://www.sermoncentral.con/sermons/its-time-for-america-to-wak-up-jim-mccutchen

2 Ibid

3 "Civilization in America: An Excellent Idea," by Davon Huss, November 19, 2013; http://www.sermoncentral.com/sermons/civilization-in-america-an-excellent-idea-davon...

4 http://www.roadtograce.net/current-porn-statistics

5 http://www.sermoncentral.com/sermons/is-americas-end-drawing-near-jack-woodard-sermon

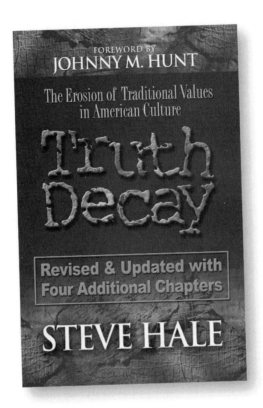

MANswers:

Empowering Men for Leadership

Some things can be addressed in a book or in a men's conference that are not so easily addressed from the pulpit. The issues covered in *MANswers* fall into that category. Steve conducts Men Who Win conferences and often puts his finger on the delicate issues and temptations facing today's men. *MANswers* is a good study guide for men's small groups or for the individual man who simply desires to take his walk with God to the next level.

SINCE 1979

Steve Hale continues to travel the nation conducting *Men Who Win* conferences, area-wide crusades, local church revivals, and Harvest Day events. His ministry office is based out of First Baptist Church of Woodstock, Georgia, one of America's premier churches.
Steve holds a bachelor's degree in journalism from Murray State University, a Master of Divinity from Southwestern Baptist Theological Seminary, and a Doctor of Ministry degree from Luther Rice Seminary.

He may be contacted at:
shea@fbcw.net or stevehale911@yahoo.com
or 770-591-0320.
Website is: stevehaleministries.com

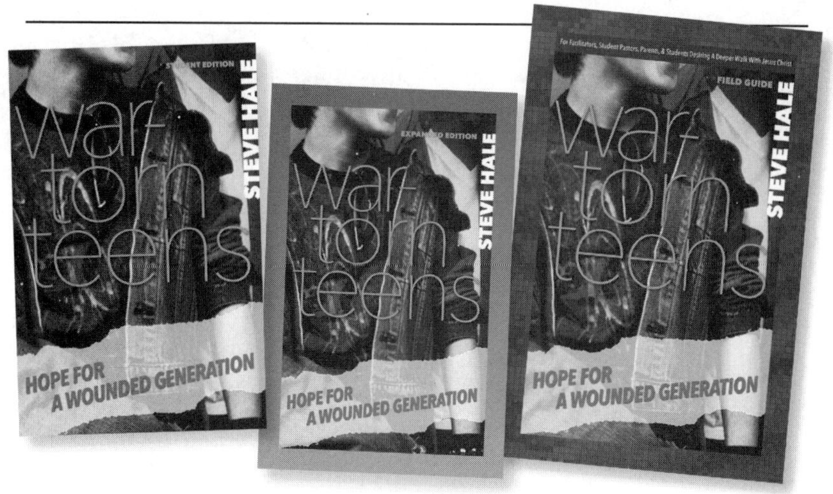

WAR-TORN TEENS:

Hope for a Wounded Generation

During the Vietnam War era soldiers were returning home from the battlefields displaying emotional symptoms for which psychologists had no diagnosis. In those days it was merely called, "battle fatigue" or "shell shock." Eventually, they coined the term, "posttraumatic stress disorder." Still today, soldiers return from warzones having witnessed their comrades getting their heads blown off, bombs exploding around them, and limbs dismembered. Symptoms of isolation, depression, flashbacks, insecurity, substance abuse, withdrawing, hallucinations are common. Psychologists are telling us that this generation of teens often display the identical symptoms of PTSD, thus, the title of *War-Torn Teens*. The title, however, is a bit misleading because the book is also applicable to young adults.

This book is an outstanding resource for mentoring another teen. It is a great tool for parents to disciple their children. It is an outstanding resource for Youth Pastors to utilize in their weekly meetings. Equipped with an extensive and separate Field Guide, each chapter in this volume is divided into five days providing the reader a guide for a daily quiet time or daily devotions. The three components of *War-Torn Teens* is a Student Version, Expanded Version, and Field Guide. The primary difference between the expanded and student versions is about 4-5 pages per chapter more in the expanded edition.

Suffice it to say, the relevant hot-button issues facing today's youth are all addressed in this volume with each chapter opening with war-stories designed to captivate the reader's attention. You will not be disappointed!

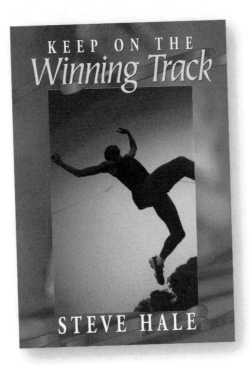